VICTORIAN EXETER
1837–1914

*E. A. Sanders, 1813-1905. Harrow and Oxford. County cricketer, keen
rider to hounds and prominent churchman. Chairman of the Exeter Bank.
Chairman of directors of the 'Devon and Exeter Gazette'. Chairman of
trustees of the High School for Girls. Member of the corporation of the
poor and the improvement commissioners. Mayor 1849-50. His political
life began in 1832 and for some sixty years he was chairman of committees
for Conservative parliamentary candidates.*

Portrait by Cape, 1889.   (By courtesy of the National Provincial Bank)

VICTORIAN EXETER
1837-1914

BY

ROBERT NEWTON

LEICESTER UNIVERSITY PRESS
1968

Printed in Great Britain
by C. H. Gee & Co. Ltd., Leicester
for Leicester University Press

Distributed in North America
by Humanities Press Inc., New York

SBN 7185 1075 5

CONTENTS

ILLUSTRATIONS

ILLUSTRATIONS

MAP

ACKNOWLEDGMENTS

F OR this study of his native city I owe much to Professor W. G. Hoskins, Hatton Professor of English History in the University of Leicester. It was begun on his sugges- tion. His advice and encouragement were always generously forthcoming. I am grateful to Mr W. D. Handcock for his friendly guidance as my Director of Studies at the University of Exeter. My sincere thanks are due to Professor J. Simmons, of the University of Leicester, for his patient scrutiny of my typescript and for his invaluable comments and suggestions. The shortcomings of this book are mine.

I am glad to record my grateful appreciation of the assistance I have received from Mr N. E. Pugsley, Exeter City Librarian, and his staff, especially Mrs M. M. Rowe and Mr G. J. Paley. I am grateful to Miss P. M. Downie, Chief Librarian, Department of Education and Science, and to Mr A. E. Fountain, for their kindness in giving me facilities to consult their records; to the staff of the British Museum and the Public Record Office for all that they did to assist research during necessarily brief visits to London; to the staff of the Roborough Library, University of Exeter; the Devon County Record Office; the Exeter Cathedral Library; to Miss D. Marshallsay, Librarian of the Ford Collection of Parliamentary Papers in the University of Southampton; and to Miss J. Lancaster, Secretary and Librarian of the Devon and Exeter Institution.

I am grateful to Dr E. D. Irvine, Medical Officer of Health, Exeter, to Mr Harold Gayton, City Planning Officer, and to Dr R. C. Blackie, for information and advice.

I am also most obliged to the Earl of Iddesleigh for the loan of papers relating to Sir Stafford Northcote, first Earl of Iddesleigh; to Mr Roger Ellis for the loan of the manuscript memoirs of Henry Ellis; to Mr George Daw and Mr Roger Daw for permission to use privately printed memoirs and reminiscences of the Daw family; to Mr G. Alderman for material relating to Colsons of Exeter; to Mr W. J. Force for volumes of notes of sales and advertisements of house property belonging to Messrs S. R. Force and Sons; to the Co-operative Building Society for papers relating to the Exeter Freehold Land and Building Society; to Mr L. J. Lloyd, Librarian of the University of Exeter, for the loan of a *Memoir of Miss Jessie Montgomery;* to Mr Stanley Wilson, Actuary of the Devon and Exeter Savings Bank, for kindly giving me access to the bank's reports.

I am obliged to Professor Hanham, of the University of Edinburgh, for advice on the problem of the true size of the early Victorian electorate, and to Mr Allan Brockett, of the University of Exeter, for advice on religious affairs. I have to thank Mr Richard Vyvyan for information about the Sanders family; and Mr H. J. Collings for giving me access to the Unitarian records of George's Meeting. I am also much indebted for information from Mr W. A. Board, of the Western Counties Brick Company; Mr Morgan Edwards, of the Rougemont Hotel; Mr R. J. McGahey, of Dunn and Baker; and Mr L. J. Seward, O.B.E., of Seward & Son (Exeter) Ltd.

Mr Vosper Arthur photographed the original portrait of E. A. Sanders used as the frontispiece and also photographed the material used for plates 1, 3, 4, 6, 11 and 14. Miss M. Hockmuth took the photograph of St David's church reproduced at plate 15. The remaining photographs of streets and buildings were taken for me by Mr G. W. Caulfield-Browne. I am grateful to all three for the trouble they took to give me what I required.

I acknowledge with gratitude the permission accorded by the National Provincial Bank to reproduce the portrait of E. A. Sanders now in possession of the bank; and by Mr N. S. E. Pugsley to reproduce material in the possession of the Exeter City Library. I am grateful to Mr R. Fry, of Exeter University, for his work on the map, and to Mrs Anne Elford, who patiently deciphered my original typescript.

Above all I am grateful to my wife who made it possible to give time to Victorian Exeter amid the problems of today.

INTRODUCTION

THE history of human communities, their growth, development and decay, cannot easily be fitted into tidy, chronological departments. The choice of the dates 1837 and 1914 as the beginning and the end of Victorian Exeter is necessarily arbitrary. Victorianism as a vigorous and complex phase of Western European history had its beginnings long before 1837 and in the provinces survived, at least in some of its less vigorous aspects, long after 1901. Exeter in the nineteenth century and beyond was only doubtfully Victorian in that it experienced neither the economic growth nor the searching intellectual inquiry which were not the least of the characteristics of Victorianism. Exeter was a provincial capital which carried far into the new era the traditions and habits of the old; it was, indeed, a social and cultural survival from pre-industrial England. A good case could be made out for treating the years 1760 to 1870 as a more self-contained phase in the history of Exeter than the period 1837 to 1914. The former period almost exactly covers the rise and decline of a provincial capital. Its symbol was the classical architecture which began to adorn the city in the reign of George III and survived in attenuated form till it came to an abrupt end about 1870.

But the year 1837 was the year in which the Exeter Liberals achieved a tenuous control of the new city council. The Whig politician, Joseph Parkes, regarded the Municipal Corporations Act as an instrument for the overthrow of Toryism, as the steam in the mill of Whig politics.[1] The Exeter Reformers hailed their victory in 1837 as the dawn of a new golden age of enlightenment. Economy and pure government were to be the offspring of the new franchise, to be guarded and nurtured by vigilant burgesses who would themselves be fully informed by a press now admitted by law to council meetings. Since the vote was all that was required for the effective exercise of rational intelligence, the burgesses would return good Reformers to the council and the results would be those envisaged by the less romantic Joseph Parkes. The Exeter Reformers were swiftly disillusioned; but in their vision of redemption through the franchise they represented a characteristic element in Victorian England. Their victory in 1837 therefore marks the beginning of a new stage in Exeter's history coinciding with the queen's accession.

The end of the period is inescapably the year 1914 since the first World War and its aftermath submerged the last vestiges of the Victorian era in so far as Victorianism in its wider sense was a phase in European culture.

In the sixteenth century Exeter had become one of the largest and wealthiest of England's provincial cities and was entering upon the most prosperous stage of a long history. By Defoe's time, in the early eighteenth century, the city had become a provincial capital 'full of gentry and good company and yet full of trade and manufacture withal.'[2] War and technical change in the second half of the century ended Exeter's prosperity as a finishing and distributing centre of the Devon cloth trade. By 1831 the city's population was described by a contemporary observer as having 'no very distinctive character as regards employment.'[3] But Devon still met at Exeter for business, politics and amusement. The old life of a provincial capital lingered on into the reigns of William IV and Queen Victoria. It was not extinct at the time of the Boer War. Richard Ford, author, traveller and man of the world, described the Exeter of the 1830s as 'quite a capital, abounding in all that London has except its fog and smoke.'[4] Lady Paterson, wife of a retired general, records in her diary for the years 1831 to 1835[5] the life of an urbane and comfortable society, though in her husband's view Exeter did not attain the standards of contemporary Cheltenham. The Patersons were not wealthy and the general found it necessary to sell his carriage. Indeed, Exeter's popularity as a place for retirement was due to a combination of good society and amenities with cheap living; and so Jane Austen chose the neighbourhood of Exeter as suitable for ladies in the predicament of the Dashwoods a generation before.

The Exeter of Richard Ford and the Patersons was still the old style, self-sufficient provincial capital fulfilling the cultural and social functions which, when the railways made travel easier and cheaper, were taken over by London. The city appeared for the last time in the old role in 1850 when Exeter was host to ambassadors and members of the nobility, to the county gentry, farmers and yeomen who visited the Royal Agricultural Show. The county and the agricultural interest were still supreme. The mayor specially elected for the occasion was the wealthy banker Edward Sanders, Old Harrovian, county cricketer, a keen rider to hounds, a good churchman and throughout the queen's reign the guiding influence in the local Conservative party. In 1850 there assembled in Exeter the older England which was losing ground economically and, more slowly, politically, as the nineteenth century wore on. Exeter in that year seemed as it always had been, at least during the past century or so, and as many hoped it always would be. Conservatives and Liberals together shared a common conservatism. Social habits and the pattern of human relations were based on the past and were not necessarily to be condemned on that account. The city remained a natural growth of the Devon countryside. The beauties of its rural setting not only inspired the raptures of the guide books but were part of an environment which shaped and explained the city's life.

In this society there could be none of the vigorous working-class radicalism of the north, no artisan pressure for improvement. The author of an essay read to the Exeter Literary Society in 1850 deplored the fact that 'from among the assistants employed by the 2,200 shopkeepers of Exeter a less number belongs to the literary societies that may be found in the service of only twelve employers.'[6] The interest displayed by artisans was even less and the Wolverhampton Mechanics Institute was held out as an example to Exeter. No evening classes for adults existed in the city at this period. Exeter was no place for the nonconformist, in the secular sense of the word; and so a bricklayer informed a meeting, in 1871, that 'a man could not express his feelings . . . as he could in larger towns'; if he did he became a marked man.[7] An assistant commissioner reporting for the Royal Commission on Secondary Education of 1894, commented to the same effect: 'whether one could expect any stirrings of life in an old cathedral city would depend greatly on the personal character of those in high position.'[8] Three men were outstanding as leaders of Victorian Exeter. Two were bishops, Henry Phillpotts and Frederick Temple; the third, Sir Stafford Northcote, was a member of county society.

Much of Exeter's nineteenth-century history is summarized by the census records. In 1801 Exeter and Leicester each had a population of about 17,000. By 1851 Exeter had a population of 32,618, Leicester 60,684. At the end of the century the population of Leicester was five times that of Exeter. In 1881 the *Flying Post*, in commenting on the census returns, acknowledged the facts: 'The population returns for the city of Exeter do not show that great increase which is seen in some places. But we must remember that we are no new centre of industry. We do not grow, simply because the process of growth as a city ceased many generations since.'[9] And in 1900 a successful and imaginative Exeter businessman explained to a working-class audience that Exeter had once been the centre of important industries which had employed large bodies of men. That golden age had disappeared. He suggested that the city had been hard hit by the prolonged agricultural depression and by what he termed 'the financial decadence' of the county families.[10] Neither statement can be regarded as typical of urban Victorianism; both summarize Exeter's economic history in the Victorian era.

There were bread riots in 1847, 1854 and 1867. By the seventies there was little occasion for the expression of civic pride which had once sturdily maintained that Exeter had no need for the Public Health Act of 1848. The problems of unemployment and destitution forced themselves upon the leaders of public opinion and were emphasized in the press. It was acknowledged, too, that in drainage and public health Exeter's record was bad.

From the period of stagnation in economic progress and civic life which set in during the sixties Exeter was at length extracted by its geographical position as the gateway to the west, a gateway which was in greater use than ever before as larger numbers of people enjoyed the opportunities of cheap travel and the holiday habit spread. The end of the nineteenth century saw the long-deferred fulfilment by the railways of the high hopes inspired by their arrival at Exeter in 1844 and 1860. It was a slow process. In 1850, when the old order assembled for the Agricultural Show, the first excursion train, from Birmingham, reached Exeter. By the time of the Diamond Jubilee and the Boer War there was a marked revival of moderate prosperity in the city and more building activity than at any previous time in the Victorian period. Railways were an important factor in the demand for the new artisans' houses, as the directories demonstrate. It was fitting that in due course a railwayman should become the first Labour mayor of Exeter. It was about this time, from the eighties onward, that there was a marked increase in wages, by local standards, expecially for the building operatives who consistently throughout the period formed the largest working-class group in the city. The great days of rivalry between the Great Western and the London and South Western railways, which provided a magnificent service to the southwest, improving standards of living in the country as a whole, including the enjoyment of holidays and excursions, revived Exeter. The city had perforce waited passively like the sea anemone on its rock; and the tide had turned.

The history of nineteenth-century Exeter is one of decline and slow adjustment. Its government and politics provide material for a study in the irony of human affairs. The achievements of Exeter as a corporate body were primarily pre-Victorian. No unleashing of the civic spirit emerged from political and administrative reform. The new régime, after 1835, erected no architectural monuments to civic pride. The extension and improvement of the canal, the impressive warehouses of the quay, the Higher Market in Queen Street, were the work of the old régime, the chamber. Victorian Exeter's legacy to the twentieth century was a university, by direct descent derived from the Royal Albert Memorial Museum and Schools of Science and Art. By 1905 Professor

Michael Sadler was inspired to see in Exeter 'the educational metropolis of the west' which inherited 'a great historic position, and no small measure of intellectual prestige.'[11] That this was so was largely due to encouragement by Sir Stafford Northcote and to the driving power of Miss Jessie Montgomery, pioneer of University Extension, niece of Exeter's Canon Cook and daughter of the Rev. Robert Montgomery whose poems had inspired Macaulay's criticism. John Buckmaster, organizing officer of the Department of Science and Art, reported that when he visited Exeter in 1861 nothing came from his visit because Sir Stafford Northcote and Sir John Coleridge were otherwise engaged and so 'destroyed the éclat which would have attached to the meeting.'[12] Urban Exeter could provide the management; for inspiration it looked to the world of the landed gentry.

The parliamentary commissioners of 1833 had found nothing of substance to criticize in Exeter for the report on municipal corporations. The chamber, as the old governing body of the city was called, was certainly self-perpetuating and restricted in its membership. As yet no Dissenter had been admitted, despite the repeal of the Test and Corporations Acts. The chamber's deliberations were conducted in secret. But no evidence of corruption or serious inefficiency was forthcoming, and when giving evidence at the inquiry Reformers were reduced to explaining that their allegations referred to some unspecified past. Yet, in the imagination of Exeter Liberals, Reform would disperse 'the mists of ignorance, bigotry and superstition' and end 'the long reign of waste and plunder.' The civic spirit would be liberated in all its pristine purity and the ratepayers' franchise would provide 'a perfect representation of popular opinion.'[13]

The Municipal Corporations Act did indeed enlarge the field of membership of the council which replaced the chamber. As a wise gesture to the new era the Conservatives arranged the election of a Unitarian ironmonger as the first mayor of the new régime. The civic spirit, however, continued to reflect the weaknesses, as well as the virtues, of mankind. Drunkenness and various forms of pressure rather than 'a perfect representation' became the most obvious feature of council elections. And, since the character of the city could not be changed by act of parliament, the Conservatives retained control of the council throughout the Victorian era, except for three short interludes amounting to thirteen out of seventy-seven years. After an initial period of trial and error in the management of the new electorate, the city's local politics fell under the control of a local boss whom both parties united in condemning at the end of his second mayoralty. This régime was followed by the domination of the licensed trade which campaigned under the banner of church and state and reorganized Exeter's Conservative party after the defeat of 1868. The Liberals came to power in 1837 on a wave of Reform which was partly emotional but which was largely engendered by natural resentment at exclusion from active participation in local affairs. The resentment was not confined to Reformers or Nonconformists. Many citizens for whom new opportunities were provided by the legislation and philosophy of the Reform era settled down as ardent Conservatives. The new Jerusalem dreamed of by the Reformers remained a dream. In political management the children of this world demonstrated that they were wiser than the children of light. On two occasions after the Conservative 'Restoration' of 1840 opposition to Conservative monopoly of power and the ratepayers' customary objections to rising expenditure brought the Liberals into power; for three years in the eighties, more convincingly for seven years in 1900. On each occasion Exeter returned to its Conservative equilibrium. As the *Western Times* stated truly in 1868, 'the tone of the city, what is called its respectability, is undoubtedly Tory.'[14]

Throughout the period Nonconformity remained the core of Exeter's Liberal party. The principles of Nonconformity, the insistence on the freedom of the individual conscience and, as a Wesleyan mayor put it in 1882, that 'the laws of a Christian state, enacted by Christian men, should be imperative,'[15] introduced to Exeter's politics moral values which had been a factor in national politics since the seventeenth century and at no time were more important than in the nineteenth. The Nonconformist conscience was at times

B

an embarrassment to politicians, as Coleridge, the 'eloquent Tractarian,' discovered when he stood as Liberal parliamentary candidate in 1864; but Nonconformity ensured that a strong minority in the city remained Liberal. Under the two-member system this minority normally secured parliamentary representation until the city was reduced to one member by the Redistribution Act of 1885.

Throughout the period the council was firmly divided on political lines. Both parties deplored the fact. Both were equally responsible for a practice which began with the first election under the new system on Boxing Day 1835. Both at times expressed hopes that the councillors might be elected, not as members of a party, but because they were the wisest and the best, the guardians of platonic philosophy. 'The Ballot Act will secure orderly polling and we hope to see the conviction that Municipal Corporations should be free from political strife growing with the intelligence of the Burgesses,' declared the Liberal *Western Times* in 1875, 'we have had forty years of political strife.' 'Municipal elections are now, to our great regret, carried on with strict and embittered reference to party politics' complained the Conservative *Flying Post* in 1886. In 1882 the *Flying Post* mourned that

'years ago men of position, wealth and leisure were proud to serve the public offices of the city, and the city was well served by men who gave dignity to the municipal life of the city. But the difficulty is to find men of position to have anything to do with public work.'

And in 1913 the mayor informed the congress of the Royal Sanitary Institute that 'for a variety of reasons those who by virtue of their education, leisure, business training or strong personality would, and should, be the most valuable members in the public service, stood aside in greater numbers and declined to serve.'[16]

Every generation is inclined to sigh *eheu fugaces* and complaints of the standard of the council were not always objective. But they had some substance. The civic spirit in all its imagined purity had not been released by act of parliament. There was much justification for the *Flying Post*'s assertion in 1875 that 'Local government is rapidly dying out before the aggressions of central authorities,'[17] and in the complaint of the *Western Times* in the eighties that centralization held local authorities 'in an iron grip.'[18]

To portray Exeter exclusively as a 'Wasteland' would be misleading. The city after all was composed 'Of all manner of men . . . Working and wandering, as the world asks of them,'[19] sincere, God-fearing, charitable and public-spirited. Henry Ellis, the jeweller, attributing his success 'under God's good providence . . .' to 'constant and steady habits of Perseverance, Diligence and Industry'[20] and taking infinite pains over the well-being of his employees; Father Galton of St Sidwell's, a conscientious and beloved parish priest though he opposed the reform of the educational charities with *'nolumus leges Angliae mutari';* R. S. Cornish, entertaining the workhouse children; William Kendall the woollen draper, a generous supporter of the Albert Memorial Museum; William Cotton, manager of the National Provincial Bank, treasurer of the Arts and Science Department of the Museum, archaeologist and antiquary, historian of an Elizabethan gild, author of *Gleanings from the Municipal and Cathedral Records of Exeter*; H. A. Willey, who sent his workmen across the Atlantic to study conditions in America; newspaper editors and proprietors like Thomas Latimer and Edward Woolmer, so different in their background but alike in their independence and integrity; men such as these, and many more, deserve to be remembered with respect. They gave of their best to their vocations and to their city.

Because Exeter was small, its social structure was inclined to be inhibiting; it could yet retain the old personal relationships between employers and men and a certain neighbourliness between rich and poor. Deprived of the opportunities and prizes of economic growth, the city was not called upon to pay the price of urban success, the impersonal relations, the wilderness of bricks and slate, the dreariness of more successful cities with their great industrial areas and the geographical separation of classes. The city's Liberalism, sometimes naïve, too often a mere protest against expenditure, and always contending with an unfavourable environment, was not a nullity. In its insistence on political and religious equality, freedom of personal judgment and the responsibility of a governing body towards the governed, it was yet a vital strand in Exeter life, as much a part of the city as its opposite.

Studies of Exeter in the city's most successful days as a semi-independent and self-sufficient *polis* exist in W. T. MacCaffrey's *The Civic Community of Exeter 1550–1630* (1958); W. B. Stephens's *Seventeenth Century Exeter* (1958); and W. G. Hoskins's *Industry, Trade and People in Exeter 1688–1800* (1935). Alexander Jenkins' *Civil and Ecclesiastical History of the City of Exeter* was published in 1806. The second edition of George Oliver's *History of the City of Exeter* came out in 1861 but virtually ignores the contemporary scene in which the author lived and laboured, T. J. Northey's *Popular History of Exeter*, published in 1885. and E. A. Freeman's *Exeter*, of 1887, in the 'Historic Towns' series, are both general in scope and perfunctory in their treatment of the Victorian city. To Freeman, Victorian Exeter was no longer historic. W. G. Hoskins' *Two Thousand Years in Exeter*, published in 1960, was the first to describe life and work in the nineteenth century and is necessarily brief.

The present work is an attempt to show 'our forefathers remote and recent, in their habits as they lived, intent on the business of a long-vanished day.'[21] Inevitably it has been necessary to be severely selective. Economic and social problems, the copious field of Victorian religious and educational controversy, in themselves can provide ample material for a book. More could have been written on the position of the clergy. The discussions and arguments over railway development have been omitted. Much use has been made of the contemporary newspapers to establish the framework, what happened and when. Newspapers do not necessarily give a true explanation of events, but they reported what was done and said with a fullness derived from the principle that knowledge was necessary for the exercise of active and vigilant citizenship, and with the corollary that, given knowledge, citizenship would respond. The great days of Exeter's press were over by the seventies. 'It is then,' wrote

Thomas Latimer, 'a great privilege to be one of the guides and teachers of the people. This privilege is conferred on the journalist.'[22] In the time of Woolmer and Trewman, Latimer and Bellerby, the Exeter press, rumbustious, hard hitting and at times reminiscent of the Eatanswill Independent and the Eatanswill Gazette did not fall far short of this ideal, as *The Athenaeum* pointed out in 1869.[23] In the later period it still continued to cover local affairs with a valuable wealth of detail and often with pungent comment.

Against the achievements and heart-searchings of Victorian England the history of Victorian Exeter is a study in quiet lives. Not for Exeter was the vigour implicit in 'the roaring looms of many-gated Leeds';[24] in Grey Street and Elswick, Newcastle upon Tyne. There was no local leader of the calibre of Joseph Chamberlain or Joseph Cowen. Nonetheless Exeter was representative of a great section of Victorian life, the world of Trollope and Surtees surviving in, and moulded by, a rural environment and, for good and ill, by the traditions of the country house and the rectory. In the last resort the city's Victorian history is a record of progress, not on all fronts, but in the improved standards of living which were at length apparent by 1914.

EARLY VICTORIAN EXETER

I

EXETER IN 1837

Prologue

IN June 1837 the citizens of the ancient city of Exeter greeted
the accession of Queen Victoria with feelings as mixed as
their politics. The announcement of a new era does not
always stand scrutiny in the perspective of history. Nevertheless, the replacement of an eccentric old Tory king by a
Whiggish young queen fortuitously coincided with a new era
in the history of Exeter. It was the year in which the Exeter
Liberals[1] captured an ephemeral control of the city council,
thus instituting the brief reign of the 'spirit of Reform' which,
it was hoped, would modernize and, more optimistically,
purify, outworn institutions. 'The fashion of this day passeth
away' as one Exeter Reformer put it with the blend of
biblical learning and optimism characteristic of his type.[2]

Reports of the late king's failing health had appeared in
the local papers since the beginning of the month. On 14
June the Whig *Flying Post* informed its readers that once
more 'after an interval of 125 years, from the death of
Queen Anne, a female wields the sceptre of these realms, and
in her we have a Princess of no ordinary promise.'[3] The
Liberal *Western Times* was enthusiastic in 'homage to the
rising hopes of old England; the coming of age of Princess
Alexandrina Guelph.'[4] In contrast there was misgiving in the
comment of the Conservative *Exeter and Plymouth Gazette*
that 'the Whig – Radicals are now soliciting the support of
the electors, and are deceitfully and impudently assuming
that the circumstance of the Queen having appointed Lord
Melbourne and his Cabinet is a proof that her Majesty is
favourable to that policy.'[5]

Exeter's proclamation of the young queen inaugurated the
new era with a characteristic touch of Eatanswill and much
that was reminiscent of Rowlandson. In St Petrock's parish

church a young clergyman caused smiles by his prayer to 'so rule the heart of . . . our Queen and Governess.'[6] The proclamation was accompanied by a civic procession formed with all the pageantry of the old-style city life, which Utilitarian dogmatism denounced as 'the silly pageantry of the big hat and the "gert" long sword of the gentlemen who strut before the men in cocked hats'[7]: The Military and the Staff of the East Devon Militia; the Trade Incorporations with their banners; the Clerk of the Corporation of the Poor, the Beadles and the Gentlemen composing the Forty Guardians of the Poor with their Apothecaries, the Blue Boys of St John's Hospital; the Staff Bearers, Trumpeters, and a Herald on Horseback; the Serjeants at Mace; the Right Worshipful the Mayor and Magistrates; Aldermen, Councillors, with the Naval and Military Officers, and 'such citizens as [felt] disposed to attend.' Eighteenth-century pageantry was marshalled to greet the new era. Flanked by constables the procession proceeded through the narrow streets for the five-fold reading of the proclamation.

Argument had raged over the person of the herald, for politics were an expression of vigorous local life. William IV had been proclaimed by one Rippon, certainly a sound Tory, allegedly the tallest tailor in the city, his Toryism inseparable from his business as 'clerical robe and cap maker.'[8] The rival candidate, George Augustus Moore, had been custodian of the flags and banners with which the Exeter Reformers had been celebrating their recent victories. Moore had been wounded at Waterloo, whereas Rippon's military service had been confined to less arduous duties with the militia.[9] The new council approved Moore's appointment. The Conservative jeweller Henry Ellis, who had no love for political enthusiasts on either side, noted that 'The Liberal party being now in the ascendant, poor Rippon the Tory herald was deprived of the office he had filled with so much credit to himself on previous occasions.'[10] The herald's supporters claimed that this new victory of enlightenment was confirmed by Moore acquitting himself 'with all that ease, grace and self-possession which those best acquainted with his melodramatic genius so fondly anticipated.'[11] It was an age when local personalities and differences, products of a vigorous local life, were fought out vigorously in terms of national politics. Whether it was a question of a Buff job over the appointment of a tollman or the appointment of the herald of a day, the assertion of moral principles and material progress was as much the justification as the cause of local strife. At the grass roots, the rivalries, ambitions and differences of individuals and groups transformed the clash of policy and principle into more tangible objects of contest.

A new reign required a general election. The prospect of a contest momentarily agitated the city. Exeter was well represented in parliament by a Conservative, Sir William Webb Follett, and a Liberal, Edward Divett of Bystock, the latter termed by his supporters a 'stern, uncompromising advocate of Reform,'[12] who was also business adviser of the ironmaster Sir John Guest.[13] Both were local men. Follett was the son of a Topsham timber merchant. Educated at Exeter Grammar School and Trinity, Cambridge, he had been called to the Bar in 1824. An accomplished speaker, 'his voice was music itself and his reasoning the most seductive and charming';[14] he was also a prodigious worker. By birth and education a Liberal and a Nonconformist, Follett became a Conservative. From 1834 to 1835 he had been solicitor-general in Peel's brief government. He had contested Exeter unsuccessfully in 1832. In 1835 he had been returned at the head of the poll and retained the seat without difficulty till his premature death in 1845, when he was attorney-general in Peel's second government, leaving a fortune of £160,000 and a reputation as one of the greatest advocates of the century.

Divett had the county connections which eased the path of Liberal parliamentary candidate for Exeter, his father having bought the Bystock estate near Budleigh Salterton in 1773. He had been brought forward for the Exeter election of 1831 by his brother-in-law, a Buller, with the support of Lord Ebrington and Sir George Bampfylde. A man with business interests, of Liberal, but independent, views and active in his constituency, Divett first stood for Exeter in April 1831, when he came bottom of the poll in an electorate of 936. In the first post-Reform Bill election of 1832 Divett took second place, defeating Follett by 502 votes and remaining a representative of the city until his death in 1864. Divett was a conscientious and able member of that section of the electorate described by a local Conservative newspaper as 'the numerous and effective middle classes of society, who are desirous only that those practical improvements in our political system should be made, which are compatible with the constitution of our country and the knowledge of this age';[15] as such he was to be criticized by the more radical for failing to support Hume's motion on parliamentary reform in 1850.

Conservatives such as Henry Ellis, who held aloof from active politics and disliked 'agitators and noisy politicians, regarded both Follett and Divett as dignified successors to the county families who had represented Exeter in the past. 'They were both men of good family and position, born and living in the immediate neighbourhood of Exeter and therefore proper men to represent in Parliament their ancient and loyal city.'[16] In 1837 a brief flutter was caused by hints that this tidy arrangement of the city's parliamentary representation might be disturbed. Charles Brutton, attorney, future mayor, friend and agent of the Earl of Devon, was suspected of designs to bring forward Lord Courtenay in an attempt to unseat Divett. If there had been any such intention the Conservatives thought better of it.

In consequence the election of 22 July 1837 was a relatively decorous affair, the absence of a contest having limited the supply of drink usual on such occasions. Even so, the proceedings were noisy and the opening of the gates of the Guildhall was the signal for a rush which speedily filled the old building. The city's leaders took up their positions on the stage, each in the role expected by his supporters.

Divett's proposer, after a suitable reference to the accession of 'our youthful Queen,' aroused Tory ire by voicing the hope that the grey hairs of the heir presumptive, the Duke of Cumberland, 'would never be oppressed by the weight of an English crown.'[17] A counter-attack was launched by 'Iron Sam' Kingdon, wealthy Unitarian ironmonger and a sound

Conservative, recently elected by his party as the first mayor of the new régime after the Municipal Corporations Act of 1835. Kingdon, whose harsh voice and forthright manner were an asset on such occasions, proposed Follett on the grounds that the candidate 'would be found the supporter of every fair and just and substantial reform – of every reform that would really benefit the nation.' The implication provoked renewed uproar. Proceedings were brought to a standstill by the speaker's praise of the Duchess of Kent and the well-justified insinuation that the Whig ministers were exercising undue influence on the queen.

Kingdon's seconder, the young banker Edward Sanders, who made his political debut on this occasion, went on to exercise a potent influence on the local Conservative party till the twentieth century. Born in 1813, Old Harrovian, county cricketer and keen rider to hounds, in 1900 Sanders was to preside over a Conservative cause based on patriotism and General Buller. He died in 1905 after sixty years of chairmanship of the committees of Conservative parliamentary candidates. Moving on easy terms with the county and cathedral society, Sanders and members of his family wielded effective influence in local politics. He was related to Ralph Barnes, bishop's secretary and chapter clerk, and Samuel Barnes, alderman and prominent surgeon.

Sander's first political speech was short and delivered with becoming modesty. Divett then rose to declare that he had supported the reform of corporations with the object of introducing into all towns and cities 'a good local government, formed in the most popular manner, and in which all persons contributing to the burthens of the place were called upon to take part.' Above all, his object was to check wasteful or mistaken expenditure. He supported the reform of the Irish Church and of Irish municipal corporations. He believed that it was the duty of the state to provide all that was necessary to bring a good education and sound instruction into the hands of every class. The bias of his mind was in favour of the abolition of the death penalty and he 'had the misfortune to differ from some of his constituents on Sabbath legislation, believing that the cheerful decorum which should characterize the Sabbath could not be achieved by legislation.'

Follett began with a polished tribute to his opponent. As to the position of the queen, 'there might be differences of opinion on certain points but there was a unanimous feeling of loyalty and attachment to the throne.' He desired that education should be made as wide and general as possible. He did not support the proposed abolition of the death sentence but he was at one with his colleague on sabbatarian legislation. He had not voted for the initiation of corporations' reform because he did not believe that the bill had been framed 'with due consideration of circumstances which existed in the various towns and cities to which it was to be applied.' He did not vote for the proposal to disfranchise the freemen because there was no good cause to deprive those persons of the privilege which they had inherited from their forefathers. He was also opposed to Irish municipal reform because 'the municipal corporations in Ireland had been placed in that country exclusively to keep up the English influence.'

Follett then touched on church rates, a subject which was currently causing turmoil in the Exeter vestries. He was ready to remove any hardship that pressed on the Dissenters but this was a question 'not so much of relief to the Dissenters, as a measure for stripping the dignitaries of the church of the possessions of the church.' On the question of reform 'he would not obstruct reform of the institutions of the country, but there was a great difference between settling some questions of conscience and upsetting all that was established in the land.'

The speeches of the candidates were temperate expressions of moderate opinion delivered by men of the world. The proceedings terminated with the customary procession of the re-elected members from Exeter to Heavitree through decorated streets. The Conservatives dined with speeches and songs at the Royal Subscription Rooms. Divett celebrated 'with a numerous party of highly respectable and influential electors' at the Half Moon. Exeter returned to its business and to face the adventures and problems of the Victorian Era.

The Setting

In 1837 man and nature, not yet divorced, had created an environment in which the citizens of Exeter could still live 'under the natural and ubiquitous influence of lovely sights and sounds.'[18] The 'spirit of improvement'[19] had been in the air since the late eighteenth century. In the eyes of contemporaries the city had much changed; but the builder-architects using local materials and the current manuals of classical architecture had achieved a harmony of old and new within a rural stting. Even the severely functional warehouses recently completed on the quay harmonized with the scene where the Exe, ending its journey from the bog and cotton grass of the Exmoor Chains, flowed through the water meadows under the cathedral towards Topsham and the sea.

Tristram Risdon in the seventeenth century found Exeter 'pleasantly situated on a hill among hills . . . very beautiful . . . in building and for quantity matchable with most cities.'[20] The Rev. George Oliver, the city's kindly and erudite Catholic priest, watched with gratification Exeter's development. His panegyric deserves quotation as an assertion of civic pride that was not wholly unjustified:

'Where do the constituted authorities display more considerate liberality in providing places of recreation and beautiful and airy walks, like Northernhay, Bury Meadow and Bonhay? What town can boast of more convenient locomotive communication with our charming watering places, and of conveyance to every part of the kingdom . . . Where [shall we] find a climate more mild, more equable and more salubrious, and where superior medical relief is more accessible? . . . No reasonable being need seek elsewhere a residence more salubrious, comfortable, polite and friendly.'[21]

Deep in trees, ringed by the seemly estates and villas of the gentry and prosperous merchants, dominated by the great towers of the cathedral, backed by the long perspectives of the Exe, the wooded ridge of Haldon, in sight of the sea, Exeter throughout the nineteenth century, and beyond, retained the atmosphere of pre-industrial England. Its history was shaped accordingly.

The city was still essentially the Exeter of the Tudors enclosed within the remnants of the old walls. From Northernhay 'tastefully laid out in walks and shrubberies under the antiquated city walls and ivy-mantled towers,'[22] fields sloped down to the Longbrook and up to the recently completed New North Road. From northeast round to southeast a thin suburban growth outside the walls extended along the roads that fanned out from the coaching terminus – London Inn Square. Working within the discipline of classical architecture Georgian and Regency architects had created suburbs of charm and taste: Higher and Lower Summerlands, Southernhay, St Anne's Terrace and Belmont Terrace; the Mount Radford estate in St Leonards, once the home of the Barings and bought and developed by the firm of William and Henry Hooper 'as a place of residence for people of independent means.'[23]

Within the walls, and between the western wall and the river, there remained much of the old medieval city, its narrow alleys and packed slums interspersed with the open spaces formed by the gardens and courts that had once belonged to the wealthier merchants and industrialists. The extensive property of John Blackmore, offered for sale in 1837,[24] included offices, walled garden, warehouses and greenhouse. The age of the intensive development of urban property was just beginning.

Tudor Exeter was tenacious of life and much was to survive until the early years of the twentieth century. Dr Shapter's story of the terrible cholera year of 1832[25] describes the narrow streets paved with cobbles, the open gutters which provided the only means for the disposal of sewage and household slops. Water was still obtained largely from private wells, an ancient conduit, cisterns and a few public pumps. An attempt had been made by the Reformer John Golsworthy to supply water through iron pipes in 1811 but the cholera revealed the inadequacies of his system. As a result of the epidemic Golsworthy's interest had been purchased and the Exeter Water Company founded in 1833 with a reservoir at Dane's Castle near the county prison. Old houses, especially in the lower parts of the city, had been converted into tenements and were occupied by five to fifteen families crowded into dark and insanitary rooms. It is not surprising that in September 1837, it was reported that smallpox was 'raging to an unprecedented extent, and with unusual mortality, especially in the lower parts of the city.'[26] The children of the poor were accordingly offered free vaccination at the dispensary.

With the development of wheeled traffic in the second half of the eighteenth century it had become necessary to widen streets and ease the gradients of the road system which made Exeter the gateway to the west. By 1837 the imposing city gates had been removed one by one beginning with the south gate, 'the fairest and most imposing,' in 1819.[27] Exeter is still hilly but the improvements that began in the coaching era have smoothed or obliterated the more prominent physical features of the city on the narrow ridge site running northeast to southwest down the axis of Sidwell Street, High Street and Fore Street and so to the river. The steep ascent up Fore Street hill was moderated in 1834. The Iron Bridge, today still giving useful service, was completed in 1835 for the benefit of the wagons and coaches from north Devon making the descent from St David's Hill to the Longbrook Valley and the ascent to North Street. In the previous year the New North Road had been completed as a link with the turnpike to Barnstaple along the Taw valley.

To remove trading in the open streets, which blocked High Street and Fore Street on Tuesdays and Fridays, the chamber had embarked on the construction of the Higher and Lower markets, two outstanding examples of classical architecture, the first designed by the distinguished Cullompton architect George Fowler and the latter largely Fowler's work. The new markets and their access had necessitated the removal of a tangle of medieval lanes and houses. The future Queen Street, so named in 1839, where the Higher Market still stands, was under construction at this period as a new means of entry to the city and a link with the New North Road and the recently completed turnpike to Crediton and Barnstaple.

C

In 1836 a contributor to the *Sporting Magazine* took it for granted that 'everything connected with public travelling had, say within the last ten years, approached as near perfection as anything of mortal mould might.'[28] The improved roads and increase in travel reinforced the position of Exeter as a centre of communications. The epic of 'The Exeter Road' had begun. From Exeter's London Inn Square the coaches left for Honiton, Cullompton and Taunton and onwards to London, Bath and Bristol. The famous Telegraph 'that very superior well-conducted fast coach'[29] left the New London Inn at 5.0 a.m. and reached London in seventeen hours. By 1832 the Telegraph had become 'quite the go in consequence of Lord Ebrington, Mr Divett and other celebrated Reformers having taken it into their patronage.'[30]

Improved means of travel and increased wealth brought to Exeter the country gentry of Devon for business and amusement, for the assizes, political meetings, concerts and balls. The city's climate, cultural amenities and cheapness attracted visitors and retired people. To meet the needs and taste of polite society the Royal Subscription Rooms, an elegant classical building, had been erected in 1821 by subscription from the gentry of Devon and Exeter, and became a centre of social life. In close proximity, in Southernhay Square, the similarly classical public baths were constructed in the same year to provide 'cold, hot, plunge, shower and medicated baths.' The Theatre Royal, facing a row of 'new genteel houses' in East Southernhay, had been rebuilt in 1820.

Technological progress brought gas, first used for street lighting in Exeter in 1817. In February 1837 the Exeter Commercial Gas Company were actively engaged in laying pipes throughout the city. A new and large gasometer had recently been erected in the Bonhay. By 1837 the gas company's office in Castle Street was offering its customers 'a very cleverly constructed and simple apparatus for cooking by gas.' The company was profitable throughout the century. Henry Ellis invested £200 at £25 in 1836; this, he recorded, 'proved a profitable speculation.'[31]

Within the 1,800 acres enclosed by the municipal boundaries lived a population of some 31,305 people. Exeter had lost the industrial importance which in the eighteenth century had made the name of the city synonymous with the serge trade.[32] By the 1830s the former source of wealth and employment had become little more than a memory perpetuated by the abandoned rack yards, the old fulling houses and drying sheds in the lower quarters of the city, and the dwindling number of fullers and weavers appearing in the electoral lists. Dr Thomas Shapter, with some exaggeration, described the Exeter of 1800 as a manufacturing city. By 1831 he wrote, the woollen manufacture had virtually ceased and the population had 'no very distinctive character.' It consisted of 'gentry, tradespeople, artisans and the ordinary admixture of the poor.'[33] Wealth and power lay in the hands of professional men, attorneys, surgeons, bankers, wine and spirit merchants, innkeepers and brewers, builders, mercers and grocers. Exeter was living, and prospering, as a centre for the distribution of goods and services and on the business derived from its position as a political and social capital.

Since the city had grown great on overseas trade the unreformed governing body, the chamber, in its later years had turned its attention to the modernization of the canal. Between 1825 and 1831 some £106,527 had been spent on this object. It was a brave decision taken a generation too late. In the old canal, vessels had been frequently delayed for want of water and none drawing more than nine feet could approach the city.[34] The new basin had been completed in 1830 with the display of enthusiasm with which the early nineteenth century greeted progress; a procession of decorated barges, gunfire and music, and the plaudits of many thousands of spectators. Freight rates were reduced by 20 per cent. The price of coal was halved. The number of sea-going vessels and coastal traders entering the port of Exeter grew substantially during the early years of the century.[35] But the advent of the age of steam was acknowledged by the new council, in 1836, with a resolution that in future all convicts from Topsham should be carried by steamship.[36] And early in 1837 a correspondent informed the readers of the *Flying Post* that he had just returned from

Bristol where the Bristol to Exeter railroad was 'going on with great spirit.'[37]

At this point in Exeter's history, amid the final erosion of an old industry and with the opportunities and uncertainties of the railway age ahead, the city was still at its peak as a social and cultural capital. Exeter could not compete with the attractions of Bath or Cheltenham. General Paterson, living in retirement in Baring Crescent, found Cheltenham considerably gayer than Exeter and, after he had given up his carriage as too expensive to maintain, he experienced no difficulty in travelling to Gloucestershire by coach.[38] But the parliamentary commissioners reporting in 1832 remarked upon 'the rows of respectable houses and villas occupied by retired officers, professional men and persons connected with the city of Exeter.'[39] The attractions of the city were recorded with enthusiasm in 1835 by Richard Ford.

'This Exeter is quite a capital, abounding in all that London has except its fog and smoke. There is an excellent institution here with a well-chosen library in which I take great pastime and am beginning my education. There is a bookseller who has some ten thousand old volumes. Here one has no vices or expenses, except eating clotted cream.'[40]

The Devon and Exeter Institution, to which Ford referred, had been founded in 1813 to promote science, literature and the arts. By 1837 it had acquired a library of nearly 15,000 volumes.[41] The Public Select Library in the High Street, founded in 1807, was intended primarily for young persons: it therefore excluded 'all books of an immoral nature, novels, dramatic productions, works on controversial divinity and party politics.'[42]. In 1835, the Exeter Athenaeum had been completed 'for the purpose of holding public lectures and demonstrations of science, literature and the arts.'[2] The promoters of the Athenaeum, however, misjudged the extent of the culturally-minded public in the neighbourhood. As Henry Ellis remarked:

'the number of gentlemen and professional men addicted to scientific pursuits being insufficient to keep it up with proper spirit . . . it finally became appropriated to the services of the humble, but more useful, Literary Society.'[43]

It was still the golden age of the amateur archaeologist, naturalist, historian and scientist. Physicians, surgeons, clergy and country gentlemen could find time for learned works:

> 'Small treatises and smaller verses,
> And sage remarks on chalk and clay,
> And hints to noble Lords – and Nurses.'

The Devon and Exeter Institution in the Cathedral Yard preserves today the atmosphere of that time: the volumes of tracts and sermons; lectures and discourses, the transactions of learned societies; correct poetry on rural scenes in the manner of Cowper; engravings of gentlemen's country seats and 'picturesque' landscapes.

Exeter had its share of men with inquiring and speculative minds seeking knowledge of their environment, human and natural, and finding relaxation in inquiry; men such as Edward Upham, member of the chamber, bookseller, mayor of Exeter, author of a *History of Buddhism*, two novels on oriental themes and *A Concise History of Turkey*.[44] Philip de la Garde, surgeon and last mayor of the unreformed corporation, member of the Devon and Exeter Architectural Society, was the author of a book on cataract as well as of many papers on archaeological subjects.[45] Thomas Shapter, mayor in 1846, wrote the section on Exeter in the Health of Towns Report of 1845 as well as *The History of the Cholera in 1832* and *Medica Sacra, or Short Expositions of the more Important Diseases mentioned in the Sacred Writings*.

People of leisure, such as Lady Paterson and her daughter, spent much of their time receiving visitors or paying calls. Margaret Paterson enjoyed walks and picnics. Her other relaxations, which would have been frowned upon at a later date, included listening to breach of promise and murder cases at the assizes.[46] Lady Paterson would hire a barouche for a trip to Topsham or accompany Sir William in a fly from Baring Crescent to Cowley Bridge to admire 'the great improvements going on in Exeter and the suburbs.'[47]

Concerts, balls and the theatre enlivened city life and entertained the families of the country gentry visiting Exeter for the assizes and politics. General Paterson and his family

were 'astonished and enraptured with the wonderful performance of Paganini' whose appearance in Exeter attracted
the *haut ton* from Torquay.[48] Samuel Phelps, who was to
make a national reputation at Sadler's Wells, made his first
appearance at Exeter's Theatre Royal in 1836 and was
'nightly honoured with unprecedented applause.'[49] In 1837
the theatre provided a social occasion under the patronage of
young Matthew Parker fresh from his victory over Lord
John Russell in the South Devon election. The proceedings
were enlivened by cheers for Parker, Sir John Buller and Sir
William Follett and by counter-demonstrations from Whigs
and Reformers. The ball at the Subscription Rooms in
September 1837 under the patronage of Lady Carew attracted
three members of parliament, including Edward Divett,
together 'with about 230 of the rank, beauty and fashion of
the County.'[50] Society danced late; Margaret Paterson
returned from an assize ball at 3.0 a.m. Fancy dress balls
were popular and were the occasion for much borrowing of
exotic garments. It was the age of the Eglinton Tournament,
of Harrison Ainsworth and Bulwer Lytton. Exeter society
adopted with gusto Turkish attire or sported vaguely
medieval plumes, armour and beards.[51]

Across the Exe, St Thomas was, and long remained, a
centre of wrestling, then a rough sport accompanied by much
shin-kicking. Shooting was popular and citizens could enjoy
'much betting and gaiety' at sparrow matches organized at
the Blue Ball on the edge of Clyst Heath. On one occasion
some seventy sparrows 'as well as jays, sparrow hawks,
shelducks and herons, were sacrificed at the trap to the
detonating propensities of the amateurs present after a
sumptuous dinner at the inn.'[52] The old custom of 'skimming-
ton riding,' a rough and ready treatment of persons suspected
of marital infidelity by their neighbours, was still maintained
and caused an affray in St Sidwells in 1837.[53]

In 1837 the working classes could congratulate themselves
on having escaped the tribulations experienced by their
fellows in town and country in the England of the 1830s.
Captain Chapman, reporting on Exeter for the inquiry into
the state of the poor laws, commented that the city had been

exempt from any marked local vicissitudes during a long series of years. Wages varied from 10s. to 12s. a week. Agricultural labourers were paid 7s. to 9s. with an allowance of 1s. 9d. for a third child.[54] The council's labourers on the canal received between 1s. 4d. to 2s. 9d. a day according to experience.[55] The watch at this time were paid 14s. a week and permanently employed skilled labourers of the council received 13s. to 14s.[56] Relatively well off were the journeymen papermakers whose demand for $3\frac{1}{2}d$. an hour and a sixty-hour week was refused by the employers in January. According to the employers the men received 18s. to 23s. a week and, with wives and children employed, might earn as much as 50s. a week.[57] A married clerk might expect £30 a year in private employment.[58] Henry Ellis, in the previous year, had increased the salary of a trusted female clerk to 20 guineas.[59]

Wages of 10s. to 12s. a week represent an annual income of £26 to £31 4s. a year. In 1841 the assistant clerk of the St Thomas Union calculated on the basis of the workhouse dietary that an agricultural labourer with four to five children would need to spend £21 12s. 5d. a year on bread alone. Other articles, such as milk, fuel, potatoes, clothing and rent, would increase the family's annual expenditure to about £30 a year.[60] Prices in 1841 were rather higher than in 1837, and 14s. a week would have represented reasonable conditions, by the standards of the time, for artisans in regular employment such as members of the watch or carpenters employed by the council. But there could have been few artisans regularly employed, especially in view of the large proportion of the working class employed in the building trade and allied activities liable to disruption by bad weather. Ordinary labourers received a maximum of 2s. a day depending on the circumstances. In normal times they survived; but in 1837 Exeter was entering upon a period of rising prices, at times of famine prices, and some forty years of economic stagnation. An advertisement for workers in the local paper industry included the warning that 'no cardmen need apply.'[61] Victorian Exeter then and throughout the period discouraged trade unions.

For the poor in hard times and misfortune there was always

recourse to the workhouse or to the uncertainties of private relief. Good employers like the Ellis family might be relied upon to assist former employees, especially those who had virtually become members of the household, private charitable organizations abounded.[62] Signs of hard times became apparent in 1838 when a public meeting was 'called to take into consideration the best plan of providing some permanent means of relieving the poor and destitute.'[63] This meeting was the origin of the Exeter Relief Society which was to be active throughout the whole of the Victorian era. The reports of the annual meetings as published in the local press provide some indication of economic vicissitudes in the city.

Captain Chapman, whose report was published in 1834, commented that Exeter 'provided a striking instance of the effects of a good workhouse combined with the means of setting the poor to work.'[64] Dr Thomas Shapter wrote that Exeter in 1831 contained 'the ordinary admixture of the poor.'[65] Shapter's own account of the cholera of 1832 is evidence that the 'ordinary admixture of the poor' included severe poverty, squalour and destitution; but evidently Exeter was free of the problems which necessitated the inquiry into the poor laws and which produced the drastic Poor Law Amendment Act of 1834.[66] Exeter's corporation of the poor, according to Captain Chapman, administered relief with firmness, efficiency and humanity. Measured by expenditure alone pauperism in the Exeter of 1837 was not as serious as it had been, or as it was to be later. Even if the extraordinary expenditure required by the cholera epidemic of 1832 is not taken into account the average annual expenditure by the Exeter guardians was still lower in the period 1837–43 than in 1831–36.

By the standards of the day, and notwithstanding the denunciations of Reformers, Exeter at the time of the queen's accession was a well-administered provincial city. Charitable organizations worked in the environment of a close-knit society. Propinquity and personal contact encouraged the observance of a man's duty towards his neighbour. Similar conditions could not exist in the barbaric conditions of the slums of Liverpool or the parish of St Mary, Whitechapel.

A humane concern for the state of the poor did not necessarily imply any great interest in working-class education. In 1838, 2,045 working-class children received education of a sort in schools, including dames' schools, which a select committee of the house of commons[67] described as 'very indifferent.' Since conditions regarded as suitable for working-class children were strictly utilitarian the description was an understatement by more modern standards. A total of 1,830 children were educated in establishments described as 'better schools.' Educational facilities for working-class children in Exeter were not as appalling as they were in some of the great manufacturing towns experiencing the problems of unmanageable growth; but they were worse in Exeter than in the city of York which, in 1832, had a population of 25,359, some 3,000 less than the population of Exeter. In York, 2,697 working-class children were educated in the better schools and 1,494 in the inferior schools. Not only did York contrive to provide education for more children but the education was superior. The predominance of the Church of England in education at this time was beyond effective challenge. Day schools in Exeter administered by religious denominations provided for 5,618 children in Church of England schools and for 162 in Nonconformist schools; 3,663 children attended Church of England Sunday Schools and 1,193 the Sunday Schools of Nonconformists.

The select committee of 1838 formed the opinion that, allowing for the children of the richer or middle classes, it should not be necessary to provide daily education for more than one-eighth of the population. Exeter failed to achieve this proportion even with the inclusion of children educated in 'very indifferent' establishments. On this issue the city stands condemned by the standards of the day. Brighton, Sheffield, Reading and York, unlike Exeter, contrived in 1838 to have more children educated in the better type of schools than in the indifferent.

Responsible people at Exeter doubtless agreed with the definition of education given by a witness to the select committee of 1838: 'sound religious instruction, correct moral training, and a sufficient extent of secular knowledge

suited to [the] station in life' of the pupils.[68] Most, too, would
have accepted the priority given to religious instruction. By
1837 Exeter was already experiencing the dominating influence which religion was to exercise on life in Victorian
England.

In 1837 the cathedral city of Exeter, and the vast diocese of
Devon, Cornwall and Scilly, were uneasily adjusting themselves to their new bishop, Henry Phillpotts. High Churchman and High Tory, a vigorous polemical writer and orator,
and an efficient administrator, Phillpotts was the last bishop
appointed by the Wellington government. Unpopular with
many for his outspoken opposition to the Reform Bill, he
was suspect to many of his clergy, and assailed as Judas by
Radicals, on the grounds that he had bought preferment by
changing his views towards Catholic emancipation in 1829.
This accusation was due to the inability of the average man
to follow a subtlety of mind and mastery of dialectics which
the bishop shared with his admirer Mr Gladstone.[69]

Philpotts's theological learning and skill in controversy
eluded the understanding of a diocese which on the whole
was Protestant in the tradition of Kingsley's Salvation Yeo.
The city's attitude to the finer shades of theological controversy was expressed by Mark Kennaway, himself an
Anglican Reformer: 'I say that the Protestant principle of
this country is that which is intelligible to the wayfaring man.
If you tell me that it consists in the Apostolical Succession,
I say that you are another pope.'[70] In practice the city knew
few Catholics. It was worthy of comment that John Porter,
elected for St Paul's ward in 1847, was a member of this
community and apparently the first to reach the council.[71]
George Oliver, the Catholic priest, was universally respected
as a man and as a scholar, but his personal example did
nothing to shake the position of the Smithfield Fires and the
Inquisition in popular mythology. In 1851 Oliver ministered
to a community which numbered only 250.

The new bishop had no illusions about the difficulties
facing him in his cathedral city. 'Cautious . . . in admitting
adverse newspapers to my table, yet the caution has not
prevented me from hearing of the extreme unpopularity of

my appointment to Exeter.'[72] So Phillpotts wrote in 1830 to
Ralph Barnes, bishop's secretary, chapter clerk and, through
his family as well as in virtue of his offices, a member of
exclusive governing circles in the city. The bishop asked,
'Does (sic) any steps occur to you which I might take to
diminish this adverse feeling?' But Barnes's meticulous
industry did not include ability to advise Phillpotts on the
delicate art of human relations and the bishop's absence
from the city during the cholera epidemic of 1832, albeit for
a long-planned confirmation programme, was used with
effect by Radicals.

An archdeacon advised the new bishop that he was
coming to 'preside over a clergy with very few exceptions
exemplary in their private lives and industrious in the performance of their public duties.'[73] The bishop's own correspondence,[74] however, reveals that throughout the diocese
there was much to reform and that many of the clergy could
scarcely be regarded as industrious in their duties, at least by
the rigorous standards of Phillpotts himself. An advertisement in 1837 for the sale of the perpetual advowson and
right of presentation to the rectory of Iddesleigh – 'six
hundred pounds a year and the spiritual duties very light'[75]
– denotes an attitude to clerical responsibilities deplored by
Evangelicals and Tractarians alike, and by the bishop who
was neither. General and Lady Paterson were clearly surprised when the rector of Heavitree called upon them for no
other purpose than to discuss the stock exchange.[76] The
Exeter clergy at this time were certainly exemplary in their
private lives and none was ever criticized for lack of industry
in his public duties. Their political attitudes were succinctly
summarized by the *Western Times*'s description of the
cathedral chapter as one of 'the most compact estates of
Toryism.'[77] This description is confirmed by the published
voting lists at parliamentary elections. The clergy included
men of marked, sometimes eccentric, character, ready to assert
their independence against bishops as formidable as Phillpotts. Dr Carwithen, cathedral lecturer, was an active Whig
who voted for Lord John Russell in 1835 and had to be
reprimanded by the chapter for expressing the hope that he

'would live to see the day when bishops were kicked out,' as he put it, 'from the House of Lords.'[78] More typical were the twenty or so clergy assembled at the great Conservative dinner in that same election to listen to Exeter's Precentor Lowe express the hope that Russell would never be their representative again.

In Exeter the Anglican revival had set in by the time of Waterloo. Between 1815, when the derelict St Olave's Church was restored and reopened, and 1830, some twelve churches were extensively repaired or rebuilt and one chapel constructed. In 1837 Phillpotts opened a meeting, with Lord Courtenay in the chair, to form a diocesan society to promote the further building and enlargement of churches.

The heroic days of Dissent in the city, and Exeter's own prominence as a Dissenting stronghold, belonged to the eighteenth century; perhaps the opening of the Mint Methodist Chapel in 1813 is a suitable terminal date.[79] Nonconformity, however, was the spearhead of the Reform movement in the city and was to be the core of Exeter's political Liberalism.[80] The Exeter Dissenters' committee issued handbills expressing gratitude to Lord John Russell 'for his enlightened advocacy of the rights of Dissenters.'[81] Church rates kept the vestries in a turmoil and were denounced, characteristically, by the Anglican reformer Mark Kennaway, as based on a law which 'arose in the dark hours of superstition and ignorance, when the clergy made the people bow before them.'[82] No Nonconformists had been admitted to the old chamber despite the removal of legal barriers. As Alderman Sanders explained to the parliamentary commissioners of 1833, though no by-law existed to ensure that none but members of the Established Church should be appointed to the chamber, there was 'a very strong feeling against it, that the sword and mace shall not be carried into a meeting house.'[83] The most significant consequence of the Municipal Corporations Act of 1835 was the admission of Nonconformists to the city council; of the first five mayors after 1835, three were Nonconformist and one an Evangelical who fell foul of the Establishment.[84] Nevertheless, in 1837 and throughout the nineteenth century, it was never quite socially respectable to be a Nonconformist or a Liberal in the city. In contrast, membership of the party of church and state conferred respectability on some whose claims to it were dubious.

Institutions and Reform

In the late thirties Exeter began to adjust its public and political life to the age of Reform. This process was not difficult. It required no change in the conservative character- istics of the city. The Conservative party was reinforced by new men who accepted the new order which, it was tacitly recognized, still required the cruder methods of influence and persuasion to achieve and hold power. A more difficult adjustment was necessitated by far-reaching change in the position of the city itself. Exeter, which in the sixteenth and seventeenth centuries stood fifth among the provincial cities of England, after Norwich, York, Bristol and Newcastle upon Tyne, was moving downwards in the scale in proportion to the rise of the new urban England. There was none of the stimulus to urban growth enjoyed by Plymouth and its sister towns of Devonport and Stonehouse, which had developed fast under the stimulus of war and continued to be stimulated by government expenditure. Exeter could not emulate the great Plymouth breakwater, completed by the admiralty in 1823, or the Royal William Victualling Yard in Stonehouse, completed in 1835 at a cost of £1,500,000. The increasingly active role of government, the growing ease and cheapness of communications and lack of economic stimulus combined to erode Exeter's importance as the capital of a remote province. There was an awareness of lost status in the council's petition to the house of commons in 1859 'to take the earliest opportunity of repealing all laws which, by centralizing power in London, have deprived the Provincial Corporations and other Public Bodies of that independence which they have hitherto enjoyed.'[85]

In the meantime Exeter was still 'a community, that is, not a political or geographical entity merely, but a miniature world of full dimensions.'[86] Here county society assembled.

The city's leaders still regarded local office as honourable advancement because, in a 'miniature world' there were no more commanding heights to dwarf the local peaks. Local government was still a suitable occupation for a gentleman as that term was understood in a cathedral city with a rural environment.

A city and county of itself by charter of Henry VIII, Exeter had risen to prosperity and importance under a system of government which had become obsolete by the 1830s but which nevertheless did not deserve the sweeping generalizations brought against it by the reformers. The famous report on the municipal corporations of England and Wales, described with good reason as 'rhetorical and unfair,'[87] contained no serious criticism of Exeter. The chamber had become vulnerable because, by custom though not by law, it had excluded the Dissenters, an active and influential section of the population, from participation in local affairs. The statement that 'the Corporation of Exeter being self-elected and conducting their affairs in private, have not gained the confidence of the inhabitants'[88] was undoubtedly valid. Inevitably secrecy gave rise to allegations of corruption and misgovernment behind closed door. Equally inevitably the admission of the press to council meetings led to the private meetings of both political parties, or their more influential members, to decide on the policy to be discussed and adopted in public.

The parliamentary commissioners of 1833 criticized over-expenditure on the canal and their report gives the impression that they made the most of faulty estimating, then as now not an uncommon practice, in default of evidence to support the more scandalous revelations which their colleagues were making elsewhere. That the report was critical at all was resented in Exeter. An Exeter Conservative who was no reactionary recorded in later years that the chamber was

'not prepared for the stigma cast upon them by the Commissioners of Inquiry when they made their final report, for they (the commissioners) had bestowed upon these worthy functionaries unqualified praise for their gentlemanly conduct evinced by them during their investigations.'[89]

The valid criticism of the old chamber is that it was obsolete, not that it was corrupt.

The parliamentary commissioners, Roscoe and Rushton, began their inquiry[90] in the Guildhall on 1 November 1833 and completed it in six days. The chamber made every effort to provide the information required. At the close of the proceedings, and in contrast to a somewhat chilly beginning, Roscoe expressed his 'very great satisfaction at the manner in which the Mayor and other members of the corporation who had taken part in the proceedings had assisted the commissioners.'[91]

The commissioners for their part received every encourage-ment from those who wished to make the most of the inadequacies of the old regime. Reformers such as John Hull Terrell, who later acted as a parliamentary agent of Lord John Russell, and the Unitarian J. D. Osborn, a retired glass and china merchant, who became an energetic member of the new council, were particularly prominent. The expendi-ture on the canal was an embarrassment to the chamber, as it was to be to the council, though the chamber had been advised by Telford himself and had acted on his advice. Osborn ventured into technical questions and was reminded dryly by Rushton that on such questions engineers alone were competent. The chamber had employed the best advice.[92] But Alderman Sanders, who bore the brunt of the cross-examination on the subject, 'was quite ready to say that if the Chamber had foreseen the heavy expenditure which it would have led to they would not have subscribed to it, even for the sake of the citizens of Exeter.'[93]

The chamber's files were examined, the commissioners noting with satisfaction that 'the accounts of each Receiver exist in an unbroken series from 1756 to the present time audited regularly.'[94] There were some discrepancies; but even the difficulty in tracing the expenditure of so large a sum as £20,000 merely provoked the comment that there was no doubt that the money had been fairly appropriated though it had not been 'clearly made out.'[95] On behalf of the Reformers, Terrell conceded that he believed the individual

members of the chamber to have been too honourable 'to
make the public trust subservient to their private interests.'
He suggested, however, that 'in olden time it was not so when
persons of low degree were sometimes admitted to the
Chamber.'[96] Exeter's Reformers were not democrats in the
modern sense. Rushton endorsed Terrell's tribute to his
contemporaries by reading a statement that

> 'we have seen the members of the Council were formerly
> of low estate; the present body are men far above any
> imputation; the charge against them is not a charge
> individually but in their collective capacities. It is a charge
> against the system.'[97]

Under the old system Exeter had been governed by a
mayor, eight aldermen and fifteen common councillors
collectively known as the chamber. The common councillors
were elected for life by the chamber itself. The freemen
elected the mayor each monday before Michaelmas from one
of two names selected by the chamber in private scrutiny.
The eight aldermen were also elected for life. All aldermen
were justices of the peace with extensive powers. As a
Reformer had occasion to point out, the chamber was
composed of 'gentlemen who met upstairs in black coats to
transact the business of the Corporation, and came down in
red gowns to act as magistrates.'[98]

The freemen on whom this superstructure was based
numbered, in 1835, only 586 in a population of 28,285.[99]
They alone had the privilege of voting at parliamentary
elections, as well as for the mayor, and they tended to
monopolize the subordinate offices of the corporation. The
Exeter freemen had not been appointed specifically for
electoral purposes, unlike those of Maldon in Essex where
1,870 freemen had been admitted in 1826, 1,000 during an
election.[100] Nor, in the nineteenth century, did they acquire
that reputation for corruption which characterized their
brethren at Barnstaple.

The substance of the complaints of the Exeter Reformers
was that the old system did not in fact include among the
'more substantial and discreet citizens and freemen' from
whom the chamber was chosen all those of discretion and

substance in the city. The admission of the town clerk, Edward Gattey, to the parliamentary commissioners, that since the repeal of the Corporation and Test Acts no Dissenters had been admitted to the corporation,[101] was in itself an explanation of the prominence of Nonconformists among the ranks of the Reformers. Resentment against exclusion from local affairs was expressed in terms of unhistorical appeals to the past. 'The institution of local government,' declared J. D. Osborn, the glass and china merchant, 'which was once the pride and boast of our citizens, shall once again be restored to that state of vigour which the great men of the early ages of English history intended it to be; . . . a corrupt group of oligarchs, the jest and scorn of all thinking men' was to be swept away.[102] Ancient tradition and ceremony were derided as 'silly pageantry . . . for the prattling tenants of the nursery.'[103] Henceforward purity of government and economy were to reign, 'swilling and guzzling' were to be abolished and, in the opinion of the *Western Times*, the 'vast extent of property' of the corporation would 'amply repay all the expenses of the future.'[104]

Too much weight should not be attached to political rhetoric which expressed in emotional form a demand for 'efficiency, cheapness, comprehensibility and uniformity.'[105] The conventions of controversy required exaggeration of expression. In 1835 Woolmer's *Gazette* had dismissed criticism of Sir William Follett as 'a mass of insolent rubbish penned by an anonymous assassin.'[106] But the Exeter Reformers tended to delude themselves with their own rhetoric.

The chamber's responsibilities had been limited in accordance with eighteenth-century theory and practice. Poor law administration was in the hands of the corporation of the poor by an act of 1696 last amended in 1788. Street maintenance, lighting, sewage and the night watch were the responsibility of the improvement commissioners whose powers had been brought up to date by an act of 1832. The improvement commissioners, sixty in number, were men of substance, having either to be in possession of land to the yearly value of £80, or of personal estate amounting to

D

£3,000, or else to be assessed at £40 annually in rates. The council was empowered to appoint six commissioners, not being magistrates. The dean and canons residentiary were also commissioners. The parliamentary commissioners of 1833 reported that the city was well lighted and well paved.

The beneficiaries of Reform, those to whom the keys of the new Jerusalem had been entrusted by the Reform Bill and the Municipal Corporations Act, were some 2,300 parliamentary electors in the enlarged parliamentary constituency and about 1,900 ratepayers.[107]

Analysis of the contemporary reports of elections makes it possible to reconstruct the parliamentary electorate in detail.[108] At the parliamentary election of July 1831 some 365 out of an electorate of 1,125 were artisans, porters, gardeners, masons, carpenters, plasterers and the like, and small shopkeepers who may or may not have employed assistants. Labourers employed as such numbered fourteen. At the time of the election of December 1832, the first held after the Reform Bill, working-class electors numbered about 421 in an electorate of 2,333. Artisans had alarmed the established order in the days of Pitt and Liverpool, but the artisans and small shopkeepers of Exeter were not given to see visions or to dream dreams. Radical tinkers and cobblers remained silent. The only journeyman tailor of note, Stephen Brunskill, rose to fortune through his assiduous canvassing for orders and sought respectability as a Conservative councillor.[109] It was an electorate dominated by professional men, merchants, brewers and wine merchants, with a second tier of bakers, boot and shoemakers, brushmakers, carpenters, smiths, hairdressers, grocers and druggists, all of whom were predominantly Liberal. The margins were usually small, but so were the majorities by which elections were decided. Throughout the century 'the respectability of the city was undoubtedly Tory,' as the *Western Times* put it in 1868,[110] a statement fully supported by the published voting lists. Clergy, bankers, surgeons and lawyers were overwhelmingly Conservative. The deferential vote, of waiters and servants, was Conservative. Cathedral vergers were inevitably Conservative. Butchers were Conservatives by a majority. Labourers were almost equally divided. Thirty-two labourers, seven of whom were freemen, voted in the parliamentary election of 1835. They provided twenty-five votes for Sir William Follett and twenty for Divett.

The electorate created by the Reform Bill normally returned members representing both the Conservative and the Liberal elements in the city, a practice which was regarded as fair by all except the more ardent political partisans. The Municipal Corporations Act was more significant in the local context because it transformed the social and economic composition of the council. It did not, however, necessarily improve the standards of individual councillors by means of the mechanical operation of a relatively democratic system, despite the assumptions of the Reformers. Whatever its failings by the test of representative government the chamber in 1835, its last year, was remarkable for the personal qualifications of its members.[111] Of the twenty-four members of the chamber in that year nine, including the mayor, were surgeons, members of a profession which had risen to the higher levels of local society and was making an honourable contribution to cultural activities. The press was represented by Edward Woolmer, proprietor of the *Exeter and Plymouth Gazette* in the days when the Exeter newspapers could be described by *The Athenaeum* as a credit to literature.[112] A moderate Tory and a man of independent mind, Woolmer represented Exeter's old patrician element on the council of the new era. Banking was represented by Robert Sanders; accountancy by the actuary of the Devon and Exeter Savings Bank. Four members came from the higher levels of the licensed trade. One was an attorney, a member of a profession which was to achieve and maintain a weighty representation on the council throughout the Victorian era and one that was notably disproportionate to the profession's numerical strength in the city. Five members of the chamber in 1835 can best be described as retired gentlemen without straining the social conventions of the time.

The first mayor of the new council was the Unitarian ironmonger 'Iron Sam' Kingdon who assumed office on 1 January as the Conservatives' nominee. The council still included five surgeons, four of them Conservative aldermen. Representation of the legal profession rose to five including three Reformers. The licensed trade had nine representatives of whom seven were Reformers or sympathetic to Reform. Another thirty years were to elapse before 'the trade' became a powerful Conservative instrument on the council. Exeter's old order was well represented on the new council. It included three wealthy bankers, W. Nation, J. B. Sanders and Thomas Snow. The surgeon, Samuel Barnes, was a member of an influential Exeter family and himself was a man distinguished for this professional ability and his literary and artistic interests. Newspaper proprietors included Edward Woolmer and Robert Trewman of the *Flying Post*, both from the higher levels of Conservative society. Trewman resembled Woolmer, 'his social position pointed him out, of course, as gentleman.'[113]

Exeter's Conservatives wasted neither time nor money on hopeless opposition to municipal reform. Henry Ellis commented that the bill had 'passed into law and, whether palatable or not, as the law of the land must be obeyed.'[114] This attitude was general. The Conservatives set themselves the task of securing control of the city under the new system without vain repining. The Reformers presented the first elections in the six wards of the city,[115] held on the 26 December 1835, as a contest between right and wrong, between 'the one party [who] actuated by the most selfish feelings, seek to perpetuate the corruptions on which they have so long gorged,' and those who 'animated by genuine patriotism, demand a purification of our ancient institutions.'[116]

To represent men like Edward Woolmer or the banker Sanders as gorging on corruption was, at best, unconvincing. In the small, tight society of Exeter too much was known of individuals for some 1900 ratepayers to be carried away by conventional propaganda. The elections returned the two parties in equal numbers, with eighteen councillors on each side. The subsequent events are obscure. All possible means of persuasion must have been employed by both sides to escape from the *impasse*. The Reformers had hoped for support from Paul Measor, the postmaster. Measor had been mayor in 1830 and was regarded by the Reformers as 'the first mayor who had ever treated the people as deserving of a political existence.'[117] His candidature for the new council had therefore been unopposed. But Measor voted with the Conservatives while the Reformers found their ranks reduced by one because a newly-elected councillor, who was also a Quaker, declined for reasons of conscience to take the qualifying oath and so became ineligible to hold office. The Conservatives' majority of one was enough to ensure that eleven out of the twelve aldermen were sound church and state men. The twelfth alderman, William Kennaway, had been a member of the chamber and had earned the respect of the city for his conduct as mayor during the cholera epidemic of 1832. Kennaway was regarded as a liberal Conservative and was sometimes styled a Whig. The Conservatives' use of the aldermen to achieve and maintain a majority on the council was henceforward a permanent feature of Exeter's political life. It was not, however, unique. In 1878 the house of commons was informed that both Leeds and Exeter indulged in this practice, the one to maintain a Liberal majority, the other a Conservative.[118]

With the control of the council in their hands the Conservatives proceeded to elect their own nominee as the first mayor of the new regime from 1 January 1836. In deference to the spirit of the times their choice was the Unitarian ironmonger, Kingdon. The Reformers for their part austerely refused on principle to attend the dinner with which by custom newly-elected mayors entertained city dignitaries and the neighbouring nobility and gentry.

The control of the council had been secured for the Conservatives by smart tactics. Whig legislation of the 1830s did not alter the fact that politics were still a struggle for power in the boroughs as at Westminster. In Exeter both parties had fought the elections in a political context. That the result was a tie was as much a tribute to the good sense of the electorate as it was an indication that the Conservatives had yet to perfect the methods which ensured their control over the city. For the moment the Conservatives had misjudged local opinion. The power which they had seized by a *coup de main* was rapidly reduced. In the elections held to replace three Conservative councillors who had become aldermen, as well as the Liberal Quaker who had refused the oath, four Liberals were returned. When the regular series of elections began in November 1836 there were further Liberal gains and the Conservatives were reduced to maintaining a precarious equality by means of their aldermen. In this situation the Reformers once more looked to Paul Measor. 'Mr Measor's good sense,' said the *Western Times*, 'and other circumstances combined gave the Liberals a decided predominance.'[119] William Kennaway, wine and spirit merchant, became the new mayor after an election hailed as 'a glorious victory for Reform.' 'Iron Sam,' described in the Liberal press as 'a man of irascible temper, overbearing manner and rugged exclamations and epithets,'[120] left the chair amid an uproarious demonstration of Reformist feeling.

In the elections of 1836, 3,453 votes had been cast for the Liberal candidates and 3,228 for the Conservatives, a result which was far from demonstrating overwhelming resentment against the old order. William Kennaway himself was no root-and-branch Reformer and his election as mayor could be regarded by the Conservatives as a safe gesture. For the time being it was expedient to defer to the spirit of Reform which, as Henry Ellis observed with distaste, 'appeared to reduce everything to the standards of utility.' Kingdon had appeared on the magistrates' bench 'unrobed and undistinguished by distinctive badge of office.' He himself is reported to have remarked that 'for his part he did not like the petticoat sort of things worn on such occasions.'[121]

The *Western Times* sneered that 'a good deal of praise was slobbered over Mr Kingdon';[122] but Exeter's first post-Reform mayor deserved the presentation of a silver salver once given to the city by the merchants of Teignmouth and sold with the rest of the city's plate as an unnecessary gesture to the age of Utility and Economy. 'Iron Sam' was no Reformer. As a Unitarian he would not have been eligible for Exeter's governing circle under the old régime. In his religious background, his forthright manner and his impatience with ceremonial precedent, Kingdon himself symbolized the significance of the act of 1835. He was a member of the new class of local businessman now admitted to positions of authority and prestige and like so many of his colleagues he became thereafter a firm supporter of the party of church and state. It was not till the second year of the new council, after the elections of November 1837, that there was a breach in Exeter's essential conservatism by the inauguration of the city's ephemeral reign of Reform.

II

REFORM AND THE CONSERVATIVE
REVIVAL 1837–1847

THE Exeter Liberals hailed the Municipal Corporations Act and the expectations it evoked in the spirit of *Shelley's* Hellas. 'The world's great age' was to begin anew through the reform of political institutions. Their victory in the council elections of November was the victory of enlightenment, destined in imagination to dissipate 'the mists of ignorance, bigotry and superstition,' to end 'the long reign of waste and plunder.'[1] Belief in the automatically beneficent power of Reform soon withered in the unresponsive soil of the local environment as the true character of the city reasserted itself and the Conservatives gained control of the modernized machinery of local government. 'The Municipal Reform Bill has at length become the law of the land, and it now behoves the people to reflect on the use they intend to make of a measure which will confer so much power on them'; so declared the *Western Times* in 1835.[2] Five years later the same newspaper was complaining of 'a scene of servility, corruption and indifference on the part of the burgesses,' of 'shameful scenes of drunkenness and debauchery.'[3]

The Reformers came to power on the assumption that the 'spirit of Reform' would of itself engender 'pure government' and a regime of economy enforced by the vigilance of the burgesses. The new council was required to live off its own traditional income, an impossibility if there was to be any extension of its functions. The Reformers' attitude to finance was expressed succinctly by Councillor S. S. Bastard, who 'held local taxation to be a great curse' and by W. J. P. Wilkinson, Nonconformist wine and spirit merchant, mayor in 1837–38, who 'would sell every stick of property before he would tax the inhabitants a single farthing – before he would inflict that most dangerous thing, a borough rate.'[4]

Exeter's Liberalism was a blend of utilitarianism, idealism and Nonconformity stiffened by a sturdy suspicion of all authority except the Bible as interpreted by the individual conscience. As a party it represented the shopocracy, men of property whose mouthpiece in the city was to denounce 'the revolting doctrines of the Chartists.'[5] Hating injustice, privilege and waste, Exeter's Liberals were second to none in their respect for the landed aristocracy – provided it was Whig; Nonconformist, or at least opposed to church ceremony and to the authority of the priesthood, dogmatic and often naïve, they looked down vistas of infinite moral and material progress opened up by the franchise, secular education, economy and hard work. They were men of probity, conscientious and public-spirited. It was a source of perpetual surprise to them that the children of this world could be in their generation wiser than the children of light. Their weakness was that they were a loose coalition born of protest – protest against church privilege, against a restricted franchise, against rising rates. The protest was usually necessary but only in exceptional circumstances could it achieve political power.

Lord John Russell had referred in parliament to the need to ensure the proper representation of the 'property, the intelligence or the population of a town.'[6] This happy coincidence, it was assumed, had been achieved in Exeter. The *Gazette*, while revealing its satisfaction that the 'loyal and conservative character of the city had been maintained under the new regime,' knew of 'scarcely any individual appointed, who may not be entitled to the distinction, as far as regards integrity, respectability, and habits of business.'[7] But acts of parliament could not change Exeter itself. Since the city was small and compact the bankers, merchants and clergy who formed the higher circles in local society lived in the same neighbourhood as did the slum dwellers of the west quarter. Between Barnfield Crescent and Tudor Street there could be no gulf such as divided, for instance, St James's Street and the east end of London. With industry on a small scale the employers could still retain close personal relations with their employees. This relationship humanized economic life; it also discouraged the growth of trade unions. Social attitudes remained deferential. Rank, wealth and status were accorded respect. The landed gentry and aristocracy indisputably took first place in society. Standards of manners and culture were set by the county. The environment was not favourable to Utilitarianism or to Radicalism.

The old system, the prejudice against the association of the sword and mace with a Dissenter's meeting house, the restriction of the corporation to the freemen, had barred from participation in local affairs a prosperous, influential and often able section of the community. It was a weakness in city life which in Exeter was hardly defended. Institutional reform and equality of opportunity within a limited circle did not, however, change social traditions and habits or imply admission to local power. Conservatism and membership of the Church of England remained necessary for all who sought power, though they did not necessarily convey full social status. Reform opened the road to local power for men of a lower social class, by the standards of the time, but builders like Henry Hooper and licensed victuallers like Joseph Harding who wielded influence in the Victorian era were church and state men. Men such as these were to capture for the Conservatives control of the new machinery of local government by means of efficient down-to-earth methods which disillusioned the Liberals for whom faith in the regenerative power of Reform tended to take the place of political organization. Local government itself became less respectable, though not less Conservative, till, as in 1882, the Conservative *Flying Post*, complained that it was difficult 'to find men of position to have anything to do with public work.'[8]

The period 1837 to 1847 has a unity in Exeter's nineteenth-century history because it was then that Conservatives and Liberals alike took the initial steps in working out the implications of the Municipal Corporations Act. For Exeter they were above all years of financial crisis when the council grappled with the debts inherited from its predecessor. The imposition of a borough rate was at length reluctantly accepted in 1847, though it had first been proposed by a Conservative member of the council in 1836. Administration was overhauled and modernized by trial and error. In 1847 the nucleus of a full-time police force in the modern sense was at length established. Apart from opposition to the borough rate, which was predominantly Liberal, there was no great division between the two parties. Differences were over men rather than measures. Arguments raged over appointments and charges of 'jobbery,' and over questions of ceremony.

In November 1836, the cathedral bells had saluted the election of William Kennaway as mayor. The elections were hailed as a proud day for the Reformers whose exertions had regained the position 'from which they had been displaced by treachery and party spirit.'[9] Kennaway was not the Liberals' first choice. He was a liberal Conservative and suspect because he had favoured compensation for loss of office for the former town clerk, Gattey.[10] In 1837 the Liberals consolidated their position. Of the twelve retiring councillors seven were Liberal and five Conservative. Eight Liberals and four Conservatives were returned. The election was hard fought. Men with placards paraded the streets. Flags and banners exhorted the partisans. The *Western Times* announced the result in language which still retained the fervour of political epic in the Age of Reform:

'We have gained eight out of twelve candidates, beating the Tories in their stronghold of St Sidwell's . . . shaking them in St David's and carrying everything else with a high and triumphant hand save in the ward of St Paul's where, through the employment of foul influences, the Tories combined to defeat Mr William Beal by the very significant majority of two, which two votes were provided by the proprietor and editor of the "neutral" *Flying Post*.'[11]

The Liberals used their clear majority to elect as mayor the Nonconformist wine and spirit merchant Wilkinson, described as 'a gentleman hitherto known in the city for his unbending firmness in the discharge of his duty and the rigid Roman-like steadfastness of purpose which has characterized his private life.'[12] The Conservatives, though they themselves elected a Dissenter for the first mayor, had seen insuperable objection to Wilkinson's election in 1836[13] when the possibility had first been discussed. In 1837 the Conservatives had no choice. Wilkinson's election was greeted with horror by the Conservative press under the headline 'Election of a Dissenting Preacher as Mayor.' He was not, in fact, a minister, though he did admit to the habit of 'expounding the scriptures to a few serious friends on Sundays.'[14] He also proved to be a Chartist sympathizer.

Wilkinson's election was expected to mark a symbolic breach with the past. By custom each new mayor attended a service in the cathedral accompanied by the members of his council. Samuel Kingdon, though a Unitarian, had observed the proprieties with such of the traditional state as had been left by the spirit of Reform. His example was followed by Kennaway who, explained the *Western Times* 'as a churchman, needed no excuse for attending the Cathedral in the usual form.' It was hoped that Wilkinson would be of sterner stuff and would refuse to bow down in the House of Rimmon. The hope was disappointed. The mayor was liberal enough to make the gesture, his friends explaining that he had been 'trammelled by the example of his predecessors.'[15]

In 1838 the Liberals maintained their position with twenty-six elected councillors opposed to twenty-two Conservatives of whom eleven were aldermen. The aldermanic elections brought a further accretion of strength to the Liberals, the Conservatives being reduced to seventeen and the Liberals correspondingly increased to thirty-one. The election proved to be the high tide of early Victorian Liberalism on the council.

For the Conservatives, 1838 was the year in which the council became 'to all intents and purposes, a Whig-Radical body.'[16] The Liberals were determined to secure the election of their own aldermen and so 'to acquire a position on the Council which could not be shaken for years to come.'[17] The Conservatives claimed that their own representation on the council was not that to which they were entitled 'by virtue of their undoubted claims to respectability, intelligence and influence.'[18] They were accused by their opponents of seeking to impose a borough rate 'which would effect the gratification of their jobbing and reconcile them in some measure to the change in municipal government.'[19]

The fight was rough. In St Mary Major's the Conservative brewer John Clench was returned at the head of the poll. This success was naturally represented by Clench's supporters as a victory of principles and 'a knockdown blow for the Radicals.' The Liberals claimed that Clench had been 'literally floated into office on a flood of drunkenness and debauchery.' This charge was supported in the following year by the publication of an election bill signed by John Clench which included such items as eighty gallons of beer, 327 grogs and 187 breakfasts and luncheons, as well as an obscure item for canvassing, amounting to £57 11s.[20] In St Sidwell's, the builder Henry Hooper, whose workshops were situated in that ward, defeated by six votes the Liberal maltster, Joseph Sayell. It was Hooper's first appearance on the council and the beginning of his climb to the position of the city's Conservative boss.

The Liberals elected Dr Edward MacGowan as mayor for 1838–39. MacGowan had hitherto taken no part in local politics. He was an Evangelical with a reputation for good works who had been persuaded to stand by the Liberal leader Mark Kennaway.[21] In his speech proposing the new mayor, Kennaway declared uncompromisingly that he had always looked upon the council 'as being of a political character,'[22] a statement apt to be overlooked by later Liberals complaining of the intrusion of politics into local affairs. Kennaway's challenge was taken up, the more eagerly because MacGowan refused to attend the cathedral, not apparently because he disapproved of Anglican forms of worship but because he insisted that any individual should have the right to refuse to attend a religious service if he wished to do so. It was a stand on principle. 'To Dr MacGowan,' wrote Thomas Latimer, 'the Liberal Party owes a deep debt of obligation – he is the first civil magistrate who has carried out the principles of religious, as well as civil liberty, in connection with that office.'[23]

The Conservatives promptly counter-attacked through a

legal flaw in the council's proceedings. The election of aldermen, of whom MacGowan was one, had taken place immediately preceding the statutory meeting of the council held at noon on the same day to elect the mayor. *Quo Warranto* proceedings were launched. The council agreed that the action should be defended and authorized the town clerk to take such steps as he might think proper to defend MacGowan.[24]

Legal matters of this nature took time. It was not till after the termination of MacGowan's term of office that the Court of Queen's Bench ruled that the election was void on the grounds that the election of the mayor should have been the first if not the only business proceeded with at the meeting on 9 November. MacGowan was presented with a bill of costs amounting to £197 and writs followed. In October 1840 the council agreed to meet the costs, which had been initially met by a personal loan from Mark Kennaway, by nineteen votes to fourteen against the strong Conservative opposition led by Henry Hooper. The decision was reversed later, leaving an unpleasant impression of *vae victis*, when the Conservatives regained their majority at the end of the year.[25] As Henry Ellis commented sardonically,

'the real question had been virtually settled six months after Dr MacGowan had fully served the office which it was decided that he was ineligible to serve. So much for party.'[26]

In 1839 the Liberal majority was reduced to four. The impetus of Reform was dwindling fast. The Conservatives, not for the last time, displayed their practical organizing ability, through the Conservative Association which took the field in 1838.[27] The election of the Unitarian wine merchant William Drewe, in 1839, proved to be the last gesture of Reform. In 1840 the Liberals fell ingloriously from power, unable, according to their own account, 'to contend against the forces of corruption and intimidation.'[28] But in truth the city had regained its equilibrium. Eight Liberals and four Conservative councillors were replaced by nine Conservatives and three Liberals. In five out of six wards there was no contest.

'To the great joy of the Conservatives,' wrote Henry Ellis, 'a Conservative Mayor was this year elected in the person of John Carew Esq. This gentleman again donned the robe of office, which had been discontinued by the preceding mayors. The cocked hat, it is true, had not been resumed, but the Sword, the Cap of Maintenance, the Maces and the old paraphernalia of civic dignity were borne before his worship as heretofore.'[29]

With cheers for queen and church and the discharge of cannon the city resumed the Conservative regime which was to be maintained virtually for the remainder of the century. Attorney John Carew attended the cathedral in scarlet robes trimmed with white silk and sable which had been presented for the occasion by a group of Conservatives. The mayor was accompanied by the town clerk once more dignified by a gown. Carew was the first lawyer to be elected mayor but he was also a member of an indubitably county family, the Carews of Bickleigh, as well as adviser and personal friend of the Aclands.

The immediate tasks faced by the new regime in 1836 had been the overhaul of personnel, the institution of the new practices and procedures required by the Act and the instilment of some order into the finances. Both parties agreed on the need for economy. The Liberals also adopted a strongly Utilitarian attitude to traditional posts and ceremonies and this was reinforced by a single-minded desire to oust Tories from office. Both parties concurred in the decision, taken on 6 December 1836, to sell the irreplaceable corporation plate, – 'all the plate, knives, forks and dish covers specified in the schedule of the personal property of the Council.'[30] An old fire engine, a piece of brass ordnance and a small quantity of wrought iron were also sold with the plate by auction in the following February and added to the impression that the bailiffs had taken possession. The receipts are presumably covered by the item 'Sundries, £834 1s. 3d.,' in the accounts for 1836–37.[31] Though much of the old ceremony was revived later the plate was never recovered for the city.

The first five permanent committees of the council,

watch, finance, navigation, market and general purposes, were instituted in January 1836.[32] The council then appointed a strong committee of twelve, drawn equally from the two parties, to

'inquire into the nature and extent of the duties performed by the several officers under the late Chamber . . . and to report thereon to the Council before any other officer shall be appointed or other salary fixed.'[33]

This committee began proceedings with a resolution that 'all persons who hold office under the Town Council should be remunerated for their services by a fixed salary so far as circumstances permit and that all emoluments arising from perquisites of office or fees are highly objectionable in principle as they afford opportunities for fraud or extortion and tend to prevent an efficient and regular discharge of their duties.'[34]

The resolution was a reflection of the views of the report on municipal corporations. Insofar as the town clerk and the treasurer were concerned, some fifty years were to elapse before these officers were paid adequately. The finance committee recommended in 1837 that the town clerk's salary should be £200 a year 'for all business except business transactions in Parliament, actions and suits at Law or in Equity; Journeys, Conveyancing; Charges of Town Agents.'[35] But the bulk of the town clerk's remuneration continued to be derived from his charges as solicitor; the work of the council was conducted from his private office by his own staff. The new town clerk's, Gidley's, bill for the Exeter Port Dues Act of 1839 included such items as 13s. 4d. for attending a meeting at the Guildhall and 6s. for 'attending Mr Hooper, the chairman of the committee, relative to fixing a time for a conference.'[36]

The modern practice of Tuesday meetings was inaugurated by decision of the council in June 1836. In the same month financial control was initiated by means of a resolution ordering that all bills should be submitted to the finance committee. Continuity was sought, and an effort made to prevent the discreet side-tracking of embarrassing decisions, by means of an instruction to the general purposes committee at its monthly meetings

'to examine the proceedings of the Council and to see that the orders made by that body be carried into execution or continued until they are so completed that no business once ordered be lost sight of.'[37]

Visiting committees began in 1839 with the decision that two councillors, assisted by the newly-appointed surveyor, were to examine alterations to council property in the Bonhay.

Changes such as these were the response of practical men to the task imposed by the Municipal Corporations Act and gave little opening for party polemics. Establishment matters on the contrary involved patronage and engendered heat. The post of swordbearer was not only difficult to defend by the standards of utility but its holder, paid £80 a year for ceremonial duties, was a Conservative, Hugh Cumming, a prominent frequenter of Mol's Coffee House in the Cathedral Close.[38] A Liberal attack on the post was beaten off in May 1836 when John Carew argued for its retention on the genial grounds that 'it was indefensible on grounds of public utility but if it did good it did no harm and there was no reason why the lovers of show should not be gratified.' A compromise was reached by which the ceremonial post of swordbearer was held in conjunction with the new post of superintendent of police. When, however, the Liberals strengthened their position on the council in November 1837 they lost no time in abolishing as 'useless and unnecessary'[39] an office which was an offence to utilitarian principles. Hugh Cumming henceforward was confined to the role of superintendent of police.

The Reformers were slow to appreciate that the financial adjustments required by the Municipal Corporations Act required more than the abolition of obsolete offices or the sale of the city plate. In 1837 the council's revenue for rudimentary administration amounted to £7,718. Of this, £2,000 was an advance on a loan. The remainder was derived from rents of property, market dues, and tolls and dues. The last were under attack by traders on the grounds of 'their partial character and their tendency to restrict commerce.' Canal dues formed an additional valuable source of revenue

E

amounting to £6,725 in 1837-38 and providing a balance after expenditure on the canal had been met which was used for the general purposes of the city. Debts in the year 1837-38 amounted to £161,127.[40]

Loans were raised by mortgages on property. It was not till 1875 that the field of financial operations was immeasurably enlarged by the facilities for loans sanctioned by the Local Government Board under the Public Health Act. For the time being the imposition of a borough rate in accordance with the provisions of the Municipal Corporations Act was the only means, apart from mortgages, by which the council could finance any extension of its activities. The imposition of a rate was first broached by the Conservatives in January 1836 but the Liberals in particular were anxious to avoid the association of the new era of enlightened local government with additional taxation. The council resolved that 'the propriety of ordering a Borough Rate . . . be considered at the next Council.'[41] It was then resolved that 'further consideration of a Borough Rate be deferred until the Treasurer shall make application for one.'[42] In May 1837 the council resolved itself into a committee of finance for the purpose of 'fully investigating the Income and Expenditure of the Body.'[43]

For the ensuing nine years committees met again and again, and 'nailed themselves to the never much altered agenda.' To avoid what the *Western Times* denounced as the 'odious impost of a Borough Rate,' council property to the value of some £17,000 was sold between 1837 and 1848. Much of this passed into the hands of councillors. In the meantime, while recommending the postponement of a borough rate, the finance committee optimistically expressed the 'confident expectation that the resources of the Council will overtake the difficulties which at present embarrass the Treasurer.'

The treasurer, Hugh Ellicombe, continued to be embarrassed, and was not assisted by the helpless admission of the finance committee in 1840 that 'it could not at present recommend any mode of paying the remainder of the Town Clerk's bills.'[45] By that date 'simple contract debts,' debts for goods and services, amounted to £166,658. Ellicombe had occasion to inform the mayor that sums due in interest, salaries and pay for the night watch amounted to £4,792.

'The present position, my dear Sir,' he wrote, 'is full of painful and shifting embarrassment which, without exaggeration, I find increasing from day to day. This, after every suggestion on my part is doubly painful to the discharge of my official duties.'[46]

The council responded to this *cri de coeur* by approving Henry Hooper's suggestion to abolish the night watch during the summer months, a decision which was swiftly reversed under pressure from the magistrates.

The financial position was made worse by the fact that in December 1837 an additional £30,000 was required to pay off debts on the new markets, including £7,000 due to the Hoopers, and to complete the market approaches.[47] The council itself was losing £1,000 a year which the former markets had yielded till 1834 and which was guaranteed to the council by the act of that year authorizing the new markets.[48] It was not till the enactment of further legislation in 1840,[49] which enabled the council to raise a further £40,000, that the financial tangle was straightened out. The capital debt was then funded at £103,000, of which £17,777 represented the capital value of revenue due to the council. All interest due to creditors after Christmas 1836, and all arrears due to the council after that date, were to be given up. In 1843 the market account was credited with its first dividend of 4½ per cent.

The council's financial difficulties remained pressing. In 1843 the long-suffering treasurer informed the town clerk that he had only £10 in hand. Ellicombe wished the council to instruct his colleague to issue no further orders for payments.[50] In the following March the Conservative brewer, Ben Salter, declared bluntly that the necessity for a borough rate should be reconsidered and that the council could no longer continue 'in such a disreputable manner.' The town clerk explained that the council had spent £25,000 'out of their own property' to meet borough expenses in the past ten years though the money 'might have been raised from the town.' He hoped that 'the town would give the corporation credit for the postponement of a borough rate for as long as possible.'[51]

Further postponement was ruled out by a crisis over the canal in 1845. The canal improvements executed by the chamber had been financed in the customary manner by a mortgage on the security of the tolls. Revenue had been improving and the tolls, which had amounted to £6,725 in 1837, were now leased to Jonas Levy, of Blackfriars, for £9,905. The cash received from Levy was required by the council to meet its day-to-day expenses; as the treasurer explained to the mayor, he had no funds 'other than what had been derived from the Canal.'[52]

With the completion of the Bristol to Exeter railway in 1844 the canal creditors became anxious over the security of their capital and interest. Legal action was brought to secure debts due to the creditors as a first charge on any funds, and to claim prior right to all canal property, tolls, rents and profits, until they had received full payment of capital and interest. The mortgagees applied for an injunction, which was granted in 1845. A receiver was appointed for two-thirds of the income derived from the canal. Legal proceedings dragged on till a compromise was reached in 1857.[53] In the meantime the council's income had been reduced by some £6,000 a year.

The council at last surrendered to financial exigencies. In April 1846 the finance committee recommended that in view of the situation the council should 'levy the Deficiency required for Borough Expenses by a Borough Rate.' In December a special committee endorsed this recommendation and point out that 'the loss of the canal income . . . has rendered the Borough Rate necessary.' The new rate, like income tax, was regarded as a temporary measure and the special committee sought to make its advice more palatable by expressing the 'confident expectation that . . . the Borough Rate may be in a short time considerably diminished.'[54] The council accordingly resolved that a rate for the sum of £1,181 11s. should be levied and a Conservative newspaper voiced the hope that 'the vigilance of the citizens would ensure that it did not become permanent.'

The new council, like the old chamber, was still regarded essentially as an organization for the management of city property. The implications of the new responsibilities latent in the Municipal Corporations Act had not yet been grasped by Exeter. The machinery for the collection of the new rate did not exist and had to be improvised. It was therefore decided to collect the rate in the traditional manner through the churchwardens and the overseers of the poor, payments to the council being made from the funds of the corporation of the poor against reimbursement when the rate was collected. This decision embarrassed the guardians because they were deprived of cash. Further, the Exeter Poor Law Act of 1788[55] provided that while the corporation of the poor could levy up to £5,000 a year, further sums could be raised only with the consent of quarter sessions. The possibility of raising the rate by means of a separate assessment through the churchwardens and the overseers was canvassed but these officers objected to the additional work involved and also to its unpopularity. It was accordingly resolved to revert to the original decision.

The new rate could not immediately solve the financial difficulties of the city and at the end of the financial year 1847–48 the council's balance on the year's operations was only £1 8s. 7d. Even this had been achieved by the failure to pay £1,052 due in arrears of officers' salaries.[56] The *Western Times* summarized the position accurately enough:

'We regret to have to report that in these days of financial embarrassment the municipal corporation of Exeter follows the melancholy fashion and stands before its creditors in a state – if not of complete insolvency, at least of as close an imitation of that sad condition as can be obtained without falling into utter ruin.'[57]

But order had been introduced into the financial confusion that had prevailed since 1836. The council was no longer so embarrassed by floating debt and had achieved a flexible source of revenue sufficient for the unexacting requirements of mid-Victorian local government.

Since the corporation was thought to be primarily concerned with the maintenance of its property and the police, there were now no issues to arouse the interest of the rate-payers except personalities and appointments. Expenditure remained low. Appeals to the civic spirit of the burgesses could elicit no response when ratepayers had little reason to grumble. The newspapers devoted more space to ploughing matches than to elections and the number of voters who polled each November markedly declined. According to the ward poll books, 1,632 burgesses polled in 1835. In the series of elections between 1835 and 1839 the total number who voted never fell below 1,325. Between 1840 and 1847 the voters on only two occasions exceeded 1,000 and the highest poll, of 1,115, was substantially lower than the lowest poll in 1835-39 when 1,325 voted in 1838.[58] Wilkinson, he of the 'rigid, Roman-like principles,' lost his seat in 1844. In that year, as in 1840, only one ward was contested.

The *Western Times* complained that the Conservatives 'as usual made up by the excellence of their tactics for the badness of their principles.'[59] By the 1840s local politics had become a matter of beer and influence rather than of principles. The mayoralty, and the council itself, continued to attract men of the class which ten years later was described as that of the 'respectable members of the party, Squires, Bankers and Doctors,'[60] men like Charles Brutton, solicitor to the Exeter Gaslight and Coke Co. and the Plymouth, Devonport and Exeter (or South Devon) railway; Edward Woolmer, mayor before Reform and again mayor in 1844-45; Dr Thomas Shapter. Men such as these represented the older governing class of the city and by their presence on the council they must have perpetuated the ideas and attitudes of the past. Even in less hierarchical days it is not unknown for change to be opposed on the grounds that it appears contrary to the experience of half a lifetime. Within the restricted confines of early Victorian Exeter the views of the city elders were more likely to be effective. In point of numbers the law had become the dominant group on the council, which included twelve lawyers in 1848, one-quarter of the entire membership.[61] In that year there were no bankers. Edward Sanders was wielding power by remote control, though he returned to the council in order to accept the mayoralty in 1850 when a socially acceptable mayor was required to act as host on behalf of Exeter in the year of the agricultural show. The licensed trade in 1848, including hops, brewing and the hotel industry, was represented by nine members but it did not yet exercise decisive control.

The active management of politics had passed into the hands of men such as the redoubtable Henry Hooper, a Conservative but the representative of a class of businessmen who resented the influence of the older Conservatives with their county contacts. It was this resentment which provoked the crisis over the choice of a parliamentary candidate in 1857. In 1848 four Hoopers, all members of one family, were on the council. Thomas Latimer painted an inimitable picture of the scene in St Sidwell's, the Hooper stronghold, in 1847 when Henry Hooper was standing for re-election. In front of the ballot box, in those days of open voting, sat Mr Alderman Hooper, returning officer and the candidate's brother. On one side sat Mr Henry Hooper, magistrate and candidate; on the other Mr Henry Hooper, Jr., high sheriff. 'The eyes of this most formidable trio glared on every voter who presented himself.'[62] Thomas Latimer was a hostile witness, but even allowing for bias and for Latimer's own idiosyncratic method of reporting there can be no doubt that many in St Sidwell's would have hesitated to cross the Hoopers in the days of their power.

Henry Hooper's presence on the council was a consequence of the Municipal Corporations Act. The Hooper family had originally prospered through the development of the former estate of the Barings, on Mount Radford, towards the end of the eighteenth century. They built Lower Summerlands and Baring Crescent, as well as houses in St Leonard's Road, buildings which stand today as nobler monuments of local taste and enterprise than the record of political strife in which Henry Hooper took a leading part. Henry Hooper himself was concerned with most buildings of importance in the early Victorian city. He built the Higher and Lower Markets, the railway station in St David's and, later, the new post office. Debts to the Hoopers bulked large in the financial tribulations of the council. Energetic and decisive, acknowledged by his enemies to have 'a clear head and a high courage,' he was also described as 'coarse of speech and unpolished in manner'[63] to an extent which alarmed the fastidious, such as members of the old governing classes of the city. Hooper and 'Hooper's men' were prominent at a riotous meeting to discuss the Exeter Improvement Bill in 1832. In that year Hooper himself was fined for an assault on an antiquarian. In 1857 he was again fined for calling the Liberal Councillor Snell a blackguard in the public street. Hooper began his political life as a Liberal and voted for Divett in the parliamentary election of 1832.[64] But while the legislation of the age of Reform provided the opportunity for men like Henry Hooper to enter public life it could not also provide the means for further advancement in Conservative Exeter. Hooper became a member of the party of church and state and, as was acknowledged on his death, 'for something like a generation he was an immense influence in the city.'[65] He was Exeter's first political boss in the new era. Between Henry Hooper and Edward Woolmer, of the world of the *Gentleman's Magazine*, or Edward Sanders with his county connections, there was no bond save party. Hooper represented a rougher class and in 1857 he took a leading part in the successful revolt against that section of the Conservative party represented by the newspaper proprietor and the banker, those whom the *Western Times* described as 'fastidious about their aitches.'[66]

If, however, the council by 1840 had regained its Conservative equilibrium, parliamentary elections continued to give Exeter's Liberalism full opportunity for self-expression. In 1841 the Conservatives made a determined attempt to capture both seats in an election which demonstrated the full strength of the Conservative resurgence at Westminster after the years of Whig rule. Exeter forecast the most severe contest for many years.

Despite the importance, in national politics, of the general election of 1841, it was not fought on clear-cut issues; nor was it even fought at all in many constituencies. There were no contests in the two county constituencies of Devon and none in the boroughs of Tavistock, Totnes, Honiton,

Tiverton and Dartmouth. In Exeter, people like Henry Ellis viewed with approval 'the rule acquiesced in here (and which was considered to have given satisfaction) that each party should have their man.'[67] But the Exeter Conservatives considered that they had an opportunity to capture both seats. A delegation to the Carlton Club as late as June[68] produced a candidate in the person of Lord Lovaine, son of the Earl of Beverley, once member for the suppressed pocket borough of Bere Alston and later eighth Duke of Northumberland.

The Liberals met the challenge by appealing to local patriotism and by making the corn laws the issue. Mark Kennaway denounced the intrusion of a candidate from Yorkshire and invoked the county paladins of the past: Baring and Courtenay, Bampfylde, Newman, Kekewich and Buck.[69]

> 'The ever faithful city was thus taken by surprise,' noted Henry Ellis, 'here was a man, a perfect stranger . . . brought down without any previous notice to be thrust on the independent voters of the city as though it had been a most venal borough.'[70]

The *Western Times* thundered that the people of Exeter would never sanction 'the unbridled insolence which dared to hint so great a degradation to the city as that which introduced this small-loaf lord to be a candidate.' The election was represented as 'a holy contest against the advocates of starvation' and the mothers of Exeter were urged to aid the queen to confound the enemies of 'her suffering and sorrowful people.'[71]

Divett took no chances. He began his canvass before the dissolution of parliament. His personal canvass was described by his supporters as 'the most active and arduous seen in the city.'[72] His opponents thought otherwise. Divett himself was usually treated with respect even in an age distinguished by uninhabited electioneering. But according to Woolmer's *Gazette*

> 'The electioneering procession of the Honourable Member . . . attracted much notice, being most objectionable to a very large proportion of the respectable inhabitants, and

disapproved of by some of the more moderate of his own friends. The big loaf and little loaf, stuck on poles, were fitted only to excite and inflame the worst passion and feelings among the lower classes.'[73]

The intruder, Lord Lovaine, behaved with decorum. Henry Ellis, beset by canvassers in his counting house and doing his best to avoid offence to important customers, recorded that the ladies of Exeter found Lovaine a 'nice young man.'[74] The candidate professed his determination 'to maintain in all their integrity, the Monarchy, Church and Constitution of the Country, and to protect the rights and privileges of the people.' He criticized the new poor law, suggested that 'cheap bread could be obtained only through a great cheapening of wages' but wisely would 'not give pledges or promises which he could not be expected to perform.'[75]

The election was a tumultuous affair and the Guildhall, where Henry Hooper presided as sheriff, was full to overflowing. The Conservatives brought a phalanx of navvies to enliven proceedings with cheers and counter-cheers. According to the *Flying Post*

'the walls of the ancient hall resounded with the ever-inspiring English cheering, and then with the most tremendous groans, while thirdly came the shrill whistle proceeding from hundreds of throats.'[76]

Because he could not make himself heard in the uproar the sheriff in vain held aloft placards calling for silence. The speeches were mostly inaudible. From the close-packed throng and the high beaver hats a steamy heat rose to the ceiling and condensed in moisture on the reporters' notebooks.

Follett came head of the ensuing poll with 1,302 votes. Divett was second with 1,119. Lord Lovaine received only eighty-three.

Both parties celebrated their victories on an unprecedented scale. Many of the Exeter shops were closed for Divett's triumphal procession in which fifty-six carriages took part amid a profusion of bands and banners. From henceforward Divett's position was unshakeable. The Conservatives held a banquet at the Subscription Rooms attended by

Archdeacon Barnes, member of an influential family entrenched in the church, banking, medicine and the law, who acknowledged the toast of 'The Bishop and Clergy of the Diocese.' The archdeacon 'did it all in honour and very much like a gentleman – rather more convivial than clerical but still sufficiently devout.'[77]

The Exeter Liberals had beaten off the most determined assault they were to experience for thirty years. In 1845 the death of Follett opened the way for a counter-attack. The vacant seat was contested by Sir John Duckworth, son of an admiral, grandson of a bishop of Exeter, and an intimate of the wealthy Rolle family of Bicton.[78] The Liberals in their turn brought forward an outsider in the person of General Briggs, who stood as a Free Trader. Once more there was 'a strong feeling in the minds of a large body of the electors of Exeter that the city should be represented in parliament by someone closely identified with the city.'[79] Briggs struck a note which was not to be heard again in Exeter till Canon Girdlestone's campaign in the late 1860s on behalf of the labourers of Halberton. He spoke for the agricultural labourers whose wages were 7s. to 10s. a week. He sought election on the grounds that he wished 'to elevate the minds of the people of Exeter to render them sensible of the privileges they possess.'[80]

Appeals for elevation of mind were not likely to be of much practical effect in the Exeter of the Hooper regime even if they were audible in an uproar which was hardly less tumultuous than that of 1841. Nor were labourers' wages a burning issue for the enfranchised of Exeter. The *Western Times*, Liberal always and occasionally Radical, reproved the Exeter food rioters of 1847, and Canon Girdlestone himself in 1869, for flouting current theories of economics by demanding more than the market was deemed able to afford. Exeter was the heart of a rural province of landowners and farmers. The city's press was busy reporting agricultural meetings which acclaimed 'the independent peasantry of old England' with 'three times three.'[81] Even in the febrile atmosphere of 1841 the *Western Times* had qualified its support for free trade with the announcement that it would 'deeply regret to see any plan proposed which would tend to depreciate agriculture as an interest.'[82] The environment of Exeter did not encourage attacks on the landed gentry in the manner of Manchester and the *Western Times* at this time commented with approval on the relations of 'the lords of the soil with the class immediately beneath.' The Exeter Conservatives for their part searched in vain, in 1846 'for either Crisis, Emergency or Expediency to justify the sudden conversion of the Prime Minister' and urged that 'a Representative has higher duties in the House of Commons than to be a puppet that shall dance whenever a Prime Minister shall pipe.'[83] Exeter's protectionism did not die in 1846, nor even with Disraeli's election address of 1852.

In 1845 the nomination proceedings in the Exeter election terminated with the sheriff's declaration, reached after understandable hesitation, that the show of hands had been in favour of Briggs. Nominations were attended by many who had no qualifications for the franchise and who were more likely to respond to a candidate's concern for labourers than were the majority of the £10-voters. At the polls Duckworth received 1,258 votes against the 588 votes cast for his opponent.

Exeter's natural conservatism embracing both parties and the majority of all classes ensured, after the brief aberration of the late 1830s, the 'Restoration' of 1840 and the local Conservative party's subsequent prolonged control of the council. In the religious field this conservatism engendered suspicion of changes in ritual or emphasis on doctrine which exalted the status of the clergy, savoured of Rome or otherwise conflicted with what the plain man was satisfied he could find in his Bible. Religious feeling in turn, whether due to dislike of change or genuine scruples of 'tender consciences,' was fomented and exacerbated by the personal feud between the *Western Times* and Bishop Phillpotts.[84] The Protestant Reformation was commemorated annually each 5 November, when the great bonfire blazed outside the west door of the cathedral, adjacent properties were barricaded and flaming tar barrels bounded down the steep streets. The opportunity was usually taken to lampoon the bishop, whom the *Western Times* enjoyed assailing as 'Pot-Boy' and Judas.[85]

Thomas Latimer's campaign against Phillpotts, though often wrong-headed and scurrilous, was born of an enduring strand in English history. In the same spirit John Stubbs the Puritan had suffered mutilation and cheered for the queen, and Cromwell's 'russet-coated captains' had ridden to war. The same spirit survived in Macaulay's England, though some of its manifestations justified the comment that the only one of the Thirty-Nine Articles in which people took any interest was the one denying jurisdiction to the Bishop of Rome.[86] By the 1840s the Tractarians were restoring old ceremonies and decorum, as well as pastoral zeal, in Devon. Phillpotts was no Tractarian. In 1842 he commented tartly that

'the Tractarians have, in my opinion, made it necessary to mark determined disapprobation of their extravagance. In the present crisis it is, I think, the part of sound church-men to manage, if possible, in such a manner as shall prevent the Low Church Party from gaining strength, and triumphing in the excesses of their opposite numbers.'[87]

In public, the bishop alluded to

'a longing on the part of many, for a return to ancient usages and ceremonial observances, which, however valuable for their significance, and edifying when properly understood, are yet regarded by a large proportion of the population as little better than the remnants of Popish superstition and the revival of them is therefore resisted with warmth, often, it may be, disproportioned to the occasion.'[88]

One manifestation of the revival of edifying observances was the wearing of the surplice in the pulpit during the sermon, a practice which was ritually and legally correct. In the west country it was regarded as an undesirable innovation smacking of popery. Helston, Cornwall, resented it to the point of riotous behaviour. Exeter followed suit. In view of the disorderly scenes which the reintroduction of the surplice had provoked, the bishop determined to enforce uniformity. Since the surplice was required by the rubric it was logical to ensure uniformity by insistence on its use and so deprive it of significance as a party badge of one section of the church. On 19 October 1844, Phillpotts consulted his senior clergy. They were divided in opinion but the bishop formed the opinion that on balance they favoured his proposal. Nevertheless, as he informed Ralph Barnes, he 'resolved to have recourse to a general chapter, whose counsel cannot fail, in this state of things, to be more satisfactory in my own mind, as well as to convey with it additional authority to others.' The presence and opinions of the non-residentiary prebendaries would be 'the more valuable as they may be able to bear testimony to the feelings of the clergy, and of the Laity, in their several neighbourhoods.'[89]

The general chapter met on 19 November. With the support of a majority decision of ten votes to six the bishop informed his clergy that 'there is one diversity for the quieting and appeasing of which I now wish to take order by requiring whenever the sermon is part of the ministration of the Parochial Clergy that the suplice he always used.'[90]

Uproar ensued in Exeter, where the *Western Times* fulminated against a 'crafty, selfish and tyrannical man.' Latimer claimed that the innovations were derived from a body of men, the Tractarians, 'whose deliberate aim is to undo the protestant reformation . . . and to subdue the minds of people to their intolerable thraldom.'[91] The chapter opposed the bishop. Canon Bull, canon of Exeter, prebend of York, canon of Christchurch and vicar of Staverton in Northamptonshire, told Barnes that the bishop had made a catspaw of the general chapter and had thus overridden the advice of his dean and canons residentiary.[92] The dean and chapter despatched a memorial to the Archbishop of Canterbury. The bishop and members of the chapter conducted an unseemly controversy in the press. Canon Bull enjoyed what for him was the unusual experience of being cheered at public meetings.

The bishop gave way and withdrew his instructions on 23 December 1844. His attempt to impose uniformity had been untimely but, in the opinion of Ralph Barnes, who had been advising both sides, the action of the dissident members of the chapter, especially Canon Bull, had been disloyal and factious.[93]. Parish meetings of St Sidwell's and St James, on 9 January resolved to request earnestly that the use of the surplice in the pulpit should be discontinued. The incumbent of St James complied. His colleague refused pointing out that he had worn the surplice in the pulpit for the past three years. Both he and another clergyman were mobbed and required police protection. On 19 January, recorded Dr Shapter, 'it is computed that a mob excited and violent in its demeanour of not less than two thousand followed the incumbent of St Sidwell's through the streets and had it not been for the superadded assistance of many others personal violence would have resulted.' At a subsequent parish meeting 'much angry and coarse expressions of opinion occurred' and the incumbent was 'received with scant courtesy.'

There was another recrudescence of trouble in 1848, after which Exeter grew accustomed to the appearance of the surplice in the pulpit for the sermon.

In the view of Richard Ford, a detached observer, the rabbling of the Exeter clergy was instigated by the 'middling classes and the rich tradesmen' animated by 'a violent, no-popery protestant feeling.' In Ford's opinion, the mob was quiet having work and cheap food. The gentry attached 'no importance to the black or white vesture.'[94] Shapter commented that the disturbance 'was solely due to the feeling of the people – fanned into anger and action by a local press violently opposed and consistently abusive of the Bishop – but more on political than religious ground.' He considered however that Phillpotts' own letters to the press had made the situation worse and 'seriously damaged the position and influence of the Bishop.'[95]

Exeter's assertions of Protestantism in the nineteenth century tended to be rough. Anything savouring of papist practices was denounced by the Evangelical *Flying Post* and the Liberal *Western Times* in scurrilous terms. But Exeter did not normally rabble the clergy though ready enough to burn in effigy Tractarians, 'Puseyites,' cardinals and Jesuits each 5 November. The surplice riots of the winter of 1844–45 were indeed factious rather than religious, whipped up by the

Western Times and the *Flying Post*, particularly by the former, and encouraged by disloyalty on the part of members of the cathedral chapter. Sober citizens of unimpeachable respectability, those who filled the best pews on Sundays with broad cloth and silk, undoubtedly tended to regard the surplice in the pulpit as another step on the road to Rome. Henry Ellis attributed with regret, wrongfully as it turned out, the resignation of 'that good man, for such he really was,' the vicar of St Pancras to a remonstrance against the vicar practising 'certain ceremonial observances which were pronounced, if not sinful, to have grown into desuetude.'[96] But, as Dr Shapter observed, the riot in St Sidwell's was caused by men who were unfamiliar with the interior of a church.

By 1845 Exeter was moving into economic troubles for which neither Conservatives nor Liberals could offer a solution. Two years later the city's poor had cause to riot in earnest. The bright hopes of human regeneration entertained by the Reformers of the 1830s had been dimmed. 'It is among the first blessings of the measure of Reform,' the *Western Times* had claimed in 1832, 'that it has tended still more powerfully to educate the people in the science of good Government.'[97] The Municipal Corporations Act was to have destroyed 'the power (*sic*) of the Corporation being mixed up with political parties' according to J. D. Osborn.[98] In the words of Mark Kennaway the act would meet the demand for 'pure and disinterested election.'[99]

Life had returned a dusty answer to these eager seekers after political verities. The council had been firmly based on political parties from the outset. The party of Reform had been given a mere three years of tenuous power. Instead of 'pure and disinterested election' the electors were offered the expenditure of John Clench and the methods of the Hooper regime. The Exeter Liberals, however, should not be dismissed too easily as political romantics. In their insistence on religious and political equality of opportunity, freedom of private judgement and on the council's responsibility to the public, they represented values which, though undoubtedly shared by some of their opponents then and later, were not always conspicuous in the council's later history. Exeter's Liberalism became effective when grievance was most felt; in the 1830s, the grievance of exclusiveness and secrecy, in later years the grievance of rising rates and the complacency of the governing party. An assertion of political and moral principles rather than a programme, it reminded the city's rulers of the obligations and accountability of power. Therein lay the value of Exeter's Liberalism in the Age of Reform.

F

III

LAW AND ORDER 1837–1847

THE England of the early years of the nineteenth century has been described as a country without police prepared to put up with 'a certain amount of disorder if it was the price of freedom.'[1] By the 1830s the price was becoming too high. In 1830, southern England saw in the flames of burning stacks the beacons of rural revolt. Elsewhere 'lying outside the orbit of the old governing class, the industrial territories were growing up as best they might, undrained, unpoliced, ungoverned and unschooled.'[2]

The thunder-charged clouds of a society under strain gave place to clearer skies over Devon where society retained a stability derived from traditional habits and sanctions. Exeter had made its own contribution to the tale of riots which had punctuated the history of eighteenth-century England. But in the 1830s and throughout the nineteenth century the city's population remained firmly within the control of its ruling classes. Traditional society, in town as in country, retained a cohesion unweakened by the stresses of the Industrial Revolution. Merchant, surgeon, lawyer and clergyman exercised an influence possible only in a small and neighbourly society.

The weight of traditional authority and the absence of large, isolated, working-class communities in the city, factors which determined the course of its nineteenth-century history, served to contain any serious disorder. Exeter long remained turbulent. The city's mayors had to be prepared to take personal command in time of riot and to tour the seething streets with constables and soldiery.

In Exeter as elsewhere soldiers and yeomanry were called in to suppress disorders which could have been prevented by an efficient police. Exeter rioters shared to the full the prevailing dislike of the yeomanry. The constabulary commission of 1839 was informed that 'the animosities created or increased, by arming master against servant, neighbour against neighbour . . . were even more deplorable than the outrages actually committed.'[3] When Captain Acland's troop rode in from Killerton to help suppress the Exeter riots of 1847 they were roughly handled.[4] The incident drew from the *Western Times* the observation that 'the mob certainly have a contemptuous dislike of yeomanry – the cause of which we do not well understand.'[5]

Prior to the Municipal Corporations Act the permanent police force in Exeter consisted of the four sergeants at mace and the four staffbearers who had other, more remunerative and less arduous, duties to perform. Such routine patrolling as existed was carried out by the night watch, an easy-going body of men under the control of the improvement commissioners and usually carrying out their duties at the end of a day's work. In consequence they were frequently in trouble for sleeping on duty. In times of disorder the mayor could call on the special constables, men of property large and small, such as those who turned out in their thousands to patrol London in the days of the Chartists.

The parliamentary commissioners had reported that the existing organization in Exeter was 'stated to form a sufficient force for the ordinary purposes of the police.'[6] But the Corporations Act introduced a new conception of the responsibility of town councils. Lord John Russell informed the house of commons that his party proposed that the whole work and business of watching the town should be placed completely under the control of the councils.[7] This step appeared 'absolutely necessary in establishing a municipal government.' The home secretary explained that 'the keeping of the peace, or, to use the words of olden times, the quieting of the town, should come immediately under the control of persons who are deemed to have the government of the town.' Accordingly section 76 of the act enjoined upon the new corporations that they should speedily take steps to appoint watch committees empowered to appoint constables sworn in before the justices 'for preserving the Peace by Day and Night.' Salaries and expenses were to be met from the borough fund.

Exeter began forthwith to institute the system which was to last till 1966. The council worked by trial and error, largely without expert guidance. The nucleus of a modern force took eleven years to achieve. It was the work of men distinguished, as the *Gazette* put it, 'as regards integrity, respectability and habits of business,'[8] engaged on a novel task. In the background was a sturdy suspicion of external interference from London. The council petitioned parliament in 1839 against the proposals to appoint commissioners of police in Birmingham and Manchester, the expense to be met by local taxation, as 'contrary to the spirit of the constitution.'[9] In 1856 there was a further petition against the Police Counties and Boroughs Bill which introduced the system of government grants on condition of inspection by home office inspectors. The council's objections were on the grounds that

'the general principle of centralization which characterizes the whole Bill, taking from the Rate Payers and Local Authorities all power and jurisdiction within their ancient limits and vesting them in individual members of a Government to whom the Bill gives absolute power, is contrary to the constitution of the country and an uncalled for and unnecessary innovation.'[10]

The watch committee appointed under section 76 of the act held its first meeting on 18 January 1836 to begin the evolution of an organization and code of discipline. They worked by the light of their own common sense since for the first four months the force had no commanding officer. The altercation over the post of swordbearer led to the suggestion that the ceremonial duties of this post might be combined with those of the officer in charge of police. Hugh Cumming, who had once served in the militia, was thereupon appointed superintendent of police, his duties being 'as near as circumstances will permit, the same as the Superintendent of Police in London subject to the orders of the Watch Committee.'[11] His salary was £120 a year.

The watch committee erred in retaining the distinction between the day and night police with a resolution that 'the Day Police with the exception of the Captains be distinct from the Night Police.'[12] The day police were the four sergeants at mace and the six staffbearers. The two junior staffbearers alone were regarded as full-time police, who were not to receive the perquisites enjoyed by their seniors for traditional duties. The two junior sergeants were regarded primarily but not exclusively as police and allowed to continue to receive their former perquisites. The remaining four officers attempted to combine their former duties with the new and, as events showed, to the detriment of the latter. The night watch was under the control of the captain of the watch, an office filled by members of the day police in rotation.

The new régime was recognized by the improvement commissioners in May 1837 with a resolution 'that from this time no more money be paid by this body on account of the Nightly Watch agreeably to the provisions of the Municipal Act.'[13] By the end of the year there existed on paper a force of twenty-five men under a superintendent. Two sergeants at mace and six staffbearers formed the day police paid at rates varying from 18s. to 21s. a week according to whether they also received a free house. The night watch included twelve watchmen paid 2s. a night and four inspectors paid 2s. 3d. a night, all on a temporary basis. The captain of the watch received 4s. a night in addition to his pay as a member of the day police for his spell of night duty.[14]

The evolution of force orders began in February 1836, when instructions for the day and night police and a summary of the duties of a police constable were approved and printed. A code of professional conduct was constructed brick by brick.[15] An occurrence book was kept at the Guildhall and laid before the watch committee at each weekly meeting. Much time was spent in discussions on clothing and equipment, which included the traditional rattle of the old-style watch, lancewood staves, lanterns and handcuffs.

The main problems were how to make best use of the force and how to impose discipline. Standards of behaviour remained those of the old-style watch accustomed 'to sit upon the church-bench till two and then go home to bed.' The records of the early Victorian watch committee in Exeter are a tale of dismissals, reappointments and further dismissals. Some sixty men were dismissed between January 1837 and November 1848, over half for drunkenness. Typical of many was Abraham Jones, fined 5s. and dismissed, reinstated and again dismissed eight months later 'for being disguised in liquor when he presented himself on duty and for being impertinent to the captain of the watch.'[16] A more ambitious performance was that of John Coles who was drunk on duty, persuaded a comrade to share a convivial glass while on duty and ended a crowded day with a coach ride to Okehampton, where he became involved in a fight. Even the experienced John Ginham, sergeant at mace, was found one night drunk and incapable in South Street. In 1846 the arrival on duty of two newly-enlisted men in a state of intoxication led to the discovery of a genial custom by which new recruits were required to pay a footing of 2s. – more than a day's wages for the ordinary labourer – to be spent on beer.[17] The watch committee resolved that 'the rule which authorizes this committee to dismiss a police constable for being drunk on duty be strictly enforced.'[18] But this resolution was not carried out. Exeter was hard-drinking in the nineteenth century. Towards the end of the century the watch committee was still concerned about drunkenness in the force.

There was no training. The porters, labourers and artisans who, as a councillor had occasion to point out,[19] had already put in a long day's work before supplementing their earnings in the watch, were left to pick up experience as best they might. Few remained in the force long enough to do so. Entry into the force was achieved by enrolment as supernumerary watchman on an approved list. The frequent vacancies ensured reasonable prospects of regular employment as watchman with further prospects of admission into the day police.

The permanent members of the force were reluctant to perform their new duties, and also tended to play off the mayor against the watch committee.[20] Four of the day police were almost wholly employed on law processes, said to be 'very tedious.'[21] On occasion the whole of the force might be occupied with the assizes.

In 1836, the watch committee resolved that it was desirable 'as soon as possible to re-arrange the Night and Day police by consolidating their duties and forming one regular police force.'[22] For financial reasons this wise decision was postponed for eleven years, until action was enforced by the pressure of events. The committee made various attempts to improve the use of the available men. In 1839 it was decided to require the night watch to patrol singly instead of in groups. The inspectors thereupon complained that this arrangement forced them to walk too rapidly on their inspection and therefore they could not 'pay that attention which is required.'[23] In 1841 the watch committee resolved that at least two of the day police should in fact patrol by day. The decision was communicated to the magistrates who were unsympathetic and refused to release men from court duties. They agreed with the watch committee that 'an efficient police should perambulate the city by day'; but they found it necessary 'to state as their decided opinion that the present police force is not sufficiently numerous to admit any of the Force being employed in the proposed perambulation even if the whole force were available.' It was not available. Two men had to be in constant attendance at the Guildhall and the others 'of necessity were engaged in other duties such as attending to the general directions of the magistrates.'[24]

Police reorganization involved expenditure, and the council was still seeking to avoid the imposition of a borough rate. Because the council was living such a hand-to-mouth financial existence, the pay of the watch was often in arrears. In 1841, after receiving no pay for ten weeks, the watch breathlessly petitioned the committee hoping

'you will be pleased to bear in mind the severe Winter Wee have endured for the Protection of Your Property and the Citizens of Exeter Wee beg most respectfully that you may be Pleased to see the cause of our Petitioning Many of us having Large Families to Support and Provisions being High and Labour Scarce as being sadly against us Wee hope and trust you will see the Necessity of paying us regularly . . .'

The treasurer explained to the mayor that

'having been urgently requested to pay the night watch, and feeling that as these men are employed they might from some means or other be paid, I take the liberty of explaining to you that the reason why I am unable to apply any of the money in my hands to this particular purpose is that the Council have positively ordered the Treasurer to retain all Money arising out of the tolls of the Canal, after paying its expenses, to the discharge of the interest on the mortgage and the Canal Debt.'[25]

With pay in arrears, continuity and experience dependent on men whose main interests lay in their traditional duties, with a superintendent who was no more than the old sword-bearer in a blue coat, and with additional expenditure ruled out by parsimony as well as by financial necessity, Exeter's first attempt to constitute an efficient police force was a failure.

The Reformers consistently urged complete reorganization. In 1837 Councillor Snell had drawn up proposals for a unified force. In 1847 J. D. Osborn prepared a scheme based on his own study of the Lambeth police.[26] The council had taken the plunge and had imposed a borough rate in the previous year. In May the bread riots provided further compelling reasons for the reorganization of the police. Osborn's proposals were accepted in principle by the council without demur and referred back to the watch committee for the elaboration of detail. On 16 June the final report of the watch committee was approved by the council without a division.[27]

By the decision of 16 June 1847 the council authorized a police establishment of thirty men: a superintendent at £120 a year; five inspectors at 21s. a week; three sergeants at mace at 18s. a week and seventeen constables at 16s. The day police and the night watch were amalgamated, three sergeants at mace and seven constables being available for day duties. The estimated recurrent cost was £1,461 4s. for pay and £164 10s. 6d. for clothing.

Important questions of principle were at length decided without difficulty. The future of Hugh Cumming and the appointment of a successor, being more tangible and arousing allegations of jobbery, gave rise to the heat which such matters still engender in local government. Cumming had been too closely associated with the old régime to be popular with Liberals, who attacked his proposed pension of £100 as excessive and a typical example of Tory jobbery.[28] Advertisement of the vacant post was opposed on the grounds that this would lead to jobbery. The arguments at one stage threatened to lead to the abandonment of the scheme; but Hugh Cumming received his pension, which he drew for twenty-eight years, dying at the age of ninety-two.

Meanwhile the town clerk had consulted Colonel Rowan, chief commissioner of the metropolitan police, asking for a recommendation of a superintendent to take up his duties in Exeter on 1 August. Colonel Rowan, hard-pressed by other town councils engaged in police reform, replied that he would make the vacancy known to members of his force but declined to take upon himself responsibility for the selection.[29] On 26 July the council approved the appointment of David Steel, a former member of the metropolitan police and currently superintendent at Barnstaple. His application was accompanied by an impressive number of testimonials from a vice-chancellor, peers and magistrates.[30] Councillor Floud, attorney, grumbled in the spirit of Sir Walter Elliott of Kellynch that the superintendent at Exeter should be a gentleman fit to associate with other gentlemen.[31] But Steel was appointed. He proved an efficient and conscientious police officer until his retirement in 1873.

Despite the inevitable protests from some of the ratepayers the reorganization was carried out expeditiously. The whole of the night police were discharged and those regarded as suitable were re-engaged. The new force paraded under their superintendent at the end of August. To ensure that pay did not again fall into arrears the treasurer was instructed to ensure that funds should be provided each Thursday for the payment of police salaries and expenses. Exeter had at last the nucleus of a modern, full-time force. But it was not till 1891 that the council submitted to home office pressure and agreed that the sergeants at mace should no longer be regarded as members of the force.[32] Government grants-in-aid, with the corollary of home office supervision, were accepted only with reluctance and after repeated refusals, partly because the interference of 'foreigners' and officials in the affairs of Exeter was always sturdily resisted, partly because home office inspectors were inclined to make proposals requiring additional expenditure.

The police had to maintain law and order in a cathedral city which was rough, disorderly and often brutal beneath the crust of middle-class culture and clerical life. Much disorderly conduct was attributable to heavy drinking in a city which contained 120 inns and public houses for a total population of 32,000. Quay porters who stopped to fight on the way home after refreshment and then knocked down the watchman who attempted to intervene were perhaps in the tradition of Mr Weller's colleagues. More dangerous was an assault on the landlord of the Royal Oak by two recalcitrant customers armed with an iron bar. Streets were unsafe after dark. A doctor in the service of the corporation of the poor found it advisable to carry a life-preserver on his night rounds and had occasion to use it with good effect.[33] In 1842 the well-known surgeon, Samuel Barnes, was knocked down and robbed on a July night while on his way from his residence in Barnfield Crescent to visit a patient near Summerlands. The assailants did not get far in rural Devon, where strangers were conspicuous. The men and their accomplice were arrested at Chudleigh, the men being sentenced to transportation for life and the girl to fifteen years. They were described as 'trampers, persons who are in the habit of attending fairs, regattas, races and places of that description.'[34]

Exeter's only sensational crime of the century had occurred in the previous summer when the city was shocked by the discovery of the body of Nathaniel Bennett, of the West of England Insurance Company, found floating in the river near Trews Weir. After visiting the Bonhay Fair, the deceased had spent a night in disreputable company, male and female, in the Cattle Market Inn and had been followed home through the streets. The subsequent arrest of William Pitts, aged nineteen, and Pitts's trial for murder, provided a sensation for Exeter. On the opening of the trial the court was rushed by spectators and so much confusion was caused that the proceedings had to be postponed till the following day. The case against the accused depended on the evidence of an accomplice turned queen's evidence whom public opinion, apparently with justification, regarded as the more guilty of the two. Pitts was accordingly found not guilty of murder but guilty of larceny and was sentenced to fifteen years' transportation.[35]

Prostitution flourished with the active encouragement or connivance of some of the many public houses. The Pestle and Mortar in Guinea Street had a particularly bad reputation for providing lodgings 'for persons of the lowest class.'[36] In proximity to the Pestle and Mortar lived Mark Elms, of Idol Lane, later King Street, a 'fence' who was eventually arrested in possession of the proceeds of a robbery near Taunton.[37] There were well-known brothels in Rockfield Place, in the malodorous courts off North Street and in the slums of St Mary Major's. In 1839 the superintendent of police was specially instructed 'not to permit prostitution, nightwalkers or other disorderly persons to loiter in public streets or footways.'[38]

The police were unpopular. One Sunday night in June 1844 a running fight between police and soldiers disturbed the peace from the New London Inn to the Guildhall. The soldiers obtained reinforcements from Topsham Barracks and in the small hours laid siege to the Guildhall. They were taken in the rear and routed losing five men under arrest. At the subsequent trial, however, the acquittal of three soldiers charged with riot was received with applause. The popular view was that the soldiers had been unnecessarily provoked by 'the busy B's of the police.'[39]

The police were further tried by the tendency of the citizens of Exeter 'to prove their Doctrine Orthodox by Apostolick Blows and Knocks' each fifth of November. In 1843 the watch committee minutes recorded 'very severe injuries' to four watchmen during the performance of their duties in the Cathedral Close.[40] In 1847 the Protestant ascendancy was celebrated in a particularly 'wild and ferocious spirit.' Men 'rolled barrels through the streets with force and arms, resisting the police with bludgeons and fighting their fiery way most savagely where they . . . encountered resistance.' Each fifth of November the mayor and magistrates assembled in the Guildhall to deal with disorder, the mayor holding state and entertaining the city dignitaries.[41] The near-riot of 1847 caused the mayor for the following year, Dr Shapter, to take firm measures to restrain the annual disturbance. Tar barrels were prohibited and the police assembled in force in the Cathedral Close. But it was not till the 1880s that the old customs were discarded.

Newspaper reports of proceedings before the magistrates and the records of the Gaol Calendar Book[42] were too often a reflection of the more wretched aspects of life in an early Victorian city. Some 350 men and 315 women appeared before the assizes and general quarter sessions between 1837–1847. There were 761 convictions, including 110 men and 59 women sentenced to transportation for periods ranging from seven years to life. In defence of property, Maria Tarbutt, aged sixteen, was transported for seven years for stealing a pair of stockings, a reticule and some other articles. John Hill, aged thirteen and convicted of his second felony, was sentenced to seven years transportation for stealing 1s. 6d. Prostitutes like 'Ducky' Marshall, aged twenty-two, and Mary Ann Herman, aged twenty-seven, were transported for fifteen and ten years respectively for stealing from clients. In 1840 John Warne, aged fifteen, was sentenced to two months' hard labour, and to be whipped three times in the last month of his imprisonment, for stealing a cake. Thomas Smith, aged fourteen, was sentenced to one month's hard labour and to be 'privately but severely whipped' for stealing a teaspoon.[43] The police returns for the twelve months ending 1 September 1848[44] – one of the results of the new superintendent's appointment – recorded that 813 persons had been charged and 528 summarily convicted. The convictions included 231 for drunkenness and disorderly conduct, 143 for vagrancy and fifty-eight for assaults on the police.

In 1837 the recorder had pointed out in his charge to the grand jury that there had been some increase in crime. He deemed it his duty, therefore, to draw attention 'to the state and condition of the people out of which the increase in crime (seemed) to have arisen.' He suggested that the cause lay not in 'cravings of hunger' but in education, which increased the capacity for crime, facilitated the means 'and would be the most noxious weed that we could sow unless accompanied by a religious or moral principle.'[45] In 1842, the year of the serious industrial disturbances known as the Plug Plot, Exeter's recorder found it necessary to say no more than that the public houses in the city required watchful attention. Three years later Mr Justice Coleridge commented that it was gratifying 'to find that while the population was increasing – and therefore, they might fairly suppose, the temptations to crime were increasing also . . . crime did not seem to grow.'[46]

These were the years when Brougham was alarming the house of lords with tales of 'pillage, alarm, insecurity of life and property, nay, wholesale massacre,'[47] when Rebecca and her daughters ranged the turnpikes of Wales and there was plotting and arson in Birmingham. Exeter remained quiet till, in 1847, the price of wheat advanced from 77s. 11d. a quarter in April to over 100s. in May, as compared with 59s. a quarter in May 1846. Lord Hardwicke drew attention to the need to prevent profiteering and pointed out that in Devon only one-eighth of the old harvest was left.[48] At the Exeter March sessions a boy aged fourteen was sentenced to fourteen days hard labour and a severe whipping for stealing three loaves; a woman received twenty days' hard labour for the theft of two pounds of mutton.[49] The recorder attributed an increase in crime to the scarcity of food, not to a lack of religious and moral discipline; 'almost all the cases in the calendar were petty thefts, in many cases most probably occasioned by want.'[50]

On 11 May 1847 there was trouble at Cullompton, thirteen miles from Exeter, where a corn dealer had his windows broken. In Exeter at about noon on 14 May, Thomas Latimer saw 'an elderly man, pale, confused and anxious, mobbed by women' who rushed past the door of the *Western Times* to seek refuge in the Guildhall.[51] The fugitive was a potato dealer from St Thomas believed to have been buying up provisions brought into the city from the country. The mob was up. It included not only the idle and disorderly 'but middle-aged elderly women who would not have been found in the streets clamouring against provisionmongers had there not been dreadful want at home.' Bakers' shops were attacked. The corn market was cleared out by a riotous mob. The windows of corn dealers were broken and farmers fled the city.

The mayor, attorney W. D. Moore, was in London attending the Lord Mayor's banquet. He returned by express train to take charge. Accompanied by the town clerk, Moore toured the streets at the head of the police, dispersing crowds and personally apprehending offenders. That night there was a public meeting in the Guildhall at which the mayor explained the dispositions of the police and special constables. The yeomanry were already partially mobilized since exercises were to be held at Exmouth on 22 May. Captain Acland was assembling his troop at Killerton. With a minimum of delay troops were mustered at Topsham Barracks under Colonel Buller.

After the initial disturbance the streets had become quieter but on 21 May it was decided to make a show of force by parading the yeomanry. The decision was a mistake. The yeomanry, as always, had a rough reception and when they were withdrawn towards ten o'clock at night there was a sudden outbreak in St Sidwell's. An attack on the Guildhall in an attempt to release prisoners was repulsed; but mayor, magistrates, police and special constables remained at their posts all night. The events of 1549, when Exeter stood siege by Catholic insurgents, were recalled as the candlelight glimmered on the bayonets of soldiers under the high fifteenth-century roof-beams. That night the crisis passed. Next day the yeomanry were brought up to a strength of six troops. Two companies of the 5th Fusiliers arrived by train from Plymouth. The examination of the prisoners began.

There were only nineteen accused and the most severe sentence was no more than one month's imprisonment, in contrast to Torquay where the riots were followed by 323

convictions including eight sentences of transportation.[52]
Against the disturbed background of England, tumults at
Exeter, Torquay, Newton Abbot, Ashburton, Totnes,
Buckfastleigh, Tavistock, Barnstaple, Exmouth and Crediton
aroused little interest. In the house of commons Sir George
Grey 'was happy to state that in consequence of the prompt
and judicious measures adopted by the local authorities,
order had been restored; and he hoped that there be no
cause for alarm in the future.'[53] By July the price of the 4lb.
loaf had fallen to $8\frac{1}{2}d$.[54]

The Exeter riots provoked vigorous criticism of the
superintendent, Hugh Cumming, and undoubtedly hastened
the re-organization of the police.[55] They were wisely followed
by a meeting at the Guildhall to organize measures for the
relief of the poor, for the disturbances of 1847 were an
outbreak of despair on the part of a population which had
little opportunity for voicing grievances in the Devon of the
1840s:

> 'We hear men speaking for us
>   Of new laws strong and sweet
> Yet is there no man speaketh
>   As we speak in the street.'

IV

SOCIAL AND ECONOMIC AFFAIRS
1837–1850

VICTORIAN Exeter differs sharply from more typical Victorian cities in that Exeter looked back with regret to the past and had no occasion to take pride in the achievements of economic growth. Dr Shapter wrote of the Exeter of 1800 as an industrial city. By 1831, he recorded, the woollen manufacture had virtually ceased.[1] The speeches celebrating the arrival of the railway in 1844 expressed the hope that the city would once more sail on the full tide of economic opportunity. Yet in 1881 a local newspaper had occasion to reflect that 'The population returns do not show that great increase which is shown in some places . . . We do not grow, simply because the process of growth, as a city, ceased many generations ago';[2] and in 1900 an enterprising local industrialist, H. A. Willey, informed the Exeter Working Men's Society that, 'as they all knew, Exeter had once been the centre of important industries employing large bodies of men, but that golden age had been followed by a period when the industries had disappeared.'[3]

In the early eighteenth century Exeter 'came to rank as the third city of the kingdom, outside London, in population, wealth and trade.'[4] But the city's prominent position was undermined by the long French wars of the eighteenth century. No longer, in the 1830s, did 'argosies with portly sail' leave the Exe, their bills of lading inscribed with the Miltonic roll of Europe's great seaports: Amsterdam, Rotterdam, Hamburg, Cadiz, Lisbon, Oporto.

By the 1830s Exeter was facing the problem of survival, at a time when other towns were experiencing the difficulties created by exuberant and often anarchic growth. In the census decades 1811–21 and 1821–31 the population of Exeter increased by just over 24 per cent. and 20 per cent., or from 18,896 to 28,242 within the municipal boundary during twenty years. In the following decades the gross increase was substantially less and by 1851 the population of the city was only 32,818.

Throughout the first half of the nineteenth century Exeter retained substantial, though ill-distributed, prosperity as a provincial capital – the centre of a remote world in which movement was still restricted. The city provided goods, services and entertainment for a still prosperous rural community and held its traditional importance as a political and social centre. The list of economic activities in the directories – foundries, breweries, corn mills, warehouses and tanneries – remained impressive and it was not the business of directories to measure the extent or prospects of growth. In 1847 the *Western Times* commented that food was regarded as a staple manufacture.[5] Distinguished visitors came to Exeter's famous inns on their way to the fashionable resorts of Dawlish, Torquay and Teignmouth. Charles Dickens, accompanied by the artist Maclise, was one of those who stayed at the New London Inn in 1842. The social world of Exeter and its neighbourhood flocked to see Macready as the cardinal in Lord Lytton's *Richelieu*. Charles Kean appeared in the *Lady of Lyons* before 'a succession of the most crowded and fashionable assemblages ever known in the city.'[6] There were packed audiences to hear Paganini and Jenny Lind. County and city society gathered for occasions such as the Race Fund Ball held at Congdon's Rooms in 1843, when the patronesses included the Duchess of Somerset and the Countess of Egremont as well as citizens' wives such as Mrs J. B. Sanders and Mrs Mark Kennaway. The assize balls were social institutions at which eligible young ladies 'came out.' In 1845 Exeter began to dance 'those wild whirling figures born of Julien's grand quadrilles,' though doubtless with more decorum than at Cremorne. In 1847, the year of the food riots, nearly 1,000 people were said to have attended Julien's concerts at the Subscription Rooms.[7] At his residence in Dix's Field Mr Mason was teaching 'the much admired new Polka of the Austrian Court' though he was careful to give an assurance

G

that it was 'free from the grossest vulgarity of those generally taught.'[8]

The attractions of Exeter's balls, concerts, theatres and assemblies are evident from Lady Paterson's diary.[9] The city's cultural and material advantages are emphasized by Richard Ford. Visitors and retired people sought the suburbs rather than the more restricted environment of the municipal area. It was represented that the virtue of the 'salubrious air of Heavitree [was] supported by the recommendation of the most eminent physicians in the country.'[10] Between 1821 and 1831 the population of St Leonard's increased by over 126 per cent. and in the following decade by over 163 per cent., from 206 to 1,129. The population of Heavitree increased by some 40 per cent. and 45 per cent.[11] New villas on Mount Radford, St Leonard's, were said to offer 'a most delightful Rus in Urbe.' Property sales emphasized Exeter's popularity for retirement: Mount Radford villa and grounds 'lately the abode of Colonel Blanchard'; Elm Field, with 'its extensive pleasure grounds';[12] No. 11, Baring Crescent, formerly the property of General Clay. Sales displayed evidence of life overseas in the form of eastern curios or 'a rare and choice collection of foreign birds and butterflies.'[13]

Solid standards of comfort in Exeter's surrounding villadom are indicated by the fact that in 1831 Heavitree with the same number of families as Crediton employed twice the number of domestic servants.[14] The proportion was slightly higher than that of fashionable Sidmouth though lower than in the select and purely residential area of the future Torquay.

Business and politics of landowners provided a prosperous living in 1841 for sixty-two attorneys, solicitors, barristers and conveyancers; there were sixty-two compared with only thirty-seven in the larger city of Leicester and twenty-six in Northampton, a town comparable in size with Exeter.[15] Surgeons and apothecaries numbered fifty-four, a high figure compared with thirteen in contemporary Leicester and twenty-nine in Northampton. Bath, of course, always a stronghold of the medical profession, had a much larger number – 104. Exeter's surgeons and doctors moved in the higher circles of the city's society. They could derive a prosperous living from the neighbouring gentry and retired people who could afford a golden guinea for a brief visit and a prescription, as Lady Paterson did on the occasion of Dr Miller's visit in 1834.[16] The legal profession provided an essential link between city and county. John Daw, from Black Torrington, near Hatherleigh, rose to prosperity and acquired status as steward to Lord Rolle at Bicton.[17] His son, John Daw II, became prominent as a political attorney, twice mayor of Exeter.

To meet the requirements of a prosperous middle- and upper-class society in the 1830s, J. Windeatt, of High Street, offered furs of sable, mink, lynx and ermine. In the 1850s Mr Sparks, of Colson and Sparks, was bringing from British and foreign suppliers 'new and fashionable articles . . . in rich silks, Shawls and Mantles.'[18] Mrs Colson, when a widow in poor circumstances, had opened her milliner's shop about 1792 and was followed by her son, John Worthy Colson, in 1812. By 1840 Colson and Sparks had become one of the leading haberdashers in the city, with a name and a reputation which were to stand for one hundred years.[19] To meet the demand for other luxuries Exeter provided in 1841 forty-five jewellers, goldsmiths and silversmiths, a larger number than in Leicester and Cheltenham and exceeding the figure for the historic county capital of York. Henry Ellis had set up his jeweller and watchmaker's shop at No. 199, High Street, in 1815. By 1834 he reckoned that his assets amounted to a clear £13,000.[20] This he recorded 'under God's good providence, I consider to have been mainly attributable to constant and steady habits of Perseverance, Diligence and Industry.'[21] But, as Ellis's memoirs show, it was also due to customers of wealth and taste whom business and pleasure brought to the city. Young Samuel Ellis, managing the shop in 1850, had occasion to write to his father: 'this being hospital day the city has been rather gay and we have had many of the Bigwigs in the shop.'[22]

Exeter's importance as a port had dwindled but with the improvement of roads since the late eighteenth century the city made the most of its position as the gateway to the west. In the great days of coaching 371 coaches left Exeter weekly, the majority from the Old and New London Inns and from the Half Moon Inn. In 1837 thirty-six coaches were advertised to leave Exeter daily for Barnstaple, Bath, Bristol, Falmouth, Gloucester, London, Plymouth and Torquay.[23] A thriving carrier trade, with Russell and Co. at its head, worked from the smaller inns and the market towns of Devon. By the end of 1837 an omnibus service had been begun between Exeter and Crediton charging a return fare of 2s. 6d.[24]

Improved means of travel had brought prosperity to Exeter. John Clench's New London Inn was assessed at £965 for rates in 1838, by far the highest assessment in the city.[25] The Old London Inn was assessed at £450, the Half Moon at £275 and Sarah Street's Clarence Hotel at £266. In comparison, John Hayman's dwelling-house and coach manufactory was assessed at £265, Ben Salter's brewery in Old Bridge Street, with its extensive cellars, lofts, counting house, water wheel and cooper's shop at £200; J. J. Tanner's 'extensive oil leather dressers yard' with pits, workshops, drying lofts and glove maker's shop at £125; and James Northam's foundry on the Coal Quay, with casting, moulding and smiths' shops, dwelling house and garden, at £92.

The demands of the great coaching industry required the services of ostlers, grooms, postboys, guards, inn servants, saddlers and smiths, farriers and corn merchants. In 1841 8 per cent. of the employed male population of Exeter was engaged in the horse and transport industry compared with about 3 per cent. in Leicester, 4 per cent in Norwich and 6 per cent. in Bath. In that year there were 207 blacksmiths in the city, twice the number in Bath, far more than York's 139.

The railway, which in 1838 the Defiance coach office at the Half Moon denounced as a 'dangerous and uncertain experiment,'[26] reached Exeter in 1844. By the following year advertisements of the Telegraph, Celebrity, Red Rover and their peers had vanished from the local papers and the Nautilus conveyed passengers from Torquay to catch the train at Exeter. From Hatherleigh a new omnibus service brought passengers through the deep lanes linking quiet villages and market towns, Jacobstowe, Sampford Courtenay, Bow and Crediton, in time to catch the 5.0 p.m. train from Exeter to London.[27] Much has been made of the 'Romance of the Road.' Railway travel had advantages of speed, cheapness and comfort, as Surtees, a realist, had occasion to point out.[28] By 1850 John Pratt, a prominent figure in the coaching world, had announced that he had commenced business as a wine merchant;[29] and in the census of 1851 the number of coach and cab owners had been reduced from thirteen to eight.

Exeter, however, continued to live by the transport industry. There were more carriers, carters, waggoners, saddlers and livery stable keepers in 1851 than in 1841; and in 1851 111 males were employed in Exeter as railway engine drivers and stokers, or were otherwise engaged in railway traffic. More than 700 males in Exeter, out of 7,556 recorded as employed in 1851, were connected in one way or another with transport. Proportionally the figure was higher in Exeter than in cities such as Bath, Leicester and Norwich.

Deprived of opportunities for large-scale industrial employment, 12 per cent. of the employed male population of Exeter were, in 1841, employed in the building trade and ancillary occupations, as builders, carpenters, bricklayers, masons, plasterers, painters, plumbers and the like. Ten years later the percentage was the same, slightly higher than in Bath and much higher than in Norwich or Leicester. The relatively high proportion of men employed in the building trade – and the figures exclude labourers – was to have its consequence in unemployment when building activity declined in the 1840s. And building was at all times liable to be affected by bad weather.

Female employment in early Victorian Exeter, and for the greater part of the period, was mainly in domestic service. In 1841 domestic service employed 2,365 women and girls or, with occupations such as laundry keepers, charwomen and washerwomen, over half the female population included in the lists of occupations. For women there was no outlet such as Leicester provided in hose and stocking manufacture and Northampton in boot and shoe making. Dressmaking and millinery were virtually the sole alternatives in Exeter. Seventy-six females in the Exeter of 1841 were employed as schoolmistresses and governesses, or as teachers of drawing, French and music.

From the census reports and the directories the Exeter of this period emerges as a city with the tone set by a small polite society with moderate and undistinguished standards of wealth, comfort and culture. There was sufficient wealth to provide remunerative employment for sixty-four surgeons, physicians and apothecaries as compared with only thirty-six in the larger city of Leicester and only thirteen in Northampton. York had sixty-eight, but Bath 117. Jewellers, silversmiths and goldsmiths in Exeter numbered forty-one. York, with a slightly smaller population had thirty; Norwich, with twice the population of Exeter, had eighteen. Schoolmasters numbered thirty-nine and specialized male teachers twelve, proportionately the same number as in Norwich but fewer than in York. The demand for teachers of music, dancing or languages in Leicester and Northampton was apparently met by only seven teachers in each of these cities. In 1841, Exeter contained more individuals of independent means than did Leicester, Northampton or Norwich but fewer than did Bath or Cheltenham. The economic underpinning of the Devon city was provided by corn mills and paper mills, breweries, tanneries, malt kilns and foundries;[30] an extensive carrying trade; and an equally extensive provision of goods and services throughout a countryside where farmers and landowners at least were prosperous even if the agricultural labourers were not.

Some indication of Exeter's relative popularity as a place for retirement is given by the presence of ten members of the Indian civil service in 1851. Cheltenham, once favoured by Josh Sedley and his colleagues, had twenty-six. Only five were returned for Norwich. There were more hotel and innkeepers of both sexes in the Exeter of 1841 than in Leicester, Cheltenham or even Bath though there were only twenty-one lodging-house keepers compared with the 144 in

Bath and eighty-one in Cheltenham. In a population of 31,305 there were fifty-four surgeons and apothecaries. Northampton, with about the same population, had twenty-siz; Leicester, with a population of 50,000, only thirteen. Bath had 104 for a population of 53,000.

Railway construction stimulated local industry and brought money into the city in the form of wages paid to the constructional gangs. By 1857 Kerslake's Bonhay Foundry had secured the contract for the supply of iron girders for bridge construction between Exeter and Honiton. In 1838 the 'extensive smithy and foundry' workshops and warehouses of the Kingdon brothers were assessed for rates at £184; James Northam's foundry on the Coal Quay, with casting, moulding and smiths' shops, at £92; Bodley's foundry, also on the Coal Quay, at £55.[31] These foundries made an important contribution to the city's economy as the railway age developed. Kerslake's foundry provided the ironwork for the fine new station of St David's completed in 1864. But the number of men returned as engaged in iron manufacture in 1851 was only seventy-eight in contrast to 117 in Norwich and 1,777 in Wolverhampton. And in that year Wolverhampton contained 361 brassfounders to Exeter's thirteen.

The census figures and the records of elections depict the continued decline of Exeter's ancient industry. There were still sixty-five fullers in 1831. By 1851 there were thirteen. The Exeter Valuation of 1838 records in the item 'sundry lengths or racks' valued at £6 10s. These were the debris of the past. In 1851 the woollen and cloth industry employed altogether forty-eight men and seventy-eight women; probably in the mills still remaining in the Cricklepit area and in Messrs Maunders' mill at Exwick. The paper industry in that year employed twenty-five men and thirty-nine women; 114 men and two women worked in the leather and skin industry. The numbers are small, but out of 7,648 employers in the southwest who completed census returns of the number of their employees only fifty-eight employed more than fifty men.[32]

Banking and the professions, hotels and shopkeeping

could provide moderate wealth. Thomas Snow, the banker, left £90,000 in personal estate; John Carew and Mark Kennaway, solicitors, left some £50,000 to £60,000; John Dinham, tea dealer, £40,000; Christopher Arden, mercer, £35,000; Ralph Barnes, solicitor, £16,000; Henry Ellis, jeweller and silversmith, £45,000.[33] Henry Ellis had first set up shop in High Street in 1814 in premises leased at £25 a year and with stock and furniture valued at about £150.[34] John Dinham, who died in 1864, had made a fortune after various vicissitudes. Both men demonstrated the practical advantages of godliness and hard work in Victorian England. Born in 1788, Dinham started work at fourteen as apprentice to a family grocer in the High Street. His early prosperity ended in bankruptcy through no fault of his. He then worked for the London Tea Company before once more setting up on his own. A fortunate speculation at the time of the 'Opium War' of 1839–42 laid the foundations of his subsequent success. When he died he left some £24,000 to various charities.[35] In character, business ability and Christian charity men such as Ellis and Dinham represented a golden strand in the complex character of Victorian England. They were of a type which elsewhere, with wider opportunities than existed in Exeter, provided the great philanthropists of the age. Neither evinced any interest in politics.

Citizens of consequence were moving out of the old city. Henry Ellis, who had lived for many years over his High Street shop, departed to the genteel suburb of St Leonard's in 1850.[36] Sam Kingdon, the ironmonger, lived at Duryard Lodge. Stephen Brunskill, the wealthy tailor, acquired Polsloe Park from Prebendary Dennis in 1848. By 1851 about one-fifth of the population of Exeter was crowded into the three urban parishes of St Edmund, St Mary Major and St Mary Steps. The great majority were artisans, 'more particularly shoemakers and labourers with their families, a very large number in receipt of public relief.'[37] It was not surprising that the average mortality rate of these parishes in the 1840s was 26.9 per thousand compared with 21 per thousand in St David's. Dr Shapter, commenting with approval on the improvements initiated since the cholera epidemic of 1831, formed the conclusion by the 1840s that 'we have every reason to believe that at this present time Exeter is far from being oppressed by a high rate of mortality,' though he added that 'we may fairly assume that Exeter as a city is hostile to infancy.'[38] The mortality in Exeter during the period 1796–1805 was estimated at 25.8 per thousand. In the year 1841 it was 24.5 per thousand.[39] In another cathedral city, under the spire of St Mary of Salisbury, a death-rate of about 26 per thousand coexisted with 'the pride and piety, the peace and beauty of a vanished world.' An objective observer came to the conclusion that the health of Salisbury was far below the average though the local inhabitants did not agree.[40] The mortality in Exeter was little better. In some cities it was much worse. In the cathedral city of Worcester the death-rate was 25.2 per thousand, in industrial Leicester 27.4. Almost half the mortality in Exeter in 1841 was of children under the age of fifteen years. In the poorer districts of the city it was 56 per cent.[41]

Exeter tended to be self-congratulatory over its water supplies, which at this period gave about twelve gallons per head, and resented aspersions on the health of the city. Technical opinion regarded thirteen gallons per head as a normal supply; favoured towns such as Nottingham and Preston enjoyed forty and forty-five gallons per head.[42] Edwin Chadwick, who visited Exeter towards the end of 1846, forcefully pointed out the dangers arising from the existence of cesspools, and a number of influential citizens had occasion to inform the corporation of the poor that they were 'seriously amazed by two extensive open reservoirs of putrifying and offensive soil etc. from the workhouse.'[43] Chadwick's meeting at the Guildhall to discuss the problems of urban health was poorly attended despite the presence of Sir John Duckworth and Viscount Ebrington. Both Divett and Lewis Buck, member for North Devon, took the opportunity during the debate on the Health of Towns Bill in parliament to defend the reputation of the city. Divett described the bill as 'involving provisions of a most unconstitutional and arbitrary character.' Buck declared that 'there was scarcely a town in the kingdom where such large sums were spent in the improvement of the city.'[44] In Exeter itself Kingdon castigated the Health of Towns Bill as rascally. Even the *Western Times* suggested that it failed to do justice to what had been accomplished in Exeter.[45] The death-rate in Exeter for the years 1838–1844 was 25 per 1,000. It fell to 23.8 per 1,000 from 1851 to 1860.[46] But in 1850 Mark Kennaway found it necessary to draw attention to the existence of ninety-two dwelling houses containing 506 inhabitants with no means of obtaining water.[47] Although in 1846 the council addressed a petition to parliament in favour of the bill for the promotion of baths and wash houses, it was not till the seventies that Exeter was effectively roused over the palpable defects of public health and water supplies.

In his contribution to the great report on the *State of Large Towns and Populous Districts* of 1845, Shapter described the old Elizabethan houses in the heart of the city as they were in the 1830s, presenting a general appearance of poverty and dirt with single rooms occupied by eight or ten persons or more where ventilation was discouraged by the structure of the dwellings.[48] Conditions were made worse by the 'deficiency and ill-construction of privies.' Dames' schools existed 'in crowded and bad situations, small, and inhabited by the mistress day and night, with the addition of a fire, winter and summer, for culinary purposes.' Here, amid conditions of 'closeness and unpleasantness' which Shapter found scarcely credible, perhaps some twenty children received what purported to be education.[49] Overcrowding, the presence of middens and offal in courts and streets, the faulty construction of houses, defective water supplies, were accepted as the inconveniences of urban life until cholera and a rising death rate reinforced the arguments of Chadwick.

The impetus which improvement received from the cholera of 1832 had dwindled. Mark Kennaway, opposing the abolition of the improvement commissioners in 1867, emphasized their economy in finance as much as their achievements. There were no pioneers of public health in Exeter. On the contrary, the *Western Times* in 1848 declared that 'the health of Exeter is, we are glad to say, thus far in a very prosperous state, and our sanitary precautions appear to win the confidence of visitors.'[50] No newspaper attempted to make any such claim in the seventies. In the period 1838 to 1844 the death-rate per thousand was higher in Exeter than in towns such as Sunderland, Wolverhampton, Norwich, Plymouth and York.[51] Exeter was one of the 'town districts' with a mortality of 26 per thousand in the list presented by Dr Farr to the select committee on the Public Health Bill and Nuisances Amendment Bill of 1849–50.

The city's health problems were not appreciably made worse by the influx of a rural population. In the Victorian era the Exeter city council never experienced the embarrassment of large-scale urban growth. This was fortunate, since there is no indication that the council could have dealt with the resulting problems more successfully than did the majority of urban authorities. Undoubtedly there was immigration from the countryside but in 1851 nearly one-half of the population had been born within the city limits. In Salisbury, where there were even fewer signs of economic growth, the proportion was rather more than half.

Wages were low and stationary. Full-time labourers employed by the council, men who were described as navvies from 1845, were paid 2s. 4d. a day throughout the period once they were deemed sufficiently experienced. They began on 2s. a day.[52] Thus John Lang appears in the paysheets in 1841 when he was paid 2s. a day for work at Cowley Bridge though his colleague Esau Griffen was paid 2s. 4d. for the same work. In the following year Lang was still paid 2s. a day for work on the canal. Most of his colleagues received 2s. 4d. In 1845 Lang was being paid 2s. 4d. and by that time was described as a navvy. He was still paid 2s. 4d. a day in the 1850s for work such as cleaning the urinals on the quay and for repairs at Head Wear. In 1852 a labourer was still paid at the rate of 2s. 4d. a day for work such as assisting a mason working at the Old Brewery. Not all labourers were paid as much. Men working at Turf in 1836 received 1s. 4d. a day and so did a man 'knocking off old plaster' at the Guildhall in 1853.[53] On the other hand a foreman employed by the council was paid 3*s*. 6*d*. a day throughout the period covered by the City Treasurer's Vouchers, from 1836 to 1856.

The council's carpenters, William Flood and William Bailey, were paid 2*s*. 10*d*. and 2*s*. 8*d*. a day respectively in 1841. By 1846 Flood was receiving 3*s*. a day but this was not the rate for both men until the 1850s. On the other hand, in 1837–38 the council was paying 3*s*. 6*d*. a day for work such as repairing the prison oven, repairing a cart, cutting rails for the canal locks, and pile driving and bracing. This was more than the 3*s*. 4*d*. a day paid to a carpenter repairing seats for the council in 1850 and was the same as the pay of a mason employed on the Old Brewery in 1850. Masons in general were paid 3*s*. a day throughout the period. The remuneration of a mason and his tender usually appeared as 5*s*. 4*d*. made up of 3*s*. and 2*s*. 4*d*. Plumbers seem to have earned more, judging by an item of 7*s*. paid to a plumber and labourer for a day's work fitting pipes and water cocks on Northernhay.[54]

After the reorganization of 1847 police constables were paid 16*s*. a week,[55] corresponding to 2*s*. 8*d*. a day for a six-day week and thus 4*d*. a day more than the pay of the labourers employed on the canal. Domestic servants were a favoured class. In general they could expect regularity of work and perhaps some assistance in time of need. By the year 1842 the average deposit of male servants in the Devon and Exeter Savings Bank was £50 2*s*. 5*d*. compared with the £40 7*s*. 3*d*. of small tradesmen, the £35 8*s*. 5*d* of artificers and mechanics and the £45 8*s*. 2*d*. of schoolmasters and clerks. The average deposit of female domestic servants was £29 13*s*. 5*d*. That of females in trade was £33 14*s*. 10*d*. The average deposit of labourers in trade and manufacture was £27 3*s*. 3*d*.[56] A skilled man like Henry Ellis's assistant, Harvey, after the termination of his apprenticeship in 1837, received 25*s*. a week and was encouraged to marry on the proceeds.[57]

In general the period 1837 to 1850 was one of stable prices. The Exeter guardians had paid an average of £1 16*s*. 9*d*. per cwt. for meat from 1831 to 1836 and £2 4*s*. 6*d*. per sack for flour. From 1837 to 1842 the cost of meat averaged £2 2*s* 2½*d*.

per cwt., and flour £2 8s. 11d. the sack.[58] Thereafter, with the important exception of 1846 to 1847, prices remained stable or tended downwards. In November 1841 beef in the Exeter pannier market was sold at 6d. to 7d. per lb., mutton at 5½d. to 6½d., pork at 5d. to 7d. Judging by the market reports in the newspapers these prices were never exceeded between 1841 and 1850.[59] The working classes at this time rarely ate fresh beef and mutton except perhaps when butchers sold supplies sheap on Saturday nights in the days before refrigeration. Bread and potatoes were the all-important staple items of diet. In 1841 the assistant clerk to the St Thomas Union calculated that over two-thirds of the family budget of an agricultural labourer was spent on bread.[60] In November 1846 the price of potatoes in Exeter rose from the more usual 6d. to 8d. a score to 5s. a score, or 3d. per pound, the highest price within living memory.[61] Thereafter the price declined but it was still 2s. 6d. a score in January 1857 and 1s. 4d. in November of the same year. Wheat, which had been sold at 8s. 2½d. the bushel in January 1837, and 5s. 9¾d. in January 1845 rose to 13s. 3d. the bushel in June 1847. In consequence the retail price of a 280 lb. sack of flour, which had been between 45s. and 48s. in January 1845, rose to 81s. and 82s. for the best quality in June 1847, and the price of 'seconds' rose from 79s. to 80s. The quartern loaf, costing 7½d. to 8d. in 1841, was sold for 10½d. to 11d. for best quality, and for 9½d. to 10½d. for seconds, in 1847.

In 1837 shoes could be made for 4s. a pair; the cost of the cheapest cloth and fur caps ranged from 4d. to 4s.[62] Moleskin trousers, such as were worn by labouring men, were advertised at 2s. 6d. at Mr Solomon's establishment in the High Street in 1845, and the jackets for 6s. 6d. Buckskin and doe-skin trousers, such as were worn by aspirants to fashion, cost 15s.[63] Good London gin was sold at 9s. the gallon, claret at 40s. to 48s. the dozen.[64] Shag tobacco cost 3s. 6d. per lb. in 1837,[65] kitchen chairs advertised at 2s. 9d. each to 3s. in 1837 were being sold for 2s. in 1850. In 1843 Mark Kennaway paid £6 10s. for a wardrobe; a washstand with two drawers cost him 18s. and, in 1848, two dozen iron tablespoons 1s. 2d.[66]

In 1837 a convenient dwelling-house in St Sidwell's 'replete with every requisite accommodation for a small family' could be leased for 20 guineas; better accommodation in Brook Green Villas, with two good sitting rooms, kitchen, four bedrooms, dressing room and large garden and a 'pump of excellent water' for 35 guineas. Both were free of taxes. Smaller houses in St James's Terrace, with two kitchens, bedrooms, attics, cellar and pump went for £21 to £25. In 1848 an adjacent house in St James's Terrace was offered for lease at £18 per annum. The new brick-built houses in Bystock Terrace were leased at £42 and £45; cheaper houses in neighbouring Little Silver at £9.

Even at £9 a year rents were high for white-collar workers earning perhaps £30 – £40 a year. Some of these had several sources of income. Henry Ellis for a time employed an accountant at the relatively high salary of £40 a year for an hour or two every morning before the opening of the bank in which the accountant regularly worked.[67] Food and clothing, however, tended to be cheaper in the 1850s than they had been in the 1830s and the trend was downwards. Beef had fallen from a prevailing price of 6d. to 7d. per lb. to between 4½d. and 6d.; mutton from 5½d.–6½d. to 4½d.–6d. A sack of fine flour, sold at 48s.–50s. in January 1841, fetched only 30s. in January 1850. The price of potatoes was still affected by the shortages of 1846–47. It was 8d. the score in mid-January 1837 and 6d. in January 1845. In 1850 it was 10d. The countryside provided in their season elderberries at 3d. per quart and blackberries at 1½d. Rabbits at this time were sold in the market at 9d. to 1s. each, hares at 2s. 6d. to 3s. 6d. Both must have been an attractive temptation to the poor man who wandered into the fields within a short distance of the Exeter slums. Tea at 3s. per pound and sugar at 8½d. to 10d. remained a luxury.

On the assumption that in 1841 an agricultural labourer with a family required a minimum income of £30 a year, canal labourers at 2s. a day, police constables at 16s. a week, or carpenters who could find sufficient jobs at 3s. per day, were all adequately paid. So, too, was a man paid by the council 2s. 6d. for stripping off old thatch in 1843[68] provided further employment was in sight.

Standards of living were not so much a question of wage rates as of the regularity of employment and immunity from misfortune. Daily work could not be guaranteed. If the artisan or labourer worked for less than an eleven-hour day his remuneration was proportionately reduced. The high proportion of the working population engaged in building work and allied activities was particularly exposed to dis-location of work. At times of bad weather – there was heavy snow in 1843 and the Exe was frozen in 1845 – work ceased. Building construction in Exeter was slowing down by the end of the 1840s and over the period as a whole the city was becoming increasingly concerned with the problems of relief and destitution. The number of families assisted by the Exeter relief society rose from 138 in 1838 to 887 in 1849 and averaged 531 a year.[69] Out-relief granted by the Exeter union rose steeply between 1846 and 1847, from 490 families or 824 persons in February 1846 to 651 families, or 1,133 persons in February 1847.[70] At the meeting held in 1847 to organize relief after the bread-riots, it was estimated that one-third of the entire population of the city required bread at reduced prices. The Famine Fund, founded in 1846 to relieve distress in specially hard winters, was reported to have assisted between 7,000 and 8,000 individuals per week for nearly two months during the winter of 1846 to 1847.[71] Casual relief, distributed in cash by the Exeter guardians, which amounted to only £71 in 1837, jumped to £173 in 1838, the year in which the Exeter Relief Fund was founded, and was £133 in 1842.[72] 'Out relief,' reported the assistant poor law commissioner in 1843,

'is at present given almost entirely in terms of money. Able bodied men applying for relief are sometimes ordered to the workhouse, but more generally are sent to work in a brickfield belonging to the Guardians, where single men are paid 4s. weekly, a man and wife 5s. weekly and, in addition, 1s. per week for each child.'

Expenditure on this form of relief rose sharply from £6,792 for the year ended 25 March 1846 to £13,363 for the year ended 25 March 1848.[73] 'There is a class of persons,' said the poor law commissioners in a circular of 1847, 'who contrive to enjoy the physical comforts of the workhouse without performing the labour, or submitting to the discipline.'[74] But the Exeter workhouse was not remarkable for physical comforts; the master of the workhouse frequently reported that of those ordered to report few or none appeared.

Economic distress in cathedral cities at the time of the Chartists and the 'Hungry Forties' did not achieve the notoriety of conditions in the great manufacturing towns of the midlands and the north. It was smaller in scale but not proportionately less. The social and economic environment of Exeter discouraged organized Chartism even in the Hungry Forties. In April 1848 a Chartist meeting was held in the Subscription Rooms with W. J. P. Wilkinson, the mayor of 1837 to 1838, in the chair. The meeting, which elected Wilkinson as delegate to the Chartist National Convention, experienced considerable interference from hostile spectators. More characteristic was the counter-meeting of six to seven hundred 'of the respectable inhabitants of Exeter' held in the Guildhall under the chairmanship of Dr Shapter. An address to the queen was approved affirming the city's loyalty and readiness to maintain the laws and promote peace. Mark Kennaway, however, secured an amendment to express the 'full conviction that your Majesty will listen to all representations of grievances constitutionally presented.'[75]

In view of the tight social discipline of a small society the bread riots of 1847 are the more significant. Economically Exeter was running down. Deprived of its former industrial strength the city had yet to come to terms with the nineteenth century. There was still money to be made, by bankers, lawyers, doctors and merchants. But there was no indication of future growth. In the 1840s the momentum derived from the late eighteenth-century environment was palpably dwindling. Correspondingly the problems of poverty, unemployment and destitution became more pressing. Opportunity, offering land, wealth and freedom from social control, beckoned from California, 'one vast district of gold for those who choose to go and look for it.'[76]

The balance sheet was not wholly loss. Human happiness eludes definition, especially by utilitarian formulae. It would be too easy to demonstrate that the life of most men in early Victorian Exeter was 'poor, nasty, brutish and short.' Yet the paternal control of small businesses and workshops, though it may have inhibited free voting and the development of trade unionism, also made possible the existence of closer relations between employers and employed. The wayzgoose, or annual outing, of firms and businesses, was celebrated with flags, music and abundant food and drink. The members of the Exeter Teetotal Friendly Society assembled for supper on 'beef and plum pudding in plenty.'[77] Children from the workhouse picnicked with flags, music and good food at the expense of the benevolent R. S. Cornish.[78] The woods and fields, the river and the ancient lanes were within easy reach of the citizens of a small city. On Sundays, citizens walked through the lanes to Heavitree, or along the Cowley Bridge Road to enjoy the home-brewed beer of the inn by the bridge and to return over the hill by Marypole Head or along the river under Exwick. Family parties took the river path for tea at Topsham. There was boating on the river, skittles at the Customs House Inn in Little Quay Lane and the Fountain public house.[79] In St Sidwell's there was wrestling for a prize of forty sovereigns. The Salmon Pool tea and fruit garden was 'a favourite resort for respectable parties.' The band played on summer evenings in Northernhay, improved and planted by the council and public subscription, and the Northernhay keepers donned their livery for the occasion. Lady Paterson's maid, Susan, went to the theatre.[80] For 1s. in the pit or 6d. in the gallery the artisan or clerk enjoyed a full programme comprising a farce, *The Spectre Bridegroom*, a pantomime, *Whittington and his Cat*, and a melodrama, *The Miller's Maid*.[81] If Exeter at this time could not offer the economic opportunities existing in the great industrial towns, and if poverty and destitution were as harsh in degree as they were elsewhere, life in the smaller old-fashioned society of the Devon city was less strange and inhuman, especially to the immigrant from the countryside. Most individuals at that

H

time would have agreed with Dr Johnson that 'human life is everywhere a state in which much is to be endured, and little to be enjoyed.' And so they would have made the more of the opportunities for enjoyment which the city offered.

MID-VICTORIAN EXETER

V

GOVERNMENT AND POLITICS
1850–1870
Exeter in 1850

THOUGH in retrospect it was evident that Exeter stood
still while the outer world was in movement, this was not
readily apparent to the city in 1850. Unemployment and
food riots were not necessarily an indication of dwindling
opportunities for growth. In the brilliant sunshine of 1 May
1844 the locomotive *City of Exeter* had steamed with a special
train of the Bristol and Exeter Railway Company into the new
station erected by the Hoopers in Pennyroyal Fields. New
vistas of prosperity and progress were opening. The efforts of
local journalism to describe the scene still evoke the sense of
wonder and achievement, of optimism and hope, which
filled the hearts of the thousands who flocked to admire the
new accomplishment of Victorian man.

A goods shed had been decorated with the flags of all the
nations and was transformed into a banqueting hall. Here
Henry Hooper, the builder, in his first mayoralty, received
on behalf of the city members of parliament; representatives
of the great landowners; the county families, Acland, Drake,
Drew, Buck and Carew. Brunel stood on a table to receive
the acclamation of his admirers. Buller of Downes hailed
railways as links 'to bind together the common European
family . . . a union which would extend the intercourse of
nations, and promote their trade, and advance peace and
civilization.'[1]

It was remembered with some misgiving that only fourteen
years before the canal had been improved at great expense
in order to invite the commerce of the world to Exeter. That
invitation all too obviously had been declined. There was
general agreement that Exeter's vitality as a city had still to

be renewed; if the canal had failed, the railways would surely come to the rescue. The revolutionary improvement of communications between Exeter and the outside world was immediate. In August Henry Ellis paid 20s. for a first-class fare to Bristol. He left Exeter at 10.30 a.m. and arrived at Bristol at 1.15 p.m. For his last visit to Bristol, Ellis had set out from Exeter in a crowded coach which left on a Friday evening and reached its destination at 6.30 A.M. on the Saturday morning.[2] Exeter's protective isolation was over. By 1850 the city saw the forerunners of the tourist invasions which in the next one hundred years reduced much of the southwest into an appanage of an urban society. In 1850 the first excursion train from Birmingham arrived at Exeter. Twenty-five shillings were charged for a first-class return, 17s. for a second-class and 14s. for a third.[3] Mary Ellis had paid 18s. for a coach fare to Bideford in 1837.[4] Exeter's first organized tourists from the midlands were found to be 'a well-ordered lot.' That same year a 'Temperance Special' was engaged to run from Exeter to Bristol and travellers from Exeter and its neighbourhood were also taken to Plymouth on 'very easy terms.'[5] To meet the demands of the new growth which the railways were expected to foster, the last important domestic buildings in the grand manner, Peamore Terrace and Bystock Terrace, were constructed to form the northern termination of a Queen Street which never fulfilled expectations.

The excursionists from Birmingham found a city which in 1850 appeared for the last time in its ancient role of a provincial capital of the old, rural England. In December 1849 Edward Woolmer had moved the election of Edward Sanders as mayor. 'It behoved the Council,' explained Woolmer, 'to select a gentleman of high standing and position, a gentleman who must possess both property and reputation, a gentleman connected with the city by the strongest ties of family and relationship.' Men such as Henry Hooper would not do when Exeter was host to ambassadors and the landed interest. Sanders, a gentleman by the most exacting social criteria of the time, descendant of Sir Edward Courtenay of Powderham, had already been made eligible for office by election as alderman in the previous October since he was not otherwise a member of the council.[6]

The occasion was the Royal Agricultural Show of 1850, a prosperous and lively year for Exeter. Hotels and boarding houses were full. Country houses in the neighbourhood entertained guests with a hospitality which owed much to the still unbroken prosperity of the agricultural interest and the yet unshaken position of the landowners. The mayor presided at an entertainment which included the choruses from Sophocles' *Antigone* set to music by Mendelssohn. The city's attractions included the much-admired camellias of the nurserymen Luccombe and Prince; these, the newspapers duly recorded, were seen by the Duke of Northumberland and members of the Russell family as well as by numerous visitors of less august status. The newspapers discoursed of stockbreeding, manures and farm implements. West country society thronged the city. The Easter Ball which preceded the opening of quarter sessions was attended by the county, who danced till dawn. The Exeter Oratorio Society performed Handel's *Judas Maccabeus*. Carter's *Grand Colossal Moving Panorama* offered visitors views of the still legendary Mississippi, Missouri and Yellowstone.

On the crowded pavements pedestrians jostled to admire the shop fronts furnished for the occasion with 'rich woods, bright metals and costly plate glass,' the triumphal and floral tributes, the flags and wreaths and 'other devices of great beauty and taste.' At the great banquet organized by the famous Soyer, where the Marquess of Downshire took the chair, Edward Sanders replied with brief felicity to the toast of 'The City of Exeter.' Soyer himself received the guests at a lavish working men's dinner.[7]

Prices were lower than they had been for several years past. That summer the markets were glutted with commodities which could not long be kept on account of the heat. By January the price of wheat had fallen to about 5s. 3d. a bushel from the high price of 9s. 2d. a bushel in January 1847. Meat was back at the level of 1844. Potatoes, sold at 2s. 6d. a score in January 1847, were 10d.[8]

'From whatever side the traveller approaches the city,'

enthused one of the copious Show Supplements,[9] 'he must be struck with the beauty of its situation and the elegance of its public buildings. Nor can he fail to be prepossessed by the general regularity and cheerfulness of its streets, as well as the numberless interesting vestiges of antiquity.'

The city 'famed for its delightful diversity of public walks and picturesque scenery' yet retained 'a large share of general commerce.' The directory of 1850 records the 'several large iron foundries, corn mills, malt kilns, breweries and tanneries; and many coal, corn, wool, timber, wine, spirits, drugs and grocery merchants.'[10] The city had been little affected by the severe financial crisis of 1847. Local share-prices had recovered from the low levels of that year. The gas company was generally paying dividends of 8 per cent. and the water company 10 per cent. though both concerns were liable to severe criticism for their deficiencies. Six to eight trains left St David's station each day. Coaches were still necessary to penetrate the country districts and the Royal Mail still left the Half Moon for Dorchester by way of Honiton and Chard. Samuel Ellis reported to his father that business was 'going on very pleasantly and on the whole briskly.'[11] Business was reviving in Exeter. The 'elegant fabrics' of Messrs Wilcocks and Brock were travelling 'far beyond the limits of the city.'[12]

Supporters of agricultural protection were claiming that the Exeter tradesmen had lost their best customers as a consequence of the repeal of the corn laws. In 1849 the agricultural interest had organized a large county meeting at Exeter. The proceedings were heated and neither Divett, nor even Lord Ebrington, obtained much support for free trade. The poor law board at this time expressed satisfaction

'that the total expenditure throughout Devon was lower than at any time since 1842, with the exception of the year 1846, and that expenditure per head of the population was lower than it had been at any year since 1834 with the exception of the years 1834 and 1837.'[13]

In Exeter the total cost of poor relief was certainly falling from the high level of £13,363 in the bad year 1847–48. The total expenditure in 1849 was £10,736. There was a sharp fall to £8,274 by Ladyday 1851.[14]

Throughout the nineteenth century there was a tendency to regard reduction in expenditure as an indication of the success of poor relief. Economies achieved by discouraging applications for relief except in grievous extremity did not necessarily indicate less distress among the poor. Private charity in Exeter had recognized that there was a wide field for activity outside the restricted operations of the poor law and for that reason the Exeter relief society had been founded in 1838. In 1850 the society assisted 1,131 poor families not otherwise in receipt of parochial assistance. The figure rose steadily each year thereafter till 1855.[15] In the winter of 1849–50 committees for the relief of the poor of St Sidwell's and St James were organized to distribute bread, meat and coals. The plight of the poor at this period was the subject of letters to the press which suggest that the situation in Exeter was by no means as favourable as the figures in the reports of the poor law board, or the descriptions of the Agricultural Show, suggest. 'It is pleasant, beyond all question,' remarked a pertinent editorial in the *Flying Post*, 'to get a 4 lb. loaf for 5*d.*; but how does the matter stand when a man has only four days' employment for a week's sustenance?'[16]

Urban expansion since 1837 had been slow, the most significant development being the northern end of Queen Street after 1844. It was in Queen Street that the post office authorities took possession of their new premises in 1850, this building, like so much else in Exeter, being the work of the Hoopers. Houses were filling in the empty spaces in the roads between St David's Hill and North Street. Sidwell Street had been built up as far as the Old Tiverton Road and along the Blackboy Road to Workhouse Lane, the modern Polsloe Road, where the open country began. In Holloway Street buildings reached as far as Larkbeare, but St Leonard's with its 'pleasant modern houses chiefly occupied by military men'[17] still held aloof. The number of inhabited houses within the municipal boundary actually fell slightly from 1841 to 1851.[18] In that period the population within the municipal area grew by only 4.3 per cent. In the larger area of the parliamentary constituency the increase of population was nearly 9 per cent., from 37,231 to 40,688, but even in St Leonard's and Heavitree the growth of population had substantially slowed down. In contrast, tales of the fabulous gold of California, and of equally fabulous wages across the sea, were appearing in the local press. The treasurer of the Exeter relief society informed the annual meeting of 1850 that Exeter was suffering more than other places from the extent of poverty because in Exeter little or nothing was done to assist emigration. And so, 'the poor remained undiminished, or rather increased.' It was admitted that the city contained 'too many beings in very great distress.'[19]

The sunshine on the Agricultural Show of 1850 was the after-glow of an old, essentially rural, social system. Exeter was entering upon a period of decline similar to that of the contemporary market towns who saw their populations dwindle, their inns half used, the decorous Georgian residences of doctor and attorney watching quiet streets roused to life only from time to time by a market or an election. For the moment the old governing society, like the city itself, was enjoying the late summer. The election of Edward Sanders, not a member of the council, as mayor, was in itself a reflection of social change within the council itself. Sanders was followed by William Wills Hooper, the first mayor since 1835 to have two years of office, and brother of Henry Hooper, himself to be re-elected in 1857.

The impression of an older England making its last bow in the summer of 1850 is heightened by the religious census of the following year, which revealed that 'a sadly formidable portion of the English people [were] habitual neglectors of the public ordinances of religion.'[20] Even allowing for those who, for various reasons, could not go to church at all on the census Sunday, it was concluded that close on 5,300,000 who might have attended church did not in fact do so. In particular the masses in the great industrial towns seemed 'by natural inclination averse to the entertainment of religious sentiments, and fortified in this repugnance by the habits and associations of their daily life.'[21] The index of church attendance in the small towns and rural areas, where religious observance was encouraged by social pressures as well as by 'natural inclination,' was 71.4. Among the larger towns, as they were classified in 1851, only three in all England could show a higher figure. These three were Colchester (89.5), Exeter (84.5) and Bath (79.1).[22] In Exeter at this time 11,963 out of a total population of 32,823, or about 30 per cent., were members of the Church of England. Nonconformists numbered 6,229, or about 19 per cent.[23] These figures can be no more than approximations. In accordance with the advice of the compilers of the census they are based on two-thirds of the persions returned as having attended religious services on the census Sunday of 30 March 1851. The figures showing the relative strength of Anglicans and Nonconformists in Exeter at this time do not conflict with such other evidence as exists throughout the period.

The determining factor in England's domestic history during the Victorian period is the inter-relation of the ancient order, based on land, and the new forces, social, economic and political, represented by the great industrial towns. In the towns were the great areas of paganism which horrified Victorian investigators, as well as the smaller pockets of sophistication which encouraged indifference or unbelief. In rural England, social habits and traditions accepted and enforced the place of religion in daily life. Religious observance was not due merely to the authority of squire or rector, or to the invocation of religion in support of the social order. The Nonconformist minister, the Bible Christian wrestling for souls in a remote Devon hamlet, were equally insistent on the importance of religious practice and belief. The religious revival of the nineteenth century could most easily take effect when fortified by 'the habits and associations' of the close-knit rural and small-town society where personal influence and example were less likely to be helpless in the face of numbers. Exeter's high index of church attendance in 1851 demonstrated the city's relationship with rural England. No attempt was made again to repeat the religious census of 1851; had it been repeated it would almost certainly have demonstrated the same pattern of religious observance in Exeter, and for the same reasons.

For the time being Nonconformity was beginning to revive after a period of decline.[24] Methodism was still distracted by the controversy which led to the formation of the Methodist Free Churches. In 1841 an Exeter Baptist minister had occasion to deplore the 'present depressed condition of the church.'[25] The Unitarian community was dwindling. By 1857 there were only fifty-nine contributors to the minister's fund of George's Meeting.[26] The Unitarians, however, exercised an influence in local life out of all proportion to their numbers. As late as 1865 the *Flying Post* complained, in exaggerated terms, of 'Soccinian councillors and atheistic aldermen perhaps elected by lot in the vestry of St George's chapel.'[27]

In an age when, in Horace Mann's words, men thought of themselves as 'swift and momentary travellers towards a never-ending destiny,'[28] conviction as well as prejudice contributed to the passion of controversy. Exeter shared to the full the revival of inter-denominational ill-feeling which was then a feature of contemporary England and had been encouraged by Lord John Russell's impulsive letter to the Bishop of Durham in 1850. The growth of Tractarianism, the Gorham controversy, and the Pope's restoration of the Catholic hierarchy in England, stirred up Exeter's most impressive demonstrations of militant Protestantism. Meetings were held in defence of the 'pure Reformed Evangelical Protestant Church.' Tractarians were denounced as a 'treacherous and nefarious sect.'[29] Church rates were an irritating reminder of the special status of the Church of England and a few staunch individuals had their goods distrained for refusal to pay. Insistence on the implications of the priestly office was denounced by Mark Kennaway on the grounds that 'the church was the laity employing certain officers as her ministers.'[30]

In 1849 Sidney Herbert, apparently busy on *The Better Application of Cathedral Institutions*, had written to Ralph Barnes that the dean's reports showed that the canonries of Exeter were 'filled by excellent men' and that this assisted Herbert himself to 'take a better stand in defence of cathedral bodies.' He suggested, however, that the chapter might move more with the spirit of the times. The good works of the chapter, as described by the dean, 'were performed by these gentlemen, not as members of the Chapter in the execution of their duties, but rather as acts of voluntary benevolence.'[31]

There was undoubted truth in the comment of the *Western Times* that the cathedral formed one of 'the most compact estates of Toryism.'[32] But by 1850 cathedral and parish clergy were conscientious priests. The Rev. Francis Courtenay, once mobbed for wearing a surplice in the pulpit, in that year received a presentation to mark the 'gratitude and esteem' of St Sidwell's.[33] The local clergy were active in good works. If they rallied to the cry that the church was in danger and, for the most part, voted Conservative, they did so in a context in which an earnest search for religious truth was still regarded by many as of supreme national importance, a search which was also entangled in controversies over the special status and privileges of a church by law established. That the Anglican Church in Exeter was an auxiliary of the Conservative party was demonstrated repeatedly by the public speeches of local clergy and by the voting lists; and so, in a cathedral city, membership of the party of church and state conferred social respectability on some whose claims to be respectable might otherwise be regarded as dubious.

Nevertheless, in the Exeter of the mid-nineteenth century, membership of church and chapel included thousands of men and women of all classes of whose sincerity there could be no question and who still, in their various ways, regarded the Christian ethic as the principle of daily life. The exceptionally high figures for church attendance revealed by the census of 1851 were not in themselves typically Victorian if they are compared with the larger towns more in the forefront of the national life. Exeter could take legitimate pride in the figures of the religious census; but not in those of the educational census of the same year. The proportion of scholars to population was 15.3 for Sunday Schools, one of the highest in the country. The proportion of day scholars was only 6.77, lower than, for instance, in York, Birmingham, Leicester and Newcastle upon Tyne; even lower than 8.57 in the grey town of Sunderland. And while 277 adults attended evening classes in contemporary Norwich, and 1,254 in Huddersfield, there were none in Exeter.[34]

Secular education for the masses was evidently not a feature of the Exeter of 1850. The successful Royal Agricultural Show of that year was a rally of an older England. The city appeared as Defoe had described it two hundred years before 'full of gentry and good company.'[35] On the council, lawyers, newspaper proprietors, doctors and surgeons represented the traditional governing circles of the city. Old Tories such as Ralph Barnes, who had once denounced the Municipal Corporations Act as 'contrary to the law and constitution of England.'[36] must have felt reassured as they listened to Edward Sanders the banker welcoming ambassadors and noblemen on behalf of the city. But Defoe's Exeter, humanized by later culture and inspired by landed gentry and aristocracy for the most part conscientious in the fulfilment of their public responsibilities, was a survival rather than an active element in Victorian urban history.

Practical Politics 1850-70

'Spirited contest, my dear sir,'
'I am delighted to hear it,' said Mr Pickwick,' . . .
'Oh yes . . . we have opened all the public-houses
in the place, and left our adversary nothing
but the beer shops.'

'Municipal elections with but very few exceptions have ceased to possess that interest which formerly attached to them,' commented the *Flying Post* in 1857. The paper added tendentiously: 'for the very good and sufficient reason that the administration of public affairs in the city has long been in the hands of a body of gentlemen who have the entire confidence of a large majority of the burgesses.'[37]

The burgesses had little opportunity to express an opinion. Between 1850 and 1870 there were only forty-six contested elections out of the 132 possible in the six wards of the city. From 1853 to 1856, only one ward was contested in four successive years.[38] Even the *Western Times*, which missed few opportunities to encourage active citizenship, found it necessary to apologize for the prominence of the annual ploughing matches over local politics.[39] In some years all the Exeter newspapers relegated reports of the council elections to an obscure paragraph. Religious issues provided an alternative outlet for energy and full scope for emotion. Bishop Phillpotts had refused to institute the Rev. Cornelius Gorham to the quiet parish of Brampford Speke, five miles from Exeter, on the gounds that Gorham held doctrines 'contrary to the true Christian faith' and to the doctrines of the Church of England.[40] The ensuing controversy threatened to split the fabric of the Church of England. The judicial committee of the privy council eventually decided in 1850 against the bishop, and the *Flying Post* expressed the hope that the day would never arrive when the Christian world would be subjected to the rule of such men as the Bishop of Exeter. The judgement was politically necessary though Gladstone thought it a catastrophe. Manning and others went over to Rome.

Exeter at this time shared to the full the revival of seventeenth-century Protestant zeal. The re-establishment of the Roman hierarchy by Pius IX evoked demonstrations of Protestant zeal reminiscent of the tumultuous days of the Popish Plot. The fifth of November celebrations of 1850 were enlivened by guys in the form of the twelve Roman Catholic bishops of England, Puseyite clergymen and former members of the church. To point the moral the procession was 'flanked by officers of the Inquisition with instruments of torture for heretics.'[41] An overwrought young lady deposed to the mayor that she had been lured into an uninhabited house 'by an elderly gentleman in black having the appearance of a clergyman.' There, in circumstances strongly suggesting the romances of Mrs Radcliffe, she was alleged to have been forced 'to recant the doctrines of the Church of England.'[42] In September 1850 the mayor and recorder attended the cathedral in state to hear Dean Lowe preach on 'the superstitions and corruptions of Rome.'[43] A memorial was addressed to the queen on auricular confession.

Activities of this kind were anachronistic but exciting.

They provided an outlet while politics were left in safe hands. Through national politics Exeter was drawn into the network of territorial influence and family relationships which controlled the political scene in Devon in the age of Palmerston. City and county interlocked through social, economic and political affairs. George Stuckley Buck, unsuccessful Conservative candidate at Exeter in 1852, was the son of the Buck of Hartland who had represented the city in pre-Reform days. His brother-in-law was S. T. Kekewich, of Peamore, where on occasion Exeter's affairs could be discussed with Exeter Conservatives of the appropriate standing such as banker Ralph Sanders and attorney John Carew.[44] At Pynes, three miles from the city, Sir Stafford Northcote, urbane, scholarly and conscientious, kept a close watch on the political scene and found time to address meetings on social and literary subjects as well as on politics. The Courtenays played the political game from Powderham. Sir John Duckworth lived at Topsham, conveniently close to the stronghold of landed wealth and old Toryism at Bicton. Serious Exeter Liberals like J. D. Osborn and Dr Miller supported Palmerston on the hustings at Tiverton in company with the sporting parson Jack Russell.[45]

Political management, tactics and intelligence were in the hands of a group of political attorneys. 'Roaring Dick' Brembridge manipulated the strings of power in Barnstaple,[46] his exposure for blatant corruption in 1852 in no way affecting his standing with the Barnstaple electorate or interfering with his subsequent re-election as mayor. Brembridge, with Riccard and Sons of South Molton, and John Daw of Exeter were members of a team of shrewd experts working together to ensure that the social conventions of politics were observed, testing the ground, advising their principals on the intricacies of legislation against corruption and keeping a jealous eye on costs. Thus Riccard and Son reported to John Daw of Exeter in 1857 on the difficulties experienced in canvassing the Rolle tenants at Chittlehampton:

'The canvassers were kindly received, and there seemed to be a great inclination among the voters to favour Sir

Stafford's return, but they had received no communication from headquarters and could not act without it.'[47] Northcote was urged to stand well personally with Castle Hill and Bicton. John Daw replied to Riccard and Sons from the committee rooms in Bedford Circus, that they should immediately canvass the Rolle and Trefusis tenantry, for there was 'every reason to believe that your canvass will not now be unsuccessful.'[48] Exeter's Charles Wescomb, now climbing to ephemeral wealth and power, reported to John Daw that 'Mr Chichester of Hall went with me to tender the votes of his tenantry for Mr Trefusis provided the Rolle tenants would vote for Sir Stafford.'[49]

Through John Daw the political strings of half Devon were joined at Exeter. Twice mayor of Exeter, recorder of Bradninch, 'attorney of the hostile canal creditors.'[50] as the Western Times put it, presented in 1846 with a silver salver for his services to the Conservative interests in the city, John Daw was a punctilious and discreet political manager. Even the Western Times described him as a liberal Tory with 'not inconsiderable' merits.[51] The circumstances of Exeter's politics did not necessitate the more blatant forms of corruption which earned notoriety for contemporary Barnstaple and Totnes. Certain rules of prudence were observed. In 1854 Henry Hooper, who knew much of the realities of political management, deemed it advisable to direct the Conservative candidate's special attention to the provisions of the Corrupt Practices Act of that year.[52] In 1857 'Roaring Dick' Brembridge's firm, in Barnstaple, was even more appropriately consulted.

Elections, however, were not likely to have been pure by any strict interpretation of purity. In 1868, the Conservative candidates Karslake and Mills spent £2,544 between them and the Liberals, Coleridge and Bowring, £2,057.[53] The four candidates together spent £385 on clerks, messengers and boardmen, the Conservatives employing 303 messengers at 5s. a day, or more than the ordinary artisan's daily wage, and seventy-nine boardmen at 3s. 6d. each. Even the loan of a table cost 10s. The hire of rooms and furniture cost the Conservatives £291 and the Liberals £221. Printing,

I

stationery and advertisements cost the Conservatives £800 and the Liberals £221. The Conservatives spent £713 on agents and advocates, the Liberals £246.

These expenses may well have been understated and were often found to be so when exposed to the scrutiny that followed an election petition. They do not include lavish expenditure on food and drink. Exeter elections remained rough, disorderly and drunken. The quay porters, voteless but tough, were in demand as party demonstrators. In 1852 the uproar in the Guildhall was such that Divett's proposer found it impossible to proceed with his speech. When Divett's seconder denounced the 'drunkenness and debauchery' of the scene the voice of old Exeter replied from the throng, 'we have a right to drink.' Yellowing testimonials to the vigorous democracy of the free and independent of those days are the printed notices in the city archives: 'If the Sheriff cannot have silence he must adjourn the Court.'

According to the parliamentary returns there were 2,501 individual electors, including 2,215 £10-householders, on the registers for 1851–52.[55] In 1865–66 the electorate numbered about ,3088. The electorate was doubled by the Reform Bill of 1867, the registered electorate increasing from 3,751 in 1867 to 6,156.[56] Owing to the inclusion of double-entries the parliamentary returns were usually inflated. According to the local reports of elections of 1864 and 1868,[57] which claimed to record all who voted or were entitled to vote at the time, the electorate numbered 2,486 in 1864 and 4,917 in 1868. Even with the exclusion of those registered in respect of two or more properties the electorate was doubled.

Sir Stafford Northcote, whose views are entitled to respect, sought to refute the Liberal claim that the representation of the working class in England as a whole had declined from about 30.1 per cent. in to 1832 26 per cent. in 1867. He informed the house of commons that he was satisfied that the number of working men on the register at Exeter was 660 and that there were also 137 others who, he explained, were 'working men to all intents and purposes, constituting some 32 per cent. of the electorate.[58] The parliamentary returns give 361 £10 occupiers, 113 freemen and thirty-eight ancient right voters, a total of 512, as the 'number of electors who come within the description of Mechanics, Artisans, and other Persons supporting themselves by daily manual labour' in 1855-66.[59]

The term 'working class' is too vague for use as a precise description – John Bright, for example, would have excluded beersellers and cart-owners, as well as tradesmen with assistants. Labourers described as such on the voting lists had numbered fourteen at the time of the parliamentary election of 1831. There were thirty-two, including seven freemen, in 1835. The local report of the election of 1864 records four labourers among those who voted or were entitled to vote. At the time of the election of 1868 the number had risen to about 200. An examination of the local records of elections suggests that Northcote may well have been correct if the working-class vote is taken as including artisans (porters, gardeners, masons, carpenters, plasterers and the like) and small shopkeepers who may or may not have employed assistants.[60] An exact answer to the problem depends on a knowledge of the circumstances of each individual voter. Acceptance of the descriptions recorded by the poll clerks in the voting lists can cover a wide range of economic and social differences.

What at least is certain is that the respectability of Exeter was predominantly Conservative. In the election of 1864 thirty-three lawyers voted for the Conservative Lord Courtenay and five for the Liberal Coleridge. Doctors and surgeons provided twenty-five votes for Courtenay and five for Coleridge.[61] This is a voting pattern which remains the same from 1831 till the last election conducted by open voting was held in 1868. The Anglican clergy were overwhelmingly Conservative, as in 1852 when, according to an analysis of the voting published in the *Gazette*, out of thirty-four Anglican clergy who voted only two voted Liberal.[62] These two were denounced as 'standing in the same ranks as Socinians, Chartists, Jews and Baptists.' None of the Nonconformist clergy voted Conservative. The liquor trade was predominantly Conservative and was overwhelmingly so by the 1870s when the licensing policy of

Gladstone's government became a political issue. The Reformer Joseph Sayell was a maltster who had controlled six public houses[63] and his colleague, the Nonconformist mayor Wilkinson, was a wine and spirit merchant, but the leaders of 'the trade' and the owners of the largest inns and hotels were all Conservative.

The deferential vote of Exeter was likewise Conservative. Only one waiter voted for Coleridge while seven voted for Lord Courtenay in the election of 1864. The latter also received the votes of six servants, a butler and a cook. The Liberal vote came from the middle ranks of the electorate. The bakers, boot and shoe makers, carpenters, smiths, brushmakers, tailors, hairdressers, grocers and druggists were predominantly Liberal. The margins were small but so were the majorities by which elections were decided. The commercial travellers voted Liberal by twenty-three to three.[64]

If the respectability of the city was Tory, not all Tories were respectable. Conservative society itself was divided, not only into various circles, of which the cathedral clergy and the bankers were the most select, but also, broadly, by the division between the older governing element in contact with the county and clerical society and the trade and business element represented by the Hoopers and the licensed victuallers who dominated the local Conservative machine by the end of the 1860s. William Wills Hooper, Henry Hooper's brother, had been elected mayor for the second time in 1846. In 1857, Henry Hooper was himself re-elected for his second mayoralty, a year in which the *Western Times* claimed that the office of councillor had 'declined in public estimation on account of the expense involved by the methods required to obtain votes.'[65]

Henry Wilcocks Hooper, the son of 'Old Harry' and councillor for his father's stronghold of St Sidwell's, resigned in 1854 to be elected coroner,[66] a post which he held till his death in 1903. In 1857, on the death of the treasurer Ellicombe, John Laidman, who had been active in Conservative politics for some five years past, resigned as councillor for St Paul's, paid the required £50 fine and was duly elected as the new treasurer.[67] The Liberals fumed over another 'Tory job' and made an unsuccessful attempt to reduce the treasurer's salary.

The social cleavage between old Toryism and new Conservatism in the city at the time of Henry Hooper's second mayoralty was brought to a crisis by differences over the Conservative representation of the city.

In 1847 Sir John Duckworth, first elected in 1845 on the death of Sir William Follett, had been returned unopposed with Edward Divett. The following general election, that of 1852, was as confused as the attitude of the Conservative leader, Lord Derby, on the issue of protection. The Exeter Conservatives determined to capture both seats. Protection in Exeter was neither dead nor completely damned though it had shifted ground. Stafford Northcote, momentarily considering the possibility that he might stand for Exeter,[68] sought to escape from the dilemma imposed by practical politics and by the strength of at least an influential section of the electorate. Stating himself to be on general grounds a supporter of Lord Derby's government he reserved judgement 'upon one question with respect to which the course which his lordship may take is still doubtful.' Northcote expressed his 'strong individual opinion that the long agitated question of Agricultural Protection [was] upon the eve of final settlement.' It was his 'full expectation that Lord Derby would perceive that the reimposition of a tax on corn was no longer possible.' If any 'protecting imposts' were revived, Northcote would find it impossible to support them.

In the event the Conservative candidates were Duckworth and Buck of Hartland. Buck's staunchly protectionist past caused some difficulty but he agreed to come forward in 'favour of relieving Native Industry from the pressure it now has to bear while it is exposed to the unrestricted opposition and untaxed labour of the foreigner.'[69] It was the line of the newly organized Devon and Exeter Association for the Protection of Native Industry which in itself was little more than a regrouping of the old protectionist interest.

The *Western Times*, urging the tenant farmers of Devon to get their rents adjusted and to accept free trade as an accomplished fact, called Liberals to arms against 'a reckless and unprincipled coalition of sham free traders.'[70] As in 1841, the issues were presented in the form of a contest between the large and small loaf. The speeches of both sides on the nomination day were drowned by 'a continuous roar of discordant sounds, whistling, catcalls, braying, cock-crowing.'[71]

Even Dr Carwithen, who had voted for Lord John Russell thirty years before, in 1852 voted for Duckworth and Buck.[72] Nevertheless, though Duckworth came head of the poll with 1,191 votes, Divett was second with 1,111. As Stafford Northcote was informed by one of his Exeter advisers, the solicitor Winslow Jones of Winslade, the election 'proved the impossibility of unseating Divett.'[73] Winslow Jones admitted that Duckworth was unpopular – he does not appear to have had the open purse required for popularity – and that the election had not improved his position, but all respectable Conservatives were reported to have the strongest feeling that his seat should not be endangered and that the party should not be exposed to the embarrassment and divisions which would ensue if a candidate of the standing of Northcote himself came forward.

Conservatives who were powerful, but perhaps less respectable, thought otherwise. In 1857 the citizens of Exeter were urged to 'refuse to be for ever dictated to in the choice of their representatives by a few proud Gentry.' To demonstrate their independence they should elect one of themselves 'a man of business habits, sound judgement and independent of all parties.'[74] This man was Richard Somers Gard. Son of a woollen manufacturer of North Tawton, once clerk in the City Bank of Exeter, Gard had gone into business in London and had made his fortune by acquiring a number of original shares in the famous Devon Great Consols copper mine. By 1852 he was the owner of a property near Honiton and of Rougemont House, Exeter.[75]

The *Western Times* reported that 'Mr Gard's advent has been considered a grave intrusion by the "nobs" of the Great Conservative Party, who treat it as a rebellion of the "snobs." ' The respectable members of the party, 'Squires,

Bankers and Doctors' held aloof.[76] All this was true. A meeting of Sir John Duckworth's supporters included the social elite of Exeter's Conservative party: Edward and Ralph Sanders, the bankers; the cathedral chancellor, Dr Martin; John Carew, John Follett, Sir William's nephew, Edward Woolmer and R. J. Trewman. Dr Shapter took the chair. Ralph Barnes, cathedral registrar and bishop's secretary, had been one of those instrumental in calling the meeting. The chairman of Gard's committee was Henry Hooper, the mayor.

Duckworth made a dignified withdrawal to avoid splitting the Conservative vote. Henry Hooper therefore had the satisfaction of nominating a candidate who was born in Exeter, who had lived within the walls of the city and having made his fortune had returned to dispense 'the money which he had obtained in benefiting his fellow citizens.'[77] Gard announced that he had observed 'the general feeling that the municipal constituencies should be represented by men whose walk had been with the mercantile interests of the country.' He regarded income tax as 'un-English.' He observed with apprehension the tendency to centralize administration in London, this being 'subversive of that unfettered action and local self-government of the municipalities to whom he attributed the greatness of the kingdom.'[78] In the words of a Conservative, Gard represented the city of Exeter but not the city's Conservative party. Gard and Divett were elected unopposed and Gard remained an undistinguished member of parliament until 1868 without having to contest an election.

Gard's adoption and election was the work of the lower social strata of the Conservative party which ruled the city under Henry Hooper. In the same year the mayor himself came under strong suspicion of having once used his position as one of the improvement commissioners to secure the expenditure of £4,000 on the improvement of access to a non-parochial area known as No Man's Land, in the neighbourhood of Fair Park, where the Hoopers held much property. The expenditure was defended on the grounds that No Man's Land was part of the municipal area; but in 1857, when receiving, as mayor, an inquiry from the poor law Board about the status of the land, Hooper purported to reply, in his capacity of overseer for St Leonard's, that the land was not within the city and so was not liable for municipal rates.[79]

The mayor's highly equivocal action was resented by both parties. Angry public meetings were held. There were sharp exchanges between the mayor and his brother magistrates in the course of which Hooper was called a liar. The mayor was charged with improving his own property at the public expense and then evading rates.

When Hooper left office in November 1857, he contrived to secure the election of his supporter, Captain Frederick Tanner, late of the Indian navy, as his successor. The proceedings were unusually stormy. Hooper's appearance in the Guildhall aroused an uproar of cheers, hisses and groans. Pandemonium followed the nomination of Captain Tanner, who was elected after two attempts to elect an alternative candidate. The meeting terminated amid 'a tornado of hisses, groans, and yells, mingled with cheers.'[80] Henry Hooper achieved the distinction of being the only mayor who was never thanked, even perfunctorily, for his services to the city. His tenure of office and the appointment of his successor were both condemned with significant unanimity by the Conservative press. 'Mr Hooper,' declared the *Gazette*, 'will retire from the chair without enabling us to say a single word in favour of the mode in which he has performed the duties of his office.' As to Captain Tanner, 'the managers of the previous mayor's nest have done more to set the citizens by the ears than any event since the extinction of the old corporation.'[81] The *Flying Post* suggested that if with the possession of power the Conservatives would not take its responsibility 'they had better at once hand over the city to the Radicals.'[82]

Hooper died in 1868. As late as 1865 there were indications that he retained his influence. Under him the politicians of the future were learning their trade. Captain Tanner's nomination had been seconded by Joseph Harding, leader of the licensed trade in the seventies. Hooper himself had launched from his base in St Sidwell's the career of his disciple Charles Wescomb, a more flamboyant adventurer with wider ambitions and lacking Hooper's base of assured wealth.

Charles Wescomb was the son of a poor widow and became a schoolmaster at Budleigh Salterton. Later he made himself useful by assisting a tollkeeper with his accounts. He then became a sharebroker in Exeter where he made money, kept a good table and acquired popularity. On the death of Edward Woolmer, in 1857, he bought the *Gazette*. Wescomb always appeared to have ample funds. He acquired interests in west country mines, bought real property and was said to have had a hand in the development of Budleigh Salterton.[83]

By 1866 Wescomb had become associated with politicians of influence and integrity such as Sir Stafford Northcote and the Adullamite Robert Lowe. He bought newspapers at Deal, Edinburgh and Maidstone and was involved with the *Globe* newspaper when it was acquired in the Conservative interest. His sudden death in London from apoplexy in May 1869, after a stormy meeting of the shareholders of the Frank Mills Mine, near Christow, was a day of mourning in Exeter. Many shops were closed. The cathedral organ played the Dead March from *Saul*. It was then revealed that his financial affairs were considerably embarrassed, that he had ruined many who had trusted him. There were grounds for the assertion that 'the public life of the poor misguided man was a painful sham, and his splendid fortune a hollow bubble.'[84]

But 'Charley' Wescomb was not all charlatan. It was recognized that he had been indefatigable in the discharge of his public duties. His ability and practical common sense made him generally respected in the council. He gave Sir Stafford Northcote sound advice on local politics. His vision ranged beyond Exeter to propose 'a fusion of the moderate Whigs with the Conservatives' in 1866.[85] He was active in forwarding the project for the Royal Albert Memorial in Queen Street and was an energetic honorary secretary of the Exeter School of Art. A man who was said to work hard by day, and to be convivial when the day's work ended, noted for his genial hospitality and for 'putting a friend up to a good thing or two occasionally,'[86] Wescomb's misfortune was that he overreached himself financially. He might have lived to old age as an honoured and affluent member of society in Edwardian England.

Henry Hooper and Charles Wescomb were both party managers of a new type, necessary to get out the vote in the larger electorates, useful to politicians, but never quite accepted socially. In the age of Hooper and Wescomb the leaders of the older generation were unfitted by reason of their background, and perhaps by their principles, for the spadework of politics. The pressure of a new element in the Conservative party, old age, and finally death, were removing the older generation from the scene. Edward Woolmer, proprietor of the *Gazette*, died in 1857, Robert Trewman of the *Flying Post* in 1861. Of both men it could be said, as it was said of Trewman, that their social position qualified them to take a leading part in the affairs of their native city. Both for some years before death had ceased to take an active part in the affairs of their papers, which, however, continued to reconcile with their party allegiance a spirit of independence and forthright criticism. Both newspapers had long been surpassed in circulation by the *Western Times* under the more dynamic management of Thomas Latimer, 'The Cobbett of the West,' Liberal and sometimes Radical, but equally individualistic and independent. All three shared a common tradition, that it was their duty to deal even-handed justice without fear or favour. Their successors were lesser men and their newspapers bound too closely to the fortunes of political parties.

'Iron Sam' Kingdon died in 1857. In 1865 the death of John Gidley, 'the learned and venerable clerk to the municipal body of the city,'[87] broke another link with the pre-Reform era and the traditions and manners of the eighteenth century. Town clerk of Exeter, judge of the provost's court, clerk to the land and assessed tax commissioners, recorder for the borough of Bradninch and member of an ancient Devon family, Gidley had been firm, tactful and hard-working, a conscientious pilot for the new council and its often strong-willed members. His tastes were described, a trifle sententiously, as 'eminently archaeological and his learning of that patristic, half-ecclesiastical, philological cast which befits such pursuits.' He was indeed a representative of the well-educated, scholarly, professional men who formed the backbone of innumerable learned societies in the age that was passing. Originally said to be a man of Liberal principles, John Gidley had become a Conservative but he retained the respect of both political parties, guided the council through innumerable lawsuits, found time to maintain an extensive practice and, as a staunch Anglican, was reputed to have written powerful anonymous letters to the press in support of the bishop during the surplice controversy. William Kennaway, Henry Hooper and John Carew all died in 1868. A new generation assumed the manipulation of power as the reign of the licensed victuallers began.

Change in personalities and social emphasis did not affect the political complexion of the council, which remained firmly Conservative. Exeter experienced the more unedifying manifestations of local politics; or perhaps the methods employed to achieve and maintain power were least concealed at this time. Charges of swilling and guzzling, of the open-handed political entertainment known as quilling, were freely made and rarely, if ever, denied. The Conservatives made no secret of their determination to maintain good party men in power. As a protest the Liberals refused to take part in the election of aldermen, who duly included two Hoopers, in 1859. In 1865 the attorney William Dennis Moore who, as mayor, had handled with vigour the food riots of 1854, resigned as alderman in order to be appointed town clerk.[88] In the following year the Conservative confectioner Cuthbertson, though returned at the head of the poll for St Mary Major's, found it necessary to deplore for the sake of both parties the 'gross, open and deliberate bribery' which, he claimed, had been employed on that occasion.[89] In 1867 it was alleged that £5 a head had been paid for votes in St Sidwell's, where Charles Wescomb was entrenched in succession to Henry Hooper.[90]

The Conservatives made a gesture in 1867 by arranging the election of the Liberal Wesleyan wine merchant, John Trehane, an 'anti-state church man,' as mayor. It was observed at the time that the office was usually given to some professional man; but on this occasion the election had been made 'with a view that the honourable offices of the municipality should be divided among the respective partisans.'[91] Gestures of this kind involved no surrender of power. Both the town clerk and the treasurer had been active partisans. Despite the gesture of 1867 the Liberals took no part in the election of Alderman King as mayor, in 1869, an acrimonious proceeding which was watched by Mark Lemon the editor of *Punch*.

The annual November elections had become contests involving power and prestige rather than programmes since the council had settled down to little more than a quiet maintenance of existing conditions. Expenditure was at a minimum. The police were the largest single item. Their efficiency and conditions of service were steadily improved under a superintendent who enjoyed the confidence of the watch committee. Discipline was still hard to enforce. Drunkenness persisted though there were also other offences, as in 1851, when a constable was dismissed for 'carrying on an improper intimacy with a female and neglecting his duty by so doing.' An inspector was also dismissed 'for visiting a female of bad character at her house and at times when on duty.'[92] With more efficient control hard work was less easy to avoid than it had been in the old days, with the consequence that at two o'clock on a December morning Constable George Cornett 'came into the station house and took off his great coat saying that he had enough of police duty.'[93]

There was still a large turnover in the force. In 1866 the superintendent complained that men joined the police 'for the mere purpose of obtaining a testimonial of good conduct as a means of obtaining employment elsewhere.'[94] An attempt was made to carry out the superintendent's recommendation of 1850 that 'in all future appointments the men should be possessed of some education and intelligence as well as strength and character.'[95] Seven years later a newly-promoted inspector had to be instructed to take pains to improve his handwriting. New technical methods were being adopted, as in 1851, when the electric telegraph was used to secure the arrest of a thief in Plymouth. In 1853, plain-clothes detectives were being used though they were not officially recognized till 1867.

Police pay was no longer allowed to fall into arrears. In the harsh Crimean winter of 1854, however, the police petitioned for an increase; a temporary increase of 2s. a week was approved 'in consequence of the higher price of provisions.'[96] To improve prospects, and to keep good men in the force, grades for constables were introduced. By the end of 1867 constables were receiving 18s. a week on appointment, 19s. a week after twelve months' service and thereafter promotion to 20s. a week at the discretion of the watch committee.[97] In normal times the force, which had been increased to a strength of thirty-three by 1863, was adequate. 'Exeter,' reported the superintendent in 1862, 'is neither a manufacturing town nor a seaport town. The population is quiet and orderly compared with such towns. I also beg to draw your attention to the absence of crime in the borough. There has not been a robbery of any magnitude for some years.'[98]

If, however, there was no serious crime problem, the Guy Fawkes celebrations each fifth of November still gave trouble to the force. In 1852 the riotous proceedings left four members of the force unfit for duty and thirteen injured with burns and bruises. More serious were the bread riots which broke out in the bitter month of January 1854, and again in November 1867. On each occasion it was necessary to call in the troops, though the police performed their duty with credit. The fundamental cause of both riots was hunger and the wretchedness of life existing under the surface of the city though in 1867 the mayor, the solicitor Alderman Head, came to the more comforting conclusion that the outbreak had been caused by emissaries from elsewhere. Head himself had had occasion to take note of two strangers who, he thought, had forced themselves on his notice for no good cause other than to become 'personally acquainted with the person in authority.'[99] Alderman Head suggested to the home secretary, Gathorne Hardy, that every city in the kingdom was at the mercy of 'roughs' if they chose to combine. Special constables were of little use on dark nights because they could not be distinguished from the roughs. Accordingly, in view of what he considered to be a 'prevalent disposition to set the law at a defiance,' the mayor proposed that a national guard should be enrolled and that the police should be armed.[100]

This irresponsible suggestion was ignored. Exeter, however, though remaining free from serious crime, long remained prone to outbreaks of riotous behaviour, particularly in the 1870s when liquor licensing became an emotional political issue.

Though the watch committee supported the superintendent in his creation of a force that was adequate by the standards of the time, the council resolutely refused to accept the control from London involved by the acceptance of a grant towards the cost of the police under section 25 of the Police Act of 1856.[101] There was some justification for what might otherwise appear merely as an example of local intransigence. Financial grants did in fact imply control. The ancient and virtually independent boroughs were becoming increasingly dependent on London, a process implicit in the widening operations of the central government and in the improvement of communications. Three resolutions in favour of an application for a government grant towards the Exeter police were defeated in 1858, the council on one occasion accepting an amendment 'That to accept money for such a purpose would give strength to the principle of centralization and tend to interfere with the freedom of local action.'[102] It was not till January 1861 that the step was taken and the council began to submit to the reports of the inspectors of constabulary, which were generally favourable.[103]

The council continued to reduce the debts inherited from the old regime and by 1869 the market was showing a substantial margin of revenue over expenditure. Sales of municipal property were continued, property to the amount of £70,065 being sold between 1838 and 1870, and the proceeds being used, on Treasury insistence, for the reduction of debt. These sales were not always above suspicion. The committee which sanctioned the sale of part of the city wall to Somers Gard, in 1857, consisted of three members of the council; one was Henry Hooper, who sponsored Gard's parliamentary candidature in that year; another claimed to be attending as Gard's attorney rather than as a member of the council.[104] The old city gaol was sold to Leon Solomon, of Dawlish, in 1863, because the council could not raise the funds required for the modernization of the building and the more enlightened treatment of prisoners. By agreement with the county magistrates the city's prisoners were confined in the county gaol on payment of a capitation charge by the city.[105]

The municipal account for 1850–51 showed gross receipts of £3,565, of which £547 represented the balance carried over from the previous year. Revenue was derived from the traditional sources, dues and rents. Municipal payments amounted to £3,675 including debt charges of £2,693. Borough receipts amounted to £4,218, of which over three-quarters was provided by the borough rate. Borough expenditure was £4,108, including an item of £1,723 for the police. Twenty years later, according to the accounts of 1870–71, municipal receipts had fallen by some 15 per cent. while expenditure had risen by 23 per cent. There was also a debt of £1,339 carried forward from previous years.[106] Borough revenue had doubled in the same period, the borough rate contributing two-thirds; expenditure had increased by 71 per cent.

Expenditure incurred by the improvement commissioners declined markedly after the initial expansion of the 1830s under the stimulus of cholera. By 1839, when their debt had risen to £63,000, the commissioners decided to restrict the scale of their operations.[107] It was not till 1865 that renewed fears of cholera impelled Exeter once more to consider the state of the city. In that year, 'with a view to an effective promotion of cleanliness,' Exeter was divided into districts under the supervision of representative committees including members of the council and improvement commissioners.[108] The latter pledged their co-operation within the powers conferred by the Improvement Act of 1832. These powers were inadequate though they had seemed impressively comprehensive thirty years previously. The council as yet still had no adequate means of raising funds for the large-scale capital expenditure required for modern improvements.

In the gloomy and unprosperous year of 1866, as the *Annual Register* styled it, cholera was sweeping westwards across Europe.[109] By the end of the year it was computed that the disease had killed 100,000 people in Austria, and some 8,000 in England. On 11 August, the surgeon, Mr Roper, reported to the corporation of the poor that a case of Asiatic cholera had occurred in the west quarter.[110] The very term was evocative of exotic pestilence and death and reminded Exeter of the horrors of 1832. The corporation began to discuss the possibility of using the Eagle Tavern, in Howell Road, as a reception centre for cholera cases. A druggist was appointed to superintend the destruction and valuation of clothing. By October the returns placed before the corporation had recorded 100 deaths from 'cholera and diarrhoea.'[111]

The disease disappeared from the city by the end of November but it had been a salutary reminder of the dangers latent in the lax sanitary administration and in the normally desultory manner in which improvements were discussed. In the following year the corporation of the poor drew the council's attention to the many nuisances endangering life and property in the city. Faced with the possibility that the council would itself take action the improvement commissioners applied formally for the adoption of the Public Health Act of 1858. The application was misconceived since the act provided that its execution should be vested in a local board of health and that in corporate boroughs the board should be 'the Mayor, Aldermen and Burgesses acting by the Council.' The council replied to the improvement commissioners' move with a special meeting held in January 1867, at which a unanimous decision was taken in favour of adopting the act. In March a committee was appointed to examine the home secretary's instructions relating to the act of 1858. The improvement commissioners were invited to 'facilitate the transfer of their powers to the Town Council and the Local Board.'[112]

The improvement commissioners did no such thing. The proposed change in what had become the traditional order provoked the customary opposition. Vestry meetings were organized to protest. This opposition, in the view of the *Gazette*, was merely factious:

'The £7,000 per annum which is now devoted to lighting, paving and drainage might be put to better use than at present . . . No ratepayer acquainted with the sanitary history of the past year, and with the real state of the borough, will say that Exeter does not stand greatly in need of improvements.'[113]

At the ensuing inquiry before the home office inspector, Arnold Taylor,[114] William Buckingham, solicitor (currently chairman of the improvement commissioners and later mayor) was supported by Mark Kennaway and Dr Shapter in opposing the proposed change. He raised the flag of local independence: 'Is no town, no city whatever the circumstances, or whatever special cause there may be – is no town or city to have any opinion of its own, but is everything to come within the general rule which the Legislature has perhaps laid down?' He urged that the election of the improvement commissioners was 'uninfluenced by any motive beyond their fitness for office' whereas the election of members of the council was 'influenced by various motives, amongst which a political motive [was] seldom or never overlooked.'[115] As to the facts of public health, Buckingham demurred to the inspector's suggestion that infant mortality might be taken as an indication of the state of public health.[116]

Shapter's supporting statement was primarily a recapitulation of what had been done in the past, especially after the cholera epidemic of 1832, and paid little attention to what was required in the future. Mark Kennaway's defence was a eulogy of economy. Having spent £124,000 on public works since 1832 the improvement commissioners had borrowed only £73,000. They were 'the best trustees of public money I

J

ever saw.'[117]

Buckingham's comments on the election of the council should be treated with respect. He himself moved in political circles and shortly afterwards he took an active part in mobilizing political support over the school board elections. But the improvement commissioners had become an anachronism. Dr Shapter himself had intimated in his younger days that increased powers were necessary if the health problem was to be satisfactorily tackled. Evidence was given that Bath and Salisbury had shown more improvement in public health than had Exeter in recent years,[118] and, if the office of sanitary inspector appeared at first sight impressive, that official was paid only £12 a year and had other duties. Despite an unconvincing rearguard action and the presentation of a petition signed by owners and occupiers of property the question aroused little real interest in the city and the result was a foregone conclusion.

In August 1867 the Exeter improvement commissioners were formally superseded by 'An Act to confirm certain Provisional Orders under the Local Government Act, 1858, relating to the Districts of Exeter, Devonport, Reading, Warley and Midgley, and for other Purposes relative to certain Districts under the said Act.'[119] The opposition to centralization, the awareness of diminishing status, were not unjustified. It was indeed an indication of changing conditions and status that Exeter should be included in orders relating to Warley and Midgley.

In April 1867 it was recommended that an inspector of nuisances should be appointed at a salary of £100 a year and that the appropriate committees should be instituted.[120] Amicable arrangements were made with the dean and chapter for the application to the Cathedral Close of 'all powers, authorities and regulations in reference to Police and Sanitary purposes.'[121] In June the new inspector assumed duty armed with a manuscript copy of the new by-laws.

It was at this point that Exeter moved decisively into nineteenth-century England and the council began the slow development of its powers and responsibilities. The change was due to a practical response to the pressure of circumstances. No party or section at that time sought election on a platform of improvement. It was not till the eighties that new methods of local government finance made possible substantially increased expenditure and the ratepayers stirred under the stimulus of rising rates. In 1870 the *Western Times* complained that the municipal government of the city had been reduced 'to the lowest ebb through the virulent party spirit'[122] which it was said, had been infused into the council in 1835 and had been maintained thereafter. The *Western Times* was partisan and the responsibility for the decline was attributed to the Conservatives just as the *Flying Post* attributed it to the Liberals. The fact was that the long domination of the council by one party, the Hooper regime and the monopoly of key posts by party partisans had extinguished the 'civic spirit.'

The parliamentary elections alone at this period were evidence of the life still existing in Liberal Exeter. The election of 1859, which returned Palmerston to power, occasioned no contest in Exeter. Divett and Somers Gard were both Palmerstonians. Gladstone, now moving towards Liberalism, was attacked by Divett for displaying Tractarian tendencies which were 'the dread of those who were disposed to advance true religion in the country.'[123] But Divett died in 1864. One of Exeter's 'honourable local gentry,' as the *Gazette* had once styled him, assured by an opposition paper in 1849 that his position owed much to 'the personal respect entertained for him,'[124] Divett attracted the Nonconformist vote without duly exciting either the fears or the prejudices of the Conservatives.

Before his death Divett had brought forward his successor in the person of John Duke Coleridge, of Ottery St Mary, the future lord chief justice. A product of Eton and Balliol, student of Homer, Virgil and Wordsworth, an admirer of Keble and Newman, Coleridge in 1864 already had presentiments that a seat in parliament would lead to the high office which Divett had never sought.[125] He was received with some suspicion in Exeter, partly because he was suspected of using politics as a stepping stone in his legal career, according to the common practice of nineteenth-century lawyers. Neither his subtlety of mind nor his leanings towards High Church theology was readily acceptable to Exeter. By Nonconformist opinion he was regarded as unsound on church rates.

For the bye-election of 1864 the Conservatives brought forward Lord Edward Courtenay, third son of the Earl of Devon. Courtenay was described in the Liberal press, fairly enough, as a young gentleman 'given up entirely to the pastime of the racecourse and the excitement of the betting ring.'[126] His interests, indeed, ended in one of the more spectacular bankruptcies of Victorian times. He went bankrupt for about £100,000 in 1870 and for some £20,000 in 1878. He succeeded as Earl of Devon in 1883 and died of paralysis at Boodles Club in 1891.[127] In the meantime he appeared at the Exeter Subscription Rooms to declare his 'warm interest in your city and its neighbourhood.'[128] He also announced his strenuous opposition to any measure for the abolition of church rates or which might tend to weaken the influence of the Church of England.

Coleridge was declared elected on a show of hands after an uproar caused by his statement that many electors had said that they would gladly vote for him were they not exposed to coercion. At the polling, however, he was defeated by twenty-six votes. This result was attributed by local opinion to the abstention of a few leading Nonconformists who disliked Coleridge's attitude towards church rates.[129] The explanation was probably correct; a High Churchman and godson of Keble was not easily acceptable to Exeter's Nonconformity.

Somers Gard retired before the general election of 1865 and Courtenay and Coleridge were elected for Exeter without a contest. With the death of Palmerston three months later, Glastone's star was in the ascendant, a phenomenon that was apparent even in Exeter. Divett had criticized Gladstone for Tractarian tendencies but a Reform meeting held in the city in 1866 resolved that Gladstone should be specially thanked 'for his persistent efforts to enfranchise the intelligent artisan classes of the country and for his noble defence of their character.'[130] By the following year Gladstone, described by the Exeter Conservative press as 'the renegade centurion of a riotous and distempered rabble' was nevertheless acknowledged in the same breath as 'the inevitable Prime Minister of England.'[131]

The events of 1866–67, which led to the enactment of the Reform Bill of the latter year, aroused no great interest in Exeter. There were public meetings but these lacked the fervour of the old days of Reform. For the Conservatives it was enough that a Conservative government at long last was in office. Disraeli's brilliant opportunism was loyally and uncomprehendingly accepted.

In 1868 Disraeli dissolved parliament in the hope that the newly enfranchised voters would show gratitude for their enfranchisement. The Liberal candidates at Exeter were Coleridge and Edgar Bowring. Whatever reservations there might have been regarding Coleridge among Exeter's Nonconformity he was not under-rated by Sir Stafford Northcote who, in 1866, had suggested to Disraeli that Coleridge's appointment to a judgeship was the best means of getting rid of 'a dangerous man in the House of Commons' and gaining a Conservative seat at Exeter.[132] In 1868 Coleridge's colleague, Edgar Bowring, was calculated to make up for any defects in Coleridge's own appeal to a section of the Liberal electorate. The son of a brilliant father, Sir John Bowring, Edgar Bowring had been educated, not at Oxford but at University College, London. In 1841 he had entered the civil service in the board of trade, where he served as private secretary to Clarendon and Granville. He was the author of an English poetical version of the Psalms, and translator of Schiller, Goethe and Heine.[133]

The Conservative candidates were Sir John Karslake, Disraeli's attorney-general, and Arthur Mills, the son-in-law of Sir Thomas Acland. Karslake was a candidate of real merit acknowledged by his opponents to be 'much respected in Exeter . . . a man of genial disposition and kindly nature.'[134] Mills had been Conservative member for Taunton from 1857 to 1865 and had been involved in charges of corruption.

As presented to the electorate, the issues were routine. Bowring's electoral address, for example, stressed his family connection with Exeter, his hearty rejoicing over the Reform Bill 'brought forward by the Conservatives under pressure,' allegiance to Gladstone and support of Irish disestablishment. Bowring viewed 'with alarm the great increase in our National Expenditure.' He declared that 'the great problem of the relation between capital and labour and the means of securing harmony between employer and employed must be grappled with.' He was ready to vote for the ballot and also 'to advocate the establishment of a complete system of national education, based on due regard for the scruples of my dissenting brethren.[135] There was something here for all sections of Liberal Exeter; moreover, the gesture of a former student of University College, London, to his 'dissenting brethren' was likely to allay Nonconformist misgivings over voting for Coleridge, the High Churchman.

Coleridge was returned at the head of the poll. Bowring came second, defeating Karslake by the narrow margin of twenty-eight votes. For the first, and last, time in Exeter's Victorian history the two parliamentary seats were both captured by the Liberals. Exeter had shared in the decisive Liberal victory which brought Gladstone to his first premiership. Plymouth, Devonport and Tiverton each returned two Liberals. But Exeter was not one of the larger towns of England which together returned eighty-nine Liberals and twenty-five Conservatives in the election of 1868. The city belonged to the urban class of 'old provincial centres . . . only partially absorbed into the world of modern industry and party politics.'[136] It was, indeed, the election of 1868 which provoked the comment of the *Western Times* that 'The tone of the city, what is called its respectability, is predominantly Tory.'[137] Thomas Latimer – the article bears unmistakable signs of his pen – went on to elaborate:

'The Cathedral and its dons (*sic*), and the Bishop and his establishment for a certain period impressed the higher class of tradesmen with awe . . . all the leading shopkeepers found it in their interest to go with the Church and the Tories. The residuum of the old freemen was another element of Toryism . . . In addition to the Church there were the lawyers.'

Influence brought to bear on tradesmen and shopkeepers cannot, of its very nature, be substantiated. The extent to which the charge can be justified must be left to experience of human nature in a small community, hierarchical and deferential in its traditions, animated by strong political and religious feelings. Henry Ellis recorded something of the pressures exerted on him by customers twenty years before.[138] The Anglican clergy were as overwhelmingly Conservative in 1868 as in previous elections. They provided thirty-nine votes for Karslake and Mills compared with four for Coleridge and Bowring and a plumper for Coleridge; in all sixty-four Conservative votes and nine Liberal. Barristers and solicitors voted Conservative by fifty-nine to twenty-two. The Conservative leanings of the freemen had been demonstrated by the previous election, that of 1864, when they cast 131 votes for Lord Courtenay and forty-three for Coleridge.[139] Among the Conservative freemen voters were distinguished county magnates such as Sir Stafford Northcote and Sir Lawrence Palk; but the Conservative supporters included humbler figures: two labourers, plasterers, a carpenter, a hairdresser and waiter.[140] The enlarged electorate of 1868 included over 200 labourers and the Liberals ensured that Bowring's nomination at the Guildhall was seconded by 'a real working-class man.'[141] There was, however, no overwhelming support for Liberalism among this class, which provided 229 votes for the two Liberal candidates and 221 for the Conservatives. Liberal support in the Exeter election of 1868 came broadly from the middle ranks of the electorate, the artisans and small shopkeepers, and from the Nonconformist vote at all levels. Even so, the Liberal victory by a total of 4,564 to 4,244 was far from a landslide.

Elections are not won by purity of principles as some of the Exeter Liberals appeared to imagine. The Conservatives attributed their defeat to faulty organization and to lack of zeal among some of their supporters at a time when large numbers of new voters, belonging to 'the artisan and labouring population almost to a man,' had been added to the electorate.[142] The new electors had not yet been organized. W. J. Richards informed a meeting shortly before the

election that a working men's association had been planned
and a code of rules had been drawn up;[143] but the practical
work had still to be done. Even so the voting record of
1868 suggests that there had been no great Liberal majority
among the 'labouring population' who had voted for the
first time. The Conservatives themselves paid tribute to the
'assiduous and pertinacious' canvassing of Edgar Bowring
who was said to have called personally on every elector.[144]
The Liberal candidates formed a strong team. Their success
by a narrow margin can be attributed to personal factors
assisted by failure of Conservative organization. The
Conservatives set themselves to ensure that their defeat
would not be repeated. They overhauled their political
machine with marked efficiency assisted by the two great
issues of the 1870s, education and liquor licensing, which
combined to arouse to the full extent the political zeal of the
two powerful elements in Exeter's life, the church and 'the
trade.'

Irony, it has been said, 'has no place in popular movements.'[145] But the Exeter Reformers were to savour the irony
of politics. Political reform, the Municipal Corporations Act
of 1835, the Reform Bills of 1832 and 1867, had enlarged the
opportunities for active participation in public life. The
result in Exeter had been to emphasize that the major
influence in the character of the city was conservative. This
conservatism was being accentuated by the city's steady
withdrawal to the perimeter of national affairs as a representative of a way of life which, though not without its
virtues, yet belonged to the past. A protective carapace of
tradition and habit had closed over the momentary breach
made by the excitement of the years of Reform. By 1870 it
had hardened. Man, 'sole judge of truth, in endless error
hurled,' was not created in the Utilitarian image.

'Corporation Reform,' said the *Flying Post* in 1835,
'unquestionably is a great boon granted to the people, but
it will prove a blessing or otherwise to the present generation according to as it is used ... all feeling of party should
be excluded, since, constituted as human nature is, it does
happen that the warm political partisan may be the most

unfit person to perform those functions which are assigned to the Council, and the prudent exercise of which is so necessary to good government.'[146]

No objective observer reviewing in 1870 the history of the past thirty-five years would have concluded that Exeter had achieved the objective which the same paper regarded as the object of the act, 'to select men who from their respectability are likely to inspire confidence, while their education, wealth and influence are such as will enable them to carry on local government free from grovelling and jarring.'[147] The widening of the parliamentary franchise in 1867 and the very success of Exeter's Liberalism in the ensuing election were to strengthen by reaction Conservatism, but not the Conservatism dreamed of by Trewman's *Flying Post*.

VI

THE GROWTH OF THE CITY TO 1870

THE 1860s were the end of a well-defined period in the cultural history of Exeter, a period which had lasted for almost exactly one hundred years. In 1768, it was recorded, 'the spirit of improvement began to manifest itself' in the city.[1] That spirit was largely classical in inspiration. There is, indeed, a good case for treating the period 1768 to 1870 as Exeter's Georgian period, with due allowance for the difficulty of applying exact chronological boundaries to human history; for the correct expression of architectural taste on classical principles was also an expression of pre-Victorian society. Within the context of that society Exeter had flourished as a provincial capital. When, in the seventies, the order and distinction of classical architecture were replaced, with almost dramatic suddenness, by the more disorderly variety and ornament of later Victorian architecture, the event marked a profound change in the city's life as a whole.

In nothing was Victorian Exeter less Victorian than in urban growth. When the British Association visited Liverpool in 1870, after a meeting held in Exeter the previous year, the contrast was described as a transition 'from the cloisters to the mart, from silence and past memories to the noise of tongues and active present occurrences.'[2] Dr Doran's antithesis was no doubt in part routine and probably pleased Liverpool. But the impression left on the minds of the visitors of 1869 was one of a 'lively, quaint, antique and attractive city,' gay with its moving crowds, its flags and banners; civilized to the extent that visitors were not faced with the 'exhorbitant demands which have not infrequently been made in other towns.'[3] Such comments, though gratifying, did not indicate that the visitors had been impressed by economic vitality. It was not an impression of a city in the van of progress as a great body of Victorian opinion conceived progress.

To those with the imagination to recognize in industrial architecture the power of a new order, as young Harry Coningsby did at Millbank, Exeter offered no more than the impressive warehouses on the quay erected in 1835. Whereas in a city such as Leeds controversy and pride in civic achievement centred on a town hall, in Exeter the major architectural controversy of the Victorian era raged round Sir Gilbert Scott's treatment of the cathedral reredos. The arrival of the railway in 1844 had failed to fulfil the apocalyptic visions of a golden age of material progress and moral advancement. In the welcome given to the London & South Western railway and the new station under Northernhay in 1860, the muted tone was not wholly due to the penetrating July rain which diluted the champagne and ruined the ladies' crinolines. In the leaking tent where over three hundred guests banqueted, William Kennaway harked back to the days before the queen's accession, to the era of Reform and its buoyant assumptions of progress; to the opening of the canal with its invitation to the commerce of the world. Danby Seymour, cousin to the Duke of Somerset and Liberal member for Poole, found the occasion more suitable for an expression of hope than for congratulations on achievement. 'Your fair city of the west,' he told his audience, 'will reap the trade and commerce developed, and will recover that importance which has been slightly eclipsed.'⁴

At the beginning of the nineteenth century Exeter had been a compact city 'picturesquely situated in a grove of trees' and almost wholly confined within its walls.⁵ By 1831 according to Dr Shapter, the city was

'no longer girt about by its original ancient boundaries, houses for its increased and increasing population had been planted in the suburbs, where shortly before avenues of trees had flourished, and it was no longer a city in a grove. The ancient character of its streets had disappeared.'⁶

The extent of the change in the first thirty years of the century was undoubtedly exaggerated. It is true that the suburbs were being developed, a process which had begun with the finest creations of Exeter's Georgian architecture,

Southernhay and Higher and Lower Summerlands, at a time when Exeter was beginning to adjust itself to the increase in wheeled traffic. But it was not till the 1880s that Exeter experienced the growth of housing estates and the spread of suburban villadom in some measure approaching the scale of development experienced elsewhere. And it was not till the early years of the twentieth century that suburban growth made any significant impact on the appearance of the city. Exeter in 1870 was still a compact city with no part further than a few minutes' walk from the water meadows of the Exe and the immemorial fields and lanes of the Devon countryside. Some hundred years of Georgian taste, modified over the years but in spirit unchanged, had created an architecturally pleasing city. The diverse styles of a long history had blended in 'an easy commerce of the old and the new,' deep in elms and ilex, ringed with orchards and market gardens, dominated by the cathedral, and looking to the hills and woods of Devon from almost every street.

The rural environment is both the cause and outcome of the nineteenth-century history of Exeter. It forms the ecology of a human community. For the Victorian city was a microcosm of one of the many aspects of social and economic life constituting the Victorian England of Surtees and Parson Jack Russell, essentially rural and provincial. The values were determined in the last resort by the clergy and the county. This was not necessarily to be deplored merely because it was so far in spirit and achievement from, for instance, 'the roaring looms of hundred gated Leeds,'[7] or Grey Street and Elswick, Newcastle upon Tyne. But Exeter lacked the dynamic energy of the true Victorian city; and so the city's importance declined in the national scale. In this respect the census figures speak for themselves.

Between 1801 and 1841[8] the population of Exeter within the municipal boundaries rose from 17,412 to 31,305, an increase of over 85 per cent.; by 1851 the population was 32,818; by 1871 it was 41,467, an increase of about 32 per cent. since 1841. The population of Leicester had increased during those same seventy years from 17,005 to 99,622; York from 16,846 to 51,480. In the decade 1861 to 1871 the percentage increase of Exeter's population was 4.2 per cent., compared with 39.7 per cent. in Leicester, 11.4 per cent. in York and 84 per cent. in what was becoming suburban Croydon. In 1801 Exeter was said to have contained 2,590 inhabited houses. By 1841 there were 5,122. The period of most vigorous growth, expressed in housing construction, was between 1821 and 1831, when the increase was over 24 per cent., and in the following decade when it was over 26 per cent. By 1851 there was in fact a small decrease. If the figures of houses under construction at each census are taken as an indication of progress the conclusions are the same. Eighty houses were under construction in 1831 and sixty-seven in 1841. The number fell to twenty-three in 1851. It rose from twenty-seven in 1861 to sixty-one in 1871. By contemporary standards Exeter's performance was not impressive even in the earlier period. Cheltenham had 173 houses under construction at the time of the census of 1841; the rapidly growing town of Bradford had 435.

The increase in wheeled traffic, and hence the need to improve the roads, greater wealth and higher standards of living, new tastes and more leisure, and finally the potent fear of cholera, had first inspired and then continued the growth of the city, its embellishment and improvement, at the end of the nineteenth century. The improvement of the road system had begun with the removal of the south gate in 1819. That stage ended between 1834 and 1839. In the former year the New North Road was constructed by the turnpike commissioners, at a cost of £7,000. The steep Fore Street hill leading to the city's western approaches and the bridge over the Exe was lowered and improved in 1836 and 1837. In 1838 Magdalen Street was widened, the houses in the neighbourhood of the ancient, and still flourishing, White Hart, were set back to a new line, and projections likely to interfere with the traffic were removed. The completion of the Higher Market in 1838 was followed in 1839 by the dedication to the public of a new road between Maddox Row and High Street,[9] the new Queen Street, planned to meet the advancing railway. By the end of the thirties the medieval road pattern had been recast in a form which was to suffice with little change for another hundred years. The improvement commissioners, impressed as much by the needs of economy as by the possibilities of further development, thenceforward confined themselves to relatively minor works, the only major work being the construction of the Bonhay Road to provide a direct link between St David's Station and the Exe Bridge along the level ground beside the river. In 1838 the improvement commissioners raised £3,000[10] for the flagging of streets, necessary in the interests of vehicles and pedestrians, and to remove the open sewers which, as the cholera epidemic had reminded the city, were a distinctive feature of Exeter's streets in 1832.

Despite the necessity for improvement impressed by the cholera in 1832, Shapter in 1845 admitted that there was still much to be done. There were still midden heaps in private courts, slaughter houses with their heaps of offal, the 'ill-arrangement of the streets,' the bad construction of private drains and 'the more general evil of driving back of foul air from great sewers.'[11] Water supplies were still inadequate. So was the law. Shapter stressed the need for more effective provision for the removal of nuisances and for ensuring that private communication with the public sewers should be undertaken at the public expense instead of at the expense of the occupier; but it was not till the 1870s that Exeter began to make further progress in public health measures and improved sanitation. Except when the dark shadow of cholera reminded the city of the retribution exacted by defects in drains, sewerage and water supplies, insistence on economy and the rights of private property tended to take precedence over improvement. Thus in 1848 the Health of Towns Bill was denounced as despotic and arbitrary at a public meeting held in protest against this new manifestation of government interference. Samuel Kingdon declared that the existing water supplies were more than sufficient.[12] A 'very large and influential meeting' in Heavitree agreed that the bill 'would be extremely pernicious in its effects to the parish, amounting in many cases to sheer confiscation of property.'[13]

Protests such as these were far from being confined to

Exeter and its suburbs. They were, however, an aspect of influential opinion with which the improvement commissioners had to contend. In the circumstances of the time the commissioners' final statement of accounts was not discreditable. When they unwillingly handed over their statutory powers they had spent a total of £112,350, including £72,294 on the widening and improvement of streets, £18,111 on flagging, £10,645 on sewers and £11,478 on cemeteries. £40,000 had been raised from the rates. The remainder had been borrowed.[14] This was a modest achievement if compared with the £2,000,000 or more spent within four years on improvements by Newcastle upon Tyne in the early years of the nineteenth century.[15] The contrast is a reflection of Exeter's status at the time.

Since the beginning of the century the expansion of Exeter had been directed to the central spine of the city along the St Sidwell's ridge eastwards from the east gate to the Blackboy turnpike. Here, by 1838, was a multitude of small courts, tenements and cottages with rateable values of between £2 10s. od. and £5 a year.[16] These lowly buildings were interspersed with the Georgian and Regency structures which survive today as the monuments of a refined and civilized domestic architecture: Belmont Terrace, St Ann's Terrace and Albion Terrace. To the south of the city the Hoopers were creating during these years the pleasant suburb of St Leonard's where the foundations of their family fortunes had been laid with the acquisition and development of the Baring estate.

The larger new houses were required for the retired people and for the professional and commercial men who were moving out into the fields and gardens on the outskirts of the city in search of something of the landed background which was the hallmark of success. Some purchased old estates. Thus 'Iron Sam' Kingdon owned Duryard House and the wealthy tailor Stephen Brunskill bought Polsloe Park in 1848. While the suburbs grew the old parishes within the city walls tended to decline. Four of the twenty-one parishes and precincts showed a reduction in the number of inhabited houses between 1831 and 1851, and eleven between 1851 and 1871.

The expansion of the city was essentially the work of the speculative builders such as the Hoopers themselves in their early days, men who worked in a local idiom using the current manuals of classical architecture and therefore creating buildings designed as an investment but admired by later ages for proportion and taste. The early works of the Hoopers surviving today include Lower Summerlands and Baring Crescent. As communications improved the pace quickened. In 1836 a group of brick-built houses were offered for sale in Nelson Place, St Sidwell's and 'excellent houses,' several of them lately erected, were being offered for low rents at Hills Court.[17] In the same year building sites were being offered for sale on the Barnfield estate, now the Barnfield Road. It was noted that at this period Heavitree was experiencing 'extensively the exhilarating hand of improvement.'[18]

The vicinity of Exeter with its theatre, libraries and concerts, its facilities for business, politics, law and administration increased the attractions of the suburban villages and was the primary cause of their growth. By the time of the queen's accession it had been remarked that there were a number of 'genteel houses'[19] in Alphington, the 'residences of many respectable families,' including the original of Mr Micawber. By that time, too, 'the vast number of genteel houses and villas recently erected'[20] in Heavitree exceeded the descriptive powers of even the writer of the contemporary guidebook.

Measured against the more spectacular urban growth which was creating the opportunities and problems of Victorian England, the growth of Exeter was far from impressive. To Exeter itself, accustomed to the slower evolutionary process of pre-industrial England, building activity in the suburbs deserved the raptures of the guide books. In St Leonard's, the number of inhabited houses increased by 62 per cent. between 1821 and 1831. In the following decade the increase was nearly 188 per cent; this was followed by an increase of 50 per cent. between 1841 and 1851. During these thirty years the number of inhabited houses in the parish rose from sixty-two to 267. Heavitree contained 211 inhabited houses in 1821. By 1831 there were 528, an increase of close on 70 per cent. In the next decade there was a further increase of just over 13 per cent., to 608. The figures are not unimpressive. They were the consequences of the city's popularity as a place of retirement which, if it could not offer the social standards of Bath or Cheltenham, was also less likely to involve the expense of keeping up appearances.

Heavitree, declared a directory of 1857, 'contains a number of neat and handsome residences occupied by persons of respectability.'[21] The expansion of Exeter in the first half of the nineteenth century was based on the demands of a class which required moderate but respectable comfort either in retirement or because it was no longer necessary to live over the shop. The unpretentious and well-proportioned houses and terraces of the time of George IV and William IV were the homes of professional men, clergy, army officers and single ladies whose inclusion in the 'Nobility, Clergy and Gentry' section of the directories was an indication of their claims to some status. The authentic world of wealth and fashion preferred Cheltenham, or the still exclusive attractions of Sidmouth and Torquay; but Exeter and its suburbs were the home of a leisured society who patronized the theatre and Mr Congdon's Subscription Rooms, borrowed off each other Indian scarves and Turkish slippers for fancy dress balls and were pleased to find in a new neighbour a former judge from Ceylon.[22] For this class Exeter never lost its attractions; but the initial period of growth created by their requirements, which had begun in the eighteenth century, was over by the 1850s both for the city within the municipal area and for the suburbs. For a time there seemed a possibility that the railways would give an additional stimulus to building. In 1847 the public were informed that 'property in St David's was likely to increase in value on account of the projected and competing railways to Exeter.'[23] Around the junction of the New North Road with the northern extension of Queen Street there arose in the 1840s a number of pleasant brick and stucco terraces, New North Terrace and Queen's Terrace, collectively named Queen's

K

Terrace in 1863; Bystock Terrace,[24] St Petrock's Terrace and Peamore Terrace. These buildings were Exeter's last major essay in domestic architecture in the grand manner.

In 1778 John Kendall of Exeter had published his *Elucidation of the Principles of English Architecture usually denominated Gothic*. Salvin had designed Gothic Mamhead in 1828; but Exeter in general had remained faithful to the classical tradition. It is at the northern end of Queen Street that evidence of the Gothic element becomes important. The buildings existing today still reflect the battle of the styles. Bystock Terrace, now the Bystock Hotel, was constructed at this period in the vaguely termed 'old English' style popularized by the architect Loudon[25], with its steeply-pitched roofs replacing the classical flat roofs and pediments, the gables, barge-boards and the windows with their flavour of the medieval. It was a Gothic influence which yet eschewed the excessive enthusiasm for decoration and colour which marked the architecture of later Victorian Exeter.

In the 1860s the classical tradition ended with the construction of Velwell Villas and Elm Grove Terrace by John and Charles Ware, builder and architect. John Ware had extensive interests in St David's. He had been associated with William Hooper in the construction of the county gaol in 1863. That same year he was pressing the improvement commissioners to construct a road and footpath in Pound Lane, the future Richmond Road.[26] In the following year he proposed the construction of a 'new road from the New North Road to behind the county gaol and offered to give up land for the purpose.'[27] And so by 1864 the short length of Elm Grove Road came into existence for the benefit of Ware's new houses facing Bury Meadow.

The houses in Elm Grove Road and Howell Road behind the trees of Bury Meadow reflect today the shadow of the Georgian traditions from which they were derived, a homogeneous group of simple stucco houses with sash windows and attics on the edge of the country and the town. Buildings such as these abound in Torquay and Cheltenham. Their construction in the Exeter of the late 1860s endorses the comment that the local builders of the southwest managed for a time to retain the old classical traditions and the simplicity of 'west country vernacular building'[28] when elsewhere change was gathering pace. Built when Bismarck was completing the German Empire, when the crinoline was giving place to the folds and pleats of its successor, houses such as these would not have been out of place as adjuncts to the Queen's Hotel, Cheltenham.

It was not till the end of the 1860s that there began to appear in Exeter the dour rows of working-class houses which were a feature of the Victorian urban scene; standardized streets without grace or character, their uniformity emphasized rather than relieved by spasmodic applications of ornament or colour. The first distinctive area of artisans' housing, Newtown, had made a tentative appearance towards the end of the 1830s on the slopes below the Polsloe Ridge. Some thirty years later the nurseryman Sclater informed his colleagues of the new local board of health that he considered himself to be the creator of Newtown though, he explained, he had given up his interest in the area twenty years previously. Newtown, said Sclater, was intended for artisans and was believed to have offered 'the cheapest dwellings that could be had for the class of persons they had to provide for.'[29] The long lines of the streets of Newtown, as they exist today, are largely the work of the late nineteenth century, though houses of the earlier period still stand at the lower end. In the meantime artisans, and working men generally, lived where they could in courts and alleys and cottages, and in the slums of the west quarter; in Wood's Buildings off Summerland Street, Skittle Alley Court off Sidwell Street, and Rope Walk off the Blackboy Road, where they were assessed at between £3 and £4 5s. per annum in 1838.[30]

By the late sixties there were 2,386 occupiers of houses in Exeter with a rateable value of above £4 and under £10. In 1838 the comparable figure had been of the order of 1,456. The figures suggest a substantial increase in the number of occupiers able to pay 2s. 6d. to 4s. 6d. a week.[31] The expansion of the city before 1870 cannot therefore have been wholly due to the requirements of the middle class and rentiers. The rent books of the water company in 1851 record the existence of little groups of courts and cottages off Sidwell Street, Warren Cottages, Strong's Cottages, Baker's Court and Gattey's Court, Nosworthy's Row, some of which were to acquire notoriety as sub-standard housing in the early twentieth century. The dates of construction remain unknown.

From the year 1867 the records of the streets committee of the local board, and later of the council, provide evidence of the activities of the speculative builders in Exeter. Between 1867 and 1870 not less than 200 new houses were approved – the minutes of 1867 and 1868 in addition to giving precise numbers, also refer to 'houses' and 'cottages.' About this time there began the development of the area between Union Road and Lion's Holt, ending with the construction of the close-packed brick and slate streets, such as Victoria Street, which exist today. In 1869, the builder William Huxtable, after considerable argument with the streets committee about building standards, received permission to construct thirty-four houses in Hilly Field, the present Napier Terrace. In the same year plans for the construction of new streets in Newtown were approved, though in fact no substantial work was undertaken in that area till the 1880s.[32]

The builders worked on a small scale, building houses in small groups in streets and terraces for loan or immediate sale. A block of four adjacent houses in Sandford Street, Newtown, was on offer for sale in 1848.[33] William Huxtable, the builder of Napier Terrace, owned two houses in Poltimore Square in 1867 and seven by 1870.[34] Thomas Pinn, joiner and builder, owned five houses in the Blackboy Road in 1851 but apparently had disposed of them by 1870.[35] The executors of the builder George Knowling offered seven houses for sale in Newtown in 1888.[36]

Of the old-style artisans' dwellings constructed before 1870 few now remain though there are still some in Newtown. Architecturally their simplicity is not unpleasing. They were not jerry-built and they lack the harsh colours and meaningless ornamentation which emphasized rather than relieved the monotony of the new streets constructed after 1870.

The maximum use was made of space and the builders chafed under the efforts of the local board to enforce the not very onerous building standards of the day. In 1868 the Exeter branch of the General Builders Association, under the chairmanship of William Huxtable, complained that the new bye-laws were too stringent and 'had a tendency to prevent the erection of new houses, particularly those of the smaller class that are so much in demand.'[37] The builder also objected to the board's insistence that a certificate should be issued before the new houses were occupied in order to ensure that the standards were observed, and urged that they should be allowed to deviate from approved plans according to circumstances.[38] In 1869, Huxtable was in trouble over the plans for his thirty-four houses in Hilly Field. There was inadequate provision for ashpits. Only thirteen water closets were provided. The walls were too thin.[39]

The impetus for the construction of superior houses came from the Exeter Freehold Land Building Society founded in 1857 under the inspiration of Birmingham. An inaugural meeting was held in that year with the old Reformer, J. D. Osborn, in the chair. The representative from Birmingham informed the meeting that freehold and land societies 'elevated the members socially and morally, and tended to reduce crime.' It was thereupon decided to form a committee of citizens 'favourable to the working class' in order to carry the project further. A month later Exeter was informed that the society 'promised to be very successful.' Over 100 working men and others had been enrolled and more members were expected to join. Shares were £40, with half shares at £20, and the subscriptions were 1s. a month.[40] By 1869, the society was offering for sale or lease in Queen's Road, Alphington, 'three newly erected semi-detached villa residences' comprising parlour, drawing room, kitchen and two W.C.s, with a flower garden in front.' The terms were £20 down with interest at $5\frac{1}{2}$ per cent. on the diminishing balance.[41] Water-closets were still an innovation, a sign of the slowly changing attitude towards hygiene which had been marked by a 'considerable demand for the new galvanized iron baths' in 1847.[42]

Building land was provided by the utilization of the fields and market gardens which extended far into the city, and by the sale of the large estates which family vicissitudes brought into the market. The break-up of large estates for building in Exeter was at least as old as the acquisition of the Baring estate in St Leonard's by the Hoopers in the early nineteenth century. Polsloe Park came into the market in 1865 after the death of Stephen Brunskill and forty-one acres were on offer as valuable building sites in that year.[43] By 1869 the builder John Wills was advertising for sale Hesketh Villas, 'two new and substantial buildings' in the former park of the Dennises.[44] On the other side of Exeter, Bowhill House was for sale with the inducement that it could be converted 'into a number of dwelling houses of a respectable class.'[45] In the year 1863, abortive plans had been made for the development of the Duryard estate on the tree-covered slopes overlooking the road to North Devon and the valley of the Exe. 'A very superb range of villas which should attract local residents'[46] was contemplated but proved too ambitious. There were limits to the demands for this kind of housing in Exeter, especially at a time when Exeter was entering the trough of its nineteenth-century existence. That side of Exeter was spared the contemporary architectural style considered suitable for a 'superb range of villas.'

By the seventies the full force of Victorian architectural diversity, an individualism approaching anarchy, was manifest in Exeter assisted by 'the scourge of the builders' catalogues which swept regional tradition into the limbo of things unwanted.'[47] Henceforward there was to be diversity at all costs: bay windows, red brick and blue tiles, the ideals of Pugin and Ruskin expressed in terms of middle-class villas and working-class houses interpreted by the speculative builder using the new mass-produced materials and the harsh texture of machine-made brick. It could no longer be said of the Exeter builders and architects that they were conversant 'with the handling of material, not only with its suitability as a means of expressing ideas, but with a nice regard for its ultimate effect amidst the natural scenery, and an appreciation of texture values.'

In the 1870s Queen Street was recording in architecture the aspirations and achievements of the period and was becoming a museum of Victorian provincial architecture. The upper section, from High Street to Northernhay, included the severe classicism of the Higher Market. The unadorned simplicity of the dispensary, completed in 1841, faced the Victorian rendering of early French Gothic in the form of the Royal Albert Museum across the street. The Victoria Hall had been rushed to partial completion in time to receive the British Association in August 1869, and to accommodate the 2,000 working men and their families who came to cheer Miss Burdett-Coutts or to listen to Professor Muller's lecture on an 'Experimental illustration of the modes of determining the composition of the sun and other heavenly bodies.'[48] The building was the scene of concerts, political meetings and lectures until public taste changed at the end of the Victorian era. The site of the old city gaol was still undeveloped. It was acquired by the Devon and Exeter Hotel Company formed in 1875, with a capital of £30,000 and the prestige of good county names, to construct the Rougemont Hotel. In the background, the great spire of St Michael's and All Angels, completed in 1868, was a monument to middle-class munificence and faith.[49] The meadows between the New North Road and Northernhay had now disappeared under the weight of the permanent way and buildings of the London and South Western railway. The market gardens and orchards on the slopes above Lower North Street had been replaced by an untidy medley of warehouses, builders' yards and commercial buildings or were being used for the extension of the railway to connect Queen Street with St David's station.

George Oliver's panegyric on Exeter had been quoted to the sceptical ear of the home office inspector in 1867. Oliver's ministry had begun in 1806[50] and doubtless it was with the Georgian city in mind that the Catholic priest eulogized the Exeter of the sixties, the great 'moral revolution in the expansion of liberal and christian feeling,'[51] the 'salubrious, comfortable, polite and friendly' environment. Urban development in the seventies inspired James Cossins to publish his *Reminiscences* in 1877 in a 'desire to preserve some account of the manners and customs of our predecessors which have been, and are now, disappearing under the introduction of railways and the telegraph.' In his view, 'if cities and towns were registered for their sociability, popularity and picturesqueness, on a plan similar to that of ships at Lloyd's, Exeter, from information gleaned from those competent to form an opinion, would be classed A.I.'[52]

Cossins's *Reminiscences* reached back to the days of the Regency, to the time when willows lined the banks of the Long Brook and boys bathed below the slopes of Northernhay, when streets designed for the packhorse were first becoming jammed by coach and wagon. In comparison with the early years of both writers Exeter could show signs of progress. Measured by the achievements of other Victorian cities Exeter's development was less impressive.

The city's aspirations were aptly summarized by Queen Street, which was described as 'an imposing and handsome thoroughfare' by the end of the seventies, though by the mid-twentieth century it was apparent to an informed observer that this street 'could not be reckoned as one of the more commercially successful.'[53] Queen Street was an expression of unfulfilled hope, a gesture towards an era of urban development and material progress based on the railways but which the railways never stimulated to the extent, or in the manner, expected. The street indeed remained a monument to great expectations and an interesting record of architectural development. Queen Street, it was pointed out by a directory of the seventies, was the modern portion of the city. After entering Exeter from that direction a visitor would be 'much struck with the picturesque old houses still remaining in the principal thoroughfares, with their timbered fronts, carved brackets, grotesque heads and overhanging storeys.'[54] Houses such as these evoked memories of Exeter's true 'Victorian' period in so far as the term in relation to cities is synonymous with enterprise and growth. In this sense Exeter's 'Victorian' era lay in Tudor and Stuart England.

What was becoming significant in the Exeter of the

seventies was not so much growth as change. The proliferation of overhead wires which encumber the rooftops of modern cities had begun in 1863 when the improvement commissioners had approved in principle an application from the United Kingdom Telegraph Company for 'leave to erect a line of Pole Telegraph (*sic*) on the tops of houses and other buildings in the vicinity of Exeter.'[55] The application of modern techniques to street improvement was first broached in 1870. In that year, on the day when the Prussian ambassador was conveying to his king news of war fervour in Paris, the streets committee discussed the acquisition of a 12-ton steam roller,[56] an experiment which was postponed till 1885 because it was deemed inadvisable to incur the expenditure of £425. The purchase of a steam roller from loan funds in 1885 was indeed a minor example of the new possibilities opened up for local authorities by the financial provisions of the Public Health Act of 1875.

In the seventies, too, the long years of the great agricultural depression had begun. 'The squire seemed struck in the saddle' and the rural provincial society of which Exeter had been the capital was in its decline. With vitality draining away from the countryside of the west, as the census returns demonstrate, the prosperity derived from Exeter's position as a centre for the distribution of goods and services also declined. The railways, once regarded as the harbingers of new prosperity for the city, so far had merely increased competition. As Surtees, an astute observer of the rural scene, observed in 1865: 'London being now accessible to everybody . . . people get sucked up to the capital almost incontinently and talk of going to town just as their forefathers talked of going to sessions or assizes.'[57] London was assuming the functions which previously had been performed by the great provincial capitals. The trips to London by people of all classes recorded by the local newspapers at the time of the Great Exhibition of 1851 were evidence of a form of competition for which there was no compensation until the reverse flow began with the widening popularity of west country holidays in the latter years of the century. Since Exeter could offer no serious alternatives in the form of

large-scale industrial enterprise, or the social attractions
which led to the phenomenal growth of Cheltenham and
Bournemouth, the city was being relegated to the side-lines
of national life.

VII

SOCIAL AND ECONOMIC AFFAIRS

1850–1870

ECONOMIC historians have formed a 'clear impression of a substantially improving standard of life between 1850 and 1870.'[1] Though this generalization may be statistically accurate when applied to the country as a whole no such clear impression can be formed of Exeter. Undoubtedly for most people above the level of the artisan, and for those artisans in good health and regular employment, conditions were improving. By the end of the period some imported foods, such as tea and sugar, were substantially cheaper. Bread was much cheaper. There were new amenities. Sewing machines could be bought for £3 15s. By 1858 it was possible to enjoy sea bathing at Dawlish for a return fare of 6d.; and in 1870 a tour of the Dart by rail and boat from Exeter cost 2s.[2] Housing was becoming improved and sanitary arrangements were being modernized. And at the bottom of the social scale the paupers in the workhouse were living under better conditions in 1870 than they were in 1850.

Yet the period 1850 to 1870 in Exeter is distinguished chiefly by two outbreaks of bread riots, in 1854 and 1867, and by stark problems of unemployment and destitution. The well-being of the city's working class cannot be gauged by the wages of some skilled men in favourable circumstances; and few even of these men could look forward to a regular income. There was certainly some improvement in wages. The carpenters employed by the council, who were paid 2s. 10d. a day till 1845, thereafter were paid 3s., a rate which was maintained till at least 1856 when the series of city treasurer's vouchers ends. By 1870 Mark Kennaway was paying a carpenter 4s. a day for eleven hours' work.[3] But he had paid a carpenter at the rate of 3s. 10d. a day for three days' work in 1838[4] and it would be rash to deduce the fact that carpenters' wages had risen from 2s. 10d. to 3s. and thence to 4s.

The essential factor determining standards of living in Exeter between 1850 and 1870 was not so much wage levels as fluctuations in prices and irregularity of employment. This factor underlay the bread riots of 1854 and 1867.

In January 1854 the city was concerned to note that the 'severity of the weather, and the dear prices of food and fuel, have fallen upon the poor with an extreme severity, that excites for them the deepest commiseration.'[5] The cold was bitter, in England as in the Crimea. Heavy snow and frost hampered traffic in the west country by road and rail. Ashburton experienced one of the heaviest snowfalls in living memory. In the opinion of local observers food had risen to nearly double its former price. Fine flour in the Exeter market was sold at 63s. to 64s. a sack, seconds for 61s. to 62s. Potatoes rose to 1s. 4d. the score. By the first week in January the price of the quartern loaf was 9d.[6] The severe weather was causing serious unemployment. There were mutterings against the bakers.

The situation was sufficiently serious to stir the conscience of the city. In the parishes door-to-door collections were made for the relief of the poor, though it was remarked that in St Sidwell's and St James' the donations were very small and did not amount, if distributed, to more than 1d. or 1½d. a head.[7] The corporation of the poor decided, with marked lack of enthusiasm, to increase the rate of outdoor relief by one-third.[8] At this time the scale of outdoor relief was regulated by a decision of 1848. Paupers over seventy were relieved at discretion. The aged and infirm under seventy received not more than 2s. 6d. a week for single persons. A man and his wife together received 4s. 6d. a week unless requiring a nurse. Mothers with bastards received not more than 1s. a week and a loaf before the birth of each child, thereafter 1s. a week and a loaf for four weeks. Able-bodied widows with one or more children were assisted at discretion during the first month of widowhood and then received a sum not exceeding 1s. 6d. for each child. Deserted women and their families were sent to the workhouse or were eligible for 1s. 6d. a week. Temporary relief, if the head of the family were sick, amounted to 2s. a week for the man, 1s. 6d. for the wife and 1s. for each child, children over the age of twelve years being excluded.

In January 1854 a meeting in the Guildhall under the chairmanship of the mayor was informed that there were at least 13,000 poor in the city and probably more, even excluding men earning over 12s. a week 'unless sick or with large families.'[9] This figure amounted to over one-third of the population of the city. It was proposed that the meeting should approve a distribution of 6d. a head, less than the price of one quartern loaf, from the balance of the relief fund. To this proposal W. H. Furlong, treasurer of the corporation of the poor, objected in forthright terms. The corporation had just agreed to increase outdoor relief by one-third. If they had been aware of the proposal to distribute a further 6d. a head, and to institute an immediate appeal for further subscriptions for relief, the corporation might have acted differently.

'It was no doubt their duty to relieve to a legitimate extent the necessities of the poor, and they had the means placed in their hands as rates, but he did not like calling upon those who paid the rates to put their hands in their pockets before it was necessary. He wished to see excluded from the distribution all those who received the one-third additional assistance, until they actually cried out that the absence of that additional relief left them in dire want.'

To this incarnation of Scrooge and Gradgrind, R. S. Cornish, whose benevolence included entertainments for pauper children, reasonably replied that the poor had already proved their need by 'suffering for some weeks.' He suggested that those who sat comfortably in warm rooms should see for themselves conditions in St Sidwell's parish, where the poor were under the pressure of a severe winter. The meeting was reminded that the extra relief proposed would begin only that week. The proposal to make a distribution was accordingly carried. It was also agreed that a sum not exceeding £100 should be allocated to soup kitchens.

In the meantime the price of wheat in Exeter rose to 11s. a

bushel, on Friday 6 January. On the following Monday the price of the 4 lb. loaf was raised to 9*d*.[10] In the slums of what the *Gazette*[11] termed the 'Alsatia' of the west quarter women were gathering in groups to discuss the situation. There were threats against the corn merchants and ominous references to the troubles of '47. Groups coalesced and were joined by men and youths. Stones were thrown, smashing windows in the Cathedral Close. The disorder spread and a mob advanced into St Thomas breaking windows and attacking shops. At Exminster, some four miles from Exeter, 'a group of ragged people, men, women and children' advanced on the house of Edwin Trood, a prosperous farmer who had been criticized for paying his labourers no more than 8*s*. a week. Trood's father had narrowly escaped death at the hands of a mob in 1797 and his son's evidence before the assistant poor law commissioners in 1843 had been remarkable for his advocacy of the whip to keep apprentices in order. He had been fined £1 for horsewhipping a girl and upon this had ordered his apprentices out of the house.[12] In 1854 there was damage and looting before the Trood household was saved by the opportune arrival of the dragoons.

The effervescence in Exeter was brief though similar troubles occurred elsewhere in Crediton, Tiverton, Taunton and Bideford. The *Annual Register* explained reassuringly that these west country disturbances were the only violent reactions to privations which 'were borne generally throughout the kingdom with exemplary patience'; they were ascribed entirely to 'the idle and depraved part of the inhabitants.'[13] The damage and looting in Exeter seems to have been the work of a relatively small number of women, youths and boys from the slums; but if the west country disturbances were unique they were the more significant because they occurred in an area which had been singularly quiescent in the stormy period of the 1830s and 1840s, apart from the riots of 1847.

Exeter's reaction was complacent. Because the city had no manufactures liable to the fluctuations experienced by large-scale industry and because the winters were usually mild, it was suggested that the poor lacked 'fortitude and endurance of great severity by want of frequent periodical experience thereof.' According to the *Western Times* the solution lay in the education of the poor, who should learn 'in so far as they blamed the bakers for high prices, that the principle of trade is to buy very cheap and sell very dear; and trade can be carried on by no other principle.' In the *Gazette's* view the poor had not only displayed ingratitude for prompt assistance given during the emergency but also a 'consummate ignorance of the laws which regulated the supply and price of bread.'[14]

This annunciation of the austere principles of orthodox economics did not help the working class of Exeter to obtain higher wages or employment in a restricted market. Thirteen years later, in 1867, the city was again disturbed by riots.

In contrast to 1854, informed opinion in November 1867 considered that there was no serious distress in the city. The weather had been mild. Labour was said to be abundant and wages rising. Yet the city was restless to an extent which could not be explained by the preparations for the annual fifth of November turmoil in the Cathedral Close. The populace was 'in a very gunpowdery condition . . . rather more than common.'[15]

In view of the rumours that a riot was likely the mayor, Alderman Head, took the precaution of issuing a notice to the press. He announced his attendance at the Guildhall to swear in 'those well-disposed citizens prepared to act as special constables.'[16] In the meantime a meeting held at Teignmouth on 1 November had developed into a riot which caused substantial damage to the shops of butchers and bakers.

On the evening of Monday 4 November curious citizens crossed the Exe bridge to look for the disturbances which, it was rumoured, were brewing in St Thomas. St Thomas was quiet; but as the crowd climbed Fore Street hill back into Exeter some of the rougher elements began throwing stones at shop windows. When night fell disorder spread throughout the city. Windows were smashed, bakers' shops as usual being singled out for attention, and there was some looting. The police failed to restore order. By midnight the mob, mostly young men and women, were roaming the city with little opposition. At the Guildhall the mayor conferred with the staff of the East Devon Militia whom he took with him, accompanied by magistrates and police, on a tour of the city which lasted till 1.30 a.m. By 2.0 a.m. troops from the 20th Regiment stationed in Devonport arrived by special train and forthwith made a show of force by parading through the city with the mayor and the police. For the time being order was restored.

The following day was Guy Fawkes Day. Exeter awaited further excitements. Elsewhere in Devon there was rioting at Torquay and some disturbance at Crediton. At Exmouth, where bakers and butchers were attacked, women and boys clamoured for cheap bread. Bakers' shops were attacked and looted in Bradninch.[17] In Exeter it was decided to prohibit the customary bonfire in the Cathedral Close. The decision was resented and the night was more than usually riotous. The special constables on duty in the Cathedral Close were forced to retreat under fire from stones and fireworks.

To restore order the soldiers marched into the Cathedral Close with fixed bayonets. For the moment the mob was cowed, but the disorder was renewed as soon as the troops were withdrawn. The yeomanry patrolling with drawn swords under the command of the Earl of Devon, Sir John Duckworth and J. H. Buller, as usual made the situation worse. Fireworks proved an effective deterrent against horses untrained in riot drill and the discomfited yeomanry were withdrawn. The mob then determined to celebrate its victory with the customary bonfire. There was a movement down to St Thomas to capture the timber wagons which an officer had wisely prevented from crossing the Exe into the city. The bridge, however, was firmly held by the truncheons of county constables backed by the fixed bayonets of the troops. A lively skirmish in the darkness followed, with hard blows on both sides, until the constables began to give way under pressure and were withdrawn to give an opening to the troops. Then the mob broke before the advancing bayonets and the disturbance died down in the small hours of 6 November.

These troubles provoked the pained disapproval of the London *Times*, which pointed out that the prices of bread and meat in Devon were moderate compared with those prevailing elsewhere.[18] The local press took the same line. The *Gazette* was shocked by the revelation of 'the unpleasant truth that we have in our country large numbers of a dangerous class ready to create tumult on the slight pretences.' Butchers and bakers were acquitted of any anti-social activities; it was, however, urged that steps should be taken to 'disabuse the working class of errors which are disgraceful to our civilization.'[19]

The mayor apparently made little attempt to probe the cause of the disturbances. He reported to the home office that there was 'nothing in the price of provisions or in the destitution of the poorer classes to justify the outbreak.' The price of food was high, 'perhaps as regards the price of meat rather higher than the market prices of fat stock justified,' but Alderman Head thought that the 'price of wages or labour was – relatively to other periods of high prices, higher.' He had received no information of destitution or want 'other than such casual cases as are always occurring in every large city.'[20] Accordingly he came to the comforting conclusion that the disturbances had been caused by emissaries from outside the city and suggested as a solution the arming of the police.

The outbreak of disturbances in the ordered world of a small cathedral city requires further explanation. The period 1850–70 may well have been one of 'rapid and nearly continuous economic advance' and for that statistical abstraction, the average wage-earner, conditions had no doubt materially improved since the 1840s. But the quiet and deferential society of small Devon towns and villages, Cullompton and Torquay, Exmouth, Teignmouth and Bradninch, would not easily have been stirred into riot, especially if the working classes had been as conscious of economic advance as were later historians. And if the underworld of Exeter was rough it was neither unpoliced nor unsupervised. Turbulence in November 1867 was doubtless influenced by the horseplay and excitement of 5 Novem-

L

ber, which was normally riotous. This undoubtedly happened in 1879. But it cannot explain the outbreaks elsewhere in south and east Devon in 1867.

Despite the weighty opinion of the contemporary newspapers there can be little doubt that the root cause of the troubles of 1867, as of 1854 and 1847, was economic. In the autumn of 1867 the corporation of the poor in Exeter was paying 7d. for the quartern loaf, at wholesale prices.[21] This was an increase of one halfpenny since March. By the following March the tender price had risen to 8d. According to the report of the poor law board for 1866-67 the average contract price for the loaf during that year was 6d. in Lambeth, $5\frac{1}{2}d$. to $7\frac{1}{4}d$. in Birmingham and $4\frac{1}{2}d$. to $5\frac{1}{2}d$. in Bury St Edmunds. Butter prices ranged from $10\frac{1}{2}d$. to 1s. per lb. in Lambeth to 1s. to 1s. $\frac{1}{2}d$. in Bury St Edmunds.[22] The Exeter corporation of the poor was paying 1s. 6d. per lb. Tea in Exeter was bought at 2s. per lb., much higher than the average price in Lambeth and Birmingham, though much less than the 3s. paid by Bury St Edmunds. Sugar on the other hand was cheapest in Exeter at 34s. per cwt. Meat according to the tenders of the corporation of the poor was also relatively cheap. Figures such as these are not conclusive but they suggest that prices in Exeter were not an insignificant factor in the disturbances, especially if accompanied by unemployment. And in December 1867 the figures for out-relief had risen to 1,046, rather more than a 5 per cent. increase on the total for December 1866.[23] By the 1870s the city was to become seriously alarmed by the extent of destitution and unemployment.

In the west country as a whole the period 1850 to 1870 was one of prosperity. It was the St Martin's summer of the old agricultural interest. The mining industry was at its peak with copper production rising to its maximum of 41,000 tons of ore in 1862.[24] Railway construction was bringing money and work into the countryside though it also hastened the depopulation of the small towns ignored by the new lines. The new station at St David's was completed in June 1864 to replace the original structure built by the Hoopers in Pennyroyal Fields twenty years previously. The building was the work of a Taunton firm of builders though the ironwork was provided by Kerslake of Exeter. The local press claimed that the new station, Doric in style, was unrivalled throughout the country for the facilities offered for passenger traffic. The claim was not unjustified. It was a period of sharp competition between the Bristol and Exeter and the London and South Western railways which resulted in rapidly improving facilities for travellers to the west country both in regard to speed and comfort.[25] Since the lines of both competitors had to pass through Exeter, the city was in due course the beneficiary. But in 1864 Exeter had ceased to acclaim railway development with the jubilation of 1844, or even with the more cautious optimism of 1860. In 1864 it was observed that the new station was brought into use very quietly. There were no flags, speeches or bell-ringing.

Building generally had shown signs of revival since 1852, with the result that there was a vigorous demand for bricks which previously had been disposed of by auction. Trade was active and in 1867 Frederick Thomas, 'The Practical Hatter' and a well-known local character placed a substantial order worth £25,000 in France.[26]

Land and building property were still the usual field of investment for those with money to spare. The solicitor advertising in the *Gazette* in 1869 'sums ranging from £350 to £180,000 to lend on freehold estates at 4 per cent.'[27] was a feature of the period. But the field was widening. By the mid-nineteenth century the city's Forsytes were finding opportunities for speculation and profit, and for some loss, in British financial operations overseas as well as in railways and west country mines. Mark Kennaway's portfolio in this period included the Lancashire and Yorkshire railway, the London and North Western and the London, Chatham and Dover. In 1861, Kennaway was buying Illinois Railway Construction bonds and New York and Erie Mortgage bonds. He held an interest in the Vancouver Coal Mining Company and was also an investor in Spanish bonds, which he was glad to sell in 1864. By 1867 he was turning his attention to Italy with a cautious investment of £50 in the Lombard-Venetian railway.[28]

Despite these signs of a widening range of investments, the failure of Overend and Gurney in 1866, and the events which led to one of the most serious financial catastrophes of the century, were watched with little more than detached interest in Exeter. The financial house of Overend and Gurney failed for more than £5,000,000 but the published lists of shareholders included few local names. Even the Exeter City Bank was not seriously affected by the disaster though Overend and Gurney had been its London agents. Prudence had been a characteristic of the Exeter banks since their foundation in the eighteenth century.

The census reports[29] indicate that there had been no fundamental change in the economic structure of the city as compared with the past twenty years or more. Boot and shoe makers, labourers, messengers, errand boys and porters, masons, paviors and tailors; carpenters and joiners; such were the largest occupational groups in the city in 1861. There was no concentration of employment in one or two industries as in contemporary Leicester where, out of 31,766 males, 3,855 were employed in hose manufacture. By 1871 over 13 per cent. of the males aged twenty and over in Exeter were employed in building and ancillary occupations, a larger proportion than in contemporary Bath, Leicester, York and Gloucester.

On the basis of the census categories the industrial class in 1871 amounted to just over 55 per cent. of the male population aged twenty and over, a lower proportion than in Leicester, Nottingham and Northampton, higher than in Bath and Gloucester. The professional class, almost 10 per cent., formed a far higher proportion than in Leicester, Nottingham, Gloucester and Northampton. It was even higher than Brighton but below that of Bath.

By the year 1861, employment was being stimulated by work on the railway line between Queen Street and St David's which was brought into use in the following year. Railway engine drivers, railway officials, railway servants and police numbered 166. Railway labourers, platelayers and navvies together numbered 240. The railways were therefore giving direct employment to some 400 men in Exeter by 1861, more than twice as many as were similarly employed in Plymouth, Devonport and Bath, though less than the number in York.

The great days of coaching were long past but Exeter still lived by its position as the gateway to the west. The railways could not deliver passengers and goods to every town and village and the number of coachowners, coachmen, guards, postboys, grooms and hostlers, carters, waggoners and carriers in Exeter increased. In 1871 over 8 per cent. of the male population aged twenty and over were engaged in the conveyance of men, animals, goods and horses, the same proportion as in Bath and York, higher than in Norwich and Leicester.

Technical change was apparent in 1861 with the appearance of nine men employed in the telegraph service. Civil engineers increased from four to twenty-four between 1851 and 1861. In 1861 five 'photographic artists' and ten gas fitters appeared in the census lists for the first time; a photographer, Owen Angel, reached the city council. In the same period engine and machine makers increased from twenty-one to sixty-two, fourteen of the latter being under the age of twenty. Thatchers were disappearing; only four remained in 1861 and all were over twenty. Employment in the traditional occupations such as skinners, combmakers, fullers and fellmongers continued to decline. Between 1841 and 1861 fullers were reduced from thirty-eight to fourteen and those employed in woollen cloth manufacture from thirty-eight to eleven. In 1861 these two occupations employed only one male below the age of twenty.

For women, domestic service, millinery and dressmaking remained the main sources of employment. In 1861, 1,848 women and girls were employed as general domestic servants and over 3,600 in all branches of domestic service including charwomen and washerwomen, more than 60 per cent. of all women in employment other than housewives. In contemporary Leicester only 1,830 out of 36,560 females were so employed. In contrast, Leicester employed 4,862 women in the hosiery and stocking manufacture, worsted and cotton, glove-making and leather. Nottingham offered employment for women in the boot and shoe industry. On the other hand the Exeter of 1861 contained 245 women classified as gentlewomen. Inevitably there were twice as many in Bath; but there were only 185 in Norwich, 121 in Leicester and sixty-eight in Northampton. The post office in Exeter had as yet no female employee. There was only one female tobacconist compared with seven in Bath; mid-Victorian Exeter could offer no opening for a lady with the varied talents of Lucy Sponge.[30]

Moderate wealth and moderate popularity as a place for retirement still distinguished Exeter. If, in 1871, there were only nine retired officers living in the city compared with 162 in Bath and seventy-four in Brighton, there were none in Leicester, Gloucester or Nottingham. In the social world of the 1870s domestic coachmen and a private carriage were an important status symbol. There were thirty domestic coachmen in Exeter in 1871 compared with eighty-five in Bath. Census figures such as these cannot be regarded as conclusive evidence of relative degrees of affluence since so much depends on the extent to which the wealthier residential areas were included within the municipal boundaries existing at the time. Carriage folk would not normally be found living in the business areas of any town or city. The Exeter figures would undoubtedly be higher if the suburbs of Heavitree and St Leonard's were included.

In a city where change was slow and economic expansion negligible wages rose slowly. Since there was no wage structure of general application, remuneration depended on the circumstances of the job and the mood or generosity of the employer. William Tuckett, a carpenter regularly employed by Mark Kennaway, and his boy, were paid 4s. 6d. for work at Hoopern House in 1857. In 1873 Kennaway paid 6s. to Tuckett and an apprentice for erecting a fence and gateposts.[31] It was not, indeed, till 1873 that the Exeter master builders agreed after a strike that all branches of the building trade should be paid at hourly rates and hence introduced a measure of uniformity. But even in 1914 there remained a wide disparity in the rates earned by artisans. Navvies working on the railway in the vicinity of

Exeter were paid 3s. 6d. to 4s. a day in 1858 and the magistrates to whom a wage dispute was referred expressed the view that 3s. 9d. was a fair wage.[32] In 1869 masons employed on the construction of the Victoria Hall, a rush job, earned from 22s. to 27s. a week, or from 3s. 8d. to 4s. 6d. a day; but evidence was given during a strike that there was no fixed rate for the job, the men being paid what the sub-contractor thought they were worth.[33] Three years later, in 1872, the Exeter foundry workers sought a pay increase from 12s. to 13s. a week, the former being the wage received by Glasgow builders' labourers in 1850.[34]

Police constables on first appointment were paid 16s. a week from 1847 to 1859 when they received an increase of 1s. In 1872 there was another increase of 1s.[35] Hours were long. Men working on Hoopern House in 1869 put in sixty-five hours a week for which they were each paid 19s. 6d.[36] In 1873 the Exeter building operatives secured an agreement that the week's work should consist of fifty-six and a half hours, including six hours' work on Saturdays terminating at 1 o'clock.[37] Shop assistants worked even longer hours, though in 1863 it was reported that some tradesmen, being 'anxious to give their assistants as much recreation as possible,' decided to close at 5.0 p.m. on Saturdays.[38]

There is indeed no clear evidence of any general improvement in wages in Exeter between 1850 and 1870. The foundry workers who received 12s. a week in 1872 in fact were paid less than the permanent labourers of the council in 1850, and less than post office porters who were paid 15s. a week in 1866. Domestic service continued to be a relatively privileged occupation, at least with a good employer. It offered food and a roof, clothes, and some training and education for young girls. In 1870 domestic servants as a class still had the largest average deposit, £34 14s. 5d., in the Devon and Exeter Savings Bank. For some domestic servants wages had increased. In 1854 a good cook was offered £14 a year with beer money. By 1871 a 'good plain cook' could earn £10 – £16 a year.[39] In 1871 Mark Kennaway paid £7 a year with beer money at 1s. 3d. a week to a maid on entering his service and £7 a year appears to have been the normal starting wage for a maid in 1871. Kennaway's butler, who was responsible for the supervision of his household, was paid £61 a year.[40]

Artisans at this time paid some £7 to £10 a year in rent. The construction of Newtown had originally been begun with the £8-a-year rent-payer in mind and by 1858 eighty houses in Chute Street were yielding a total rent of £800.[41] Strong's Cottages, Sidwell Street, described in 1857 as 'modern, brick-built and slated' were leased at a gross rent of £44 per annum or £7 4s. 4d. each. This rent is comparable to the £7 rent 'clear of all taxes except Property Tax, Land Tax and Church Rate' received by Mark Kennaway in 1868 from William Clement, policeman on the Bristol and Exeter Railway, for No. 6, St David's Hill.[42] A grocer, one Mr Hill, had paid £15 a year for a 'good eight-room house in Melbourne Street' in 1851.[43] In 1852 houses in St James's Terrace with two kitchens, coal cellar, two sitting rooms, three bedrooms, two good attics and water were available at £20 per annum with all taxes paid by the landlord. The rent was apparently unchanged in 1865.[44] Houses in Dix's Field were leased at £30 in Southernhay and St Leonard's, houses; were available at a rent of £60 to £70.[45]

In 1873 a letter to the press stated that 'the mechanic is compelled to pay just one-quarter of his income for the shelter of a roof.'[46] This certainly seems to have been the case for the lower-paid artisans living in Chute Street in 1858. But, as the sanitary committee of the Local Board reported in 1870, there were also examples of five to six persons 'sleeping, eating, and in some cases working together, in a single room'; and in 1869 a widow who lost her savings in Charles Wescomb's ventures lived on 3s. a week out of which she paid 1s. 5d. for lodgings in Gatty's Court, St Sidwell's.[47]

Market prices tended to rise. Beef, which could be obtained at 4d. to 6½d. a lb. in 1850, had risen to 7½d. to 9d. by 1870; mutton from 4½d. to 6d.; pork from 7d. to 9d. The meat purchased for the corporation of the poor cost £1 16s. 10d. a cwt. in April 1850, and £3 12s. 10d. in April 1870. But tobacco, sugar, tea and rice were all substantially cheaper.[48] The cheapest tea advertised in 1850 cost 3s. per lb.; in 1870 it was 2s. 4d. The price paid by the corporation of the poor for roll tobacco and shag, which was 4s. 2d. and 3s. 7d. per lb. in 1850, fell to 3s. 10d. and 2s. 11d. by 1870. The cost of cheap dip candles on the other hand rose from 4s. 8d. to 5s. 6d. for twelve gross.[49]

Clothes were becoming rather more expensive. Police boots, for instance, cost the watch committee 12s. 9d. per pair in 1849, 13s. 6d. in 1852 and 15s. in 1871.[50] Moleskin trousers and jackets which could be obtained from Mr Solomons of High Street for 2s. 6d. and 6s. 6d. in 1845 were offered at 3s. 9d. and 8s. 6d in 1870. Corduroy, an important material for workmen's clothing, cost the corporation of the poor 1s. 2d. a yard in 1850 and 2s. 0½d. in 1870.[51] Trousers in winter tweed were offered at 6s. to 8s. 6d. in 1850, and made to measure 'at a trifling advance on the prices quoted' for 12s. 6d. in 1870. In 1850 a cheap workman's suit could be bought for 14s. 6d. In 1870, the cheapest men's black cloth suits advertised cost from 25s. 6d. The ubiquitous silk hats cost as little as 2s. to 4s. 6d. in 1850 though the superior French silk hats ranged from 6s. 6d. to 9s. 6d. Thomas, 'The Practical Hatter,' offered to the more discriminating French silk hats at 10s. 6d., a price which remained unaltered throughout the period.[52]

It is hazardous to attempt the comparison of prices for articles of clothing which may have differed substantially in material. If, however, police boots, corduroy and moleskins can be taken as a guide, it would appear that the cost of men's clothing in Exeter between 1850 and 1870 rose at least as much as wages. An attempt to obtain evidence of economic trends from women's clothes is more hazardous. It was the age of the crinoline and the Lincolnshire couturier Worth. The leading Exeter drapers and modistes continued to deal direct with Paris. In 1870, for example, Messrs Colson and Gates could still 'respectfully announce that Mr Gates is now in Paris making additional selections of the latest novelties in rich silks, mantles, jackets and costumes.' Mrs Treadwin returning from Paris a month later, solicited 'an inspection of Novelties in Lace and Millinery' at No. 5 Cathedral Yard.

There is a distinction between the cost of living and the cost of fashion, and by the end of the period the fashions were changing as the crinoline moved round to the back to become the bustle and looped skirt of the seventies. 'Good useful dresses' could be purchased for between 2s. 9d. and 7s. 11d. each in 1870 and may perhaps be accepted as analogous to print dresses from 3s. 6d. to 7s. 6d. and twill dresses at 1s. 8½d. to 3s. 10d. available as far back as 1836.[53] In the social and economic circumstances of Victorian Exeter few women could aspire to following fashion. For those who could, Mr Tucker 'naturalist and plumasier' of Queen Street, required 'game and wildfowl of all kinds . . . for making into the new and fashionable hats as worn in Paris and London.'[54] England was entering into one of its more blatant periods of conspicuous consumption and 'elegant firescreens' adorned with the slain birds of Devon, were regarded as 'suitable for New Year, Birthday or Wedding Gifts.'[55]

In 1855 the corporation of the poor appointed a new porter at 5s. a week. In addition the man received an issue of rations which included 18 lb. of meat, 28 lb. of potatoes and 32 lb. of bread, besides groceries.[56] On the basis of Exeter market prices, or the advertised prices of groceries in the newspapers, at this time the cost of the porter's ration scale would have been of the order of 17s. 8d. a week. On the same basis the cost in 1870 would have been £1 1s. The test is rough and ready. It suggests an increase in prices of about 33 per cent. There was certainly no general rise of wages in Exeter to this extent between 1850 and 1870 though artisans such as the carpenters and joiners on 3s. 8d. a day in 1873 would not have been badly off by the standards of the time provided that they enjoyed regular employment and some freedom from the vicissitudes of human existence. Official market prices do not in any case necessarily represent the prices paid by housewives with the time and skill required for bargaining in the conditions of the 1870s. Nevertheless, Exeter artisans at this period could not have been regarded as prosperous even if they were fully employed. The ordinary labourer competing with the low agricultural money wages of Exeter's countryside, and without the compensations of an allotment or other traditional perquisites, was infinitely worse off. Exeter with a static economy and without the competition from industrial towns in the vicinity remained a low-wage area and the mass of its wage-earners had no prospect of the rewards which the fortunate might receive elsewhere.

For some, even in Exeter, there were new opportunities for regular and remunerative employment. The post office was expanding. Its chief clerk received £100 a year with annual increments up to a maximum of £170. First-class clerks were paid £100 x £4 – £140; second-class clerks £80 x £4 – £100. Sorting clerks received 20s. a week rising to 30s. Of the eleven letter carriers, one was paid 22s. to 26s. a week, the remainder 16s. to 20s.[57] A firm of wine merchants at this time offered £50 a year plus commission for 'a middle-aged person' to undertake office duties and to travel occasionally.[58]

There were other means of earning a living in Victorian England. According to the superintendent of police the streets of Exeter in the 1850s 'swarmed with prostitutes' mostly between the ages of fifteen and seventeen.[59] In 1863 the first meeting of the Exeter Home for Reclaiming Fallen Women was informed that some of these girls could earn from £30 to £40 a month.[60]

In 1870, when the problem of unemployment forced itself upon the public notice, a builder informed a meeting at the Guildhall that there was always substantial unemployment during the winter months, 'for the reason that many trades could not be carried out during the winter.'[61] The statement emphasizes the difficulty of deducing annual income from individual daily earnings. It also explains the problems faced by a city in which some 13 per cent. of its male labour force aged twenty and over were employed in building and allied activities. The weekly average of outdoor relief according to the records of the corporation of the poor was 757 between December 1856 and December 1857. By 1869 the average was 1,160 and by 1870 it was 1,241. 1,256 persons were in receipt of outdoor relief on 4 January 1870. The conjecture of worried councillors in 1854, that almost half the total population of the city was in need of relief, was almost certainly exaggerated but the extent of destitution was serious. And on a day in the cold February of 1869 it was reported that some 3,000 'soup hungry souls' came to the soup kitchen, many of them in vain.[62]

Many lived perforce under the shadow of the workhouse. The corporation of the poor had appointed a committee in 1856 to inquire into the relief system in the St Thomas union 'in order to lessen the inducement of the poor of the surrounding district to be removed into Exeter which at present exists and also to protect the interests of the city.'[63] The committee found that the scale of relief in Exeter was higher than the union scale. Accordingly the restrictions on cash relief were reiterated. The old principle that able-bodied males should be set to work was emphasized. Outdoor relief for able-bodied widows, deserted women and their families and for temporary relief was reduced by 20 per cent.

The Exeter guardians slowly improved conditions and discipline in the workhouse, not without a constant stream of exhortation, admonition and advice from the poor law board which were not always well received. In 1860 the board found it necessary to point out that the allowance of bread for able-bodied men was smaller than that usually allowed. The guardians and their medical officers were requested 'to have the goodness to consider the propriety of increasing the allowance.' The request was complied with.[64] The request that a treasurer should be appointed as a salaried officer instead of from among the guardians was resented. Hard words were said about centralization and the corporation took a year to comply.[65] The decision to construct a new wing to the workhouse hospital with improved amenities, such as the construction of water closets, was taken in 1856. In 1859 the corporation was asked to do its utmost to encourage the general adoption of vaccination but it was not till nine years later that a public vaccinator and a vaccination officer were appointed. Money was spent on the improvement of children's dormitories and schoolrooms and in 1862 it was decided to give books as prizes 'for good behaviour and advancement in learning.'[66] Much time was given to the problems of pauper lunatics and the novel proposal to apply the methods of mesmerism said to be used in India received anxious consideration.[67]

Discipline recalled the world of *Oliver Twist*. In 1856 a committee reported in severe terms on the management of the house. Two years later a female with two illegitimate children, after being admitted for the twelfth time, had a third child within the house. Inquiry elicited the fact that the female in question had been found on the men's side in a state of intoxication.[68] There was a further report of 'a great want of vigilance and control' in 1858. Rations had been sold and exchanged. A half-paralysed man had been flogged with nettles.[69] Two months later the keys of the front gate were stolen and the master and matron were accordingly asked to resign. The corporation had some difficulty in finding suitable successors and the next couple appointed had to resign because the poor law board refused confirmation.[70] The new master, Mr Dunn, eventually appointed was in due course admonished because he had 'forgotten his duty as the Master of the Workhouse . . . and lowered himself as a Father of a Family.' The master had given a dance to entertain the female paupers. A fiddler was hired at his expense and the festivities continued till midnight in the presence of Mrs Dunn and Master and Miss Dunn. 'Plenty of Beer and plenty of Fun were had on the occasion. All enjoyed themselves and all got jolly,' including two women dressed in men's clothes.[71] In June of that year there was a more serious incident. Referring to the treatment of one of the female paupers the guardians 'could not but express their surprise and indignation that anyone would have been so brutally used.' The incident had been a 'gross outrage' and a 'disgusting business.' Unfortunately owing to the delay in making a complaint the guardians were deprived of the opportunity to inflict a punishment. One of the assistants concerned had left the house and the other was said to be dangerously ill.[72]

It is not altogether surprising that the house was unpopular or that at almost every meeting of the corporation of the poor the master reported that of those ordered to present themselves for admission few or none had appeared. But progress was made. By 1869 the poor law board commissioners reported on

'the fidelity with which the Guardians were discharging the onerous duties they had undertaken . . . The efficiency of the Officers employed in the establishment, the order and cleanliness which is a credit to their diligence and ability . . . the Provisions good (the Bread remarkably good), the ventilation excellent, the cleanliness of the persons remarkable.'

The situation of the sick wards was described as 'expressive of practical benevolence.' The regulations were practical 'being as far from grinding down on the one hand as from maudlin sentimentalism on the other.'[73]

By the 1870s practical benevolence was gathering strength in Exeter with a growing awareness that the city was in part a noisome slum. Public baths and wash-houses had been opened in 1852 and had been used by 140,000 people by the time they were closed for repairs in 1858.[74] In that year the filth of the Exeter slums was forced on the unwilling attention of the magistrates in the Guildhall. A woman appearing before the court on that occasion 'was so dirty and the effluvia emitted from her person was so offensive' that she was ordered to stand in the doorway.[75] Five out of the eight persons admitted to the workhouse one day in June 1860 had 'the itch' and three had venereal disease.[76] Effluvia is the prevailing note in the records of the city at this period: the stink of river where the effluent from the St Leonard's sewers discharged above the surface of the water; the open gutters of Tudor Street and the open drain under the Iron Bridge; 'the offensive and unwholesome state of the public urinals for the want of a continuous supply of water.'[77] In 1870 the magistrates at the Guildhall again had occasion to note the unhealthy condition of the city and complained to the sanitary committee about the 'most noisome and offensive smell' from the closets, which had made it necessary to remove a prisoner from the cells in the vicinity.[78] The reports of the medical officers of the time are a tale of diarrhoea, scarlatina, overcrowded rooms, and nuisances caused by the existence of piggeries in residential areas. The death-rate in Exeter in 1861–70 averaged 25.3 per thousand. It was higher than in York, Derby and Plymouth. In Cobden's Manchester the death-rate averaged 32.7.[79] Exeter as a whole received water on an average of five hours a day. Many houses had to rely on cisterns that were inefficient and unwholesome.

In 1869 the *Gazette* summarized the causes of high mortality under three heads: 'the precipitation of the sewerage into the rivers; the foul condition of the poor; and the unfavourable circumstances under which the city is supplied with water.'[80] The sanitary committee agreed. The committee also pointed out that the lack of adequate accommodation was a 'great evil from both a sanitary and moral point of view.' The situation was brought to the attention of the mayor 'with a view to the furtherance of a plan for the erection of dwellings for the labouring classes' and the press was requested to draw public attention to the problem.[81]

If in 1850 Exeter had stood proudly before the world as a provincial capital, by 1870 the city had plunged to its nineteenth-century nadir. The railways had been greeted as the harbingers of material prosperity and moral progress; but the reality was destitution and unemployment. No one in 1870 apparently recalled Buckingham's quotation from George Oliver, in 1867, that 'no reasonable being need seek elsewhere a residence more salubrious.'[82] Worse conditions could no doubt have been found in Exeter a generation earlier, or elsewhere in the England which had reached the peak of its economic power in the 1870s. But the cathedral city and ancient provincial capital which had once stood in the forefront of national life and still prided itself on a civilized tradition had discovered that even by contemporary standards it had little to its credit.

LATE VICTORIAN EXETER

M

VIII

TRANSITION - EXETER IN 1870

BY the end of the sixties the tides that had been sweeping through the main channels of national life and had raised the country as a whole to the peak of its economic power, had now reached the remoter creeks and inlets. Scarcely discernible at any one point in their quiet motion, they had reached a level at which the cumulative effect was apparent. Most of the older generation who had wielded influence in Exeter in the days of Reform were either dead or withdrawn from active life. With them had gone the hopefulness which remembered the city's great days as a provincial capital and looked forward to their revival in the future. For the first time the dominant note of the city was not one of civic pride but of doubt and self-criticism. Exeter was being seen for what it was, a survivor from a declining society which could offer few prospects to the bulk of its citizens. And even the rural society of which the city was the centre was beginning to lose its economic prosperity and social and political position.

In November 1869 Mr Burt of Torquay had advertised for lease or sale a

'highly desirable family mansion . . . having a spacious Italian corridor and staircase, five lofty and elegant reception rooms . . . vineries, hot-houses, Italian gardens, lawns and pleasure grounds . . . the seat of the late Right Reverend the Lord Bishop of Exeter.'[1]

The formidable Henry of Exeter had died in September 1869, aged ninety-one. 'That devil of a bishop,' Lord Melbourne had once written, 'who inspired more terror than ever Satan did . . . of whom, however, it must be said that he is a gentleman.'[2]

An able administrator, and brilliant controversialist, Phillpotts had the ruthlessness not uncommon in those who seek earnestly for truth by the 'Dark Lanthorn of the Spirit' and, having found truth, seek to impose it upon others. The bishop had raised the prestige of the church throughout his diocese. He had striven, with little understanding from the zealots of either side, to hold the balance between Tractarians and Evangelicals. Though over-ruled by the judicial committee of the privy council in the Gorham case, a political decision which was probably essential to retain the Evangelicals in the Church of England, the bishop's fame stood high. Despite opposition among the laity and clergy of his cathedral city, he had organized and brought to a successful conclusion the Exeter Synod of 1851, in itself a protest against state interference in things spiritual and a demonstration of vitality within the church itself. Hated, feared and respected, Henry of Exeter was Exeter's outstanding contribution to national history in early Victorian England.

The diversity of opinion on Henry of Exeter reflects the complexity of his character. Melbourne's comment, coming from a Whig magnate, implied respect as well as impatience with a man who added so much to Melbourne's own work. To the Evangelical *Flying Post*, the bishop had appeared 'cold and repulsive'; to the Liberal *Western Times* he had been a man with 'an unbridled lust for power.' In Gladstone's eyes he had been 'a great practical divine.' Dr Shapter, a moderate Anglican, recorded in later years that Phillpotts had been 'throughout his administrations a consistent churchman looking solely to the law of the church as his guide and alike condemning those who succeeded and those who failed in their fulfilment of it.' And when news of the bishop's death reached the edge of Dartmoor a Nonconformist congregation were told by their minister that Phillpotts had been

'a great and good man who had swept away abuses with a strong hand and left many good works to testify of him. It was said of him that his charity was deficient, but it was not for them to judge one who had so humbly judged himself.'[3]

Ralph Barnes, bishop's secretary and chapter clerk, had died shortly before the bishop himself, aged eighty-eight and working to the end. Barnes had been an enigmatic figure, a member of the family network of bankers, surgeons and clergy which the Sanders and Barnes families maintained in the higher circles of local power. Industrious, cautious, austere, learned in the classics and a terror to law students, Barnes appeared cold to strangers and was respected rather than liked. His discretion had been such that he was the subject of tributes from all the Exeter papers on his death in May 1869. Even the *Western Times* praised his 'talents and abilities of a high order, [his] strong sense of duty and his untiring energy and industry.'[4]

Less eminent figures than that of Phillpotts had left the stage by 1870. The newspaper proprietors Woolmer and Robert Trewman were both dead. James Bellerby, who took over control of the *Flying Post*, retained something of the old tradition. The *Exeter and Plymouth Gazette* after Woolmer's death had become a party instrument. Dr Shapter lived till 1902, at length dying blind and forgotten in Surrey. His reputation seems to have suffered in consequence of his acceptance of a legacy in circumstances which led to an inquiry by the commissioners of lunacy who criticized Shapter adversely.[5] Attorney John Carew, who had brought a county family to the mayoralty at the 'Restoration' of 1840, died in 1869 leaving a will proved at under £50,000.

Mark Kennaway, in contemporary opinion a Whig of the old school, had made his last important public appearance, on behalf of the improvement commissioners, in 1867. He died, aged eighty-one, in 1875. 'Favoured with a good voice, an excellent delivery, fluency of speech, but, above all, with a degree of self-confidence which is essential to a public speaker,'[6] Kennaway was one of the dour school of Utilitarians rather than a Whig. Pre-eminent as Liberal leader in the days of Reform, he was never mayor. He had his last chance for office in 1866 but was apparently kept out by unrelenting Conservative opposition. Though the Liberals, like the Conservatives, frequently deplored the intrusion of politics into council affairs, it was Mark Kennaway who had declared in early days, when the Reformers were riding high, that 'the election of councillors was a political act.'[7] The

Western Times, still under Thomas Latimer, was reduced in these days to mourning the passing of the paladins of the old battles for Reform; men such as Joseph Sayell, maltster and Reformer, 'possessing those qualities which make the bone and brain of our middle-class society and give tone and timber to the body politic'; Samuel Segar Bastard, one of 'those Liberals whose lives, like his, cover the period of the mighty stir that accompanied the preparation of the Reform Bills, [and had] a firmness of texture in their political constitution not always to be met with in the younger generation.'[8] Men such as these belonged to a generation which believed that publicity and an extended franchise would necessarily lead to government by the wisest and the best. By 1870 the *Western Times* was asserting that the city was 'in a sad state of discontent; and traders and others who have a stake in it will do well to consider the heavy penalty they are likely to bear for neglecting the duty which belongs to their station.'[9]

Phillpotts' successor at Exeter was in all respects Victorian, unlike Phillpotts himself, and was to exert his potent influence to bring the city into line with progressive Victorian thought. The appointment of Frederick Temple to the see of Exeter, like that of his predecessor forty years before, raised a storm in the diocese. But the new bishop's orthodoxy was in question, not his politics. Temple's moderate contribution to the controversial *Essays and Reviews*, studies in liberal churchmanship published in 1860, was alleged in angry letters to the press to have been responsible for souls 'carried off in the whirlpool of unbelief.'[10] Archbishop Tait was asked whether there were any means of preventing the prime minister, Gladstone, from pushing matters to an extremity since he had 'chosen the worst diocese in England to practise on.'[11] The chapter itself was divided, the bishop being elected by thirteen votes to six. Dissident clergy, including the sub-dean and the archdeacon, published a protest.

The laity of the city were not greatly stirred by the controversy. They were impressed by Temple's personality. In the misty cold of 29 December 1869, the new bishop made his first appearance in the cathedral pulpit. Discarding his prepared sermon he declared to the great congregation, 'I have, since I first was told that it was my duty to labour in the diocese of Exeter, desired with an exceeding desire for the day to come when I might meet you face to face.'[12] Temple, like Phillpotts, feared no man. In the pulpit on that day there appeared an aspect of Victorian England of which Exeter hitherto had experienced little. The congregation looked up at a new leader, Victorian in his association with Rugby, his share in *Essays and Reviews*, his work for educational reform. Rugged in manner, forthright in speech, a firm teetotaller, a man who had known poverty and manual labour – and a Liberal – Temple was a new phenomenon among Exeter's bishops. It was significant that shortly after his enthronement the 'mitred Radical partisan,'[13] to use the words of the *Flying Post*, was to clash with Exeter's traditionalism by suggesting the need to reform the city's endowed schools.

Though the replacement of one generation of leaders by another had its effect in making the end of the sixties the great divide in Exeter's Victorian history, the hinge between the old and the new, the changes which were becoming apparent were too far-reaching to be ascribed wholly to the influence of individuals. The last lingering traditions of classical architecture had ended abruptly. Exeter's streets began to display the proliferation of style, colour and ornament which was a feature of Victorian ebullience and individuality, and also of the increasing abundance and cheapness of new materials. The technical virtuosity which had been a feature of the Great Exhibition of 1851 had reached the city. Interests and amusements were becoming more varied. In the press sporting affairs were no longer confined to the reports of runs with foxhounds and staghounds, to brief records of wrestling matches and of rare birds shot in the neighbourhood. Archery had become popular in the fifties. In the next decade cricket scores were reported prominently. By the seventies bats, balls and pads were on sale in the High Street. When the Exeter Safe Path Temperance Society celebrated their annual picnic in 1869 they marched behind the militia band from Smythen Street to Duryard Park for archery, cricket and dancing. The university boat race was first reported in 1869 and was the subject of a leading article two years later. Heralds of a new mobility and freedom, and of release from some of the strictness of social restraint, were the new velocipedes advertised in 1870 at prices ranging from £5 5s. to £10 with free tuition in their use.[14]

Exeter could no longer be regarded as offering provincial society something of what London had offered Dr Johnson – all that life could afford. Bookings for London theatres and hotels could be easily arranged by letter or telegram. There were indications that the assize balls and the Christmas balls were no longer attracting the county and the aristocracy on the scale of the past. In compensation, Exeter was beginning to draw upon circles that were wider but socially less select. The Bristol and Exeter railway had begun to advertise special return fares from Tiverton, at 2s. 6d. and 1s. 6d., for the Christmas pantomime.[15] It would soon be noticed that special trains were bringing large numbers of visitors from Exmouth and Newton Abbot for the Christmas season.[16] This period saw the tentative beginning of the development of Exeter's adjustment as a social and business centre of a new type, socially less restricted, based on a more widely diffused purchasing power, higher standards of living and new standards of taste. It was not till the Boer War that the social and economic changes which this development implied took full effect, coincidentally with laments for the diminished purchasing power of the county. In the meantime the life of the older Exeter was running down. When, in 1873 the mayor, Charles Follett, Sir William's nephew, revived the practice of entertaining the judges, he was attempting to restore the faded glamour of the past.

The city had shown little sign of growth since the development of the northern end of Queen Street in the late forties. The increase of population between 1861 and 1871 was only 4.2 per cent. as compared with 7.4 per cent. in Norwich and 11.4 in York. Between 1831 and 1871[17] the number of inhabited houses in the municipal area had increased from

4,056 to 5,864. In Leicester the increase had been from 8,348 to 19,800 in the same period. Sixty-one houses were under construction at the time of the census of 1871, a negligible figure compared with the 203 of Leicester and the 268 of Brighton. Hills Court and Edgerton Park were still rural though the first redbrick houses were beginning to appear in the Lion's Holt area, a presage of the new working-class suburbs which were to come. The Polsloe Road, linking the Blackboy Road with the Heavitree Road, formed the eastern limit of urban life. St Leonard's was still outside the municipal area. Orchards and market gardens filled most of the angle between the Magdalen and Heavitree Roads. Economic activities were still varied; tanneries, bone mills, iron and brass foundries; paper mills and breweries, a canal capable of taking vessels up to 400 tons. The list gives an impression of greater vigour than was the fact. There was an archaic flavour, an echo of Bath at the time of Sir Walter Elliott of Kellynch, in a directory's description of Exeter as a place where 'the salubrity of the air, and its proximity to many delightful watering-places, tend greatly to enhance its eligibility as a place of residence for the invalid, as well as the nobility and gentry.'[18]

'Society was regulated on well-defined lines,' wrote Sir John Daw of the Exeter of the seventies. 'The Mayor, Aldermen and Councillors formed one element, and the clergy formed a close corporation, whose family circle was not supposed to be invaded uninvited . . . The professional classes, Law and Medicine, were tolerated on the fringe of most circles.'[19]

Society and governing circles, almost but never completely identical in the days of the chamber, had moved far apart. In 1868 only the banker Thomas Snow represented Exeter's old upper class on the council. By 1870 the *Western Times* had good reason for a denunciation of the rule of the wine and spirit merchants. The law, then as always, maintained its quota but 'the trade' had taken up the entrenched position from which it exercised a decisive influence on local politics until the twentieth century. Its representatives on the council in 1870 included Joseph Harding with his two partners W. J.

Richards and H. D. Thomas, William Birkett of the Clarence Hotel, Thomas Gardner of the Half Moon and Robert Pople of the New London Inn, all church and state men. Standing aside from open involvement in council affairs, Edward Sanders, great-grandson of a Courtenay of Powderham, maintained the link between city and county until the last days of the county's political and social influence.[20]

The council itself, and a section of public opinion in the city, were becoming more concerned with the responsibilities of local authority for the well-being of the citizens other than the provision of police and lighting. Powers were being exercised as urban sanitary authority. Inspectors were reporting on sanitation, water-supplies and over-crowding. The sanitary committee was busy answering inquiries from London about the prevalence of fever and diarrhoea. Unemployment was giving rise to more publicly expressed concern than it had done for some years. Ratepayers were restive over rising rates and expenditure. Both the parties represented on the council had insisted on economy though the principle had been more prominent in the Liberal programme than in that of the Conservatives. Since 1835 the assertion of the principle had been a matter of routine rather than a reaction to pressure from the rates. When, in the late sixties, a wider conception of the responsibilities of municipal government began to be reflected in the annual estimates, the principle of economy became a heartfelt personal objection to rising rates. The borough rate, which had amounted to £4,400 in 1866–67, rose to £7,200 in 1872–3.

By 1870 the number of cases assisted by the Exeter relief society had risen to 3,584 from 2,542 in 1867. A further 1,597 were receiving relief from the corporation of the poor in January 1870. By the following January the latter figure had risen to 1,667.[22] Even for those in employment times were hard. In February 1871 an artisan stated at a public meeting that the cost of maintaining a family of five amounted to 14s. 3d. a week.[23] But, he explained, many were employed for no more than nine months in the year and their average wages were said to amount to only 11s. 3d. a week, less than the wages of labourers in the regular employment of the council twenty years before. In the meantime the market price of meat had doubled and bread, though cheaper, was still expensive at 6d. for the quartern loaf.

An unemployed labour fund was opened in 1870 under a committee of management to deal with the crisis. The distress was attributed to the cessation of building activities in Exeter and its neighbourhood. The number of buildings under construction at the time of the census of 1871 was in fact substantially lower than it had been at the time of the censuses of 1831 and 1841. New buildings authorized by the streets committee declined from ninety-four in 1869 to sixty-five in 1870 and went down to under thirty in 1871. Of the 549 men on the register of the labour fund committee, 342 were described as labourers.[24] Most of these men were connected with the building trade as painters, paperhangers, carpenters, masons and plasterers. With their dependants 1,262 persons were receiving relief from this source. In the opinion of the committee only five hundred men were genuinely out of work. These were employed on stone-breaking, digging drains and road-making, work for which not all of them were physically fit, for nine hours a day at 2d. an hour. Despite suggestions that the extent of unemployment was exaggerated it appears that over five thousand persons, or about one in seven of the total population of 34,650 in 1871, were receiving assistance in one form or another, including those assisted by the relief society and an average of 1,241 on the outdoor relief handled by the corporation of the poor.

The labour fund committee in the manner of the time suggested that one reason for the distress of 1870 was 'the want of industry and temperance, and improvident habits of many of the men.'[25] The unemployed leader, John Ponsford, the first working man to achieve momentary prominence in nineteenth-century Exeter, was apparently a good Conservative since he attributed the situation to the policies of Gladstone and John Bright and also to the 'abuse of trade unions in discouraging employers and restricting trade.'[26] The Rev. John Galton of St Sidwell's, an estimable parish priest and active in making collections for the poor of his parish, agreed with Ponsford that, as he told a meeting in the Guildhall, working men were 'in bondage' to the trade unions and their misfortunes were of their own making. Speaking, it is recorded, with emotion, he informed the meeting that he knew of cases 'where men receive 14s., 15s., 18s., 20s., aye, even 30s., a week, and scarcely 5s. of that goes home to the wife and family.'[27] Drunkenness was indeed a serious social problem, as it remained till the twentieth century, though its causes were more complex than a mere taste for drink. But Galton opposed public charity with a bleak restatement in theological terms of the economic thesis which had been preached by the newspapers to the starving poor of Exeter in 1854. Misfortune, he stated categorically, was never due to what was called ill-luck, it was due to the judgement of God which followed inexorably 'in one form or another' human transgression.[28]

Doubtless in the Exeter of 1870 there were some who sought relief rather than work as there were others, products of the harsh conditions of the time, who spent the bulk of their pay on drink. The intelligent working man of Victorian politics was not a universal paragon, though he undoubtedly existed. The hard fact was that Exeter had still found no alternative source of livelihood since the final collapse of the cloth industry towards the end of the eighteenth century. The railways had as yet failed to create new opportunities for the city; they had, on the other hand, destroyed the protective isolation of the old provincial capital. Building and allied activities remained the largest source of employment in Exeter; this was vulnerable to the vagaries of weather and credit and, to prosper, required an effective demand for houses which the city's economy could no longer produce.

Economic vicissitudes were endured as the lot of man. More disturbing to the social conscience of the city were the palpable inadequacies and obsolescence of Exeter's educational system. These defects called in question Exeter's traditions of culture and good society and, since they forced themselves on the notice of a small town, aroused feelings of humanitarianism and practising Christianity. In 1869, the mayor, 'Scientific' Ellis, called a public meeting to discuss the problem of neglected and destitute children.[29] He urged that measures should be taken for the moral and physical welfare of the numerous children who either did not attend school at all or, if they did, left without even a modicum of education. The mayor was supported by the dean who informed the meeting that he had been surprised, on his arrival in Exeter, by the number of vagrant children in the city. Private charity in the past had endeavoured to deal with the problem. Ragged Schools had been founded in 1850 'to elevate the condition of the poor and ignorant children' on unsectarian lines.[30] An industrial school had been opened on Exe Island in 1863 with Mark Kennaway's son, George, as one of the honorary secretaries. What was new was the realization that unschooled and ragged children in the streets were a reflection on the standards of a city that had prided itself on its standards of civilized life, that the haphazard humanity and charity of the past were not enough. The Ragged School – a term which the *Western Times* at least deplored in 1870 – in West Street was reported to have sixty boys and youths in 1870 with ages in the wide range of seven to nineteen. Although Miss Burdett Coutts's agent in the management of such schools and benevolent institutions expressed himself gratified at what he saw there he also suggested that there was still inadequate accommodation for the destitute children of the city.[31] Close on one child in every four at this period was either receiving no education at all or education of negligible value, often under grossly insanitary conditions. Religious denominations and endowments and private charity provided education for 3,236 poor children, the greater proportion in Church of England schools.[32] The figures do not imply that all children on the registers received adequate education, even by contemporary standards. It was acknowledged at the time that there was always 'too wide a margin between the number on the register and the number in attendance at all elementary schools, but it broadens as one goes down.'[33] In a report on the West of England Church Schools in 1869[34] it had been suggested that the clergy managed these schools with a wisdom which had practically disposed of religious difficulties; but the Elementary Education Act involved Exeter, like the rest of England, in sectarian controversies which were to inflame religious feeling and impede education for another generation.

In the provision of elementary education for the poor Exeter had never claimed to be in advance of its time. The development of secondary education was part of the traditions of a historic city. Like so much else in Exeter at this period there was little more than a façade and a tradition, the shadow without the reality.

'An old and not very prosperous grammar school, in poor premises, with very few boys, a hospital school of the charitable type . . . one school [Hele's] which was considered a superior school but offered an education little better than that of elementary schools in the eighties,' thus succinctly the state of Exeter's education at this period was described to a select committee in 1886. The grammar school's headmaster had sturdily refused facilities for inspection for the purpose of the Taunton Commission of 1868 holding it 'beneath the dignity of the school to be put on the same platform with other schools which he understood had been examined.'[35] The commission was informed that the grammar school in point of fact had not been able to hold its own against the upper or middle class private schools of the city which were said to be numerous and several of which were good.[36]

Of these private schools the best in 1870 was the Mansion House School of James Templeton, from Aberdeen, which catered for between forty and fifty boarders, sons of professional men, clergymen, surgeons, and 'the better class of farmers and goods tradesmen in the county towns' who could afford fees from £40 to about £60 a year.[37] There were also some fifty day boys. Templeton suffered much from parents' limited conceptions of the range of education for their boys; as to the boys' sisters, these, he informed the commission, received education of a sort from governesses. In the Cambridge Local Examinations for junior students the Mansion House School headed the list of local schools and obtained seventeen certificates during the years 1864-66.[38] Holloway House private school came second with eleven. Hele's School followed with nine.

The Church of England training college, founded in 1840, was palpably unsatisfactory thirty years later. The college had been designed to 'supply a system of education for schoolmasters on the basis of the church differing in some points from the old grammar school system.'[39] By 1870 the college had trained some 445 students, though in that year the principal was unable to say how many students in fact were teaching in elementary schools. The standards were undistinguished. The students in the practising school were reported to be deficient in tact. The maintenance of good order in class was 'often beyond their power.' Their penmanship was 'very bad.'[40]

All thinking men were agreed on the moral basis of work and education. 'God has ordained work as the condition of success,' the Exeter Science School was reminded in 1872, therefore, 'Resolve earnestly on work and rest assured, even in this world, that it will not pass unnoticed or unrewarded.'[41] But the endowed schools in which Exeter took pride were outdated. As the bishop had to remind the city they had been designed to meet temporary needs and the needs had changed. Reform was in the air following the policy of Gladstone's government and not without stimulus from Bishop Temple himself. Approaching change aroused the traditional religious and political differences, as well as the traditional conservatism of the city.

In the meantime the initiative provided by county leadership had begun the development of Victorian Exeter's major bequest to posterity, the University College of the Southwest, which grew largely out of the inspiration of Sir Stafford Northcote. It had long been a reproach that Exeter, unlike Torquay and Plymouth, had no museum. In consequence, as the artist John Gendall had occasion to inform a public meeting, art and science collections valued at some £100,000 had been forfeited by the city.[42] The Exeter School of Art had been founded in 1854, inevitably under the presidency of Northcote. In 1863 it had been decided to organize science classes at a time when there was no certificated teacher of science in all Devon. On the death of the Prince Consort in

1861, Sir Stafford Northcote again took the lead in urging that Exeter should constitute a museum combined with an art and science centre as a fitting memorial to Prince Albert.

Where Sir Stafford led Exeter usually followed. Delays occurred. Funds were raised with difficulty. Exeter could not emulate the princely donations which the growing wealth of industrial England provided for philanthropic and other purposes. In 1868 it became possible to hold science and art classes in the completed section of the new building. In August 1869 the Royal Albert Museum was opened by Mayor Ellis in the presence of members of the British Association whose meeting had been held in Exeter that year. Exeter it was now claimed, was approaching at a humble distance no less a model than the ancient museum of Alexandria.

'Living agencies as well as dead examples,' the city was informed, 'will come within its scope, comprising as it will a School of Art, a Free Library, and a Reading Room, in addition to a Depository of National History and Antiquities. Many organisations of a useful character will cluster round it.' Exeter was to become 'the grand County Centre of Art and Science.'[43]

In so far as the museum was to grow by stages, first into a university college and at length into a university, the exuberant prophecy was fulfilled. It was the vision of the old humanist society of the county on the eve of its eclipse. In this respect Exeter was indeed a city of the past as the British Association found in 1869 and as the historian Freeman described it in the year of the Diamond Jubilee. Sir Stafford Northcote once more indicated the goal, in one of the several major speeches which he found time to deliver in Exeter in the early weeks of 1870. 'Is it possible,' he asked the Literary Society, 'to establish a sort of university of the middle classes in Exeter?'[44] It was indeed possible though not perhaps in accordance with the social classifactory system of Victorian England. In that period of Exeter's Victorian history when past status was lost and no new prospect was in sight the foundations of the city's main bequest to the twentieth century were being prepared.

For the moment Exeter had little time for visions. The city had drifted into the full tide of the Victorian era under pressure of wind and current. There was no discussion of ultimate destination, no focus for pride. It was sufficient to keep the craft afloat with out-of-date equipment; but it was beginning to be appreciated that the owners had some responsibility for conditions in the steerage. The owners were the old firm under new management still trading under the sign of church and state. Management had passed from Henry Hooper the builder to Charley Wescomb the adventurer, and thence to the licensed trade headed by Joseph Harding, brewer, and his partner W. J. Richards. The management was middle-class but it failed to provide the middle-class leadership and self-assurance which existed elsewhere in Victorian urban England. Contemporary Birmingham raised Joseph Chamberlain to a national figure. Contemporary Newcastle upon Tyne had Joseph Cowen, Radical industrialist, newspaper proprietor and an influential politician in the North.[45] In Exeter, the inspiration of leadership was provided by a bishop and a representative of the landed gentry.

The year 1870 ended as it had begun – in gloom. Cold weather set in early. By Christmas there was skating on the Exe. Those fortunate enough to be in regular employment were entertained in the old fashion at the expense of their employers. The employees of the Trews Weir Mill dined at the Port Royal Inn. For others the soup kitchen was opened. By the end of the winter, funds were exhausted and the organization was in debt. Hospital wards were reported to be fuller than usual. Exeter, reading of Paris under siege, showed little of the wonted Christmas cheer. The man of the year was Bishop Temple who was said to have lived up to his reputation as an 'honest, hard-working man.'[46]

POLITICS AND GOVERNMENT

1870–1900

FOR Victorian Exeter the seventies were years of depression, bad trade and unemployment, contaminated water supplies and a sorry record of public health. They were also years which saw the end of the prosperous rural society from which Exeter had derived business and culture. There was always some immigration into the city from the small market towns and the villages of Devon whose populations were dwindling so rapidly in the heyday of Victorian England, and Exeter was never a barren field for enterprise. Men who rose to moderate wealth and to positions of local influence were often newcomers to the city. The Daw family came from Black Torrington at the end of the eighteenth century to provide a succession of able and influential lawyers. Richard Somers Gard came from North Tawton. Robert Pople was born in Bridgwater, where he had once worked in a tile factory[1] before coming to Exeter in 1868 to acquire the New London Inn and to be mayor for three years in succession. Walter Pring, the brewer, was another immigrant from Somerset. So was John Hancock, the brick and tile manufacturer, who was born in Taunton, where he was employed in a brickyard at 6d. a day,[2] and left a fortune of £120,000 when he died in Exeter in 1906. William Brown the draper, mayor in 1844–85, was a native of Kirkcudbright; James Templeton, headmaster of the most successful private school in the city, was from Aberdeen.

Exeter did not attract large-scale immigration nor, in consequence, the adventurous spirits who were contributing to the achievements, as well as to the miseries, of Victorian England. Exeter's immigrants accepted the environment as they found it and introduced no change. There were no longer the opportunities which had set the Barings on the road to fortune in the eighteenth century. The only Exeter fortune derived from the conditions of urban growth and expansion characteristic of Victorian England was that of John Hancock and it was not till the later years of the nineteenth century that conditions favouring enterprise of this type existed in the city. Most businessmen followed the traditional paths, not ineffectively but certainly without conspicuous success by contemporary standards.

In consequence Exeter remained conservative. Political Conservatism retained control of the council, unadventurous but pragmatic, never looking far ahead but in the last resort accepting the need for innovations under the pressure of events. In the same spirit Exeter's old Toryism had accepted the Municipal Corporations Act without useless – and expensive – opposition. Wealth was a weighty recommendation for the mayoralty judging by the *Western Times*' statement in 1882 that mayors were required by custom to spend up to £1,000 a year.[3]

Health statistics reinforced by the physical presence of cholera, had provided compelling reasons for the council, as urban sanitary authority, to supersede the improvement commissioners in 1867. Full use was made of the financial facilities available under the Public Health Act of 1875. A programme of improvements was inaugurated with markedly beneficial effects on the city but involving an increase in expenditure which contributed to the shaking of Conservative rule in the 1880s and to its dramatic, though temporary, overthrow in 1900.

Except in special circumstances the environment could offer little encouragement to an effective challenge to the party of church and state:

'When honest hands and honest hearts
To Church and State are true
Defiance we may surely bid
To Dilke and all his crew.'[4]

The path to local advancement and social status continued to lead through Conservatism and membership of the Church of England. Exeter's political warfare throughout the Victorian era was waged under the banners of national issues,

Reform, Free Trade and Protection, the position' of the church, Ireland and the Boer War. To some extent these issues, and others, represented genuine divisions in the minds of sincere men of both parties. Whether what was morally wrong could be politically right was a factor in the politics of the Gladstonian era, as Parnell was forced to recognize. The political cleavage was inextricably mingled with personal and social differences and aspirations. Normal politeness and friendly intercourse in business could not shake the assumption of the social superiority of Anglicanism compared with Nonconformity, nor confer on Liberalism the social prestige of Conservatism. Political controversy was sharpened by the virtual monopoly by one party of both political and social power. When, in 1868, Edgar Bowring complained of the attempt to denigrate him politically by false rumours that he was a Unitarian[5] he was combating social values which remained dominant in the city till the end of the century. Resentment at exclusion from the governing regime was increased by the long monopoly of power exercised by the controlling group within the Conservative party, the 'Monopolists,' 'Junta' or 'Cormorants' as they were variously styled by their opponents, whose banners in political contests bore the device of Church and state. This resentment became effective at the polls in 1883, and again in 1900, when the unpopularity of the regime was increased by the growth of expenditure and the consequent rise in the rates.

In the 1870s, two powerful elements in Exeter's Conservatism, the church and the licensed trade, were forced into incongruous alliance by the policies of Gladstone's government as expressed in the Elementary Education Act of 1870 and the Licensing Act of 1872. 'The trade' and associated activities, such as hotel-keeping, had always been predominantly, though never exclusively, Conservative. By the seventies 'the trade' dominated the council as well as the local political machine. Its leaders were the cousins Harding and Richards, partners in brewing and politics. Joseph Harding, founder of the Exeter Licensed Victuallers' Association, mayor in 1871, rose to local prominence at this time

and was active in marshalling 'the trade' against Liberal
candidates in parliamentary elections. His partner, W. J.
Richards, was son-in-law of John Laidman, the Conservative
councillor elected city treasurer in 1857. Richards was also
the prime organizer of the Conservative political organization in the city in 1868 and chairman of the Conservative
Working Men's Union from its foundation in that year until
1886. The Conservative victory in the parliamentary election
of 1873 was ascribed to Richards' untiring energy and zeal.[6]
When he died in 1903, it was recorded of him that he had
'maintained the Conservative ascendancy with no serious
challenge.'[7]

Henceforward the considerable influence of 'the trade' and
all its skill in political management were to be exerted against
the Liberals at every election. In 1910, when the brewer
Alderman Pring occupied Richards' old position as president
of the Working Men's Conservative Union, parliamentary
candidates were still being harried over their views on
licensing policy. The genuine issues of principle summarized
by Bishop Magee's[8] declaration in favour of England free
rather than sober engendered passions which submerged
principle in the confused waters of vituperation and misrepresentation. Though in Exeter the Anglican clergy were
not wholly at one on the issues of the day, the traditional
Conservatism of the great majority was roused in opposition
to the religious and educational policies of the Liberal
government which took office in December 1868. These
policies, combined with Bruce's Licensing Bill of 1871,
which regulated the closing hours of public houses, created
the alliance between High Churchmen and licensed victuallers
– the Rits and the Vits of Liberal political journalism –
which must have been embarrassing to many sincere Conservative churchmen. If the church was indeed in danger it
was unlikely to be saved by men such as Joseph Harding who,
as mayor in 1871, presided over a meeting of the Church
Defence Organization and took the opportunity to proclaim
his devotion to the principles of church and state.[9] His
devotion to other interests put Harding in an invidious
position in 1872. A meeting, with Bishop Temple in the

chair, held to discuss the licensing question, was broken up by 'West Gate toughs' headed by employees of Harding and Richards.[10] The meeting began badly. The bishop, apologizing for a temporary loss of voice, was advised to try some rum and water. Some of the rougher supporters of the licensed victuallers moved in, 'a wrestler, a few fighting-men and some brickmakers' were seen among them and what was described as 'a smart and sanguinary struggle' took place. The bishop was hit by a bag of flour and the meeting broke up in disorder. Harding subsequently brought an action for libel on account of the comments contained in a letter published in *The Times*. The trial judge, Baron Bramwell, was not notably sympathetic when the case appeared before him at Bristol. Harding was awarded ten guineas out of the £1,000 claimed.[11]

In September 1872, the year of Harding's libel action, a far more serious affair took place. On the 17th an article appeared in the *Gazette* attacking the Licensing Act. The Exeter working men were encouraged to strike a blow for 'beer and baccy.' It was pointedly suggested that they were victims of class legislation. When public houses were closed each night the poor had nowhere to go while the rich could enjoy their wine without restriction in their clubs. A poster in a High Street window intimated that those who frequented taverns might satisfy their thirst after closing hours by recourse to the haunt of privilege, the Country Club in Northernhay. Acting on this hint a crowd of some 500 persons decided to try their luck and were duly dispersed by the police. On the following Monday there were further demonstrations. An attack on the club was thwarted, so the mob marched down the hill and over the bridge to St Thomas, breaking windows on the way. Across the river there was more damage to property and a set-to with the county police. Near midnight the rioters attempted to return to the city but found their path blocked by police who held the bridge with truncheons. Their zeal wore off in the small hours during an enforced detour of a few miles to return to the city by Cowley Bridge.[12]

Exeter under the rule of 'the trade' was acquiring a

reputation for rowdiness. The *Western Times*'s description of the city as a 'den of ruffianism, ignorance and brutality' was journalistic exaggeration, as was the *Flying Post*'s complaint that the name of the city was being 'dragged in the dirt all over England,'[13] But the 1870s were not an edifying time in the city's history and much tumultuous behaviour was due to the drink question. In surveying the local scene the press was unanimous in expressing distaste for what it saw. Nonconformity included an element with austere views on drink and had a teetotal wing which enforced a 'teetotallers' choice' on the official Nonconformist candidates for the school board in 1871. In this respect Nonconformity found a powerful ally in the bishop.

It was at Bishop Temple's urging that the decision was taken to found a branch of the Church of England Temperance Society in the city. Some temperance activities and language were reminiscent of the Brick Lane Branch of the United Grand Junction Ebenezer Temperance Association; in contrast there was still a trace of the old High and Dry distaste for enthusiasm among Exeter's clergy. The Rev. Henry Bramley asserted in his bishop's presence that teetotalism had too often been exalted into a religion and abstention from drink into a god.[14] Galton, of St Sidwell's, attended a licensed victuallers' dinner and deplored attacks on the trade as a whole. His speech was intemperately described by the *Western Times* as a 'tirade ornamented with the choicest rhetoric of Billingsgate.'[15] It was therefore in an atmosphere charged with recrimination and rowdiness that the church and 'the trade' stood shoulder to shoulder in the seventies in an alliance which did much to ensure the Conservatism of Exeter's parliamentary representation for the remainder of the century. The strength of the alliance was soon demonstrated.

In December 1873 Coleridge was appointed lord chief justice, thus necessitating a by-election in Exeter. The Conservative candidate was Arthur Mills, educated at Rugby under Arnold, and at Balliol, a lawyer and son-in-law of Sir Thomas Acland of Killerton. In 1852 Mills had been returned for Taunton after an election which was subsequently

declared void for corruption. The Liberal, Sir Edward
Watkin, was a new type of candidate for Exeter, a creator of
a modern world in which the city had little share. A northern
businessman, born at Salford, general manager of the
Manchester, Sheffield and Lincolnshire, and other railways,
Watkin was in fact a prominent railway magnate both in
Britain and Canada. He has been described as spending 'a
restless life in extending and amalgamating companies which
rarely paid much to the ordinary shareholder.'[16] His later
interests included an enthusiasm for the Channel Tunnel.[17]
Watkin had been Liberal member for Stockport from 1864–68
and in the opinion of Sir Stafford Northcote was 'something
of a snob.'

The Conservatives welcomed the by-election as an
opportunity for a trial of strength before the next general
election. For five years, declared the Flying Post, they had
been preparing for the fight.[18] The newspaper announced
that Edgar Bowring's majority was to be broken down by
the system based on Conservative meetings and club rooms,
by their 'coffee and politics for the working man.' Ever since
the defeat of 1868 the Conservative 'borough and ward
organizations [had] been patiently labouring at the task.' As
to the licensing question, the Flying Post decided to say
nothing because the editorial 'We' was perfectly satisfied
with the result of the appeal to the two candidates. No
Liberal candidate, however dexterous, could satisfy 'the
trade.' And so Mills was proclaimed the favourite candidate
of that 'excellent institution which has suffered so much
abuse and misrepresentation' – the licensed victuallers. This
organization, it was explained, was not political, though
its members were.

The Exeter licensed victuallers met to consider the answers
of the two candidates to the questions put to them on
the licensing issue and regretted that they could not advise
their members in Exeter to accept the answers of the Liberal.
At a meeting at Heavitree the banker Ralph Sanders
attempted to clear Mills of any association with corrupt
practices at Taunton. The meeting was attended by Archdeacon Woollcombe, Prebendary Barnes and other clergy.[19]

The Rev. Henry Bramley made a fighting speech in support of Arthur Mills, at a meeting incongruously held in the Temperance Hall. It had been suggested, he said, that a clergyman had no right to take part in elections but he maintained the right of every Englishman to come forward in support of the cause which he thought just. Alderman Harding presided at a meeting of the Exeter branch of the Licensed Victuallers National Defence League held at the Clarence Hotel. There it was resolved 'to cast aside all party politics in the present contest' and to advise 'the trade' in Exeter to 'exert all its strength in support of the candidate who had shown himself a friend of the trade.'[20] The appeal to abandon politics implied, as not infrequently happens, an invitation to agree with the politics of the speaker. The Liberal H. C. Edwards, an official of the league, responded by declaring that he would support the Conservative candidate. Richards followed with a challenge to any member of 'the trade' in the city to say that 'he had directly or indirectly canvassed in favour of any candidate.'[21] This assertion of political objectivity was doubtless justified if applied to house-to-house canvassing but in spirit it was hardly consistent with Richards' own rousing attack on Watkin at a public meeting a few days before or with his political record.

The Conservative organizers brought down a suitably picked working man, one Leach of Stalybridge, to attack Watkin's reputation as an employer and to assure Exeter that 'the working men of Lancashire, Cheshire and Yorkshire had their eyes directed to Exeter.'[22] Probably more influential than the testimony of Leach, who the Liberals claimed had turned from abstention to heavy drinking, from Liberalism to Conservatism, was Dean Boyd's letter to Edward Sanders, which was read out at a public meeting.[23] The dean wrote that he had put a restraint on himself in denying himself 'the pleasure of being at Mr Mills' side' at the meeting to which he had been invited. However, his sympathy and 'heartiest wishes' were with the Conservative cause. The dean knew that many of the working men of Exeter might wish that he should help to fight the battle, 'a battle in which the best interests of our most sacred institutions require to be fought out to the last,' but he was certain that they would give him 'credit for a scrupulous regard to maintain the warfare on his own special grounds.' The dean's letter savours of casuistry but Gladstone's policies on religious and educational issues had in fact aroused in sincere men the fear that the church was once more in danger. In 1868 an elector in Ilfracombe had informed Stafford Northcote that, although hitherto he had always voted Liberal, he could no longer do so because Glastone's policy on the Irish Church was unjust and impolitic.[24] The clergy of a cathedral city in a rural environment could not be expected to be supporters of the 'unmuzzled' Gladstone.

Stafford Northcote, in surveying the Exeter scene, informed Disraeli that the prospects were most uncertain with both parties having an equal chance of victory.[25] But the full weight of Exeter's influence and respectability was thrown into the scales and was backed by careful organization.

The electoral addresses of the candidates themselves were understandably cautious.[26] Both agreed on the inquisitorial nature of income tax. Mills expressed himself in favour of 'the utmost freedom of thought and action consistent with the maintenance of law and order,' the extension of education and the maintenance of the right of parents to secure the religious training of children in their own faith.' He suggested that 'the recent alterations of the Licensing Laws, though attended with some advantages, [had] not realized all the anticipations of their promoters.' Watkin refrained from mentioning the licensing question. He expressed himself in favour of an extension of the county franchise, of parliament's close attention to the game and land laws, and some 'generous change in the clauses of the Education Act to restore union between the Liberal Churchman and Nonconformist.' His electoral address could hardly be other than on the defensive in the Exeter of 1873.

In view of Exeter's reputation for rowdiness police reinforcements were brought from Bristol, Devonport and Plymouth for an election which was rougher than usual and ended in a decisive Conservative victory. Mills obtained 2,346 votes, a majority of 321 over his opponent's 2,025.

Some 70 per cent. of the electorate voted.

The by-election of 1873 was the first election fought in Exeter under the provisions of the Ballot Act of 1872, which introduced secret voting. The analysis of election results had therefore become more speculative. Liberal disappointment was patent. The *Western Times* had long insisted that the introduction of the ballot would remove influence and victimization and thus free the assumed innate Liberalism of the Exeter electorate. The Conservative victory was therefore attributed to dishonest means. It was claimed that some voters had received money, that the distribution of beer had been 'most unblushing.' It was suggested that the 'celebrated leap in the dark should be styled a leap among the degrading elements of beer, blankets and charities.'[27] The Conservatives, with more justification, attributed their success to 'the existence and thoroughness of the Exeter Working Men's Union.'[28]

Allegations of corruption could have been tested only by proceedings following petition. The initial steps were taken. A petition was prepared; but in January 1874 Gladstone took his controversial decision to dissolve parliament. The petition lapsed. This was the only occasion after the Reform Bill of 1832 in which a serious attempt was begun to substantiate allegations of corruption in an Exeter election. Since the assertion that Mills's election was obtained by bribery was never tested, no conclusion is possible on its merits. Indulgence in free beer was no new feature in Exeter elections and is unlikely to have been a decisive factor in 1873. The capture of both seats by the Liberals in 1868 had been a *tour de force* in exceptional circumstances which was unlikely to be repeated. It had been achieved by two strong candidates with local associations. Doctor Johnson once remarked that 'When a butcher tells you that his heart bleeds for his country he has, in fact, no uneasy feeling'; but defence of the church and freedom to sell and buy drink were tangible issues in the Exeter of 1873. They were calculated to arouse genuine feelings and, with the prompting of an efficient organization, to turn out the vote. The respectability of the city remained Conservative even though some clergy may have been embarrassed by their political allies. Moreover, to poll the lukewarm and the undecided, the Conservatives, as the Liberals admitted, were 'backed up with an organization of a very perfect character, and for electioneering purposes far more efficient, than that possessed by the Liberal Party.'[29] As to cruder appeals to self-interest, it was a Conservative newspaper which described the licensed victuallers as 'cellarers and butterers of the working men.'[30]

The Conservative victory at the by-election of 1873 was confirmed at the general election of 1874 when both Liberal candidates were defeated, Edgar Bowring losing by sixty votes. Gladstone attributed his party's defeat throughout the country to a 'torrent of gin and beer' and to the controversies aroused by the Education Act. At Exeter there is no doubt that the drink controversy ensured that the powerful influence of 'the trade' was thrown against the Liberals; as the *Western Times* expressed it more colourfully, the 'Tory Vits' had resolved that 'every innkeeper whom they could bully or gammon should be pressed into service.'[31] Gladstone's defeat in the country has also been attributed to massive Nonconformist abstentions from the polls but there was no sign of any significant abstention in Exeter, in contrast to the election of 1865 when Coleridge had found it difficult to reconcile High Church views with Nonconformist Liberalism. The Exeter Liberals themselves attributed their defeat to their not unusual defect, lapses in organization, as well as to the fact that they had been caught unprepared by the dissolution.

W. J. Richards was the acknowledged organizer of victory and acquired thereby a local fame which he retained till his death in 1903. He himself asked Sir Stafford Northcote for some form of recognition, suggesting that he might be appointed organizing secretary for the county of Devon and, in that capacity, undertake 'proper manipulation of the sources of influence which Conservatives possess in Landed Properties, M.P.s' Associations, Clubs, etc.'[32] Northcote passed on the request to Disraeli with the comment that Richards had 'done wonders in the way of organization down here.' The new Conservative organization had been expensive and in Richards's view the cost of elections had become 'simply enormous.' The cost of the Exeter election of 1874 was certainly above the national average. The Conservative candidates acknowledged an expenditure of £1,143 and £1,158 respectively, the Liberals £871 each.[33] The figures were in fact slightly below those of 1868 but the returns of election expenditure at this period were often far from revealing the whole truth.

The next election, the general election of 1880 which returned Gladstone to power to deal with the problems of Ireland, Egypt and South Africa, was also the last contest for two seats in the Exeter constituency. On that occasion Exeter returned to the sensible practice of returning one Liberal and one Conservative. The national trend which gave Gladstone an impressive victory was perceptible in Exeter to the extent that the Liberal candidate, Edward Johnson of Farringdon, was returned at the head of the poll after taking last place in 1874. The Conservative Arthur Mills, who had headed the poll in 1874, now came last and lost his seat. He was replaced by H. S. Northcote, son of Sir Stafford of Pynes and, since 1877, secretary to his father, the chancellor of the exchequer in Disraeli's last government.

In 1880 the liquor question was once more to the fore. Exeter's temperance leaders pressed the candidates to declare themselves and added the threat that they would vote against any who failed to give adequate assurances in support of temperance. Mills and Northcote could not be forthcoming. Johnson was hesitant and his insistence on adequate compensation for publicans who might suffer loss through restrictions was not popular with the out-and-out opponents of the trade. After some hesitation, and, apparently, pressure from the local Liberal politicians, the temperance leaders decided not to refrain from voting but instead to support the Liberals since they could clearly expect nothing from the Conservatives. Arthur Mills himself had not been a popular member and the Liberals themselves, with only one candidate in the field, contrived a concentration of votes which secured victory and provoked an unusual admission from their opponents of something less than the customary efficiency of the Conservative machine. According to the *FlyingPost*[34]

Edward Johnson received 2,732 'plumpers,' Mills only thirty-three and Northcote, faced with the usual difficulties of a new candidate in Exeter, forty-two.

Exeter's reversal of the election results of 1874 was the more surprising because Devon, as the *Western Times* complained, made no effective contribution to 'the great demonstration of Liberalism' in 1880.[35] Throughout the county of Devon there was a net Liberal gain of only one seat. This election introduced the series of contests in which the heady imperialism of declining Victorianism ostensibly, for there were always local issues, dominated the political scene. At Exeter's great Conservative rally of March 1880, H. S. Northcote and Mills, Edward Sanders, the dean and numerous clergy were grouped in front of a large map of the eastern hemisphere showing the route to India. The walls were decorated with 'a number of good old constitutional watchwords and mottos.'[36] Gladstone in Mid-Lothian, Chamberlain's Radicalism, and economy, were for the moment more likely to appeal to strong sections of the Exeter electorate. But the Irish question was breaking the old political pattern in Devon. County leaders in the Whig tradition were becoming estranged from the new Liberalism. In Exeter 'the upper range of society, the county gentry and the employers of labour' were not only virtually united against Gladstone, as the Liberals suggested,[37] but were drawing closer together under the rising pressure of Radicalism and Labour. Strictly the Conservatives and their allies should be termed Unionist after 1886 but they remained in fact the old Conservative party with a right-wing Liberal accretion and it is convenient to retain the old style. When the Conservatives rallied their supporters to the cry of 'Unity of Empire' the Exeter electorate was unmoved by the appeal of 'Justice for Ireland.' They listened to Lord Salisbury himself describing Ireland as ultra-protectionist and ultra-clerical and declaring that 'the flowers should not be plucked one by one from the diadem of empire.'[38]

In three parliamentary elections from 1886 to 1895 H. S. Northcote was returned with an average majority of over 460. The Liberal minority was kept in being by religious and educational issues, the latter in themselves religious, and by the liquor licensing controversy. The election of 1892 was distinguished chiefly by the appearance of Councillor A. E. Dunn as Liberal candidate, the only local politician to contest the constituency since Somers Gard had been jobbed into parliament without a contest in 1857; and Gard had not previously taken part in local politics. In the Exeter context, Dunn was an outsider, a lawyer without the professional distinction and social connections of John Duke Coleridge. The Liberals themselves were divided and disorganized in 1892 and Dunn did well to obtain 3,329 votes to Northcote's 3,888. He did not stand again though he succeeded on the more congenial ground of Camborne in 1906 and so shared the Liberal triumph of that year. Northcote himself was appointed governor of Bombay in 1899 and became Lord Northcote of Exeter. His successor as Conservative member for the city was the Edwardian figure of Sir Edgar Vincent who increased the Conservative majority to over 600 in 1899. Vincent's successful appeal to patriotism in the election of that year was reinforced by the exploits of Exeter's neighbour General Buller and of the Devon troops in the South African war among whom, as the candidate reminded the city, Exeter was proud to count relatives and friends. That close on half the registered electorate still voted Liberal in these circumstances was a tribute to the persistence of old habits and social patterns in the city.

The reorganized political machine by means of which the Conservatives had recovered from the electoral setback of 1868 continued to maintain the party's power in the city. After the elections of 1874 the Liberal councillors were reduced to ten. The elections of the following year were remarkable for the fact that no public house was opened specifically in the interests of any candidate, though drunkenness was still a feature of democratic processes and was notable in the parliamentary elections of 1895. The liquor trade, however, remained prominent and influential. In 1877 Alderman Thomas, the third partner in the firm of Harding, Richards and Thomas, was elected mayor. In that year the Conservative stronghold of St Leonard's was absorbed by the city and the size of the council was increased to fourteen aldermen and forty-two councillors.[39]

Towards the end of the seventies the Conservative monopoly of local power, their open jobbery over important appointments and the malodorous condition of the city provoked a brief reaction. 'The trade's' influence on the council was resented. Yet another licensed victualler had been elected in 1877, as councillor for St Paul's, where the mayor's business was situated. In the following year hisses from the public gallery in the Guildhall expressed disapproval of the election, as sheriff, of Samuel Jones, wine, spirit, ale and porter merchant.

Misgivings that effective power in Exeter was wielded by a caucus working in secret were expressed in 1877 when the Liberal R. C. Wilkinson attacked the election of Alderman Thomas as mayor on the grounds that the real decision had been made in the Conservative committee room. Most important issues require private discussion before public debate and to that extent the criticism was unjustified. But it was a symptom of the prevailing malaise over the standards of local government. 'The Burgesses had never need of greater vigilance than at the present moment,' warned the *Western Times*, which added 'On all sides we have complaints of the neglect of public duty at the Guildhall.'[40] A year later the newspaper complained that the licensed victuallers were over-represented on the council and pointed out that the mayor, Alderman Thomas, was one of three partners of one firm on the council. Heated arguments were raging over the defects in the water supplies and the proposed acquisition of the gas company by the council. There were hints of pressures from private interests. When, in 1876, Alderman Cuthbertson, chairman of the gas company, was proposed as mayor the proposer, Alderman Buckingham, displayed evident uneasiness over the tactlessness of the nomination.[41]

More damaging to the Conservatives had been the sudden retirement of David Steel, superintendent of police, in 1873. This followed hard on the heels of an incident when a meeting held to discuss the disestablishment of the Church of England was broken up to the strains of 'John Barleycorn.'

Plate 1. *High Street, about 1835. From a water colour by E. Jeffrey. (By courtesy of the Exeter City Library)*

Plate 2. Albion Terrace, constructed about 1830.

Plate 3. Clifton Street, Newtown. Artisans' houses constructed in the late 1830s.

Plate 4.   Exeter from Clifton Hill, 1847. (By courtesy of the Exeter City Library)

Plate 5.   St David's from Northernhay, 1847. (By courtesy of the Exeter City Library)

Thomas Shapter, 1847-48   *Joseph Harding, 1871-72*

Robert Pople, 1895-98

Plate 6.   Three Exeter mayors. (By courtesy of the Exeter City Library)

Plate 7.   Howell Road. Houses built by John Ware (1868-69) in the classical tradition.

Plate 8.   Lothair Villas, St Thomas. Built by the Exeter Freehold Land Society 1870-71 and described as 'replete with every modern convenience'.

Plate 9.   Follett's Building. 'Commodious and healthy dwellings for the poorer classes' completed by the Exeter Improved Industrial Dwellings Co. in 1874. Tenements leased at 2s. 6d. to 4s. 6d. a week.

Plate 10.   Middle-class solidity. Houses at the foot of Clifton Hill completed in 1878. Now the local Labour party headquarters.

Plate 11. *Victoria Street. 'By-law standardised street' begun in 1869 and completed about 1876.*

Plate 12. *Springfield Road, at the junction with Prospect Park Road. First developed in the late seventies and completed about 1876.*

Plate 13. Business premises, 1884. Buildings at the junction of North Street and Fore Street, contemporarily described as 'among the many fine improvements which have given a new and distinct character to the interesting architectural features of the main thoroughfares'. (By courtesy of the Exeter City Library)

Plate 14. Radford Road, constructed 1880-90. Houses designed for lease at £9 a year to artisans earning 25s. to 30s. a week.

Plate 15. Toronto Road, constructed 1889-90. Superior houses for artisans occupied in 1901 by railwaymen, accountants, carpenters, smiths and policemen.

Plate 16.   Mansfield Road. Completed in 1895 and described in that year as a street of 'convenient £14 houses'.

Plate 17.   Rosebery Road. Houses built 1896-98 and let at £15 to £16 a year.

Plate 18. St David's Church. Designed by Caroe and consecrated in January 1900. The last monument to middle-class wealth and church-going in Exeter.

Plate 19. Inauguration of the electric trams by the mayor, E. C. Perry, April 1905.

Plate 20. Isca Road, St Thomas. The first council housing scheme, approved in 1904 and completed in 1907. Houses designed for lease at 4s. 9d. a week.

An employee of Harding and Richards had been prominent leading cheers for the redoubtable Conservative twin brethren under the mistaken impression that he was breaking up a temperance meeting. The police were eventually called but the disorder continued until the gas was turned out and the meeting dispersed in confusion.[42]

There was much discussion as to whether or not the police might have acted more efficiently and successfully had it not been for their reluctance to offend ruling circles in Exeter. When, a month later, a brief minute of the watch committee[43] recorded a decision that the superintendent of police should be superannuated, public meetings were organized on Steel's behalf. Public resentment not only took the form of expressing confidence in Steel but seized the opportunity to give voice to a reluctance to pay rates which, if it served as a useful check on unnecessary expenditure, sometimes threatened to deprive the council of any scope for action whatever. Thus one speaker, after denouncing the rates, went on to explain that he was opposed to pensions of any kind, 'a man should be given his full value and afterwards take care of himself.'[44] *Western Times* went so far as to accuse the mayor, Charles Follett, of showing himself 'either blinded by partisan feeling or deficient in moral courage.'[45] Steel himself behaved with dignity and restraint though, since it was put out that he had intimated his desire to retire, he made a special visit to the office of the *Western Times* to explain that he had never been consulted in the matter.

When the affair was debated in the council it was argued that the police had become inefficient. Figures were cited to show that out of twenty-one cases involving the dismissal of constables in recent years eleven had arisen out of drunkenness. Yet there had been no previous indication that the council had become concerned over police discipline. On the other hand the *Flying Post*, though denying the intrusion of local politics into the affair, suggested cautiously that there had indeed been a tendency for the magistrates and the watch committee to interfere with the superintendent.[46] Incidents of this kind can be resolved, if they are resolved at all, only in the circumstances described by Kipling:

o

'Sometimes in a smoking room, through clouds of "Ers"
and "Ums"
Obliquely and by inference, illumination comes.'

The subsequent actions of the council further increased suspicion. Steel's successor,[47] Captain Thomas Bent, had recently been chairman of the St Leonard's Ward Conservative Association, and was now appointed without delay to the vacant post by a majority vote of the watch committee. Bent's future conduct was consistently embarrassing to his employers. Two years later, according to the version of the story accepted by the watch committee,[48] he became an unfortunate victim of circumstances through an encounter with a London prostitute and his subsequent behaviour before a magistrate in Marlborough Street. In 1880 damages and costs were awarded against him in a case brought for malicious prosecution and false imprisonment. In 1882 he had a brush with the bishop when a meeting to discuss the Sunday closing of public houses, with the bishop in the chair, was broken up, in what was becoming the traditional manner, by a crowd of young roughs using stink bombs and pepper. Captain Bent was singularly unhelpful and it was necessary to call in the mayor. In the following year the superintendent had to apologize for disrespectful language to the town clerk. In 1884 he appeared before a special meeting of the council on a charge of disrespect and insubordination to the mayor. In 1885 he was suspended for two months for 'reprehensible behaviour.' In 1886 he was at last retired on the grounds of ill-health after the reinstatement of a police inspector whom Bent had improperly suspended.[49]

The circumstances of Steel's superannuation and of the appointment of his successor as the first chief constable contributed to the impression, which the Exeter Conservatives at this period gave, of a party with a single-minded and unconcealed determination to retain control of the levers of power. In 1874 Alderman Gidley, an active and influential member of the party and son of the first town clerk, resigned his position as alderman and was subsequently elected town clerk.[50] In 1879 the city treasurer, the former Conservative Councillor Laidman, resigned after the discovery of a shortage of £2,000, caused by the dishonesty of one of his clerks.[51] This gave the council an opportunity to make some effort to modernize the duties and conditions of service. The salary was raised to £600 a year and the council provided an office. The treasurer himself remained responsible for appointing and paying his clerks.[52] The Liberals on the council protested, pointing out that in Plymouth the treasurer was paid only £300 a year. They urged that in Exeter this officer should at least devote his whole time to council business instead of combining it with his profession. These arguments were disregarded and a Conservative, Councillor W. G. Rogers, solicitor, was appointed to the vacant post.[53]

The personal integrity of Gidley and Rogers was never in issue but the evident determination of the Conservatives to retain control of key posts justified the reiterated charges of jobbery. The scale and scope of municipal activity were increasing. The Exeter Water Company was acquired by the city in 1878. By 1881 the local government board had sanctioned loans amounting to £43,000, including £20,870 for street improvements.[54] The introduction of trams was being discussed. In these circumstances it was inevitable that allegations should be made that it was profitable to belong to the ruling party. Even if all Conservatives were blameless their long tenure of power had made them careless of public relations.

To this situation Exeter responded by proclaiming once more the old ideals of 'pure municipal government,' economy, and freedom from political parties. A Ratepayers' Association was formed in 1879, its first candidate, Henry Hexter, proprietor of the Queen's Hotel, standing as an independent for Trinity Ward in that year. The *Flying Post* complained that the Ratepayers had assumed the duty of 'opposing anyone who dared to accept the nomination of either political party,'[55] but the movement against 'The Junta,' 'Cormorants' and 'Monopolists' gathered strength. In 1881 six Ratepayers stood for election. A seventh candidate described himself as non-political. The Liberal George Finch contested St Mary Major's on what were described as 'municipal grounds.' It was an indication of the discontent with the long-established Conservative regime that George Finch, one Ratepayer and one Independent were returned at the head of the poll for their respective wards in 1881. In that year the opposition secured a majority of four among the elected members of the council. In deference to the situation the new mayor was the Wesleyan accountant T. C. Andrew, vice-president of the school board. In the following year the elected councillors consisted of 'twenty-five Economists and seventeen Cormorants,' to use the terms employed by the *Western Times*.[56] In 1883 the Liberals took full advantage of the Municipal Corporations Act of 1882 which included a provision depriving out-going aldermen of the right to vote for their successors. Seven Conservative aldermen who had come to the end of their term of office were replaced by Liberals and the majority party symbolically initiated the new regime by the election of Alderman Wilkinson as mayor, as they had inaugurated the regime of 1837 by the election of his father. The use made by the Liberals of the act of 1882 was the occasion of a naïve outburst of hurt feelings by the Conservatives who hitherto themselves had shown no hesitation in using the aldermen to maintain their control of the council. According to the *Flying Post* there was strong condemnation of the rejection, on political grounds, of aldermen who had 'long enjoyed the confidence and respect of the citizens.'[57]

The new Liberal regime was a passing expression of disillusion and discontent and was backed neither by social prestige nor economic power. A programme of purity and economy, in the circumstances of Exeter, was no substitute for organization. No individual could maintain himself effectively on the council without the backing of a party. The *Flying Post* expressed its view at this time that 'municipal elections are now, to our great regret, although invariably so to all appearances, carried on with strict and embittered reference to party politics.'[58] The complaint forms the *leit-motiv* of Exeter's council affairs since 1836 and neither party could disclaim responsibility. In the eighties the Ratepayers had no effective party organization. The movement rapidly dwindled or was absorbed by the Liberals.

A. E. Dunn, later the Liberal leader of the council, was described as non-political when he was first returned for St Mary Major's in 1888. The Conservatives retained control of the council until the end of the century with an ease which engendered complacency. Active interest in municipal elections dwindled. Only two wards were contested in 1895. None was contested in 1897; only one in 1899. The council minutes for this period are noteworthy for their frequent record of the lack of a quorum.

The city, however, was making progress in the evolution of its administrative machinery and in the extension of municipal activities. The first was a product of the second. Old habits still lingered. In 1882 the town clerk, Gidley, presented the council with a bill because, on instructions from the watch committee, he had appeared in court on behalf of a police constable. The dispute which ensued was referred to the arbitration of John Daw who held that since the town clerk was in fact conducting the business of the council he was not entitled to a fee.[59] When Gidley died, in 1888, his successor's salary was raised to £660 a year. The council undertook to provide offices and to pay the salaries of the three clerks who received £20, £80 and £120 a year respectively. Henceforward the office was to be opened at stated hours, from 10.0 a.m. to 6.0 p.m. on five days a week and from 10.0 a.m. to 2.0 p.m. on Saturdays.[60] The town clerk was becoming a professional, a change that was enforced by the growing complexity of local administration. But the older tradition, that local administration required the direct participation of councillors themselves, was revived briefly in 1905. When Gidley's successor died in that year, A. E. Dunn was appointed temporarily without pay on the understanding that neither he nor anyone connected with his firm would be a candidate for permanent appointment.[61]

By 1880 the deadweight of the canal bondholders, a legacy of the law suit of 1845, had become intolerable. Urgent work was delayed while the council and the bondholders wrangled over its necessity. When the double locks required immediate repair nothing could be done until the bondholders had taken a second legal opinion as to whether the projected work was to be regarded as normal maintenance or to qualify as extraordinary expenditure.[62] Two years later matters were brought to a head by the anguished appeals from the master and owner of the coaster *Mary* which had been unable to enter the canal for several days. The town clerk had much difficulty in ascertaining whether or not the bondholders would agree to the required dredging. He was eventually informed that they would not. In consequence the council put in hand measures to resume full control of its property.

The police reforms of 1847 were at length completed in 1891 when the council, under pressure from the home office, agreed that the sergeants at mace should no longer be regarded as members of the force.[63] By that time the old riotous customs of the city had been abandoned. Exeter's last serious riot occurred on 5 November 1879, when the authorities decided to prevent a wagon load of timber in St Thomas from being brought into the city for the customary bonfire. The wagon was guarded by men armed with cudgels. Disorder spread from the resulting fracas and the police lost control. The barricades, erected as usual for the protection of the City Bank, were torn down, and repeated attacks were made on the bank itself. Troops were called upon to assist the civil power and the Cathedral Close was eventually cleared in the small hours by the threat of bayonet.[64] Thereafter the Protestant ascendancy ceased to be celebrated in the manner of Lord Shaftesbury and the Green Ribbon Club in the seventeenth century. After 1894 there were no more bonfires in the Close; it was suggested that 'Young Exeter' had become more interested in cycling. For a few years the Salvation Army replaced Roman Catholicism as an excuse for rough behaviour in the streets.

In the eighties the council, in addition to wrestling with the temperamental chief constable, was tentatively feeling its way to modernization of procedure and methods and dealing with such matters as Messrs Veitch's novel application, in 1882, to erect a pole on the roof of the Higher Market to carry telephone lines. The chief constable had to wait for a telephone till 1901. In 1883 the council had been informed that a telephone exchange was established in the city, and that Exeter was about to be put into direct telephone communication with London.[65] It was in 1880 that the estimates of all committees of council were made subject to the scrutiny of the finance committee and the financial year first ran from April to March.[66] It was also resolved that 'new Municipal Buildings should be erected . . . in the proximity of and in connection with, the Guildhall,' a decision which was never carried out. Modern developments of this nature, however, did not affect the enduring realities of local politics. A petition was presented to the house of commons by Edward Johnson, M.P. to protest against the abolition of the right of aldermen to vote in aldermanic elections, a right which had been consistently used in Exeter in the interests of the party in power; and in 1883 the council made a bid for popularity by approving a rate lower than that recommended by the finance committee.[67]

In April 1882 a stretch of horse-drawn tramway, operated by a private company, was completed between St Sidwell's and Heavitree. The line from St David's station to the Blackboy turnpike was completed the following year. Portentious memorials from 'clergy, Nobility, Gentry and Residents in and about Exeter and from owners, lessees and occupiers of houses and shops in High Street and Queen Street' protested against any extension of the new system into the main streets of the city.[68] The venture was not a success and, as was admitted later, the original proposals were successfully opposed and emasculated by 'carriage folk and shopkeepers.' The total length constructed was only two miles and two furlongs. By 1894 it was necessary for the council to come to the rescue and to undertake repairs of the track on payment from the company of £400 down and thereafter £50 per annum.[69] Nevertheless, the first trams were the harbingers of the modern period of the development of the city and encouraged building activity.

Another long-delayed reform was achieved under the stimulus of the appalling disaster of September 1887, when over 130 people were burnt, suffocated or trampled to death in the fire which destroyed the Theatre Royal.[70] This disaster led to the institution of a municipal fire brigade. The council forthwith acquired the engines and equipment of the Sun and West of England Insurance companies, which hitherto had been responsible for fire-fighting, and appointed a superintendent in 1888. By that time electricity had reached Exeter. In January 1888 the surveyor was instructed to arrange for the experimental illumination of High Street, Fore Street and Queen Street by the new method. The experiment was followed by the council's decision to terminate the old agreement with the gas company in order to be given a free hand to deal with the question of street lighting.

New methods in street lighting are not necessarily an indication of vitality in a city but there were signs that Exeter was moving out of the stagnation which had prevailed since the end of the sixties. Council affairs remained dull as the last ripples of the ratepayers' revolt of the early eighties died away and the Conservatives settled down to the resumption of their traditional supremacy with a complacency which in due course brought its own retribution. 'Citizens will have learnt with dismay,' remarked the *Flying Post* in 1887, 'that after all the beautiful and clever runs on the word economy, which have been made by some of the leading soloists of the Guildhall choir, the general district rate that is to be levied is 2s. 4d. in the £.'[71] But Exeter remained a city of long memories. Though business was improving and the council was in safe hands there was a consciousness of lost independence and status. The Local Government Act of 1888, particularly as originally drafted, indicated that old county boroughs as small as Exeter were of doubtful relevance to the administration of the modern England. The act constituted sixty county councils with councillors elected by household suffrage. Boroughs with a population of not less than 50,000 were given county status. The original proposals involved a loss of status for ancient cities such as Exeter which did not have a population of 50,000. The Exeter council protested against a loss of independence and dignity which had been enjoyed for centuries. It was regarded as an insult, for instance, that according to the bill the sheriff of Devon would be the returning officer for county council elections while the mayor was appointed deputy in his own city. The bill was stigmatized by the town clerk as 'a blow at the ancient municipal institution of the county [of the city of Exeter], whose antiquity and tried capacity for self-government might, one would have thought, have saved them from the slight which the Bill puts upon them.'[72]

Exeter was not the only city whose dignity was at stake and the problem of the doubtful viability of the smaller boroughs in modern England was merely postponed. The mayor had the satisfaction of informing drawing the attention of the council to the announcement of the president of the local government board that the government had found it impossible to ignore the position of Exeter and certain other cities, counties of themselves, which, although falling in population below the limit fixed, had much claim on historical and other grounds to be retained as counties.[73]

For the moment the threat of recognition of an undoubted decline in status and importance was averted. By the end of the century political circumstances and reviving prosperity gave an illusion of the restoration of the life and activity of the old provincial capital as it had been when communications were slower, government less complicated and Whitehall less fitted to interfere with local affairs. In 1892 Exeter had the unusual distinction of a visit from Lord Salisbury. Gladstone had turned his attention to social problems and had announced his Newcastle Programme. The dissolution of parliament was at hand. In Exeter the old order assembled for the finale to the not-inappropriate strains of *Iolanthe*. Some 10,000 people were reported to have assembled to see the Conservative leader supported by Lords Clinton and Morley, Sir Henry Northcote and Sir John Kennaway, and to hear him express the new imperialism of the age.[74] Tributes were paid to Edward Sanders for a leadership of Exeter's Conservatism which had begun long before the prime minister was an undergraduate at Oxford. Sanders, recalling the reorganization of 1868, in his turn praised the chairmen of wards and committees who had done so much to ensure a Conservative majority in parliamentary elections. Grand finales do not usually reveal the secrets of production.

Sanders, himself a man of integrity and honour, aloof from the day-to-day work of city administration and politics, epitomized the best of that tradition of church and state which had maintained power in the city by harnessing social prestige to the down-to-earth practical politics of the men who had reinforced the party since the old days of Reform. By the last year of the century that tradition and its recruits were facing a resurgent Liberalism.

X

RELIGION AND EDUCATION
1870–1914

The Background

'England has no police tyrants like France,
no petty spies like Germany, but it abounds
in religious zealots.'[1]

'IT was odd but impressive,' observed the *Western Times in* 1871, 'to hear bystanders talking of the martyrs of old, and reflecting that it was only last year that we had an "infallible" Pope proclaimed by a General Council . . . Four centuries have rolled away into eternity since a General Council caused an Emperor to break his plighted word and burn alive the Reformer Huss in a great pile not unlike the one that lit up the cathedral yard so wonderfully last night.'[2] The bonfire and annual tumult, the refrain 'a rope, a rope to hang the Pope,' with which the fifth of November was celebrated in Exeter continued to perpetuate the enduring folk memories of the Reformation, of Fox's *Book of Martyrs* reinforced by the vigorous Protestantism of Charles Kingsley's *Westward Ho!* Exeter's new bishop was insisting, as he was to inform the meeting of the Devonshire Association in 1872, that 'there must be some deep connection between Science and Christianity, between truth given by reason and truth given by revelation,' that 'the scientific spirit and the Christian spirit must have something in common';[3] but the action of the Emperor Sigismund at the Council of Constance, in the fifteenth century, was still a potent influence on thought and behaviour in the Exeter of the 1870s.

Demonstrations of religious zeal, though exasperating to educational reformers, were an expression of the importance

which religion was to retain in daily life for another generation. The riotous behaviour each fifth of November was far
from being inspired wholly by religious feeling – it was also
an outlet for high spirits – but the great body of respectable
citizens would have assumed as a matter of course that
religious truth should be the indispensable basis of all
conduct in this world. The Wesleyan Thomas Andrew, when
as mayor he found time to speak to a working-class audience
on 'individual responsibility,' urged that

> 'the laws of a Christian state, enacted by Christian men,
> should be imperative' and suggested that 'only in this
> context could any individual rightly comprehend his
> relation to society, his duty to man, and his fitness for life.'[4]

The intimate relation of religion to practical life, and even to
political issues, was unquestioned outside what the census of
1851 had demonstrated to be the large area of pagan England.
If its less desirable consequences were the bitterness of
denominational differences over religious issues and, among
Anglicans, an intemperate opposition to Ritualism, the
religious context of daily life also sustained a high level of
religious observance.

The Church of England itself was entangled in politics by
its history. In a cathedral city such as Exeter it tended at this
time to be an influential wing of the Conservative party.
Exeter's Canon Cook informed a meeting of the Church
Defence Association in 1871 that 'after a long life and much
study he did not believe that the Church of England was in
danger.'[5] This detached wisdom was rare. Its growth was not
encouraged by the speeches of opponents of establishment
then or thirty years later. That the church was indeed in
danger was an essential plank in Conservative opposition to
Gladstone's policies and cemented the alliance between the
Church and 'the trade' which maintained Conservative
political supremacy in Exeter. In organizing Conservative
tactics for the school board elections of 1871, Alderman
Buckingham correctly assumed that 'the gentlemen who
would be nominated by the Nonconformists would probably
all be of Liberal opinions . . . no doubt Churchmen generally
were Conservatives.' Buckingham added, not without a touch

of condescension, that 'there were no doubt some good and highly estimable men of Liberal opinions.'[6] It is true that in 1870 the *Western Times* suggested that the fires of religious controversy were dying, that the church of late years had gained an increase of strength from the growth of 'indifferent-ism.' According to this argument the commutation of tithes 'had detached a large body of sympathizers from Non-conformity' and the abolition of church rates had 'closed the Exeter vestry against the recusant ratepayer.'[7] The Exeter newspapers however provide little evidence of 'indifferent-ism,' even in the years just preceding the Elementary Education Act. Apart from the controversies provoked by educational policy there was a brief recrudescence in the seventies of the old trouble over church rates. In 1874 humble men in the parishes of St. Mary Steps and All Hallows on the Walls resisted the payment of Dominicals, an obsolete charge inherited from the middle ages and involving householders in the payment of a few shillings a year. The clergy concerned may have been tactless in insisting on their due though, as they pointed out, their income from this source was included for rating purposes. Angry public meetings ensued and an auctioneer entrusted with the sale of distrained household goods was mobbed.[8] The affair blew over but, as the *Flying Post* observed with some truth, it provided 'political capital for local radicalism.'[9] The same newspaper rejoiced to see churchmen meeting at the Clarence Hotel 'in agitation against the encroaching spirit of the political dissenters' though Bishop Temple disapproved of public meetings for such purposes.[10]

Within the church itself the aftermath of the Tractarian movement was having its effect in the revival of old practices and an emphasis on the significance of ceremonial observ-ances unchecked by the disapproval of bishops or by the opposition of a strong section of laity. Ritualism did not in Exeter provoke the riots which followed the reintroduction of the surplice into the pulpit in 1845 and were a feature of ritualistic controversy elsewhere in England; but the Protestantism which harked back to the burning of John Huss observed with distaste that the rector of St Olave's crossed himself at the service inaugurating the restoration of his church in 1874 and some years later the appearance of real candles on an altar was vigorously criticized.[11] The *Western Times* and the *Flying Post*, though politically in opposition, were at one in their use of language which confused plain speaking with vulgarity in denouncing new religious trends. Memories of the old inconoclastic puritanism were revived in the seventies by the reredos presented to the restored cathedral by Dr Blackall and Chancellor Harrington. The reredos was adorned with the figures of saints and therefore, it was suggested, might lead men astray in the direction of ritualism. The chancellor of the diocese, a son of Bishop Phillpotts, took proceedings against the dean and chapter on the grounds that the reredos was contrary to the law. Religious passion could obfuscate common sense to such an extent that even Temple was accused of excessive tenderness to the Ritualists, but on this occasion the bishop held that the reredos had been erected without a faculty or other authority and so was illegal. This judgement and the objections to figures of saints, declared Archdeacon Freeman, 'would bring the Church of England under the imputation of having been for three hundred years a grossly idolatrous church,' a prospect which the opponents of the reredos accepted without misgivings as long as the cause of religion did not 'suffer in order that we may see how clever man may be in the imitative art.'[12] The *Gazette*, usually the mouthpiece of a cooler Anglicanism, deprecated the attempt to 'bring English churchmen of the nineteenth century under the operation of an absolute law passed under the Calvinistic principles of the preceptors of Edward VI.'[13] This in effect was the opinion of the judicial committee of the privy council which decided that the reredos did not endanger the faith of frequenters of the cathedral by encouraging idolatry; it was not illegal.

The revival of old ceremonies and symbolism in Exeter was unchecked by opposition. By 1904 the Women's Protestant Union, meeting at the Barnfield Hall, was informed that Exeter had become a 'hotbed of Popery in the Church of England.'[14] The strength of the church in Exeter towards the end of the nineteenth century owed much to clergy who revived old forms of ceremony, or as some preferred to express it, introduced scandalous innovations, but who were also exemplary and conscientious parish priests. By 1870 nine out of the fourteen incumbents had taken orders since 1850 and could have been influenced by the higher conception of clerical duties that owed so much to Tractarianism.

If, as the Rev. Henry Bramley declared in 1871, more church work was being done and more people were coming to church, this was in great measure due to the example and labour of the city clergy, hard-working and upright parish priests: Archdeacon Sanders 'a decided High Churchman . . . true blue to the backbone';[15] Galton of St Sidwell's, who had defended the licensed victuallers in 1872, a leader of the High Church movement in the city, to the regret of the *Flying Post* which, however, acknowledged that he left 'lasting evidence of his self-denial as a parish priest';[16] Canon Lee, an outspoken opponent of Gladstone's religious policy, generous in charity, beloved as a priest, with a reputation for a profound knowledge of the Bible and ecclesiastical law; the Rev. Theophilus Toye of the wealthy and highly respectable parish of St David's who, echoing Newman, told his congregation,

'It might be that the Church of God – whose rulers at least in this land, were found among the princes and nobles and her members among the godless and graceless – would go down to the dust and be exposed to hate and persecution on the part of many, before the world saw the value of that truth which faithless Christians unworthily upheld.'[17]

Labouchere's denunciation of 'fat canons,' at the Devon Liberal Club in 1890,[18] was at least a generation out of date.

The relative position of the Anglican and Nonconformist communities remained as it had always been. According to the figures published on the occasion of the Sunday School centenary of 1880, church schools at that time contained 4,422 children and the nonconformist schools 3,693, of whom 1,422 were in the Wesleyan schools. In 1838 there had been 2,470 children in the church schools and 1,193 in the nonconformist.[19] C. E. Rowe, mayor in 1902–1903, said on the occasion of the laying of the foundation stone of the new Congregational chapel in Heavitree that 'the Anglican church provided for 25 per cent. of the population of Exeter and the Free Churches for just over 11 per cent.'[20] In 1851 about 30 per cent. of the population at that time were members of the Church of England and about 19 per cent. were Nonconformist. There is no prospect of statistical accuracy. The most that can be claimed is that there is evidence of religious growth in later nineteenth-century Exeter which points to the probability that all denominations at least kept pace with the increasing population. The ethos of Exeter's prevailingly middle-class society, untouched by industrialization, little affected by the hedonism of a section of Edwardian England, or by science and the higher criticism, remained Christian.

Religious feeling and political differences combined to revive and excite interdenominational strife after 1870. The diminution in religious controversy which the *Western Times* professed to observe in 1870 was certainly short-lived. Yet the broad trend was towards mutual tolerance and respect between religious denominations.

Initially, interdenominational discord was restored in 1870 to the old level of passion which had marked the era of Reform by the Elementary Education Act of 1870 and by the reorganization of the endowed schools under the Endowed Schools Act of the previous year. The Elementary Education Act was designed to ensure that England should not 'become over-matched in the workshops of the world'[21] by reason of lack of skill and education. Good schools were to be increased without prejudice to the interests of the ratepayer but 'there was no intention of releasing the parent from all payment for the education of the child.' The act instituted school boards financed from the rates existing side by side with denominational schools eligible for treasury grants. The boards were authorized to make their own decisions as to religious instruction and whether education was to be compulsory.

It was necessary to fit into the new system the ancient and obsolete endowed schools, to 'render any education endowment most conducive to the advancement of the education of boys and girls' having regard to the 'government, management and studies of endowed schools.' A liberal education was to be put in reach of all classes. Governing bodies were to be reformed to include 'local knowledge and interests with freedom from local prejudices and influences.'[22] What were considered to be the ill-effects of gratuitous education were to be removed. In all this the endowed school commissioners had the powerful support of Bishop Temple who deplored the tendency for gratuitous education to lower the standard of education itself and firmly advocated 'intelligent adaptation' of the old foundations to the needs of the time.[23]

As the commissioners remarked, one aspect of their work, which created difficulties 'on account of the keen and almost irritable interest felt in it by not a few persons,' was the 'doctrinal or denominational character of the endowments.[24] The reaction to the commissioners' proposals aroused in Exeter interest which was certainly keen and not infrequently passed from irritation to heated anger. It was alleged that sacrilegious hands were being laid on institutions hallowed by time. The traditional benefits enjoyed by the few were to be more widely dispersed. Even worse, girls' education was to be financed by the reorganization of the old endowments. Governing bodies were to be diluted by the admission of strangers from the county of Devon. The very moderate fees were to be raised.

The schools which held an honoured place in Exeter's educational and religious tradition were the St John's Hospital or Blue School, the Blue Maids' Hospital, the Exeter Grammar School and Hele's.[25] The Blue School had been founded in 1629 to teach 'the principles of religion, writing and accounts' to local boys 'especially such as should be, or were likely to be, chargeable to their parish.' By the 1840s, only twenty boys were receiving free education and were 'maintained, clothed and occasionally apprenticed.' The master also had forty paying boarders.[26] According to

P

the banker Ralph Sanders, who opposed reorganization, 'the class of boys applying for admission were found to be the children of artisans or the better class of labourers, a class above the central or other Charity Schools.'[27] The grammar school was derived from a foundation of 1602 and was founded in 1629. By the mid-nineteenth century it was preparing pupils for the universities, the learned professions and the commercial pursuits, and had eighteen exhibitions to Oxford and Cambridge. A modern department had been instituted in 1853 'directed with a view to the examinations for appointments in the Army and Navy, and Her Majesty's Civil Service, and those of the East India Company.'[28]

Hele's School, derived from a charitable trust of 1632, had been founded in 1840 as part of the reorganization of Hele's Charity. Its buildings in the New North Road had been erected in 1848-49. It provided a 'semi-classical' education for day boys coming from a distance of up to one mile from Exeter. Fees were from one to two guineas with small charges for stationery and drilling. According to a sample analysis the pupils at Hele's were the children of 'small shopkeepers and tradesmen, innkeepers, drapers, builders and accountants.'[29]

By the seventies the Exeter endowed schools provided an inefficient and obsolete education; they drew on too restricted a field for their pupils. No adequate provision was made for girls' education. But they were traditional institutions. The proposals for reorganization therefore aroused a violent opposition. This was the opposition for which the Rev. John Galton spoke at a public meeting in the words of medieval barons resisting encroachments on feudal privilege, *nolumus leges Angliae mutare*.[30] That the reorganization was completed by 1875 owed much to the powerful advocacy of Bishop Temple. And so by the twentieth century Exeter could take pride in Professor Sadler's warm tribute to the city's secondary educational system 'due in no small measure to the reforms carried out in Exeter about thirty years ago, largely under the influence of Dr Temple, who was then Bishop of the Diocese.'[31]

Temple himself became Bishop of London in 1885 and

Archbishop of Canterbury in 1896. Rugged in manner, forthright in speech, administrator, educationalist and teetotaller, he was justly bracketed with his predecessor Phillpotts as a 'mighty and masterful prelate.'[32] His clergy did not always agree with him, and often said so. His views on the drink question were unpopular in influential quarters in the city. But he provided the leadership which assisted Exeter's transition from early Victorian England. Edward Bickersteth his successor, poet and hymn writer, was not one to create or ride the storms of controversy. In the days of Phillpotts and Temple the personality of the bishop had been a factor in the life of the cathedral city and often was dominant. Henceforward Palace and Guildhall tended to go their own ways on terms of mutual respect. This trend was not wholly due to the change in the personalities of the bishops. It marked a change in the relations of things spiritual and temporal which as a factor in the history of western culture transcends the history of a single city.

Educational Reform and Religious Revival

When Exeter began to prepare for the elections for the new school board of 1871 there was a delusive hope that a contest might be avoided by amicable agreement.[33] As events were to show, however, the Nonconformists included a radical wing which was not disposed to accept arrangements made by their habitual leaders. The Conservatives for their part made it clear that the school board elections were a political issue and that the decisions on representation were primarily a matter for the politicians as such rather than for the school managers. The church school managers held a meeting in early January 1871, at which it was apparently assumed that agreement might be reached on the denominational representation on the board. The Conservative political leaders then moved into action from the ranks of banking and the law. A further meeting held at the Clarence Hotel, at which the local politicians such as Alderman Buckingham were present, was followed by a public meeting. Buckingham declared that as

'the city had elected the Town Council members who were

supposed to represent them in public affairs, they would naturally expect that body would not only in those matters which came within their cognisance, but in all matters affecting the city, act so as to secure a sound footing on which to work.'[34]

In other words the composition of the new school board was too important to be left to school managers. Alderman Head, solicitor, mayor from 1864 to 1867, and once accused of being a mere instrument of the Hooper regime, moved at a public meeting that the proportion of Churchmen on the school board should be in the proportion of six to three. He explained that there were at that time some 2,700 children in church schools while the nonconformist schools provided for some 700 pupils. In support of the resolution Buckingham returned firmly to the political theme: 'The gentlemen who would be nominated by the Nonconformist would probably all be of Liberal opinions.'[35]

The Nonconformists leaders were not adverse to the principle of an Anglican majority on the board but they saw no reason why the majority should necessarily be Conservative. They were therefore anxious to ensure that one Anglican should be a Liberal. In consequence they were charged with an attempt to secure a Liberal majority. 'The Nonconformists demanded a contest, and the Church Party accepted without hesitation,' explained the *Gazette*.[36] The Conservatives were charged, on no obvious evidence, with intending to take the church schools from the control of their managers in order to 'clap them on the rates.'[37] The *Western Times* reported correctly that both sides accused each other of making the issue political. This being so 'the Tory junta transferred the management to the electioneering squad who controlled the elections.'[38] As for the Liberals, the newspaper roundly denounced their 'petty contentions, their small ambitions, their desire for a petty pre-eminence' and found it difficult to understand how, 'since they were split up into so many sections, each so exacting, any arrangement could be made for reducing the Liberal candidates to five.'[39]

The acerbity of the *Western Times* was caused by the

nomination of the Rev. John Jones as one of the Liberal candidates at a disorderly meeting which thwarted an attempt by the Wesleyan Theophilus Knapman to avert an open conflict. The *Western Times* explained that

'a section of the Liberals put up an independent candidate, a reverend gentleman who had been a Wesleyan minister, but who is now administering to a congregation who are independent of any of the great Nonconformist organizations. But as there was a section of the party who had been at war with the leaders of the Association, the reverend gentleman was taken up.'[40]

The Rev. John Jones administered to the Combe Street community, a small tabernacle founded in 1769[41] which had at first been Calvinist, then Baptist and finally had become Independent Methodist. Jones was the 'teetotal candidate.' He was of the lineage of those tender consciences who had embarrassed religious and political managers alike since Cromwell's day, whose stubborn insistence on the rights of the individual conscience had created the dynamic of English Protestantism.

A further complication was introduced by the nomination of the bishop's sister. The suggestion that Miss Temple might be a useful member of the board appears to have been thrown out by the *Gazette* without consultation with the party managers. Miss Temple was nominated by a group of working men as 'Miss Temple, The Palace, Lady.'[42] The nomination embarrassed the party managers on both sides. It was explained with truth that Miss Temple's 'virtues and her philanthropic labours and sound judgement . . . [were] admirably suited to make a most serviceable representative of the interests of the working class in respect of female education';[43] but the bishop's sister could hardly be regarded as an addition to Conservative representation on the board, while the Liberals were already experiencing enough trouble in their attempts to limit the nomination of their own candidates to five. An escape from embarrassment all round was provided by Miss Temple's dignified withdrawal on the grounds that doubts raised as to the legal correctness of her description might lead to the legality of her position being questioned. Accordingly she asked that no votes should be cast for her.

In the ensuing election there were eleven candidates for the ten places on the board, five church candidates, five official Nonconformists and the Rev. John Jones, 'the teetotallers' choice.' The Conservatives organized the elections with their accustomed efficiency. Edward Sanders, chairman of the church committee, issued a notice to impress upon churchmen that in view of the cumulative vote it was 'essential that they should act with unanimity and follow the directions which the committee proposes to give as to the distribution of votes.'[44] The Exeter Conservatives were apparently well aware of the tactics which carried the church party to an unexpected triumph in Birmingham.

Though the Conservatives were determined to ensure that the Church party was adequately represented on the new board by organizing their campaign with the skill acquired in the rough and tumble of local politics, they showed a wise moderation and made no attempt to swamp the board with their nominees. Since it was uncontestable that Exeter was overwhelmingly Church of England the representation of the two main groups of religious opinion proved to be such that the elections increased neither political nor interdenominational bitterness. The five church candidates were all elected: the Rev. Henry Bramley; William Barnes, banker; William Townsend, accountant; William Buckingham, solicitor; B. C. Gidley, solicitor and mayor. The Liberal members were Thomas Andrew, Wesleyan and accountant; the Rev. John Jones, Independent Methodist; William Mortimer, Unitarian and sharebroker; John Trehane, Methodist and wine merchant; Charles Westron, Liberal Churchman and tea-dealer. On the Liberal side the Rev. John Jones received the highest number of votes. Francis Dymond, a Quaker and one of the official Liberal candidates, was defeated.[45]

The new board settled down to work without delay. William Barnes was elected chairman at the first meeting, held on 2 February 1871. Thomas Andrew was elected vice-chairman in view of his position as 'representative of the largest body of Nonconformists in the city.'[46] The board set out to acquire a formidable quantity of official literature, including all the minutes of the council of education since 1847. A fulltime secretary was appointed in the person of John Austen, schoolmaster, at a salary of £135 a year. A sub-committee was also appointed to obtain the statistical facts upon which the board's policy was to be based.[47]

The facts were, according to the information obtained from the parish overseers, that the number of children of school age between the ages of three and thirteen was 6,500. Of this number, 1,385 children were already receiving education in higher grade schools. Efficient elementary schools already provided for 3,494 children and existing schools which might be made efficient would increase this number to 4,199. The board therefore proposed to provide additional accommodation for 950 children.[48]

The programme was adopted after sharp exchanges on religious issues. The bulk of the existing schools were Anglican and Andrew pointed out that to regard accommodation in these schools as adequate was based on a denominational criterion. Jones supported Andrew with a statement that the programme was 'utterly indefensible in principle and practice.'[49] It was, he said, as if the Catholics were in power and had maintained that there was no justification for providing more schools because there was already ample accommodation in their schools. Westron, the Liberal churchman, therefore moved that instead of the proposed programme of five infant schools and one girls' school to supplement existing buildings there should be three boys' schools, three girls' schools and three infant schools.

Westron's motion was seconded by John Jones. The debate was then adjourned, thus giving time for agitation to develop in the city. It was resumed on denominational lines with the support of representations from the Bible Christians of Providence Chapel and 450 Nonconformists, including most of the Nonconformist clergy.[50] Westron urged the adoption of the amended programme on behalf of those whom he described as being neither High Church nor Ritualist clergy. The existing church schools were already under the control of the High Church party and Westron felt justified in voicing the interests of the moderates and Low Churchmen. Henry Bramley asked for fair play for the establishment. He thought that the amended scheme would be 'launching into needless extravagance.'[51] The amendment was defeated on party lines and the original programme was adopted.

The board disposed of other matters amicably enough. Regulations were approved. Fees in the board schools were fixed at 1d. a week for each child under five and 2d. for each child above five. Schools were to be opened and closed daily with singing and prayer. The Authorized Version was to be read daily 'with such explanation and instruction in morality as was suited to the age and capacities of the children.' All religious books were to be first approved by the board.[52]

At the end of the first year of its existence, in August 1872, the board reported that there were 3,623 children on the books of efficient elementary schools, an increase of 736 compared with 1871.[53] In 1875, the opening of the new board schools in Holloway Street completed the programme approved in 1871; 1,790 places had been provided.[54] The new schools, blue-slated and red brick, austere and with a suitable flavour of Gothic, had arrived on the Exeter scene. They taught, according to the board's secretary, 'order, punctuality, ready obedience, thrift and neatness as well as elementary subjects of the three R's.'[55] They also perpetuated an undesirable emphasis on social distinctions. As the Rev. Henry Bramley informed his colleagues in 1871, 'in the schools which were entirely the Board's he believed the lowest class of children would be found. The higher artisans and some shopkeepers would not care to send their children with street Arabs.'[56]

The provision of school places within the meaning of the act of 1871 did not necessarily imply adequate education even for the children described as street Arabs. Dames' schools and similar institutions remained though these were reduced in number from fifty-three schools providing for 1,024 children in 1871 to thirty-four, with an attendance of 553, in 1875.[57] The majority of these schools continued to be conducted in unhealthy and otherwise unsuitable premises such as Dr Shapter had described thirty years previously. Since the act provided that it was not compulsory for a child to attend a public elementary school if he were being sufficiently instructed in some other manner, and since the ratepayers did not encourage an expensive educational programme, unsatisfactory and perfunctory education continued. Moreover the loss of children's work or earnings could be a serious matter. In St Thomas it was found that the dames' schools were 'used by certain of the lower classes as buffers between them and the stringency of the Act.' Children were liable to be withdrawn from dames' schools at any time to mind the baby, to run errands and help with the family or merely 'to graduate in the gutter for days at a time.'[58]

Nevertheless after the initial furore over religious and political issues, the Exeter school board settled down efficiently with mutual respect between members and with a commendable sense of duty. The standards deemed necessary at the time were enforced. Even the rector of St Mary Steps received a stern ultimatum that if conditions at the Ewings Lane school under his management were not improved the board would have no option but to declare the school inefficient. By 1888, when the total number of children on the rolls of the board and voluntary schools numbered 5,036 in a population of 37,665,[59] the committee of council on education were informed that in the southwest the programme of school accommodation, except in the growing towns, might be said to be complete. Exeter was not growing. The towns in the south-west where more accommodation was required were Plymouth, Portsmouth, Bournemouth and Southampton.[60] In 1884 the inspector had commented on the high standards prevailing in the city's elementary schools, as expressed in terms of places in examinations.[61] Average attendance figures in the nineties were higher in Exeter than in the cathedral cities of Canterbury, Gloucester and Lincoln, though lower than in York.[62]

The voluntary school system, and hence the Church of England's share in education, remained supreme. By 1900, 5,231 children were attending elementary schools in the city, 3,231 in the voluntary schools and 1,700 in the board

schools. Accommodation in the voluntary schools provided
for 4,824 children, twice the number of 2,324 children for
whom there was accommodation in the board schools.[63] It
was becoming evident that the voluntary effort could not be
maintained much longer. In 1900 the voluntary contributions
in Exeter amounted to 5s. 3d. per scholar on the basis of
average attendance. In contemporary Derby voluntary
contributions averaged only 2s. 1d. per scholar, in Gloucester
2s. 9d., in Lincoln 4s. But Bath could raise an average of 11s.
per head and Brighton 9s. 5d.[64] The surveys carried out by
the education committee of the council after Balfour's
Education Act of 1902 indicated that in general the voluntary
schools could not provide the higher standards accepted at
the end of the nineteenth century. Already by 1900 the school
board had been spending on each child £1 7s. 2d. from the
rates.[65] In 1906 Dean Earle explained in a vigorous sermon
that the council schools were spending more money on fewer
children than were the non-provided schools, the former
voluntary schools.[66] The dean's point was that council
education added to the burdens of the ratepayer; but the
real issue was whether educational standards were to be
subordinated to financial limitations.

The controversy aroused by the institution of the school
board had been acrimonious but brief. The denominational
control of elementary education had been at stake. That the
Anglicans triumphed was a reflection of the social structure
and traditions of the city, and of the numerical superiority
of the Anglicans themselves. Once the issue was decided both
sides settled down to a competent administration of the act
and controversy subsided until revived by government
policies in the early years of the twentieth century. The
opposition to the reorganization of the endowed schools was
equally passionate; it was more difficult to handle because it
came from the party of church and state, from Exeter's
'establishment' itself.

As Bishop Temple explained, the reorganization was
intended 'to provide a complete system of schools from the
highest to the lowest.'[67] There was to be a three-tier system
which in theory at least would form a ladder from the

elementary school to the university. On the lowest rung was St John's School designed as an elementary school and also as a model school for the training college where students 'could watch and study the best methods of teaching.' Hele's School was to be a second-grade school for boys between eight and sixteen destined for 'practical life.' The grammar school was to be a first-grade school drawing students from beyond the boundaries of Exeter as well as from the city and, through exhibitions, opening a door to the universities. The reorganization of the Episcopal Charity Schools, founded in 1709, was to provide for girls' education. In addition, a girls' high school was to be founded.

The bishop explained the merits of the proposals. He pointed out that wealthier citizens could afford to send their sons and daughters to be educated at a distance, but the great body of the middle class, who were now to be rated for the first time, had no efficient schools of their own.

As to the grammar school, Exeter was being treated as the cathedral city of Devon and Cornwall, not as an ordinary county town. The school would therefore admit boys from the county of Devon but the city would hold eight out of twenty places on the governing body. This change would be in the interests of the school itself since abler men would be attracted to the staff and 'men of learning and ability are often keenly alive to the dignity and position which they are asked to occupy.'[68]

The suggestion that the funds of ancient endowments should be used for girls' education, perhaps for a ladies' college on the lines of the one recently opened at Cheltenham, was greeted with cries of shame at a public meeting.[69] Dean Boyd, born in Londonderry and regarded as one of the ablest of the Low Church clergy, 'could not conceive a proposition more monstrous.' The bishop remarked sardonically that he saw nothing especially incongruous in providing an upper school for girls. He did not see how it was to be maintained that the middle classes, including shopkeepers, did not require efficient schooling for their girls as well as for their boys.[70]

Opposition was voiced at a meeting at which Mayor

Joseph Harding the brewer raised the flag of defiance.[71] To the accompaniment of cheers and applause he asserted that 'if the will of the nation is against the commissioners notwithstanding Acts of Parliament, the wishes of the people ought to be carried out.' The Liberal Unitarian William Mortimer, a member of the school board, had the temerity to cite the bishop as 'a gentleman whose judgement on the matter ought to command respect.' In view of Temple's experience in the educational field the comment was incontrovertible but Exeter's bishops could not flout tradition with impunity. Mortimer was howled down amid hisses and uproar. The Rev. John Galton followed with an attack on the bishop for his previous association with the Whig Lord John Russell and for being one of those

'whom the French called doctrinaire, that was to say, men who had a pet scheme and were determined that everything should bow before that scheme. Without entering into high politics he would simply state that men in high position at the moment were doctrinaire.'

In the circumstances it is not surprising that the proposals were defeated with only eight brave voices raised in their favour.

The banker Ralph Sanders, echoing Dean Boyd, declared that 'the proposal that £5,000 of the funds given for the clothing, maintenance and education of the poor should be applied towards the erection of a Ladies' College was monstrous.'[72] A large section of the respectability of the city was evidently not in favour of experiments in secondary education.

The reaction was due in part to affection for old institutions as such, to fears that the low fees would be raised, especially at Hele's, to a deep-seated suspicion of innovation and perhaps to the disappearance of the patronage arising out of nominations to free education. The council's opposition was reinforced by the support of Bedford, whose mayor informed Exeter that 'the Trustees of [the Endowed] schools and the Corporation of Bedford contemplated the most determined resistance to the aggressive policy of the Commissioners.'[73] The scheme could not, however, be opposed indefinitely by a mere veto. Exeter still had cultural traditions which were not blind to the advantages of reform, and the bishop's advocacy was both powerful and persuasive. Some amendments were made and the proposals were finally approved by the committee of council on education on 20 March 1875.[74]

The final scheme[75] embraced the charities and endowments of St John's Hospital, Hele's Gift, the Blue Maids' Hospital and 'the playing field and New Site Fund of the Exeter Free Grammar School lately raised by public subscription.' A capital sum of not less than £8,000 was to be applied to the new grammar school at which secular instruction was to be given 'so as to render the school an efficient school of mathematical and natural sciences and of modern languages.' A school for girls, the future Maynard's School, was to be established to provide 'secular instruction on a plan to give a sound liberal education to about one hundred girls between the ages of ten and eighteen.' Hele's school was to be continued to provide secular instruction 'calculated to give a sound practical education.' A new public elementary school, to be known as St John's Elementary School, was to be established for about 150 boys.

In 1885 a select committee on the Endowed Schools Act[76] was informed that five large schools had been established in Exeter; the Grammar School, the High School for Girls (Maynard's), Hele's School, raised in status and reorganized as an intermediate school between the grammar school and the elementary schools, a corresponding intermediate school for girls and St John's Elementary school for boys. As the mayor wrote with satisfaction, it had become possible for a boy to begin his education at the elementary school and to pass thence through Hele's School and the grammar school to a university, thus fulfilling Professor Huxley's conception of a 'ladder from the gutter to the university.'[77]

By the nineties, Mrs Armitage, reporting on secondary education for the Royal Commission of 1894, wrote that the 'higher castes' in the city were sending their girls to the high school.[78] Children of professional men were in a majority at the school but tradesmen's daughters also attended and traditional objections to the mixing of classes had to this extent been overcome. Because people of social distinction had from the first sent their daughters to the school it had been a success and had largely extinguished the work of private governesses. This example had also apparently overcome the misgivings of those who complained that the High School encouraged 'a want of modest bearing and a fast and slangy style among our girls.'[79] Mrs Armitage justly attributed the achievement to the influence and example of Bishop Temple.

In 1904 Professor Sadler reported that the proportion of 24.8 per thousand boys and girls receiving education in public and private secondary schools in Exeter appeared to be the highest in the country.[80] The grammar school had gained 'a remarkable series of distinctions at the universities.'[81] Sadler paid tribute to the affection with which Hele's School was regarded in Exeter – as it still is; but its curriculum had become obsolete, the buildings were inadequate, the staff badly paid.[82] Sadler's report made it clear that the Grammar School, the Girls' High School and Hele's all required modernization in various ways, Hele's the most urgently. His report was accepted in Exeter without difficulty. By 1907 all the schools had been recognized by the Board of Education as eligible for grants and therefore became liable to state supervision.

In Sadler's vision Exeter was on the road to becoming the cultural capital of the west. At the time of his report the Royal Albert Memorial College, so named after the visit of the Duke and Duchess of York in 1899, stood at the peak of the city's educational structure. That this was so was due to the inspiration and energy of the 'higher castes' upon whom Mrs Armitage commented in 1894. Sir Stafford Northcote had first suggested the possibility of a university for the middle classes in Exeter. The essential backing for the Albert Memorial Museum had come from the county. The development of the future University College was due to the fortuitous assemblage of educational facilities around the museum, to the aspirations of the 'higher castes' and the support which this aroused among merchants and 'higher tradesmen.'

Since 1869 the museum's science and art committee had organized the school of science and evening classes. University extension lectures supported by Cambridge began in 1875 at the urging of Miss Jessie Montgomery, 'one of the pioneers of the University Extension Movement,'[83] and as niece of Canon Cook a member of influential circles in the city. With the encouragement of a letter from Bishop Temple the first lecture was given in the presence of the mayor.

The original plans of the sponsors of the museum had been circumscribed by lack of funds; Exeter never enjoyed munificence on the scale that was possible elsewhere in Victorian England. By the eighties expansion had become essential. A public meeting was held and funds collected which made it possible for Mayor Andrew to lay the foundation stone of the art gallery extension and other improvements in 1882. The new building was opened two years later.

The museum committee and the university extension committee continued to work side by side till in 1893, again under the urging of Miss Montgomery, the council, the extension committee and the Cambridge Local Lectures Syndicate approved a plan for the merging of all educational activities under one principal. The extension lectures and the art and science classes were henceforward held in one building. Thus the Exeter Technical and University Extension College came into existence with a salaried staff and 400 students. As the Royal Commission on Secondary Education reported, university extension teaching had reached its most permanent organization in the University Extension College in Reading and the Exeter Technical and University Extension College. Reading was Exeter's model.[84] In 1895 a new wing was opened by the Duke of Devonshire in the middle of a general election which took up most of the space in the press. This extension was indebted to a bequest of the Unitarian, Kent Kingdon, who left £6,000 for the purpose. In that year Exeter was informed that the city's memorial to the Prince Consort begun thirty years before was at last complete. It was hoped that with the additional space provided the museum would become still more useful and that the College of Technical Instruction, 'an institution of great possibilities,' would have a home within its walls.[85]

In 1899 the Duke and Duchess of York opened a further extension of the college between Queen Street and Upper Paul Street which had been constructed to mark the jubilee of 1887. The principal informed the gathering that the occasion marked

'the realization of an ideal towards which the citizens of Exeter, and some of their friends, [had] been labouring for more than a generation, namely, the establishment of a comprehensive centre of higher and special education under the same roof with the Museum and Free Library. Henceforward the building was not only the Albert Memorial Museum but also the Albert Memorial College.'[86]

The final step in the development of the college was taken in 1901. In order to make its equipment complete as a local university college, such as existed at Nottingham, the council granted a 1*d.* rate. Attached to the college was the new Manual Technical College, founded to give instruction in technical subjects for boys who had passed through elementary or secondary schools. The governors of the Royal Albert Memorial College outlined a scheme to

'provide for efficient instruction under the ordinary heads of arts and sciences such as is required for University and other Higher Grade examinations, and at the same time as an integral part of that scheme, for that thorough guidance in Manual, Technological, and Technical, including Commercial Instruction, which is one of the great necessities of the time.'[87]

The council accordingly agreed that the mayor should be requested to convene a public meeting to discuss the measures required to extend the work of the college on the lines proposed.[88] This decision led to the construction of new buildings, including a college hall, which were opened in Bradninch Place in 1911. In 1922 the college became the University College of the Southwest of England.

The University College of the Southwest was the supreme achievement of Victorian Exeter, the inspiration of the old, restricted society, the world of the county and the close, supported by the professional and business men, Anglican and Nonconformist. Citizens who fostered the enterprise with time and money included William Kendall, the woollen draper; 'Scientific' Ellis, fellow of the Royal Astronomical Society, secretary in his time of the School of Art and the Albert Museum and vigorous collector of funds for the cathedral restoration; William Cotton, treasurer of the Arts and Science Department, and the Diocesan Board of Education, archaeologist and antiquary, National Provincial bank manager, historian of an Elizabethan gild and author of *Gleanings from the Municipal and Cathedral Records of Exeter*. Kent Kingdon was one, a member of a family of influence in Victorian Exeter; H. A. Willey was another, an industrialist in the modern fashion who gave generously to technical education, sent his workmen across the seas to study conditions in the United States and spoke to Exeter working men on the economic situation of the city. Of this group Willey alone represented the class of business men whose drive and imagination were not only bringing them fortune in wider fields than Exeter could provide but were also contributing leadership in local government and politics. The others who were 'in trade' were not typical members of the nineteenth century 'shopocracy,' they represented the old tradition of a city which had also been a centre of culture as well as of business and administration. It was for their like that the Devon and Exeter Institution had been founded in 1813. The demand for education in Exeter was inspired from above and owed nothing to pressure from, for instance, working men's associations and institutes. The development of the Albert Memorial Museum was the bequest to posterity of the old restricted governing society of the city. Michael Sadler, pondering on the historical processes, concluded his report on secondary education in Exeter with his expression of his 'sense of the vivid contrast between things old and new, sometimes estranged and yet in their true essence not irreconcilable.'[89]

By the time Sadler was investigating secondary education in Exeter the Education Act of 1902 had revived for the last

Q

time the old recriminations between Anglicans and Nonconformists which had impeded educational progress for so
long. The act constituted the counties and county boroughs
as education authorities. The board schools became council
schools. The denominational character of the voluntary
schools, henceforward styled non-provided schools, was
maintained, but they were to be managed by boards of whom
two members were to be appointed by the new local education committees. The Exeter diocesan board of education
welcomed the bill on the grounds that the scheme would
provide some financial relief for the church.[90] As Sir John
Kennaway admitted elsewhere in Devon, the voluntary
schools were 'in a tight place financially.'[91] For that very
reason the new system was opposed root and branch by the
Nonconformists. The president of the Southernhay Congregational Church in Exeter called for a 'protest against the
prostitution of political power to sectarian ends' on the
grounds that money was being taken from the pockets of the
people while power remained with the priests. J. A. Loram,
Liberal councillor and Nonconformist, urged all Nonconformists who had interest or influence in wards contested
in the current municipal elections to support those who were
prepared to opposed the new legislation.[92]

The opposition, though vocal and often bitter, did not
delay reform. In September 1903 the council, at that time
having a Liberal majority, approved the constitution of an
education committee of thirty-two members, including ten
appointed 'from among persons of experience in education
and persons acquainted with the needs of the various kinds
of schools in the city.'[93] An investigation into the sanitary
condition of fourteen voluntary schools providing for some
4,000 children was at once put in hand. It was discovered
that in no instance did a school 'quite reach to the full
standards of excellence set forth in the building rules of the
board of education.'[94] Some were distinctly bad. The
Cheke Street School, a private undenominational school for
ninety-five infants in 'somewhat unsuitable buildings,' had
neither lavatory nor cloakroom.[95] The cloakroom windows
of Hoopern Street school, for eighty girls and fifty infants,

were not made to open; the sanitary arrangements were 'very objectionable.'[96] Schools such as St David's school in Exe Street and the Wesleyan school in the Mint were cramped and crowded.

Exeter's non-provided schools could scarcely have been expected to anticipate the more exacting standards of the twentieth century. It was a frugal city in its attitude to expenditure, private and public alike, and the denominations who had endeavoured to meet educational needs for the past thirty years had no money to spare for trimmings. Despite defects the non-provided schools as a whole bore witness to devoted and conscientious effort. The Episcopal Schools and St Sidwell's Parish School were 'very pleasantly situated and had ample playgrounds'; the Rack Street Infant's School was 'modern and satisfactory.'[97] Nevertheless, overcrowding in schools had to be reduced, teaching standards and accommodation improved. The education committee set to work efficiently and with little friction. Despite the recrudescence of denominational storms as a result of the Liberal government's policy in 1906 and the hard things that were said in Exeter, the committee was a refreshing example of local government working harmoniously. Men and women from outside council circles were introduced to public life. Education tended to widen the field for active citizenship in contrast to other spheres of council activity which tended to be the jealously guarded preserves of council committees. By 1908 elementary education in Exeter was available for 3,250 children in eighteen provided schools and for 3,793 in twenty-two non-provided schools.[98] The rising cost of education from the outset raised problems of its own. In 1909 the council,

'having in view the heavy financial burden placed upon the ratepayers by the continuous and inevitable increase in the cost of education caused by the higher standard of efficiency . . . and realizing that the continued increase of the Educational Rate jeopardizes the progress of education works,' expressed the view that 'a far larger share of the cost of education should be borne by the Imperial Exchequer.'[99]

It was no longer possible to maintain an attitude of sturdy independence of authority in London.

Progress and practical co-operation in education combined with a growing tolerance, which did not yet imply indifference on religious issues. In 1906 Sir George Kekewich had attacked Lord Salisbury and the church in the language of early nineteenth-century Radicalism. The government would die

> 'stinking of drink. There would not be many at the funeral but those who attended would go arm in arm. The mourners would include the bishops and the brewers, the deans and the distillers, the priests and the publicans.'[100]

To the end of the Victorian era, Rome and Ritualism, educational policies and the newer issue of Welsh Disestablishment aroused antique drums. But the stridency of national politics which were a feature of the early years of the twentieth century concealed a growing interdenominational tolerance in Exeter. As early as 1883 it was observed that

> 'the ministers of the various churches exchanged pulpits, and thus the somewhat novel and pleasant experience was witnessed of Wesleyan ministers conducting the services of the Baptist and Free Church assemblies, the Congregationalists preaching to the Wesleyans and Free Methodists.'[101]

The denominations were coming together in practice in the face of problems common to all. The drink question had encouraged co-operation. When, in 1903, Bishop Ryle led a delegation to the licensing magistrates to support strict control of public houses, the delegation included the president of the Free Church Council and the bishop explained that all denominations, including the Church of Rome and the Salvation Army, 'were on this occasion absolutely united.'[102] In 1890 a clerical and lay conference held in the College Hall, South Street, had discussed the attitude of churchmen towards the labour question and was informed that preachers of the Church of England 'should not be prevented by fear of decreased contributions from speaking the truth plainly to the wealthy.'[103] And in 1894 the mayor, the surgeon E. J.

Domville, displayed a breadth of view which would have been inconceivable for the representative of Exeter a generation before when he spoke to a meeting of the Church Congress of a church which 'has numbered among its saints a Pusey, a Simeon and a Maurice, and is Catholic enough at the present day to take in Lord Halifax and Dr Barnardo.'[104]

True that in 1889 a meeting of the United Methodist Free Church representatives had discussed 'How can we fill our places of worship?' and in 1902 a conference of the deanery of Exeter attributed a neglect of Sunday observances and church attendance to increasing opportunities for pleasure.[105] For the first time in the Victorian era there were signs that religious leaders in the city were concerned with diminishing attendances rather than with the provision of accommodation for increasing potential congregations. As yet these signs were scarcely perceptible. It was this period which transmitted the Victorian Sunday of fact and fiction to the post-war world.

On all sides after 1870 there were signs of growth in religious observance. Already in 1867 it had been necessary to extend accommodation in the Mint Chapel. By 1875 the Baptist chapel in South Street had become too small for the growing congregation. The Anglican church of St Matthew's in the working class area of Newtown, was completed in 1887; the Congregational church in Friernhay Street in 1899. Substantial additions to the Bible Christian chapel, Mount Pleasant, were undertaken in 1903 to 1904 and the large Wesleyan church in St Sidwell's was completed in 1905. When the new Congregational church in Southernhay was opened in 1887 it was reported that membership had increased by some 200 in the past fifteen years.[106] The growth of the Catholic community was marked by the completion of the Church of the Sacred Heart, South Street in 1887. By 1900 the Exeter Wesleyan Circuit exceeded one thousand persons for the first time after a steady increase for some years. Wesleyan church-going would have been double this figure.

In the years before the first World War Exeter was experiencing the culminating point of a period of religious belief and observance which had exercised an immeasurable influence on the life of Victorian England.[107] The decorous family groups on their way to church and chapel, the bells ringing out over a small city in the silence of a Sunday morning, these bequeathed to a succeeding generation a memory and a tradition. At this point, at high tide before the ebb, Exeter's middle-class wealth and respectability erected its finest monument to the age in which that class had been formed. The new church of St David's, designed by W. D. Caroë, was consecrated on 9 January 1900 in the presence of mayor and council. In the opinion of a modern authority 'St David's church is the only church of the last one hundred years to stand up against the cathedral.'[108] It was also the first church in the city to be lighted by electricity. But it was noted, on Good Friday 1914, that 'hundreds of motor cars' passed through the city. It may be assumed that they were not on their way to church or chapel.[109]

XI

SANITAS SANITATUM 1870–1900

Economic Change

WHEN, in 1881, the census returns did not reveal that increase in population which was still apparent elsewhere, Exeter was reminded that the city was not growing 'simply because the process of growth, as a city, ceased many generations since.'[1] So, in 1899, the *Western Times* commented nostalgically that 'Exeter could not be described as a hive of industry though time was when that city was a thriving industrial centre.'[2] Even H. A. Willey, the enterprising creator of a successful industry, harked back to the past. 'They all knew,' he informed a working-class audience in 1900, 'that Exeter was once a centre of important industries which had employed large bodies of men, but that golden age had been followed by a period when the industries disappeared.' Willey added that the 'financial decadence' of many of the county families and the 'severe disaster and loss in connection with agricultural produce' had hit the city, and especially the working class, very hard.[3]

Exeter had known hard times before but since the disappearance of its old industries the city had been sustained by the prosperity of its surrounding society. This prosperity, and the society itself, were crumbling. Disaster had not come in 1846, but now at last 'the squire seemed struck in the saddle' by the agricultural depression which began in the seventies. Sir John Duckworth informed the annual general meeting of the Devon and Exeter Savings Bank, in 1879, that 'It was the most depressed time within our recent recollection.'[4] In the nineties the citizens of Exeter were exhorted to raise their eyes from the streets to the surrounding Devon hills where they would see their 'agricultural brethren struggling with misfortunes which no skill of theirs [could] temper or avert.'[5] In 1903 Willey returned to the theme of loss of rural purchasing power:

'Exeter men, and particularly those who have handled the industries and commerce of the place, know perfectly well that not a tithe of the money which the county used to spend in Exeter comes to it now.'[6]

The Hon. Mark Rolle had occasion to tell the world that he could no longer maintain the Stevenstone foxhounds. Since the Rolle estates at that time included 55,000 acres in Devon, worth £47,000 per annum in 1883,[7] the economy may have been little more than a gesture; even so it indicated some fears for the stability of the old order among the great Devon landowners.

The *Flying Post*'s description of the year 1879 as 'sunless, cheerless and melancholy'[8] fits Exeter's history in the seventies. Bad times were far from being the unique experience of the Devon capital. There was a severe economic depression throughout the country in the late seventies and another in the eighties. In 1879 the *Annual Register* recorded the distress caused by large-scale unemployment aggravated by a severe winter, conditions which were said to have brought close to starvation thousands of families who had lived 'in decent comfort.'[9] Exeter, however, had had little share in the prosperity which ended in the seventies and the depression which followed deepened the impression of a society in decline. The well-known Exeter coachbuilders, Standfield and Cross, went bankrupt in 1876. On Monday 9 December 1878 the West of England and South Wales Bank suspended payment after rumours which had led to a run on the bank on the previous Saturday. Some of the bank's local customers were left destitute, though the Exeter Freehold Land Society prudently withdrew its balance at the last minute.[10] Mayor and bishop together launched an appeal to relieve destitute shareholders.

The year 1880 was marked by the bankruptcy of Frederick Thomas, 'the practical hatter' and one of Exeter's more ebullient characters; of Palmyra House, Queen Street, Exeter; of New Bond Street and Barclay Gardens, London; of High Street, Barnstaple; hatmaker, dressmaker and costumier of Newcastle upon Tyne; contractor, peat exploiter and financial agent.[11] Thomas's failure was due to an unfortunate speculation in mining shares and no blame was attached to him personally by his business peers but his failure necessarily deepened the gloom which overhung Exeter at the time.

In the cold winter of 1878–79 Exeter once more found it necessary to relieve 'the miseries of poverty and extreme cold by the distribution of bread, cheese and coal tickets.'[12] By 1879 the number of cases relieved by the Exeter Relief Society had risen to 3,430, a figure which was only twice exceeded in the twenty years from 1850 to 1870: in 1855, the year following the bleak Crimean winter, and in 1870, when 3,584 cases had been assisted. An adverse balance in the society's funds was attributed to lack of work and destitution caused by 'the more than ordinary trying period which they had passed through.'[13]

It is perhaps too easy to infer from contemporary reports and comments that the economic situation at this period was one of inspissated gloom. The minutes of the streets committee indicate that there was a revival of building in the years 1878 to 1881. But in the ten years from 1870 to 1880 Victorian Exeter touched the lowest point of its fortunes. There had been bad times before, as in 1847, 1854 and 1867. The Exeter unemployed and slum dweller would have deemed it pointless to have been asked to choose between different periods of hard winters, unemployment and semi-starvation. What was new was the prevailing note of nostalgia for the past and the loss of the old pride and assurance of an ancient borough. Local self-government appeared to be 'rapidly dying out before the aggressions of Whitehall.'[14] It was complained that 'centralization held local authorities in an iron grip.'[15] Reflections on Exeter's diminished status in the roll of cities were provoked by the fact the Prince of Wales could not find it possible to do more than pause on his way through the city to an engagement in Plymouth in 1893. In the seventies there were few indications of faith in the inevitable and benevolent march of progress. The parliamentary franchise had been extended; the Municipal Corporations Act had offered an opportunity to respectability and substance to take part in local affairs under the stimulus and scrutiny of a vigilant press. After thirty years of opportunity for the 'civic spirit' Exeter found itself with a polluted river and inadequate, contaminated water supplies, overcrowding; neglected children and bad drains; a deathrate which had risen from 23.8 per thousand in the decade 1851 to 1860 to 25.3 per thousand.[16] These problems, it is true, were not confined to Exeter; but not all cities enjoyed the setting and natural amenities of Exeter, or its traditions of urban civilization.

Yet by 1900 Exeter enjoyed a more widely diffused prosperity than had existed at any time since the disappearance of the old woollen industry. This economic revival is not attributable to changes in the economic pattern of the city itself despite the industrial enterprise which made Willey and Co. not only the largest firm in Exeter but 'one of the largest engineering firms in the west of England.'[17] The census returns show that the broad categories of occupations did not change in any fundamental respect between 1851 and 1901. In the later decades of the nineteenth century the population of Exeter was still much as it had once been described by Dr Shapter, 'of no very distinctive character . . . a collection of gentry, tradespeople, artisans and the ordinary admixture of the poor.'[18]

In 1871 the professional class in Exeter formed a substantially higher proportion of the male population than in the more industrialized cities of Leicester, Nottingham and Northampton though it was lower than in Bath.[19] The industrial class formed over 55 per cent. of the total male population, far less than in Leicester, Nottingham and Northampton, larger than in Bath, Brighton or the then somnolent cathedral city of Gloucester. Large-scale concentrations of industrial employment did not exist. Firms such as Garton and King, and Vicary's, ironmongers and ironfounders, probably employed the bulk of the 147 men returned as employed in brass and iron manufacture. The largest occupational group remained that of building and allied activities, which employed over 13 per cent. of the employed males aged twenty and over. In contemporary

Norwich the proportion was about 10 per cent. Males engaged in the conveyance of men, animals, goods and messages formed about 8 per cent., much the same as in York and Bath, more than in Norwich and Leicester. The old staple industries of Exeter were close to extinction. There were only six fullers left in 1871. Woollen cloth manufacture employed five men and worsted manufacture one. In compensation 211 men were employed on the railways, about half the number employed in contemporary York and in the much larger industrial Leicester.

The pattern of female employment remained unchanged with some 70 per cent. of the total female population employed in domestic duties. In Leicester other forms of employment were available for women, with the consequence that the proportion of women in the domestic class was 63 per cent. and over 30 per cent. in the industrial class. Gloucester had an even higher proportion of females in the domestic class.

In the seventies Exeter remained a city with a livelier tradition as a social and administrative capital than, for instance, Leicester and Nottingham, but without the relatively large-scale industrial opportunities offered by the midland cities. More active economically than Gloucester, it contained also a leisured class and evidence of wealth that were significant but less so than in Bath.

By the twentieth century the basic economic pattern remained the same; but it was reinvigorated. The largest single source of employment in 1901 remained building and works of construction which employed 1,891 males a proportion of 1,120 per ten thousand.[20] This proportion, though lower than in York and Bath, was appreciably larger than the 918 per ten thousand of Leicester and the 916 of Norwich. Food, tobacco, drink and lodging took second place with 801 per ten thousand. Third came railways with 541 per ten thousand. Only ten of the major towns and cities of England had a greater proportion of males employed on the railway at this time. These included famous railway centres such as York, with 970 per ten thousand, and Derby with 1,009. Employment on road conveyance including 289 coachmen, grooms and cabmen, and 361 carriers, carters and waggoners, gave a proportion of 395 per 10,000. This was above the average. Though it was exceeded in twenty-one other towns the proportion of 395 per ten thousand. This was above the average. Though it was exceeded in twenty-one other towns the coaching days was being revived in a modern idiom.

Engineering and light industry in 1901 employed 424 men per ten thousand, a modest figure less than in York and Gloucester but larger than in Leicester where male employment was dominated by the 2,330 per ten thousand employed in boot and shoe making. General and local government gave a proportion of 211 per ten thousand, far larger than the 144 of York, the 102 of Leicester or the 115 of Nottingham. The proportion of males in merchantry and banking, 317 per ten thousand, was larger in Exeter than in York, Gloucester, Bath, Leicester and Norwich; and the proportion employed in professional services was also higher in Exeter than in the other cities with the exception of Bath.

The traditional female occupations, domestic service, charring, laundry services, milliners and seamstresses, shared the decline which had been a feature of the national economy as a whole after 1891. Nevertheless domestic service still employed 1,287 females per ten thousand, a much larger proportion than in a city like Leicester, where so many women were employed in hosiery, but smaller than in the growing residential towns such as Brighton and Hastings. After domestic service, laundry services, dressmaking, tailoring, charring and teaching were the major occupations for women. Female employment in commercial occupations had begun. It was still insignificant everywhere. In Exeter the proportion, thirty-three per ten thousand, was slightly lower than in York, Gloucester and Norwich, and significantly lower than the fifty-five per ten thousand of Leicester. Even in teaching the proportion of 143 per ten thousand was not remarkable. The proportion was higher in York as well as in prosperous residential cities such as Bath and Brighton. It was not yet the custom for married women to take outside employment.

The city's former importance as a centre of transport and communications was reviving fast, assisted by the vigorous competition between the Great Western and South Western railways. Nineteenth-century Exeter's role was undistinguished in the history of cities but railway rivalry gave it the first express trains in the world.[21] In 1904 the Great Western's *City of Truro* recorded a speed of over 100 m.p.h. on the run from London to Plymouth, at a time when the company was encouraging the growing numbers of holiday-makers to visit the newly-styled 'Cornish Riviera.'[22] More goods and passengers were flowing in and out of the city along the lines whose original construction had raised hopes of economic salvation when Queen Victoria was young. Houses for railwaymen contributed to the building boom that began in the nineties. The railwaymen themselves led Exeter's working class as an independent political force.

Thus through all vicissitudes the city's geographical position remained its primary asset and began at length to make up for the lack of the industrial resources and raw materials which had stimulated the growth of other cities. The loss of the purchasing power of the county, and the parlous condition of agriculture, were deplored with good reason in the early years of the twentieth century; but there was some compensation in increased expenditure on goods and services, including holidays in the west country. Exeter began to pay serious attention to tourist possibilities in the modern manner in 1898 when a meeting was held at the Guildhall to discuss a scheme for 'securing for Devonshire a larger share of the travelling public.'[23] The attendance was poor. Exeter as a whole was slow to take up new ideas, but the meeting foreshadowed a significant development which brought money to the city and plunged it into the intractable traffic problems of fifty years later.

Much of the evidence of economic revival at the turn of the nineteenth century is provided by building, which in itself was not so much a reflection of an increasing population as of higher standards of living and a more effective demand. The population of Exeter increased by only 5.5 per cent. between 1871 and 1881,[24] despite the inclusion of St Leonard's in 1877. In the following decade the increase was 4.6 per cent., and in 1891–1901 it was no more than 3.1 per cent.

Population growth had slowed down everywhere compared with the phenomenal increase earlier in the century; but in 1891–1901 Plymouth achieved a growth of 21 per cent. and the growing suburban town of Croydon one of 30 per cent. In Exeter's own suburbs growth was still marked. The population of Heavitree rose by 37 per cent. between 1881 and 1891, and by 20 per cent. in the following decade. The population of St Thomas increased by over 33 per cent. in 1881–91 and by 14 per cent. in 1891–1901. These figures were in accordance with the trend in Devon as a whole, where urban growth at this period was most marked in the holiday and residential areas.

In 1869 the streets committee had approved ninety-seven applications to build new houses; forty-seven of these were in respect of artisans' cottages. The figure was as low as fifteen in 1875. In 1878 ninety-eight applications were approved and in the following year 103. There were peaks of 162 in 1889, of 110 in 1895 and 238 in 1896. The annual average of new houses approved by the streets committee rose from fifty-four between 1878 and 1887 to eighty-six in the next ten years. In the years 1898 to 1907 the average was 165.[25]

The Barnfield, Denmark and Blackall Roads were substantially completed, and were named, in 1876 and in that year plans were approved[26] for the so-called Rougemont estate with its main thoroughfare to be called College Road. Powderham Crescent was declared a public thoroughfare in 1880 and four houses in this monument of comfortably pretentious architecture were completed by 1883. Similar development began in 1884 in the same area in Pennsylvania Road and its off-shoot Edgerton Park.

Houses such as these were required for middle-class clients. In 1877 the Exeter builders again turned their attention to the artisans' settlement of Newtown. Plans for the continuation of Sandford Street, John Street and Clifton Street were laid before the streets committee in December of that year. In 1878 the builder Septimus Hitt produced plans for a new street, to be called Portland Street, which were approved in 1878.[27] Progress was slow, the builders constructing houses in ones and twos and often employing the same architect. By 1901 the five main streets of modern Newtown, Portland Street, Sandford Street, East John Street, Chute Street and the Clifton Road, contained about 450 houses.

To the north of Exeter the lay-out of Gaol Field as a new street was approved in 1882, the streets committee approving a relaxation of the by-laws to allow a 28-foot road because the houses to be erected were of a class 'much required in Exeter.'[28] They were required primarily for railwaymen who occupied half the houses in Hoopern Street by 1901.

The nineteenth century's major contribution to the growth and appearance of the city was the angular rows of brick houses with their irrelevant ornamentation which appeared on the crest and northern slopes of the ridge carrying the Taunton road. In 1896, the streets committee approved the lay-out of the Mount Pleasant estate approved by a con-sortium of builders and planned by the architect J. A. Lucas,[29] Councillor Lucas from 1901. In 1896 permission was forth-coming for the erection of forty-seven houses in the Rosebery, Herschell, Salisbury and Iddesleigh Roads. The roads were adopted in 1899 and 1900; they contained 161 houses in 1901. Toronto Road, a new street for artisans, was begun with approval for nine houses in 1899.

Beyond the Conservative stronghold of St Leonard's similar development took place in this period when the streets committee approved the lay-out of the Larkbeare estate planned for the express purpose of providing houses at an annual rent of £9 for artisans earning 25s. to 30s. a week.[30] Construction begun in the future Radford, Temple and Roberts Roads, and in Dean Street. By 1901 these streets contained 178 brick houses occupied by carpenters, plumbers, gasfitters, railway employees and bricklayers.[31]

There was also a demand for middle-class housing according to Robert Pople, who said in 1897 that

'there were many who sought to live in Exeter if only they could find suitable houses at a rent of between £60 and £120. There were, indeed, many premises to let in the city but these were devoid of modern conveniences and

advantages or arrangements of modern houses.'[32]
The minutes of the streets committee indicate the attempts
that were made to provide these amenities: the additions of
bathrooms to houses in the Salisbury Road and Iddesleigh
Road, of box rooms and bay windows. Exeter had evidently
taken to heart Ruskin's enthusiasm for bow windows[33]
which became a reiterated motif of the period, not only in
neighbourhoods such as Blackall Road but in some of the
streets constructed for artisans.

In 1884 it was remarked that many buildings during the
past few years had 'given a new and distinct character to the
interesting architectural features of the city.'[34] In that year
Messrs Brock's new premises in 'what is known as the Queen
Anne style'[35] were completed at the top of Fore Street.
Messrs Wippell's new building in High Street was completed
in 1883; Messrs Hepworth's premises in North Street in
1891. The year 1899 saw the formation of the Exeter Brick
and Tile Company with a site on the Polsloe Priory Estate
and designed to manufacture 100,000 bricks a week by the
latest machinery.[36] It was completed in time for the expansion of brick-built Exeter. The appearance of Fore Street,
it was suggested at this time, had been greatly improved by
the new premises of Walter Otton, iron and steel merchant,
builder and general furnishing ironmonger.

The growth of the city by the end of the nineteenth century
was negligible by the standards of Victorian England which
had viewed with mingled awe and horror the onslaught of
progress on the countryside. In 1896 foxhounds meeting at
Farringdon could still run over farm land and kill in St
Leonard's.[37] Even after the first World War, Exeter was still
a relatively compact country town. But to contemporaries
about the time of the Diamond Jubilee there were signs of
growth such as had not been remarked for a generation.
The *Western Times*, commenting on the proposals to extend
the tramway system, noted that in recent years the suburbs
had grown considerably. Across the river the same trend
was observed in St Thomas where new rows of houses had
almost established contact with the village of Alphington.
Improved methods of transport increased the always close

economic and social contacts between Exeter's suburbs and the city itself until, in 1900, it was a logical step for Exeter to endeavour to absorb both Heavitree and St Thomas. As H. A. Willey had occasion to inform a public meeting the introduction of the trams, even the rudimentary system inaugurated in 1882, led to a substantial increase in property values.[38] But improved communications in themselves could not promote growth without the effective demand for houses for artisans and clerks. When a number of the new artisans' houses in Upper Sandford Street, Newtown, were offered for sale in 1881, potential purchasers were informed that they were let at a rent of £13; but the recently constructed houses in Jubilee Road were still available at £8 a year plus rates in 1900. Toronto Road, where a house with five rooms and a bath could be rented for £17 a year in 1904, was the domain of railway employees, carpenters, warehousemen, cabinet-makers, joiners and booking clerks.[39] The 'convenient £14 houses,' as they were described, in the new Mansfield Road, where construction began in 1893, were occupied by railway employees, police constables, grocers, tailors, accountants, engine drivers and railway guards; and by an inspector of Posts and Telegraphs occupying, in 1901, 'a conveniently arranged and well-built dwelling house with an entrance lobby, two sitting rooms and three bedrooms, bath, kitchen and offices' which had been let at £15, not £14, in 1898.[40] Larger houses in the new residential areas of the Mount Pleasant Road were let at £26 a year; in Prospect Park at £28, and at £38 in College Road.[41]

Georgian Exeter had been created to meet the requirements of prosperous merchants, professional men, and retired people in the higher ranges of society and the county. The new Exeter appearing towards the end of the nineteenth century was the creation of a shift in effective demand and reflected new standards in taste. From the business point of view the result was the same. From the records of Messrs S. R. Force and Sons, whose advertisements of houses for lease or sale first appeared in the local papers in 1870, it is possible to derive detailed information of house values and rents at the end of the nineteenth century. Revived prosperity

R

offered a return of between 6 per cent. and 8 per cent. on capital. Six per cent. was the return offered by the Exeter House and Land Co. when the purchase and renovation of dilapidated tenements was first broached in 1887; on a 'well-built brick and slate terrace of twenty-two houses' offered for sale in 1904; and on a pair of substantially built 8-room villas with fitted bathrooms and good gardens.[42] Six per cent. was the return on villas offered for sale at £550 in Mount Pleasant in 1899.[43] A block of 'five well-built houses let to good tenants and producing a net rent of £50' gave a return of 7½ per cent. But the Rougemont Hotel, established with the backing of a galaxy of county names in 1878, could as yet offer nothing more substantial than improved prospects 'of making the hotel a dividend-paying concern.'

The Condition of the People

'We live in a sanitary age,' declared the *Flying Post* in 1880, 'and whether they like it or not, Municipalities are called upon to spend money freely. Sewerage works, water supply and gas supply are the three leading questions before every municipal constituency in the kingdom.'[45] This reminder of the responsibilities of local government was doubtless intended as a rebuke to the restlessness over expenditure which was beginning to make inroads on the Conservative hold on the council; but it was also a reflection of a new attitude in the city which had been gathering strength since the seventies. Criticism of inadequate standards of public health was no longer regarded as a reflection on the reputation of the city as it had been in the days of Edwin Chadwick. Sanitary reform and civic improvements never became an electoral programme. No member of the council emerged as a leader in the cause of civic improvements. But the contemporary newspapers were united in drawing the attention of their readers to a situation which may have been worse in some of the new industrial agglomerations but were an affront to a city priding itself on its tradition as an urbane and civilized capital. The quarterly returns of the registrar-general showing the death-rate at Exeter in relation to that of other towns and cities were published and discussed. Exeter's varying position on these health 'league tables' was followed with keen interest and the appropriate lessons were deduced. The council, in the capacity of urban sanitary authority, set itself with painstaking pertinacity to improve standards. Despite the frequent expressions of regret that there had been, it was alleged, a decline in the calibre of councillors, there was no disposition to regard the health standards of the 1840s as good enough for the 1870s. Progress was slow. But the climate of opinion was more favourable to improvement than at any time since the cholera of 1832. That progress was made was undoubtedly due in great measure to the officials who had been active in local politics, and so carried weight behind the scenes, and to the representations of the medical men who also stood high in the social hierarchy.

There is much that is repugnant in the conspicuous consumption characteristic of the later nineteenth century when 'society' posed against heaps of slaughtered game, and stuffed birds added weight to women's hats. The ladies' column of an Exeter newspaper in 1891 had occasion to inform its readers that the newest fashions had been borrowed from the period of Louis XV and Louis XVI. The resemblance in contemporary fashion plates to the elegance of de Pompadour or du Barry is not obvious. In the extremes at either end of the social scale there is some parallel. Conditions at the lower levels are portrayed in the pictures of Sir Luke Fildes and William Mulready, in the report of the Royal Commission on Housing, of 1885, and in Rowntree's study of poverty in York. Exeter – and its county neighbours – had little contact with 'society' as exemplified by Marlborough House or Park Lane. Local wealth was never ostentatious. But under the surface of respectable traditions was the world of King Street in 1890, where female 'pugilists' fought before an admiring audience, and where dirty and verminous children were investigated by the inspector of the Society for the Protection of Children in 1899. Nostalgic reminiscences of the 'Ever Faithful' city by members of the middle classes were offset by the revelations before the magistrates in the Guildhall; and by the writer of a letter from Ontario in

1879: 'Much as I would like to see the dear old city, I should not like to starve for another fifteen years.'[46]

The city's social problems were muted and softened by a close-knit and still neighbourly society, which also inhibited protest. Artists aimed to please rather than to comment on the social scene in the manner of Fildes and Mulready. Exeter indeed had an interesting tradition in art since the time of Thomas Leakey and John Gendall. William Traies was hailed as 'the Claude of Devon' when he died at his house in the Topsham Road in 1872. Thomas Mogford, who lived for sixteen years in Exeter, had painted portraits such as that of the Earl of Devon, regarded as 'worthy of a high place among the pictorial records of England's older chivalry.'[47] Stephens, the sculptor, who died in 1882, left among other works the bust of Follett in the Devon and Exeter Institution, Prince Albert's statue in the Museum, and the Deerstalker on Northernhay. These artists lived to please, not to comment. They were followed by William Widgery the elder, who had begun life as a mason, and painted the romantic and the picturesque. William Widgery's son, Frederick John, was Liberal mayor of Exeter in 1903–04. His prolific output of paintings reproduced the seas and moors, the mists and colour of Devon. The Widgerys in particular were the forerunners of the host of lesser artists catering for the demand for the picturesque on postcards and calendars.

If no citizen acquired fame or notoriety as a social reformer, and if council elections, outwardly at least, were primarily an issue between the ins and outs or were fought over economy, public nuisances were at least more than inconveniences in the corners of some great slum. In a small, compact community a stinking river with its dead fish and irridescent water was a palpable offence to the eyes and nose of many respectable citizens. So was the smell from the gas works. The newspapers still retained much of their old role as public censors. It was the newspapers which in 1869 drew attention to the city's death-rate and pointed out that it was higher than in towns such as Cheltenham, Devonport and Ipswich; and in 1872 the *Flying Post* deplored the fact that the last return of the registrar-general showed that the annual mortality was 'five more than in London, eight more than in Portsmouth, six more than Birmingham' and was 'worse in the last quarter than Bradford, Leeds, Hull.'[48]

A report to the local board attributed the mortality of 1869 to inevitable fluctuations in sanitary standards and to the prevalence of measles and other infantile diseases. It was suggested that such things were in part the necessary concomitant of living in cities. But the report also drew attention to the defective drainage, overcrowding, ill-cleaned streets, bad water supplies and, more doubtfully, intimated that the smell from the Gas Ammoniacal Liquor Distillery and Manure Factory, in the Bonhay, endangered public health.[49] More to the point was the suggestion in the *Gazette* that 'the precipitation of the sewerage into the river' was an important contributory factor to the death-rate.[50] In the following year a fine was imposed for poisoning fish by flushing waste and chemicals into the Exe. During the proceedings a witness drew attention to the presence of dead dogs and cats in the water. The evidence is not perhaps proof of habitual pollution but it is clear from contemporary complaints on the state of the river that the Exe under the walls of the city was no longer merely remarkable for salmon.

The corporation of the poor recommended the appointment of a full time medical officer in 1879; but it was not till 1913 that the council became convinced of the necessity for this step. Reforms were not instituted until the need for them was demonstrably overwhelming. But when the need for action could no longer be ignored the council usually set itself to the task with practical common sense. Local politics and nineteenth-century jobbery merit criticism. The expansion of the council's social responsibilities and the persistence with which it set itself to improve conditions deserve acknowledgement. The period of domination by the licensed trade was marked by increasing vigour and efficiency in the council's measures to improve drainage and water supplies. It was also a period when Exeter's social leaders made a vigorous and practical contribution to the improvement of housing.

Since the inception of the urban sanitary authority in 1867, doctors and inspectors had been drawing attention to the squalour existing in the west quarter and elsewhere in the courts and side streets of the city. For this reason a public meeting at the Guildhall in 1873 launched the City of Exeter Improved Industrial Dwellings Company with a capital of £15,000 and the object of 'providing commodious and healthy dwellings for the poorer classes.'[51] £13,000 of the initial £15,000 required was forthcoming within twelve days. Sites were purchased in the old Mermaid Yard, and in the Blackboy Road, in order to construct tenements for lease at 1s. to 1s. 3d. a week. By November 1874 the first block, in Mermaid Yard, was opened. This building consisted of tenements of two to four rooms with larder, scullery, water supply, coal cellar and water closet. The rents were higher than was originally intended and ranged from 2s. 6d. to 4s. 6d. a week but, in that age of price stability, the full cost of the new buildings amounted to only £11,500. C. J. Follett, mayor and chairman of the company, informed his audience in the authentic accents of Victorian England that the project had left a balance of £3,700 and 'would tend to the moral and sanitary well-being of the city.'[52]

So Follett's Building was completed, a gaunt and austere construction which still today looks down from its commanding position upon the Inner By-Pass and the Exe. Kendall's Building in the Blackboy Road followed in 1876. A third block, Cotton's Building in Mermaid Yard, was completed in 1877.

Water supplies and sewerage were more intractable problems. The allegiance of the water company was to its shareholders and the regularity of its 6 per cent. dividend was an indication that in this respect at least it was efficient. But the company was unable to guarantee the supplies required by more demanding standards of health. Public opinion was aroused against a body which was accused, in the still robust language of public controversy, of 'wrongheaded and tyrannical obstinacy.'[53] In 1868 the company had been unwilling to guarantee water supplies for a minimum of two hours daily, and had showed itself equally unwilling to give the sanitary committee any information at all.[54] Discussions with the sanitary committee were desultory and profitless. The company's directors refused to allow themselves to be diverted from normal routine and the sanitary committee recorded the 'great disappointment of the Committee at the delays caused by the Water Company referring correspondence to monthly meetings of the directors.'[55]

Uncertain water supplies led to nuisances such as 'the offensive and unwholesome state of the public urinals from the want of a continuous supply of water'[56] and the council was driven to attempt to buy out the water company. The first attempt in 1871 failed, with the council offering £64,000 and the company demanding £94,000. In 1877 the council adopted a firmer line with a resolution that the time had come 'when it is necessary for the city to obtain its water supply from an unquestionably pure and unpolluted source, and that this supply should be in the hands of the Sanitary Authority, and, inasmuch as the first step in this direction would be the acquisition by the Town Council of the existing water company the Committee for the purpose recommend to the Council that the Water Company be asked whether they are willing to state their terms to the Council or to refer to arbitration.'[57]

The company gave way. In 1878 the council resolved to promote a Bill 'for empowering the Mayor, Aldermen and Citizens of the City and County of the City of Exeter to acquire the undertakings of the Exeter Water Company.' This resolution was followed by an immediate invitation for plans and suggestions for an improved supply. By the end of the century, and with the vital assistance of loans sanctioned by the local government board, the daily water supply in Exeter had been increased to thirty gallons per head. In 1901 the medical officer of health could report that the city's reservoirs were filled exclusively with filtered water.[58]

Sewerage was more controversial and difficult. The defects of the existing system were patent and offensive. It was asserted in 1872 that

'the sewerage of some fifteen or twenty thousand people

passed into an open leat or gutter through the most densely populated districts rendering whole parishes so foul that one unaccustomed to the pollution turns sick as he passes through the neighbourhood . . . after poisoning the district of the leat the filth all run into a bend of the river and is kept there as it were in a basin.'[59]

The St Thomas local board had occasion to complain to the city council about the smell from the Exe. This complaint was followed by a communication from the Earl of Devon drawing the attention of the council to the Rivers Pollution Act and adding firmly that the stench at Powderham and Starcross was certainly not caused by seaweed 'unmixed with other matters.'[60]

Defective domestic sanitation, or its complete absence, added to the malodorous and unhealthy state of the public sewers. Improvements were not encouraged by the water company's insistence that special charges should be imposed for water supplied for sanitary purposes. For new buildings the streets committee was imposing more adequate standards; but much of Exeter was old. Many house owners were reluctant, or unable, to incur expenditure. In 1876 the surveyor was instructed that 'particulars be obtained as to the working and result of the use of earth closets in Birmingham, Manchester and Hull' and to report on the best means of providing 'proper privy accommodation for the inhabitants of Badger's Row and other portions of the Commercial Road in which no adequate sewer existed.'[61] In the following year, the year in which the local government board expressed concern over the 'fatal prevalence of scarlet fever in Exeter,'[62] the surveyor reported on the alleys of Exe Island as 'wretchedly narrow, ill-paved, tortuous and utterly without ventilation.' In Garden Square there were five closets for eleven houses placed in a ground floor room which itself was 'wretchedly dark and indescribably filthy.' Investigations of a 'bad fever of a low type' in Saddler's Lane disclosed that 'the stench from the water closet in the room below stairs in the living room was unbearable.'

Without efficient sewers and adequate surface drainage the numerous wells still in use in Exeter could be lethal. In

1878, the sanitary committee directed the attention of the council and the public to the large number of wells 'the water of which has been found to be so impure as to be quite unfit for human consumption.'[63] Handbills were issued to impress the public with the need for the frequent and regular cleaning of domestic cisterns; even so the close proximity of water closets and water cisterns in slum conditions endangered health. In 1885 instructions were issued that drinking water should be disconnected from domestic sanitary systems. Some hundreds of domestic supplies were improved by the owners.

The disposal of sewage and its economic use had long been debated since the era of Edwin Chadwick. Schemes were advocated for converting sewage into fertilizer and so turning sewage disposal into a source of unlimited profit. In June 1870 the town clerk reported that a gentleman had desired him to state that

'he with others were planning to form a company which was prepared to construct all works necessary for the disposal of sewage on whatever plan might be adopted by the Local Board of Health (the Council) but without expense to the Board provided that a grant of the sewage were made to the company on terms to be mutually agreed upon.'[64]

The unnamed gentleman turned out to be Mr Walter Friend, solicitor, Conservative councillor for St David's ward, and an active figure in local politics. Mr Friend was persuasive and pertinacious. His proposals offered a worried council the prospect of solving the sewage problem at a profit. There were inevitable mutterings about a Tory job but a lease of the whole of the sewage of the city was eventually granted to a public company for twenty-five years. The sewage was to be treated by what was known as 'the irrigation principle.' It was to be conveyed by a conduit under the Exe and then to be pumped by engines to irrigate some six hundred acres of land.[65]

The prospectus of the Exeter Sewage Manure Irrigation Company was seductive. The company would fully utilize, and in utilizing purify, the sewage in order 'to grow all kinds of market garden' (*sic*) and to support a dairy farm. The promoters modestly disclaimed the prospects of profits in the first year of operation but expected a dividend of 'upwards of fifteen per cent' in the second.[66]

The prospectus evidently convinced the council but not prospective shareholders. No sooner had the agreement been formally sealed than the contractors ceased work for the sufficient reason that they were not paid. In February 1871 the contract was cancelled. In the following August the sanitary committee announced that 'the company having passed into liquidation and otherwise violated the terms of the grant of sewage the works so far constructed had become vested in the Local Board.'[67] Exeter was back at the beginning. Sanitary inspectors and the press continued with their variations on a distressing theme.

In 1880 the sanitary committee was informed by its medical advisers that

'typhoid was theoretically a preventible disease, so that as an abstract propostition there would be none if a perfect state of hygiene existed . . . practically it is always prevalent in large centres of population.'[68]

This advice suggested that there was little point in attempting the eradication of disease. Between 1871 and 1880 the death-rate in the city, 24.1 per thousand, was equal to that of towns and cities which had few of the advantages provided by Exeter's natural setting or its traditions of urban civilization. In Sunderland, for example, the death-rate for that period was 24.0 per 1,000. In Huddersfield it was 22.4 and in Cheltenham 19.3.[69] According to the minutes of the sanitary committee admissions of typhoid cases to the sanatorium averaged over seventeen a year, there were thirty-nine in 1882 and twenty-five in 1883. Cases of scarlet fever average over twenty-eight and over 250 in the years 1891 to 1894. In 1899 the implications of the pollution of the Exe were emphasized by an outbreak of typhoid in Exeter which resulted in eighty-five cases between 1 July and 11 September of that year. Three-quarters of these cases were children who had visited Exmouth and there had 'partaken of raw cockles gathered from the foreshore.'[70] Since an analyst reported that the diet of the cockles themselves consisted of sea-water and untreated sewage the moral was obvious despite the difficulty of apportioning blame between Exeter and Exmouth. Dead fish floating in the river below Exeter itself in 1887 had also been a patent reminder of the need for improvements though it was uncertain whether the cause had been the operations of the Trews Weir Mills or the cleaning of the open sewer of the old mill leat in the city itself.

Nevertheless no further action was taken to deal with the basic problem during this period apart from the raising of a loan of £4,322 for sewerage and street improvements in 1882. It was not till 1896 that the city was driven to pioneer a modern system of sewage treatment devised by the city surveyor, Donald Cameron. This was the septic tank system which the council adopted in that year on the advice of the sewage disposal committee and for which the great sum of £88,000 was required. The public acclaim was enthusiastic. 'Mr Cameron's septic tank system,' it was claimed in 1897, 'continues to grow in popularity and favour, and spreads the name and fame of Exeter to the ends of the earth.' Congratulations were lavished upon 'our talented surveyor for the discovery of the septic tank.'[71] The system was approved by the local government board 'as a practical mode of dealing with a difficult problem'; and because any great increase of population was considered 'a rather remote contingency'[72] the sewage problem was regarded as solved. Once a decision had been reached the work was carried out with despatch. In 1900 the water closets and drains which had discharged into the mill leat and the river were at last connected with the main intercepting drains.

The gas works did not affect public health but they undoubtedly contributed to the smells which formed a topic for comment and argument in the seventies. In 1874 the mayor had found it necessary to issue a notice requiring persons noticing the smell from the direction of the river to 'accurately note the time, the direction of the wind and all other circumstances tending to prove its source' and to send the particulars to the town clerk's office.[73] In the following year the sanitary committee noted that there were still offensive smells prevalent in the city and the surveyor reported that the gas supplied for consumption was 'heavily charged with sulphuretted hydrogen.' The committee observed that 'the inconvenience, if not personally experienced by all members of the Council, was at least only too apparent to many of their friends and could easily be verified.'[74] The magistrates dismissed a summons against the gas company but this setback did not deter the town clerk from declaring categorically that the result of the investigations made had been to 'confirm my opinion that the fearful stench which has been so long and so loudly complained of arises on the company's works.'[75]

An expert called in to advise on the state of the gas works reported in scathing terms. Whatever might have been the merits of the original buildings they had been added to haphazardly until the confusion of buildings and plant had become 'painful and distracting.' The apparatus was 'miserably insufficient.' The gas-holders should have been abandoned years before. No manager could reasonably be asked to take charge of works such as those at Exeter which had been 'starved and stinted in every essential particular.'[76]

This forthright report concluded with a recommendation that 'the Council of Exeter may very properly follow the example of so many other local authorities in acquiring the works and business of the gas company.' Negotiations were begun but the council's decision to acquire the property was frustrated by vigorous opposition headed by the formidable figure of the chairman of the company, Ralph Sanders. The terms approved by the council were generous. The shareholders were to be guaranteed the maximum dividend authorized, redeemable at twenty-five years' purchase. The company was to proceed with the private act required for the extension and renewal of its undertakings but the expenses were to be borne by the council. On this basis the company was to be acquired by Midsummer 1878.[77] The council accordingly resolved to promote a parliamentary bill for the purchase of the company.

The gas company, notwithstanding its shortcomings, was

a relatively prosperous undertaking. Despite the precedent of the water company there was no enthusiasm in Exeter for control of public utilities as a principle. The council therefore surrendered to the opposition with a resolution that

'inasmuch as the owners of property and the Rate payers of the City have on poll taken refused to consent to the purchase of the works and undertakings of the Exeter Gas Light and Coke Company by the Corporation no further steps be taken towards the completion of the purchase.'[78]

The gas company survived and prospered, reducing prices and increasing profits.

The improvement in public health since 1870 was demonstrated by the reduction of the average mortality to 16.4 per thousand in 1896. Smallpox was virtually eradicated. After a minor epidemic in 1896, when thirty-one cases were admitted to the sanatorium, there was only one case in the years 1897 to 1900. But throughout the period measles, scarlet fever and scarlatina dominated the minutes of the sanitary committee and the reports of the medical officers. The scarlet fever epidemic of 1891 resulted in 783 cases in three years with no less than 433 cases in 1893. Slum conditions, overcrowding and defective drainage continued to contribute towards disease; another factor was the easygoing habits of the population. There were complaints of 'the great want of care to prevent infection' when measles were prevalent in 1880.[79] An outbreak of typhoid in Gills Court, Cheeke Street, in 1888, was attributed to a patient whose friends had refused to allow her to be removed to the sanatorium.

The council moved conscientiously with the times. An analytical chemist had been appointed to 'test the illuminating power of the gas' in accordance with the Exeter Gas Act of 1865. The first full-time city surveyor was appointed in 1873 at a salary of £500 a year. Posts of inspector of gas meters, an inspector under the Workshops Act, and an inspector of petroleum were all in existence by 1870. Anxiety over the mortality rate in the city in 1879 led to strong representations from the corporation of the poor, advocating the frequent analysis of milk and other foods, the suppression of brothels and the appointment of a full-time medical officer of health. These representations were followed, in the same year, by the appointment of the first medical officer of health for the whole city in the person of Dr John Woodman at a salary of £100 a year for part-time duties. In this respect as in others Exeter was correct without being adventurous. Of the twenty-three cities and boroughs from which information was obtained for the guidance of the sanitary committee[80] at this time only three, Chester, Cheltenham and Warrington, employed a full-time medical officer.

Improved sewerage and water supplies could be secured by vigorous action from above. They required little more than the preliminary convincing of educated men. The reduction of infantile mortality, though depending in part on the progress of medical science, required above all a fundamental change in the circumstances and attitudes of a host of individuals for the most part living in the conditions of poverty and ignorance which, as revealed by a report of the corporation of the poor in 1879,[81] existed in a small cathedral city. The investigations of the corporation of the poor disclosed that in the illegitimacy rate Exeter had an unwelcome pre-eminence. For the seven years ending August 1878 the proportion of illegitimate births to legitimate was sixty-seven per thousand. It was forty-five per thousand in contemporary Leicester, forty-seven in Coventry and fifty in Plymouth. The high infantile deathrate in general, according to the report of the corporation of the poor, was due to a widespread ignorance among mothers of all classes regarding the treatment, clothing and feeding of children. Narcotics and drugs were used liberally. Gin, brandy and other preparations were commonly administered as sedatives. Illegitimate children fared the worst. Out of 502 illegitimate births in seven years the deaths had numbered 163 or 324.7 per thousand. The corporation's committee reported that it was a common practice for illegitimate children to be put into the hands of foster-mothers in return for a lump sum down. Too often, it was feared, it was in the interests of both parties for the child to die. In the year 1875 there was a notorious baby-farming case in Newton Abbot which shocked Devon and drew from the *Western Times* the comment that 'guilty mothers are not infrequently best pleased with the nurses that soonest bury'[82] the children. Doctors suggested, too, that syphilis existed in Exeter to a greater extent than in other towns though they were doubtful about the influence of syphilis on the infantile death-rate.

Infantile mortality in Exeter long remained abnormally high in comparison with other towns. In 1885 the sanitary committee noted that the average rate in the city was 184 per thousand though the average for the fifty towns with which Exeter was classed was 143.[83] Four years later the committee was still expressing concern over 'the practice of giving soothing syrups and opiates, frequently of an improper character.'[84] The infantile death-rate was reduced to 143 per thousand in Exeter by 1903 but it had fallen to 135 per thousand in over one hundred other large towns.[85] The high rate in Exeter in the early years of the twentieth century was attributed to bronchitis following measles and to 'that regrettable cause, improper feeding.'[86] There remained, too, the dirt, overcrowding in old houses and bad sanitation to which excessive infant mortality had been attributed in the seventies. As Dr Shapter had commented some sixty years before 'We may fairly assume that Exeter, as a city, is hostile to infancy.'[87]

There were of course towns with much worse conditions than existed in Exeter. Urban concentrations such as the growing industrial town of Wednesbury were grappling ineffectually with scarlet fever and smallpox. High infant mortality was common to Europe as a whole. But Exeter had taken pride in the relatively healthy environment which had attracted visitors since the end of the eighteenth century. Higher standards of health were expected than those of a raw industrial town or in the mining villages of Durham and Glamorgan.

Though infantile mortality presented special difficulties, the general death-rate in Exeter had been reduced to 17.9 per 1,000 by the end of the nineteenth century from an average of 24.1 per 1,000 in 1871–80. This sign of progress was but one factor in the all-round amelioration of conditions which was taking place with growing momentum after the seventies. Another factor, though less marked, was the rise in wages. Labour itself was unorganized. Only the building trades, representing the largest single block of employment in the city, were responsible for such strikes of significance as occurred in Victorian Exeter.

In 1873 a meeting of the Exeter carpenters and builders at the Phoenix Inn, Goldsmith Street, charged the Exeter master builders with failing to introduce a nine-hour day in accordance with a previous undertaking. The builders were asked to increase the basic rate of pay, which seems to have been the equivalent of 5*d*. an hour for a fully skilled man. A further source of grievance was the allegation that local contractors brought into the city labourers who were paid at a higher rate than were local men. The mayor arranged for a delegation of the men to meet the master builders who refused any concession other than a reduction of working hours from 58½ to 56½ hours a week. The strike lasted for three weeks and ended with an agreement to raise the average wage from 5½*d*. to 5¾*d*. an hour. Rates in future were to be based on the hour and the working week was to consist of 56½ hours, including six and a half hours on Saturdays terminating at one o'clock.[88]

Despite the references to average wages the concept still had little practical significance. In the eighties some Exeter carpenters and joiners earned 21*s*. a week according to the board of trade.[89] Bricklayers earned 31*s*. 9½*d*. a week in summer and 28*s*. 5*d*. in winter. In 1857 the carpenters in the regular employment of the council had been paid 3*s*. a day or 18*s*. a week.[90] If it can be assumed that this was an average wage, the council was never particularly generous, the wages of carpenters in Exeter had risen by 15 per cent. in close on thirty years. The board of trade's statistics of 1888 cannot be accepted as evidence of the rates earned by all artisans in the building trade of Exeter at this period; but they confirm that Exeter was a low-wage area and support the reiterated complaint of men on strike that higher rates were paid elsewhere. Of the 269 towns for which statistics were compiled only one, Penzance, appears to have paid lower wages than did Exeter.

The agreement of 1873 remained in force for seventeen years. In 1890 the woodworkers, carpenters and joiners demanded shorter hours and an average wage of 6d. an hour. At that time the men worked for 61 hours a week in summer and for 54½ hours in winter.[91] The strike which followed when the men's demands were rejected had a sympathetic press. It was noted that the men lacked speakers capable of explaining their case. Strike pay was fixed at 15s. a week for unionists and 12s. for non-unionists. Some working men in the city contributed with difficulty 1s. a week to the cause. Though funds were hard to raise the men remained out during July and August. In August they agreed to arbitration. The award accepted by both sides was that

> 'the standard or average rate of wages to be paid to competent carpenters and joiners was to be at 6d. an hour, but it shall be lawful for employers and employed to enter into any special agreement to increase or reduce wages in individual cases of employees either possessing particular or extra skill or not being fully competent.'[92]

As the *Western Times* pointed out,[93] the strike of 1890 disclosed the weakness of trade unionism in the city. It had cost the strike committee £525, out of which £470 had been spent on strike pay and £25 on 'sending men to situations.' A relatively substantial donation of £139 18s. was received from the Carpenters and Joiners Union, £20 from the Amalgamated Engineers and £3 from the Brassworkers and Plasterers' Society. The strikers' balance sheet was presented to a meeting by A. E. Dunn, solicitor and rising Liberal politician.[94] Dunn was the first local politician to show serious interest in working conditions and for activities of this kind he was accused of Radicalism. Mark Kennaway, in the different circumstances of a previous generation, had been content to urge the virtues of hard work and thrift.

A short strike in 1892 was settled by amicable agreement which brought the wages of carpenters, plasterers and painters to 6½d. an hour. A more serious strike in the building trade began in July 1896 and lasted till September. This brought pay in the building trade to the level recorded by the

S

report of the board of trade's investigation of 1906.[95] Earnings varied from 28s. 11¾d. a week for painters, 33s. 5¼d. for plasterers and 35s. for plumbers. Carpenters and joiners earned 33s. 5¾d. The bricklayers received the highest hourly rate of 8d. an hour. Some artisans, such as the painter, carpenter, plumber and mason employed by the city asylum, were still receiving less than these rates in 1914.

James Kelly, the organizing secretary of the General Railway Workers' Union, paid two visits to Exeter in 1890 to form a local branch of the union. He informed the Exeter railwaymen that they were lagging behind Plymouth and Taunton, which already had railway unions, and claimed that the railway workers in Exeter were worse off than they were in other towns.[96] Men on the London and South Western railway were said to be working thirteen to fourteen hours a day for 15s. a week, the amount which had been distributed in strike pay to the Exeter woodworkers. A few railway porters at this period were certainly paid no more than 10s. to 15s. a week, though the great majority received 15s. to 20s. Guards and brakesmen for the most part received 25s. to 30s. a week and the majority of engine drivers 30s. to 40s.[97] These rates were not generous as compared, for instance, with the pay of the council's scavengers, which had been raised from 18s. to 19s. a week as far back as 1877; and in the nineties John Martin, a plasterer of drunken habits, was reported to be earning 30s. a week before his appearance in the magistrates' court.[98] But railway pay was based on a prized regularity of employment. To this extent the railwaymen were better off than the majority of artisans in Exeter and their position does much to explain the demand for artisans' houses which gave impetus to building activity in Exeter at the end of the century, and also the relatively large numbers of railwaymen recorded by the directories in the new brick streets. In the background were the agricultural labourers of Devon with an average cash wage of 12s. 11d. a week and total average earnings of 16s. 11d. In Northumberland and Durham the average was as high as 20s. 2d. and 20s. 9d. respectively;[99] but Devon in general, and Exeter in particular, could not offer the employment in industry and mining which stimulated wages in the north.

In 1891, as in 1871, domestic servants still held the highest average deposits in the Devon and Exeter Savings Bank.[100] The figure had risen from £34 14s. 5d. to £38 16s. 7d. Wages in domestic service had undoubtedly risen substantially between 1870 and 1900. General servants who, for the most part, were paid £7 to £14 a year in 1871, depending on age and experience, could expect £10 to £18 a year in 1900. The wage offered a 'plain cook' rose from £10 to £15 a year.[101] Domestic service on any terms was no longer quite as attractive as it had been in the past. It was sometimes necessary to attract applications for employment by explaining that servants were required to work in small families or that washing was sent out. The Exeter housewife had begun to feel the competition from hotels which offered as much as £20 a year for a housemaid. In 1896 an indication of further opportunities for women appeared in Messrs Lipton's advertisement in the local press seeking 'a respectable girl of about sixteen' for the firm's cash desk in Fore Street.[102] The cash desk offered a window onto a more exciting world for girls than that suggested by a contemporary advertisement for a 'thorough domesticated mother's help.' Commercial firms, too, did not normally interfere with the private lives of their employees to the extent suggested by the frequent insistence that applicants for work in domestic service should be churchwomen or not Dissenters. By the end of the nineteenth century 378 female assistants were employed in eighty-seven establishments in the city.[103] Pay might be exiguous but a new source of family income had been established to contribute to the marked improvement in standards of living which was apparent in the years before the first World War.

No survey of working-class conditions was ever undertaken by Victorian Exeter and no authoritative study of a household budget exists. During the building strike of 1890, however, the *Western Times*[104] published the weekly budget of an artisan earning 26s. a week, an income which was far from universal in Exeter even in 1914. In general, prices rose and real wages therefore declined after 1890. An artisan on 26s. a week would have been relatively better off in 1890 than after the Boer War though there were other factors which contributed to later improvement in the conditions of the Exeter working class as a whole. Exeter remained a cheap city in which to live.

According to the budget published in the *Western Times* weekly expenditure on 26s. a week was as follows:

Rent	4s. od.	Tools	6d.
Trade club	6d.	Bread	4s. od.
Sick society	7½d.	Vegetables	1s. od.
Clothing and boots	3s. od.	Tea	10d.
Sickness	9d.	Meat	4s. 6d.
Coals	1s. od.	Soup	4d.
Gas, oil, candles	6d.	Milk	7d.
Sugar	8d.	Butter or lard	1s. 4d.
Soda, pepper, salt	4½d.	Rice, oatmeal, fruit	8d.
School fees	4d.		

There were apparently only two children each incurring 2d. a week in board school fees. No provision is made for beer or tobacco. There is no margin for contingencies. In contemporary York, families with incomes of between 21s. and 30s. a week and three to four children were considered to be just above the poverty level.[105]

It was possible to exist, with care and good luck, on low earnings. Intemperate habits could lead to disaster. This was the fact which inspired the too easily derided zeal of the temperance movement. Exeter remained hard-drinking. A total of 110 persons were prosecuted for drunkenness in 1873 and 161 in 1900.[106] Prosecutions were unlikely to have been instituted unless drunkenness caused a serious public nuisance, and allowance must be made for varying zeal on the part of the police. In 1891 the porter at the Exeter workhouse was not only drunk but was reported to have been unsteady on his feet for several days.[107] Members of the new fire brigade turned up drunk at a fire in 1901.[108] Drink was a factor in too many of the cases involving cruelty to, or neglect of, children, such as a plasterer and his wife, of Gatty's Court, with their neglected children 'filthy, stinking, flea-bitten and verminous'; a hawker of Smythen Street who sold his horses, cart and furniture for drink and varied drunkenness with assault and felony; a Preston Street mother prosecuted for neglect of her children by reason of her addiction to drink.[109]

Shenton Thomas, whose astringent comments first appear in the report of the local government board for 1897–1898, commented that 'if the condition of the poor were the only factor in determining the amount of pauperism, the West of England would figure more favourably in the Poor Law returns.'[110] In 1899 he insisted that Exeter was prosperous. Food prices in general were lower than they had been for many years and food itself was more varied. Dairy products and vegetables, according to the local market reports, remained at about the same level from 1870 to 1900. Potatoes, sold at 14d. to 16d. the score in January 1870, were sold at 8d. the score in January 1900. The quartern loaf ranged between 4d. and 5d. in 1900 and at that time was cheaper than ever before.

By 1871 the shops in Exeter High Street and Fore Street had begun to advertise imported meat which was much cheaper than the local product. Bacon, available at 1s. per lb. in 1875 to 1880, was being sold by Liptons at 5½d. to 6d. per lb. in 1900. Tea was offered by Liptons at 1s. per lb. in 1900, perhaps half the price of the comparable quality in 1870. The corporation of the poor, which had paid 2s. per lb. wholesale for tea in March 1870, paid 1s. 2d. in September 1900.[111] In 1870 men's suits had been offered from 25s. 6d. upwards. In 1900 ready-made suits for men and boys could be obtained at prices ranging from 15s., and suits made to measure from 30s.

Opportunities for amusement had become more varied and gave greater opportunities for individual tastes and personal freedom. Roller skating had become popular in the seventies with the opening of the Devon and Exeter Skating Rink in the Magdalen Road. Girls who would not have been allowed to attend a public ball appeared at the rink unchaperoned. The status and popularity of cycling were marked by the attendance of the mayor and sheriff at Cycling Club dinners. Bank holidays and cheap rail travel were giving new opportunities for travel and enjoyment to clerks, shop assistants and artisans. By the nineties the Whitsun bank holiday enabled over 6,000 persons to leave the Exeter railway stations for Bristol, Bath and Bournemouth.[112] Some 3,000 went to Exmouth which was then beginning its modern period of development. In contrast some of the more genial customs which had ameliorated the hardships of life for the poor were disappearing. In 1898 the licensed victuallers announced the end of the traditional practice of providing ham and rounds of beef at Christmas for the housewife who had brought her jug regularly for the dinner and supper beer.[113] The bakers, who had followed a similar custom, ended it at the same time.

Leisure was still precious and hard-won. In the seventies agitation in favour of earlier closing had been met by angry refusals to submit to dictation by shop employees.[114] In 1875 the council had been petitioned in vain to allow the closing of the markets at an earlier hour than 10.30 p.m. on Saturday nights.[115] It was argued at the time that in most Devon towns markets were never kept open after 9.0 p.m. In 1890 many Exeter shops did not close till 8.0 p.m. and suggestions that shops should be closed at 7.0 p.m. on Mondays and Fridays in summer had no effect. Two years later Tiverton was declared to be more progressive than Exeter because its shops were closed regularly at 7.0 p.m. on Mondays and Wednesdays, and as early as 6.0 p.m. in the summer. The Exeter Early Closing Society had respectable backing. In 1894 the sheriff presided at a meeting which he informed that in regard to early closing Exeter was more backward than Plymouth, Torquay, Taunton and Barnstaple.[116] In this respect, however, Exeter refused to reform itself and effective action to secure early closing could not be taken until the shop hours acts of the twentieth century.

Improving conditions of living were accompanied by signs that the confident Victorian assumption of the connection between moral and material progress was weakening. There were suggestions that 'the great boon of a free press [was] not without its drawbacks, not to say its evils.' The young were said to be tempted by 'the most pernicious publications which [were] openly or covertly vended in alleys and byways.'[117] These publications apparently included books such as *Three Pretty Sisters; or Paris after Dark*, which was advertised in the local press of 1895 for 1s. as a 'startling new form of sensationalism.'[118] In the same year a female 'young person' appearing as witness in an assault case shocked the magistrates by admitting her addiction to cigarettes. Even the existence of the intelligent artisan appeared to require more qualification than political reformers might have admitted in the past. When lectures were planned for artisans on 'Social teaching of the Victorian Era,' in 1898, it was sorrowfully acknowledged that 'not a dozen of the artisan class attended.'[119]

The problems of the twentieth century were already taking shape at the time of the Diamond Jubilee. Nevertheless, Exeter was beginning to present a picture of a more widely diffused prosperity and, insofar as anything so illusive can be assessed and measured, of greater happiness than at any previous period in the Victorian era. Hard times in the old sense were far behind but their memory was not so faded that wider opportunities for enjoyment and better standards of living were not prized. The tone of the city was still set by the county and professional classes. The atmosphere was still that of a slow-moving society based on the Devon countryside and expressing itself in the Devon speech. The county was hard hit economically and politically but for a brief spell Exeter appeared once more as a provincial capital. It was the era of General Buller, of Colonel Kekewich in beleaguered Kimberley, and the Devons charging under Colonel Park at Waggon Hill. Visitors were flocking to the Victoria Hall to pay their sixpences to see Poole's *Myiorarama* of the battle of Colenso with 'General Buller in the thick of the fray carrying a wounded soldier to safety'; or even to watch 'dissolving views and cinematograph and the latest war pictures.'[120]

For a brief and final moment Exeter in 1900 recalled the sunshine of the agricultural show of 1850, even though the resemblance was short-lived and illusory. With revived prosperity the long rearguard action of the old society was ending. It had been maintained by economic immobility, by difficulties of intellectual and physical contact with the outer world. A presage of more rapid change was already marked when in 1899 a motor car 'in the shape of an ordinary four-wheeled carriage with a hood' was observed in difficulties on Fore Street Hill.[121] Exeter's great days as a provincial capital had been based on the improvement of roads and the growth of wheeled traffic in Devon at the end of the eighteenth century. The railway train and the motor car at last brought new life to the city and with it the end of the society and traditions fostered and protected by the age of McAdam and the horse.

THE END OF AN AGE

XII

EXETER IN 1900

A SPEECH by H. A. Willey to the Exeter Working Men's Society in 1900 was a curious echo of the views expressed at the time of the British Association's Visit in 1869, and repeated in the historian Freeman's book on Exeter, published in 1887, that Exeter was essentially a city of the past.[1] Willey was an imaginative and successful businessman whose operations were on a sufficient scale for some 800 employees to be taken by special train for the firm's annual outing in 1900. It was therefore the more surprising that his remarks to the Exeter working men[2] should have been coloured by regret for the passing of the city's industrial power nearly one hundred years before, and for the decline in the purchasing power of the county, rather than by emphasis on the return of prosperity that was apparent in 1900.

If the attempt is made to arrest at any moment of time the almost geologically slow movement of Exeter's Victorian history in order to portray the city, the year 1900 is the first point at which it is possible to form a firm impression of new vitality and growth, of widening prosperity and vastly improved conditions of living. In 1837, and again in 1850, the city had been overshadowed by the problem whether, and on what terms, it could adjust itself to the new and increasingly industrialized and urban England. Neither the social life and culture which characterized the city in 1837, nor the brief second flowering of an old-style provincial capital in 1850, could conceal the failure to devise a substitute for the loss of the old woollen industry. The city continued to live on the impetus derived from the retention of old habits and tastes and the survival of the tastes and influence of a landed society. By 1870 even this impetus had died away.

Thirty years on it was evident that the city had come to terms at last with the England created by the Industrial Revolution and the extension of the parliamentary franchise.

It had done so as decisively as the larger cities standing in the forefront of Victorian England though less dramatically. With this adjustment and revival of material prosperity there was also a revival of the city's attracting power as a provincial capital.

By the end of the century the agricultural interest had been shaken economically and was losing the remnants of its political and social power, though Rider Haggard, writing of the years 1901–02, came to the conclusion that Devon was not suffering from economic difficulties such as prevailed in the corn-growing counties of eastern England, especially in the rich lands surrounding Exeter and despite the exodus of agricultural labourers seeking better pay and more varied life in the towns.[3] Exeter's geographical position remained. New wealth and new opportunities flowed down the roads and railways converging on the lower reaches of the Exe. It was significant that the Exeter Corporation Act of 1899 provided powers for the replacement of the elegant eighteenth-century bridge by a modern structure. Though the motor car had already made its appearance, and within a few years Exeter was to see the aeroplane, the old inns of the city were still performing their ancient functions as the departure points for the waggoners and carriers setting out to the small towns and villages of Devon. From the Bull, the Crown and Sceptre, the Black Lion and the White Hart there was daily contact by carrier with Crediton, Exmouth and Dawlish. From the Black Lion the carrier went four days a week to Sidbury and Sidmouth.

Within the framework of the railways the economy was still based on the horse. On Fridays the principal inns of the city rang with the clangour of wheels and horse-hoofs on the cobbles and the farmers came in by gig and trap for the most important market of the week. The carriages of the county magnates still brought tradesmen respectfully to the door. Exeter was a west country city. The Devon dialect was the natural voice of the streets and, subject sometimes to parental reproof, of the children of the gentry. Only one in five of the population was born outside the county. The largest contingent of foreigners, 610 males and 809 females in 1901, came from London.[4]

Fortunes that were moderate by contemporary standards were derived from the traditional professions and trades with two significant exceptions. John Hancock, the brick and tile manufacturer, left over £120,000[5] in personal estate; this in itself was an indication of Exeter's belated participation in the urban expansion of Victorian England. The Hoopers had also risen to wealth through building but that had been towards the end of the eighteenth century, in the classical age of Exeter as a provincial capital. H. A. Willey left over £90,000 in personal estate. Edward Sanders the banker left over £120,000. Other fortunes followed the established pattern. Personal estates of brewers, wine merchants and hotel proprietors ranged between £13,000 and £35,000; the law, coach-building, hat making, printing, the trade of tobacconist, jeweller and draper, between £10,000 and £50,000. Church furnishing yielded £82,000.

Estates such as these were an indication of an expanding demand for consumer goods and services which Exeter could meet as an administrative capital and a centre of distribution at a time when the railways were making their long-delayed contribution to the city's economic life. Prosperity was the note of the Exeter share list[6] at this time, with the shares of the Exeter Gas Company, St. Anne's Well Brewery and Kennaway and Co. all standing at a substantial premium. Even the city's market bonds, a relic of the unhappy state of semi-bankruptcy at the beginning of the Victorian era, stood at £105–£106. The chairman of the Devon and Exeter Savings Bank announced that receipts and investments were increasing and suggested that 'thrift among the working classes was more pronounced than before.'[7] According to the report of the local government board for the year 1899–1900, trade was generally prosperous throughout the southwest despite the acknowledged difficulties experienced by the farming community.[8] It was an indication of prosperity and business activity that the Rougemont Hotel was showing signs of fulfilling the expectations of its promoters. A modest profit in 1899 had been ascribed to the Bath and West Agricultural Show, which had been held in the city in

that year, and to social occasions such as the visit of the
Duke and Duchess of York and the reception for Sir Henry
Northcote.[9] In 1900 the hotel declared a dividend of 3 per
cent. The general prosperity of the city at this period and its
moderate wealth is suggested by rating assessments. Exeter's
assessed value amounted to £5 8s. od. per head of the
population, lower, it is true, than the figure for Bath, Brighton
and Cheltenham but higher than the figure for York, Leicester
and Norwich.[10]

Exeter lived not solely on the proceeds of trade and
industry but also on the more intangible attractions provided
by a provincial capital. By the beginning of the twentieth
century there had been some revival of the circumstances of
the old days when the county had flocked to the city to vote
for Lord John Russell or young Mathew Parker, to celebrate
victory or to find solace after defeat. The analogy cannot be
pressed too far; nevertheless Exeter's political and social
importance, and the resulting economic benefits, at the turn
of the century owed much to the course of politics and to the
activity which followed Lord Salisbury's visit in 1892. The
by-election of 1899 when Sir Edgar Vincent replaced the
newly-made peer, Lord Northcote of Exeter, and the general
election of 1900, were conducted in the city with all the
traditional skill: the bands and the crowded meetings; the
working men pulling the Northcotes' carriage in procession
through the streets; the throngs cheering for General Buller,
acclaimed at a Conservative meeting as one of the greatest
generals of the day and presented with a sword of honour by
Lord Clinton. The scale was not the same. The splendour of
the Subscription Ball of 1837, attended by three members of
parliament and 'about 250 of the rank, beauty and fashion
of the county,' was not quite repeated for the 160 who
attended the Christmas Ball at the Rougemont in 1900. But
the *Flying Post*, reflecting in 1901 that the late queen left a
'happier, busier and more prosperous England,' found no
occasion to make an exception for Exeter. Pride was evident
even in such mundane matters as public health. The chamber
of commerce assembled to hear a paper describing the city's
successful adoption of the septic tank system, an occasion

marked by a reception by the mayor.

Exeter had been once more caught up in great events and had emerged from the years of obscurity. When, in January, the mayor presided at a public dinner for the Devon Yeomanry and the Volunteers, the city was also anxiously awaiting news from Ladysmith where Colonel Kekewich was prominent in the defence. There was a sense of personal involvement when the city was decorated on 19 May for the relief of Mafeking and the crowds thronged the streets to sing 'Soldiers of the Queen.' General Buller, massive, hard-riding and a paternal squire of the old tradition, was Exeter's neighbour, and also the city's hero to an extent that was reinforced by the general's differences with authority in London. Kekewich, Drew and Park and the two battalions of the Devonshire Regiment were fighting in South Africa with the panache which could still infuse war with romance and inspire an almost Elizabethan pride in the men of Devon.

Trade benefited from the revival of social and political life in these years. Shops such as Tucker's, fashionable and relatively expensive, made money from the requirements of the wives of country gentry and citizens attending the reception for the Duke and Duchess of York in 1899, the entertainment for Lord Northcote, or the annual ball of the Yeomanry. Establishments such as the Exeter Arcade were doing well. Despite the difficulties experienced by landowners and farmers, for the numerous gradations of the middle classes life was becoming more comfortable and apart from domestic service, more cheap. High standards of personal service were the accepted concomitant of daily life. The proportion of domestic servants to the total number of separate occupiers or families in the city was 24 per cent.[11] In prosperous Torquay it was 42.8 per cent. but it was only 17.6 per cent. in Plymouth. In Heavitree, Exeter's residential suburb, the proportion was 28.2 per cent. Pillar boxes were cleared seven times a day on week days and twice a day on Sundays. Milk was delivered twice daily.

In St Leonard's a 'handsome detached house' with a good garden could be bought for £1,650. In Pennsylvania a detached house with three reception rooms, five bedrooms and a bathroom could be bought for £1,050 or leased for £60. One of the modern houses multiplying along the Polsloe Road could be bought for £375.[12] Angular rows of brick houses were spreading on the outskirts of the city from Lion's Holt in St David's to the Mount Pleasant estate in St Sidwell's, in Heavitree and Larkbeare, and across the river in St Thomas. For houses such as these the rents paid by artisans ranged from 4s. to 5s. 6d. a week. Despite the new streets, Exeter was still a compact country town. The deep elm-shaded lanes, the water-meadows with their kingcups and yellow flags, were no more than a short walk from any cottage or tenement.

The theatre was enjoying a prosperity such as it had not known since the 1830s. It was even providing unprecedented opportunities for Exeter's society. Irene Vanbrugh, daughter of Prebendary Barnes of Heavitree, was a star of the Edwardian stage. The old theatre in Bedford Circus had been burnt down in 1885 and replaced by a drill hall opened by the Duke of Cambridge. Its successor in Longbrook Street had been destroyed in its turn by the terrible fire of 5 September 1887. It was promptly replaced by a new building complete with a modern fire curtain, and electric light, which was opened with a performance of *The Yeomen of the Guard* in 1889. Large audiences came to see the Savoy Operas or the repeated revivals of *The Sorrows of Satan*. Patriotism which for a later generation was to be evoked by *Cavalcade* was aroused by *The Ladder of Life, or Gordons to the Front*. This was the heyday of the pantomime when special trains from Exeter's hinterland brought the country audiences to enjoy the spectacular effects and topical humour. The demon kings and fairy queens, the wicked uncles and all the other genial and long-descended denizens of the world of folk lore and tradition were still safe for another generation.

Market prices suggest that the cost of living was cheaper than it had been in 1870, thirty years before.[13] Eggs, in January 1870 and January 1900, could be bought at one dozen for 8d; butter was cheaper, at 16d. per lb. compared with 18d. to 20d. Rabbits cost 6d. to 8d. each in 1900 instead of 10d.; potatoes 8d. the score instead of 14d. to 16d.

According to the tenders of the corporation of the poor the price of soft soap had fallen from 30*s*. 6*d*. to 24*s*. per cwt. and oatmeal from 16*s*. to 11*s*. 3*d*. Roll tobacco was bought at 3*s*. 6*d*. per lb. instead of 4*s*. though shag had risen from 2*s*. 11*d*. to 3*s*. 4*d*. The strong local cider cost 9*s*. 6*d*. for a hogshead in 1900. Bass cost 2*s*. 6*d*. the dozen.

For women such as Mary Lock, of Harding's Buildings, Exe Lane, attempting to maintain four children on the 15*s*. a week provided by a drunken husband,[14] and for many others, life was hard. The Salvation Army met a real need by providing breakfasts for 1,000 poor children in 1900. Even in 1908 an examination of 1,800 Exeter school children disclosed the uncomfortable fact that 3.3 per cent. suffered from rickets and 3.5 per cent. were insufficiently clothed.[15] But in comparison with the past, 1900 was a prosperous time for men in employment. Public health had improved sufficiently for the sanitary committee to be emboldened to suggest that the Royal Institute of Public Health should be invited to hold its annual congress in the city in 1901. The old custom of the wayzgoose survived. W. J. Southwood and Co., engravers, entertained about eighty of their employees in London. James Townsend and Sons took some 160 employees to Southampton.[16] It was remarked by 1901 that many people failed to remember the significance of the Fifth of November; but 6*d*. secured admission to patriotic entertainments at the Victoria Hall or to watch Devon play Durham on the county ground. The annual sports organized by the Exeter Cycling Club were cheap and popular.

Though the prosperity of Exeter in 1900 and the revival of its attracting power as a provincial capital are apparent, the traditional social and political pattern was crumbling fast. Despite the superficial resemblance with the days when the county came to Exeter to oppose Lord John Russell or defend the corn laws, 1900 was the year of the most striking political transformation in the Victorian history of the city. It came at a time of prosperity and imperialism when Sir Edgar Vincent seemed entrenched as the city's parliamentary representative. It was itself born of prosperity. There were no premonitory warnings other than the usual grumbles over

T

rates and rising expenditure.

With the absorption of the populous part of St Thomas into the Exeter municipal area by the act of 1899[17] and the consequent rearrangement of the city's wards, Exeter had been divided into fourteen wards with between six and seven hundred electors in each. The council elections of November were required to elect three councillors for each ward. Out of forty-two only ten Conservatives were returned. In seven wards no Conservatives were returned at all, though St Leonard's maintained its reputation as a Conservative stronghold by rejecting all three Liberal candidates; so too did St Petrock's. The election was a decisive defeat for those whom the Liberals usually described as the 'Tory monopolists.'

For the Conservatives the election result was the shattering overthrow of the old order by lesser men. The Jacobins were in the saddle. The city was now represented by 'a number of men to whom the majority of its citizens could scarcely give a moment's thought in ordinary times. Faddists, extremists of all sorts, and men of parochial minds.'[18] It was noted that council meetings were henceforward to be held in the evenings 'for the men of the new class,' men who could not afford to give up a day's work. This change had been included in the Liberal programme since 1893 when a meeting at the Victoria Hall had passed a resolution that council meetings should be held at 7 o'clock in the evening in order that 'artisans, mechanics and business men should become members of the Council.'[19]

The causes for the unexpected Conservative debâcle were patent. The *Gazette*, lamenting the 'overwhelming Radical majority,' explained that the Conservatives had virtually been in power since 1835. They had 'governed the city on their own lines' but it was claimed with justification that their general administration had been on the whole beneficial to the community despite 'some mistakes.' This Conservative majority had fostered complacency. The 'Radicals' had always been present on the council in full force. The Conservatives did not have a good record of attendance and the number of the occasions on which the council minutes record the lack of a quorum in the later years of the nine-teenth century is not in itself an indication of healthy local government. Moreover, the Liberals 'had the advantage of a strong and effective card, and they played it in connection with the growth of expenditure.' Their strongest card was the fact that the rates 'had increased by 1s. in the £ in the last ten years.'[20] The Conservatives had taken for granted the permanence of their control of the council and had not asked themselves whether it was likely to be maintained by force of habit in the circumstances of 1900. The *Flying Post* acknowledged that the Liberals had campaigned with unusual vigour. E. J. Domville, the Conservative leader, informed the Constitutional Club that 'the Radicals had shown what combination and good fighting could do.'[21]

The overthrow of the traditional Conservative regime was in fact one of those revulsions against men who have held power for too long which from time to time can stir a community. *Le peuple s'ennuie* is not the least of the factors behind political change. Of the abuse of power by the Conservatives there is no evidence, though local politics being what they are, the phalanx of architects and others interested in building on the council, at a time when Exeter was expanding relatively fast, aroused suspicion. In the 1870s the Conservatives had undoubtedly appointed active party members to key posts. The charge of Tory monopoly was an effective political slogan and, since it had been reiterated for thirty years or more, doubtless had cumulative effect. It could have been answered only by an attention to public relations and a demonstration of devotion to the public weal which the Conservatives made no attempt to provide. The progress made in sanitation, education, lighting and street maintenance was not in itself enough. On the other hand wider economic opportunities were increasing the number of independent voters outside the city's traditional patterns.

The brief Liberal successes of 1837 and 1881 had been due in large measure to the demand for economy; but economy, in the sense of lower rates and decreased expenditure, was a vain aspiration in later nineteenth century local government.

Expenditure in the Borough Fund Revenue Account had risen from £13,473 in 1870 to £31,473 in 1900.²² The city's expenditure as urban sanitary authority had increased to £38,215 from the modest £12,483 of the local board of health in 1870-1871. Loan for sewage disposals amounted to the then unprecedented figure of £41,000 in 1898 and a loan of £36,000 for improved water supplies had been approved in 1899. The district and borough rates, which had been 3s. 11½d. in the £ in 1896, had in fact risen to 4s. 4d. in the £ by 1900.

The Conservatives' mortification over their supersession by men of a new class was born out by the facts, though the change lay in individuals rather than in broad occupational categories.²³ The new council included the usual phalanx of solicitors, seven in all, of whom five were Conservative. The Liberal leader and mayor, A. E. Dunn, was himself a solicitor but he was not a man who moved on the fringes of county society in the manner of the leading representatives of the profession in the past, Carew and Brutton, Daw and Buckingham. Dunn, too, had associated himself with the working class to a greater extent than his predecessor Mark Kennaway who was no democrat in the modern sense.

Brewers, wine merchants and hotel proprietors numbered five, one fewer than in 1899. They included only one Liberal in the person of Thomas Howard, proprietor of the Seven Stars on the Okehampton Road.

F. J. Widgery, the artist, had been a councillor in 1899. One of his colleagues, Henry Noble, was a professor of music whose appearance on the council might well have caused raised eyebrows in a city used to representation by trade, commerce and the professions. Tom Linscott, the pawnbroker, had also been a councillor before 1900. Builders, architects and house-agents were reduced to five including the Conservative John Stocker, like Henry Hooper a builder, unlike Henry Hooper both in the fact that he was not a wealthy man and in the solid reputation he left as a public-spirited and painstaking member of the council. Men of a new type appeared in the persons of J. Campfield, divisional superintendent of the Great Western railway and

John Bates, the brass caster, both of whom were Liberal. The election of John Bates, the first working man to be a member of the council, was itself a portent and no doubt did much to provoke the shocked generalizations of the Conservatives on the social composition of the new council.

The *Western Times* had once commended the Liberal maltster Joseph Sayell to the electors on the grounds that he had 'a large stake in the city as an owner of house property;'[24] but property was no longer regarded as a relevant commendation to the electors. The Liberal members on the council in 1900 were not men of property in the old sense. They were the forerunners in a local form of the men who were to supply the great Liberal majority in the parliament of 1906. Of those of the class of 1900 who became mayors during the period of Liberal predominance, Dunn, Widgery, Perry and Linscott, solicitor, artist, Liberal agent and pawnbroker, none measured up to the social and financial standards, by local usage, of their predecessors in the chair.

The Liberal victory in the Exeter municipal elections of 1900 was the point at which the slow erosion of the rural framework within which the city had lived became at last apparent in political form. 'We look to the Conservative working men of Exeter for the maintenance of those old institutions of which we are so proud – the Cathedral, the Guildhall and the remains of the castle'; so Sir Stafford Northcote had informed the city in 1884.[25] In the circumstances of the time the working men may have had little freedom of choice. The election of 1900 was a sign that Exeter, though still a small city, was yet becoming too large, and its population too fluid, for the retention of the old control and influence of the clergy, or the county representatives who met at the castle in quarter sessions. The political Conservatism which elected Sir Edgar Vincent in 1899 and cheered for General Buller was a new development, a local manifestation of national attitudes personified by Joseph Chamberlain and Cecil Rhodes. This Conservatism implied no revival in Exeter of the days of Sir William Follett. But county and city society also remained conservative in a more fundamental sense than can be inferred from the political catchwords in vogue at the time of the Boer War. It remained the conservatism of rural England and the county, reinforced politically after the first World War by many of the professional men, traders and shopkeepers of the class which had once maintained Liberalism as a political force in the city; 'men of the new class' who supported Campbell-Bannerman and Asquith and later rallied to Baldwin. The change took place when religious privilege and the extension of the franchise ceased to be political issues. Exeter's nineteenth-century Liberalism never showed active interest in the 'condition of England question.' The *Western Times*'s criticism of Canon Girdlestone's efforts to improve the conditions of the labourers of Halberton in itself shows the limit of the range of Liberal imagination in Exeter. Exeter's Conservatism, political and social, retained the diminished heirs of the old county tradition, but its new recruits came from those who were the chief beneficiaries of material progress in a world that yet remained aloof from the tensions and problems of industrial England.

XIII

POLITICS AND PROGRESS 1900-14

THE general election of October 1900 – the khaki election –
returned Sir Edgar Vincent as Conservative member for
Exeter for the second time in fifteen months. With a well-
founded pride in the performance of Devon soldiers on the
veldt and a strong local patriotism which found a focus in
General Buller, the electorate was unlikely to reject Vincent's
pronouncement that Dutch supremacy should be 'disposed
of finally and blotted out from the book of South African
problems.'[1] It was, however, a tribute to the strength of old
political allegiance that, with 80 per cent. of the electorate
voting, the Liberal Allan Bright received 3,309 votes to
Vincent's 40,001. Bright himself left the field. He returned to
his own Welsh marches to study *Piers Plowman* under the
Malvern Hills and became for a brief spell member for the
Oswestry division of Shropshire in 1904.

Vincent introduced Edwardian England to Exeter. He
moved in the glittering world of high society, entertaining
friends of the king, as well as some of his constituents, in his
house at Esher. Vincent and Follett, at the beginning and end
of Victorian Exeter, had much in common. Both were men
of the world working within the necessary over-simplifica-
tions of politics. Of Vincent it was said that he was unfitted
for a parliamentary career, 'for his rapidity of perception
made him see every side of a question and stood in the way
of a whole-hearted acceptance of general principles.'[2]
Sharing with Follett an imposing presence and a command of
felicitous speech, Vincent had the adventurous mind of the
type which at that period was making fortunes in South
Africa and which brought Vincent himself to fortune as
governor of the Imperial Ottoman Bank in Constantinople.
The Conservative party of the early twentieth century could
not contain him. Defeated later at Exeter in the election of
1906, Vincent was returned as Liberal member for Colchester

in the stormy electoral year of 1910. In 1914, as Lord D'Abernon, he acquired the title by which he became known to diplomatic history.

In 1905 the prime minister, Balfour, abandoned the hopeless task of maintaining the unity of a government shattered by Chamberlain's campaign for tariff reform. Vincent's Liberal opponent in the ensuing election of 1906 was an aberrant member, politically speaking, of county society, Sir George Kekewich. The son of Samuel Trehawke Kekewich of Peamore, near Exeter, grandson of William Buck of Hartland, both county members of parliament, George Kekewich had entered the education department as an examiner in 1867. From 1900 to 1903 he had been secretary of the board of education until his resignation following disagreement with Conservative educational policy.[2] Despite his social background and his recent membership of the Carlton Club, Kekewich introduced to the local scene the language of a Radicalism in the style of Labouchere and Lloyd George. He enveloped the licensed trade and the Anglican clergy in the fervour of his invective. In the sympathetic atmosphere of the Bible Christian Hall at Exeter he denounced the government's educational policy. Elected an honorary member of the National Union of Teachers he told the union's conference at Buxton that it was the absolute right of the state to acquire church schools.[3]

The election of 1906 was fought on the classical ground of religion and free trade. Local Nonconformist leaders had called for war to the knife over Balfour's Education Act of 1902. Sir Charles Follett, once mayor of Exeter, returned to denounce Cobden and the Cobden Club and to assert that free trade had ruined the city. For the Liberals the foundations of their philosophy were at stake. The battle was for religious freedom and for the free trade which in the Victorian heyday had been regarded a moral principle arousing visions of peace and prosperity among the nations of the world. The drink question also still aroused strong feeling. On the one hand the *Flying Post* sought public sympathy when, on a Sunday night in April 1903, 'ten public houses shut their doors for ever . . . ten men found themselves without the living which the state had up to then especially permitted them to take.' The other point of view was that of Bishop Ryle and the interdenominational delegation which he had led to impress upon the magistrates 'their conviction that the intemperance of the land was that which was filling their workhouses and asylums.'[4] The magistrates themselves had ample evidence, in the cases brought before them, of the connection of drunkenness with crime, and especially with cruelty to children.

The issues were such that, as the Conservatives acknowledged, the Liberals were backed by the full strength of Nonconformity in the city.[5] Kekewich later was to observe, somewhat sourly, that in Exeter 'the majority of electors were either crusted Liberals or crusted Tories.'[6] More restrained, and to a great extent accurate, was his comment that every man's party politics were stereotyped both for parliamentary and municipal elections.[7] In 1906 the revival of old issues was in itself a reason for the full mobilization of the various components of Exeter's Liberalism. Reinforcements came from the new red-brick streets, the home of electors who were unlikely to have been stereotyped Conservatives – artisans, clerks, small shopkeepers and railwaymen. Five of these streets, for instance, could provide 249 electors on the roll including fifty-five railwaymen.[8] Kekewich's name itself was an asset despite the known opposition of his own family. The song, 'For Kekewich is a Liberal man' brought his supporters into the streets and to the polling stations. According to Exeter tradition some were under the impression that they were supporting the hero of Kimberley. George Kekewich was returned by a majority of eighty-eight votes.

Radical principles alone proved to be austere fare for the electorate and were inadequate for the retention of a small majority. Kekewich himself was an unsatisfactory candidate. He complained of the assumption that parliamentary candidates for the city should be men of means who could be open-handed on behalf of good causes. He claimed that money was essential for success, especially in the south of England; that he could not afford adequate contributions to local political bodies, societies and charities in the same proportion as his opponent.[9] There were humiliating dissensions in Liberal circles, duly reported in the press, as to whether Kekewich had made his promised contribution to electoral expenses. The *Western Times* accused the Liberal member of avoiding the city. Kekewich himself was reported to have declared that the Exeter Liberals required a relieving officer rather than a member of parliament.[10] In these circumstances Kekewich declined to seek re-election.

For the parliamentary elections of 1910, when the power of the house of lords was the over-riding issue, the Liberals turned to another member of a county family in the person of Harold St Maur, a relation of the Duke of Somerset, educated at Wellington and Sandhurst, master of foxhounds, member of the Marlborough and Cavalry Clubs, volunteer in the South African war. It was a return to the fading Whig tradition. The Conservatives broke new ground. Their candidate was Henry Duke, the future Lord Merrivale, son of a clerk of the granite works in a small Dartmoor village. Duke had been to neither public school nor university. After working as journalist for the *Western Morning News* and in the press gallery of the house of commons he had read for the bar. By 1897 he had become recorder of Plymouth and Devonport. From 1900 to 1906 he had been Unionist member for Plymouth.[11]

In December 1909, the house of commons resolved that the rejection of the budget by the house of lords was a breach of the constitution and a usurpation of the rights of the commons. Parliament was dissolved. The first of the two general elections of 1910 was held in January. Though the national issue was that of the lords versus the people, the rival levies in Exeter were marshalled for the fray under their old banners bearing the well-worn devices of Free Trade and Protection, Disestablishment and religious education, the Demon Rum. Once more the ghost of Cobden walked as Lord Northcote denounced Cobdenism. The Conservative press lost no opportunity of presenting free trade as a blow below the belt of British working men for the benefit of lower-paid foreigners, usually depicted as Germans. Placards

were posted throughout the city to show that British workmen were paid 5s. a day compared with 3s. 9d. received by
Germans.[12] The building boom that had followed the end
of the Boer War was over. Unemployment was becoming a
relatively serious problem. In the county court, Mr Justice
Wilson was reported to have commented on the 'simply
appalling' state of indebtedness of 'the lower orders.'[13] Once
more the licensed trade threw its considerable weight on the
Conservative side. The Exeter and District Licensed Victuallers presented the candidates with three leading questions
to which only Henry Duke could reply with an unequivocal
'yes.'

Duke crept to victory by a majority of only twenty-six in
a poll of 9,778 out of 10,383 registered electors. He promptly
began negotiations to buy a house in Exeter[14] and so became
the first resident member since Richard Somers Gard. The
language of Lloyd George, the allegations that Lansdowne
House had usurped from Buckingham Palace the sovereignty
of Charles I, were more suited to the Radicalism of urban
England, to the crofters of Scotland and the small farmers of
Wales, than to the rural England of the southwest. The
kindly occupants of Castle Hill, Powderham and Pynes, in a
countryside retaining a shrewd knowledge of personalities,
were too well-known to look convincing in the part of
pantomime ogres. For the cynical there was no doubt caues
for comment in the ingenuous juxtaposition of headlines in
the *Flying Post* 'Lords rejection of the Budget' followed by
a report that Exeter's neighbour Lord Poltimore had given
£300 to provide Christmas dinners for the poor of the city.
The newspaper suggested that 'his lordship may have been
originally stimulated to his £300 gift by a reference in the
Flying Post of fifty years ago to the generosity of his parents.'[15]
Exeter's conception of the landed aristocracy and gentry was
not based on their charity but on the performance of public
duties by Aclands, Courtenays, Fortescues and Northcotes,
who had come and gone in the city each in his generation.
Misconceptions about distant grouse moors had little
relevance to a county where hunting united classes in a
common interest and a Lord Portsmouth had earned respect

as much for the sport he gave with the Eggesford hounds as for his Whig principles.

It has been pointed out that the attack on the house of lords 'antagonized a county with a traditional deep respect for the landed aristocracy. Even the chapel goers . . . forgot their own ancient traditions of Dissent, and voted with the Church people on the side of the House of Lords.'[16] Yet it is doubtful whether this traditional respect, which Exeter fully shared, made any significant contribution to the result of the election. Exeter's Liberalism put forth its full strength and lost by a small margin. If anything the election demonstrated the truth of Sir George Kekewich's statement that Exeter voting was stereotyped.

The first election of 1910 also demonstrated, as *The Times*[17] did not fail to point out, that Exeter was not a safe Conservative seat. Throughout the country the two political parties had been conducting their campaigns with a bitterness which had not been seen in English political life for over a generation. Society itself was divided. It was a period which was to end with the Curragh incident and the threat of civil war over Ulster.

Parliament was again dissolved towards the end of November. In London the ultimate fate of the political parties was regarded as dependent on those constituencies where there had been small majorities in the January election. In Exeter the election was fought to a finish on the straight issues of home rule for Ireland, and the house of lords. The old war-cries of so many elections were muted. The votes cast were only 210 fewer than in the previous January. When polling was completed on 3 December, the first count, declared at ten o'clock at night, gave the Liberals a majority of three. Duke's agent accordingly insisted on an inspection of all votes recorded for St Maur. The inspection was followed by a recount. At two o'clock on the Sunday morning it was announced that St Maur had been returned by 4,786 to 4,782, a majority of four.

The result was a shock to the Conservatives. It was 'really inexplicable,' due perhaps to political ignorance on the part of the working-class voters who hitherto had usually been complimented on their political sagacity. Alternatively it was attributed to the dislike of the middle classes for activity in electioneering, in contrast with the country districts where they were said to be active on one side or the other. In Exeter, it was suggested, the tradesmen, professional men and 'the higher grades of salaried people' were found only exceptionally among the active political workers.[18] What the Conservatives attributed to lack of political wisdom was for the Liberals a proof of the reverse. The result of the election was a sign that working-class electors 'were no longer going to allow themselves to be downtrodden by those people who imagined themselves to be their betters.'[19]

There had always been some in Exeter who disliked political enthusiasts and electioneering, as the memoirs of Henry Ellis testify. But throughout the Victorian era there is ample evidence that tradesmen and professional men, especially the latter, were active in both local and parliamentary elections. 'Salaried people' hitherto had not been important. If there was any truth in the Conservatives' reference to the dislike of the middle classes for electioneering it was an indication of the growing professionalism of politics. The city had grown in size. The population was no longer small enough for amateur politicians to regard electioneering as an exercise conducted among friends, neighbours and employees, between shopkeepers and customers. The electorate itself was less amenable, and less accessible, to the old methods of persuasion and influence.

In December, as in January, of 1910, both parties had put forth their full strength. Throughout Devon there had been a net Unionist gain of four seats. Exeter therefore had run against the tide; but the exiguous Liberal majority suggests that the result was due to normal election hazards rather than to any marked change of political allegiance. In the event the Conservatives regained their position by other means. They presented an election petition objecting to the employment for reward of ninety-two persons by St Maur and alleged that some of the Liberal election agents had voted contrary to the law. The case[20] was heard in January 1911 by Mr Justice Ridley and Mr Justice Channell.

Sir Edward Ridley was an unfortunate choice for the conduct of such an inquiry at any time, and especially when political passions were unusually high. He was a member of the great Northumbrian family which had provided members of parliament for Newcastle upon Tyne for a period of ninety-two years. He himself had been elected for South Northumberland in 1878 in circumstances not greatly dissimilar from those of the Exeter election. There had been a tied vote and Ridley had been declared elected after a scrutiny. His political prejudices were known and though he was also noted for his sense of honour, the details of an election petition provided ample opportunity for the exercise of political bias by a strong-minded man.

Direct bribery and corruption in the uninhibited manner of nineteenth-century elections were not in issue. The Conservatives' claim was that all the votes cast for St Maur were not valid votes, that if a scrutiny of the valid votes was taken it would be found that Duke had been returned. Under the severe judicial examination, improper practices were found to have occurred on the Liberal side, though the wilder accusations made in the heat of the moment by citizens on the fringes of Exeter's political world were withdrawn in the chillier atmosphere of the inquiry. A tailor with qualifications in two wards who had boasted that he had voted twice found his votes disqualified and himself admonished. Four votes were removed from St Maur's total for the illegal, but not necessarily corrupt, payment of election bills. Few elections at the period would have stood the test of such severe scrutiny. By the end of the first day's proceedings Duke had a majority of one. On 11 April the proceedings ended. The judge announced that it was their duty to report 'that upon scrutiny Mr Duke ought to be returned as a member for Parliament because he had a majority of votes.'[21]

Duke's agent had secured victory. Exeter's Liberalism with good reason felt ill-used and expressed disappointment by booing the judges, Ridley being specially singled out for disapprobation. The affair ended with an incident at the railway station which has passed into Exeter's legends. St Maur leaned out of the carriage window to assure his supporters that they would meet again when the city had been cleared of men such as those who had brought charges against him and when the land had been cleared of unjust judges. At this point the other occupant of the carriage emerged from behind his newspaper to disclose the outraged features of Mr Justice Ridley. The two men were observed in heated altercation as the train left for London.

The elections of 1910 demonstrated that Exeter's Liberalism was as strong a political force at the end of the Victorian period as it had been in the days of Divett and Follett. Its core remained Low Church or Nonconformist. The Liberals' capture of both seats in 1868 had required unusual circumstances including issues capable of uniting into an effective force the very diverse elements which formed the party. The situation was similar after 1900 at a time when the growth of the city and expanding economic opportunities were loosening the influence of old social patterns. In normal circumstances Exeter remained Conservative.

In local affairs, events demonstrated once more that Liberalism was a protest rather than a programme. In part a protest against rising rates and expenditure, in part against the monopoly of power, and always a salutary reminder of the responsibility of governors to the governed, it could not provide the cohesion and perseverance required for the maintenance of power. The insistence on economy had little relevance to the administration of twentieth-century Exeter. The council elections of 1900 were followed by an immediate review and subsequent increase of wages and salaries paid by the council, the first of several. New posts multiplied. The total expenditure on personal emoluments, approximately £10,260 in the financial year 1900–01, rose to £21,873 by the financial year 1913–14.[22] The expansion of the Albert Memorial College itself accounts for an increase from £834 to £6,273. Salaries in the health department increased from £675 to £1,195. The department's one permanent, full-time senior official in 1900 was an inspector of nuisances, foods and drugs at £210 a year. By 1907 the sanitary committee after mature consideration had come to the conclusion that Exeter required a woman health visitor and intimated that 'much good would come from the appointment provided a suitable person was appointed.'[23] Three months later Miss Weaver was appointed, at 25s. a week. In the surveyor's department, expenditure on salaries rose from £1,543 to £2,156. The recurrent cost of elementary education rose from £4,300 to £14,000 in the short period of 1900 to 1904.

This increase in expenditure may appear negligible to a later generation; but at a time when the penny and halfpenny were coins of significance it was unprecedented and to many alarming. The district and borough rates, which had been 3s. 11½d. in the £ in 1896, and 4s. 4d. in 1900, rose to 5s. 4d. by 1904. By 1908 they were 5s. 10d. in the £. There was a further increase to 6s. 2¾d. by 1914.[24] Inevitably the party which had attacked the Conservatives as 'cormorants' for the alleged squandering of the ratepayers' money were themselves under fire in 1904 for 'radical recklessness in civic matters.'[25] The singing of the Dead March by the triumphant Liberals when the Conservative mayor relinquished office in 1900 may have appeared appropriate in the excitement of the moment; but if the Conservative regime was ailing it was far from dead.

By 1904 the Conservatives were demonstrating their customary resilience and the city was beginning to return to equilibrium. In that year thirteen out of fourteen wards were contested. Many of the gentry lent their carriages to bring voters to the poll. For the first time motor cars were used for the same purpose.[26] The Conservatives gained two seats. The mayor-choosing on that occasion, when the artist mayor, Alderman Widgery, was succeeded by E. C. Perry, was distinguished by an uproar of hooting and shouts in the Guildhall which at least indicated the revived vigour of party politics.

The Conservatives continued to make steady gains. The elections of 1907 left the Conservatives with nineteen elected members opposing nineteen Liberals and five Conservative aldermen against the Liberal nine. In 1908 the Conservatives regained full control of the council. In 1911, and again in 1912, there were no contests. 'Yesterday's silence in regard to the municipal elections,' observed the *Flying Post* with tendentious satisfaction, 'is the practical consummation of the efforts of the Unionists to restore the superiority in the Council which they had lost in 1900.'[27] During the seventy-seven years from the first year of the new council instituted by the Municipal Corporations Act of 1835 to the first world war, the Liberals had controlled the council, more or less tenuously, for thirteen. Except perhaps for the sale of the city plate and the abolition of old ceremony in the first flush of Utilitarian enthusiasm they had accomplished little that could be ascribed to the initiative of Liberal policy. It was a Conservative-dominated council which made the breach with tradition by the abolition of the improvement commissioners in 1867. It was the Conservatives who had taken advantage of the financial opportunities offered by the Public Health Act of 1875, thereby provoking the exasperation over rising rates which was an important cause of the ephemeral Liberal revival in the eighties. And in 1910 the Conservatives were again in power when the council began the city's first extensive slum clearance scheme in the modern manner. Nevertheless Liberal endeavours had been a healthy reminder of the accountability of power. It was their role to keep alive the democratic principles of local government and to prevent its degeneration into a monopoly answerable only to a self-appointed political machine. But to achieve power they required an effective grievance; and for the majority of the citizens there was no obvious cause for grievance in this period.

Although H. A. Willey had recently deplored the loss of the purchasing power of the county he also informed the Exeter and District chamber of commerce in 1901 that from his own personal investigation the trade of the city had never been better. Anyone walking through the streets would see evidence of 'great prosperity' and a greater number of men were being employed in industrial undertakings than ever before in the city's history.[28] The statement about industrial undertakings is difficult to substantiate though Willey's own firm is said to have employed some eight hundred men at this period. According to the census of 1901 only 717 males were employed in engineering, less than the number employed

U

in dress and on the railways.

Building activity was certainly at a high level. The streets committee approved the construction of an average of 239 houses a year from 1902 to 1908; 460 new buildings were approved in 1905 and 406 in 1907.[29] Approval of building did not always imply that building would begin, least of all in the year in which approval was given. The special committee of council appointed to investigate unemployment reported that the monthly average of houses under construction in the three years 1906 to 1908 was 169, 144 and 131 respectively. According to the reports of the medical officer of health, which unfortunately do not include figures for the whole period, the peak year was 1908 when 249 dwelling houses and six buildings 'of the warehouse class' were constructed and 134 buildings were under construction at the end of the year.

In 1902 the Exeter Building Estates Company began the development of the properties known as the Mount Radford House and St Leonard's estates. Mount Radford itself, once the home of the Barings, was last owned by Edward Knapman the draper. By June 1904 the grounds were already being built on; the house itself partially demolished, was a gaunt ruin. Some two hundred houses were planned for the two estates of Mount Radford and Grove Park in 1902, each house at a rental value of about £14 a year.[30] In the same year the former property of Ralph Sanders, of the banking dynasty, was also under development.

Across the Exe, St Thomas was rapidly taking the form it retained until after the second World War. In 1905 the builders Triggs, Sanders and Sleeman began the development of the Parkhouse estate which ended in the construction of the long rows of streets known as Churchill Road, Coleridge Road, Barton Road and Cowick Lane. The middle-class houses of Thornton Hill, in St David's, were approved in 1907; by 1912 Messrs Veitch's nursery gardens in the same area were giving way to the future Velwell Road, developed by the Streatham Hall Building Company. In these years the great gardens in St David's looking out over the Exe and the hills of St Thomas were fast disappearing. Plans for the development of the Beech Hill and Knightley's estates were approved in 1907 and 1908. In the latter year the working-class street of Looe Road began to take shape on the Lower Knightley Estate.[31]

This expansion of the city required improved transport. The latter encouraged the former. The old horse-drawn tram system, installed in 1882, had remained embryonic and amounted to little more than a link between St David's station and the Heavitree road with an extension up Sidwell Street to Mount Pleasant. In 1901 the council's consultants advised that the council should purchase and operate the tramway system, that an overhead system of electric traction should be adopted and that no such system could be success-ful which did not pass through High Street.[32] The ratepayers were consulted by means of a card vote. 5,187 replies were received in favour of the proposed system and 1,384 against. 4,950 agreed to the introduction of trams into the main streets of the city and 1,621 were opposed.[33] In the following year the council's electric traction committee formally recommended that 'an electrical system of trams be introduced within the municipal boundaries of the city and the suburbs thereof' and that the council should promote a parliamentary bill to construct, equip and work a system of electrical tramways, or of motor buses, or to lease the same to a company.[34]

The reference to motor buses is a reminder that even in 1902 the internal combustion engine had begun the revolution of transport and social habits, and perhaps of town planning. Willey's restless imagination had turned to the possibility of a motor industry in Exeter and it was due to his initiative that a representative of the Coventry motor industry reported to Exeter's chamber of commerce on the prospects. The expert, Mr Sturmer, was not enthusiastic. A large amount of capital was required and Exeter did not have the right type of labour. Nor would he advise anyone to try the cycle industry as an alternative since this was full. The tentative estimates placed before the chamber of commerce are still of interest. The estimated capital expenditure required was £47,500 to £65,000. It was suggested that 300 cars annually might be sold at £500 each less a 15 per cent. trade discount. With costs worked out at £300 a car the gross profits were estimated at £37,500 and the net profits at £25,000.[35]

The council's committee in 1902 indeed considered the introduction of motor transport but though it 'made every effort to find a service of motor vehicles in this country and on the continent it failed to do so.'[36] It was noted that Plymouth had a system of motor buses in operation, but this was in private hands. In the following year a meeting of property owners and ratepayers met to endorse the promotion of the bill to empower the council to lay down and maintain tramways.

The new tramway system which, when completed, linked Exeter and St Thomas, was inaugurated in April 1905 by the mayor, Councillor Perry. Amid the cheers of the crowd he headed a procession of decorated cars through 'Rhubarb Land' where the fruit trees in the gardens along the Heavitree road were coming into blossom. This new step in progress was celebrated in the old way, by a dinner accompanied by songs and speeches at the New London Hotel. In the following month Archibald Lucas, architect and surveyor, and member of the tramways committee, offered for sale six hundred building sites on the Babbs Barn estate of St Thomas[37] thus giving practical endorsement of the relation between improved communications and building speculation. In the same year a new bridge replaced the graceful Georgian structure across the Exe.

The new trams were at once popular and a commercial success. Over three million passengers were carried in the first year of operations and the profit was nearly £2,000. Exeter's hold on its suburbs was tightened and by 1913 the independence of Heavitree could be maintained no longer. In November 1913 the Heavitree U.D.C. was incorporated in Exeter by the Exeter (Extension) Order, and brought with it reinforcement of the Conservative majority on the enlarged council.

H. A. Willey died in 1904, aged forty-one, before the completion of the developments which had owed so much to his vigorous support.[38] His imagination and versatility had been unique in the Exeter of his day. He had expanded his firm of Willey and Co. till it became one of the largest engineering firms in the west of England. He had attended science and arts classes at the museum and had sent some of his workmen across the Atlantic 'in order that through them the whole of his employees [might] become acquainted with the condition of things in America.'[39] Shortly before his death he had bought a car in Paris, driven it to the French coast and then on from Southampton to Exeter; an adventurous journey at that time. Alone of the city's leaders he had reached out beyond the traditional economic pattern seeking for the city and his firm the new openings provided by technological change. It was symbolic that it was for him that the streets committee approved the construction of the first private garage in Exeter, in 1904,[40] the year in which Exeter became a licensing authority for cars.

Two years after Willey's death visitors to Exeter found that one of the interesting sights in the city was the presence of four to five vehicles standing in the cathedral yard. In 1907 the New London Inn finally turned its back on the coaching days which had brought it fame and opened a garage for fifty vehicles. In the following year a significant increase in motor traffic had been remarked. Over thirty vehicles an hour had been counted 'in and out of High Street.'[41] For a city which depended on its position as a centre of communications the new age was offering possibilities as well as problems. Special trains brought thousands on their way to the control point in Whipton Fields for the aircraft following the railway line from Bristol to Stoke Canon in the race round Britain in 1911.

Exeter's revived prosperity faltered briefly in 1907. It was necessary to open the soup kitchen for seventeen days in the winter of 1907 to 1908 and for twenty-five days in the following winter. Private charity distributed 21,000 farthing breakfasts for poor children from November 1907 to April 1908. Towards the end of 1908 some 200 trade unionists were said to be dependent on the funds of their societies and it was assumed that another 400 unskilled labourers were out of work.[42] In the following March the register of the council's committees for unemployment showed that 495 men were out of work, representing about 3 per cent. of the total males in occupations according to the census of 1911. The local government board reports, which tended to regard the problem as financial, reported that in the year 1907–1908, though there had been a 'remarkable increase of pauperism in Plymouth,' Exeter was benefiting from a policy of strict administration. Some deterioration was noted in the following year though it was observed with evident relief that 'local subscriptions had been sufficient to meet the distress and that no special works had been necessary.'[43] Exeter was experiencing what a later generation was to term a recession. Even so, the highest figure of cases assisted by the Exeter relief society, in the year 1909, was only 2,099,[44] the same total as in 1852 and one that was exceeded in the 1850s and 1860s. By 1911 the newspapers were reporting a meeting held at the Guildhall to discuss the promotion of tourism under the headline 'Booming Exeter.'[45]

In 1907, the gas company, after declaring its usual 10 per cent. dividend, had reduced prices to the lowest level in its history. Consumption continued to rise and after another prosperous year in 1913 prices were again reduced. The net profits of Messrs Colson's rose by 10.8 per cent. from 1902 to 1903. There was a rise of 13.29 per cent. between 1911 and 1912.[46] The theatre was still earning a profit of 5 per cent. The receipts of the Exeter trams, which were always given full publicity in the local press, reached a record total by 1913. It was remarked in 1912 that St Sidwell's was expanding rapidly as a business area.

Money wages were rising rapidly in the city. Not all shared the widening prosperity. In 1913 the *Flying Post*[47] reported the case of a man who was summoned for the maintenance of a child in a reformatory. He had a sick wife and five children. When in full employment he earned 16s. a week, out of which 4s. a week, or 25 per cent. of his income, was paid out in rent. The newspaper did not record his average earnings over a year.

In the country as a whole real wages had increased between the seventies and 1900. Thereafter there was an advance in prices, though wages were picking up again by 1914.[48] In Exeter there were no conclusive signs of an increase in money wages, primarily in the building trade, till the nineties.[49] The increase in prices between 1900 and 1914 is demonstrated by the tenders accepted by the corporation of the poor in March 1900 and 1901.[50] The cost of beef supplied to the corporation, at wholesale price, rose from $6\frac{1}{2}d$. to $7\frac{1}{2}d$. per lb.; leg and shoulder of English mutton from $6\frac{1}{2}d$. to $7d$.; butter from $1s$. to $1s$. $1\frac{1}{4}d$.; milk from $9\frac{1}{2}d$. to $10d$. per gallon; sugar from $14s$. $6d$. to $14s$. $11d$. per cwt; roll tobacco from $3s$. $4d$., and shag from $3s$. $3d$., to $4s$. $1d$. per lb. The price of tea had risen slightly by one farthing to $1s$. $2\frac{1}{4}d$. per lb. in the Exeter market, superfine flour, which had been sold at $23s$ to $25s$. the sack in January 1900, cost $27s$. to $29s$. a sack in 1914.

Though the national trend at this period was, broadly, one of rising prices with wages following behind, the impression given by Exeter is still one of greater opportunities, improved standards of living and less hardship than at any previous time since the 1830s. Wages were admittedly low and this fact had been regarded as an argument in favour of the proposed institution of a motor industry in the city in 1902. A comparison of the pay of the Exeter police with the rates in other cities, undertaken in 1911, disclosed the fact that in Exeter constables received $2s$. a week less than in comparable forces elsewhere. Sergeants' pay was less by $3s$. per week and inspectors' by $5s$.[51] In 1913 the chief constable's pay and allowances amounted to only £265, a derisory figure compared with, for instance, the £525 received by the chief constable of Worcester or £397 by his colleague at Scarborough.[52]

The Exeter council, however, was actively increasing wages and salaries throughout the period 1901–1914. Police pay was increased in 1911. Thereafter constables were paid $24s$. instead of $22s$. $6d$. during their first year of service and received $30s$. a week after ten years' service. The rates for sergeants and inspectors were correspondingly improved. The wages of the council's dustmen were raised from $21s$. to $21s$. $6d$. in 1904. By 1913 the city surveyor was able to report that with the exception of five sweepers and three lavatory attendants no artisans or labourers in the employment of the council received less than £1 a week.[53]

By 1906 Exeter artisans such as bricklayers, carpenters, masons, plasterers and plumbers were in general earning between 35s. and 35s 8d. per week for a 53½ hour week in summer.[54] Their labourers could earn 22s. 3½d. per week. Current rates in Plymouth were higher. The Exeter post office, which had become a major employer, employed over a hundred sorting clerks and telegraphists. The former began at 15s. a week and reached a maximum of 49s. 6d; the latter began at 17s. and could reach 52s. a week. The 124 postmen were paid 15s. to 17s. a week with allowances.[55]

Not only were wages rising but opportunities for more skilled employment, and consequent prospects of higher earnings, were increasing substantially. When, for example, it was observed that the recently established business of Messrs Reid and Evans, motor engineers, already required additions to premises and extra staff, it was an indication that Exeter was beginning to emerge from the basic occupational pattern which had existed with little more than superficial change for over seventy years. The post office was employing more girls and women; and if female sorting clerks began on no more than 12s. to 14s. a week, the employment provided a new source for the implementation of some family incomes and so an increase in the effective demand for consumer goods and services. The expansion of the town clerk's department and the higher salaries paid in the period 1900–14 was not only a consequence of the increasing complexity of local government but also of competition from business. In 1900 the department consisted of five clerks, paid £18, £30, £40, £117 10s. and £185 respectively. By 1914 there was a chief clerk at an annual salary of £230 and seven subordinates whose salaries ranged from £21 to £60 a year.[56]

In 1914 the council began to consider another round of wage increases for their employees, including an increase in pay of the canal labourers from 21s. 2d. to 22s. per week.[57] Half the gang of canal labourers repairing Trews Weir in

1836 were paid 2s. 6d. a day[58] so the money wages of these men at least had risen by some 46 per cent. in seventy-eight years. But the uneven progress of wages in Exeter at this period, and hence the caution required in generalizing from individual examples, and even from the board of trade's statistics, can be demonstrated by the following examples of wages paid by the Exeter City Asylum in 1901 and 1914:[59]

	1901	1914
Storekeeper	21s., rations.	23s.
Coachman attendant	20s., rations.	20s., uniform and cottage.
Cook	20s., rations and clothing.	25s., rations and clothing.
Assistant cook	17s., rations and clothing.	20s., rations and clothing.
Sculleryman	15s.	18s.
Tailor	25s.	26s.
Plumber	29s.	29s.
Carpenter	29s.	29s.
Stokers	23s.–25s.	25s.–27s.
Gardener	20s.	20s.
Assistant gardener	15s.	—
Farm labourers	14s. 6d., cottage	18s.–19s.
Night watchman	24s.	26s.

Standards of living are not wholly a question of money wages, and the well-being of the city as a whole was being substantially improved by new standards in public health and housing. The corrected death-rate for the city as a whole was reduced to 12.52 by 1914 compared with 13.7 in ninety-seven major towns.[60] Infantile mortality remained high and was disproportionately high compared with the rate elsewhere. In 1896 the infantile death-rate in Exeter had been 164 per 1,000 compared with 148 per thousand in sixty-seven large towns which included the main industrial centres. In 1902 it rose to 167 per thousand due, in the opinion of the medical officer of health, to measles and improper feeding. By 1914 the infantile death-rate had been reduced to 84.73 per thousand.[61] There was a minor typhoid epidemic in 1906; but the scourges of the early twentieth century were scarlet fever, which caused ten deaths out of 533 cases in 1901, and measles, which caused sixty-eight deaths in 1907. The deaths reported in 1907 were of children from the poorest quarters of the city. Forty-five of the parents were labourers.[62]

The council was curiously reluctant to appoint a full-time medical officer of health. The custom of appointing part-time officers was trenchantly criticized at the inquiry into the proposed annexation of Heavitree in 1912[63] and an appointment was made in the following year. Yet the council was conscientious and active in the improvement of housing. In 1911 the medical officer of health summarized conditions in the west quarter in terms which were repeated in subsequent reports:

> 'Many of the houses are occupied by people of the very lowest class; the mode of living of this class of people is so well known to sanitarians that I need not describe them; they are a terror to landlords and a continual source of trouble to the sanitarian authorities.'

The worst conditions existed in the little courts and cul-de-sacs, corners such as Johnson's Court in Combe Street, where six families sharing two water closets between them paid rents of 2s. 4d. to 2s. 7d. a week. Another bad area was the maze of old lath and plaster buildings off Paul Street.[64]

In 1904 the council decided to adopt section 3 of the Housing of the Working Classes Act of 1900 and to apply for a loan for the construction of working-class houses. In the following year the local government board approved the construction of forty-two workmen's dwellings in a new street off the Alphington Road, the future Isca Road. These houses were ready for occupation in 1907 at rents which were originally fixed at 5s. a week but were subsequently reduced to 4s. 9d. inclusive of rates.[65] In 1910 a major scheme of slum clearance was put in train in the Paul Street area. The scheme, as subsequently approved, affected some 411 'persons of the working class' paying annual rents varying from £3 to £16 in respect of houses occupied by not more than one family and from £3 12s. to £10 8s. in respect of tenements of one room or more.[66]

For the poor during this period accommodation of a sort

was still obtainable at little more than 1s. a week though rents at this level were likely to have been a reflection of the bad state of the building. For the ordinary artisans, clerks, telegraphists, railwaymen and the rest, the equivalent of the £8 houses of a previous generation, as in Sandford Street in 1874, were the houses leased at £12 to £15 a year. Rents for accommodation of this type changed little between the nineties and 1914. The 'convenient £14 houses' of the Mansfield Road of 1895, with three bedrooms and a reception room, were still leased at £14 in 1908. In Portland Street, Newtown, houses were leased at £13 to £14 in that year and sold for £220 to £225 – they were still leased at £14 in 1914. In neighbouring Sandford Street there were houses to let at £9 to £10 10s., and in Hoopern Street at £12 in 1914. All these were primarily streets for artisans. Houses in Lyndhurst Road were let at £13 to £13 10s. at the end of 1913 and were sold at £180. In Hoopern Street rents, at £12 a year, were lower. Superior houses in the recently developed Knightley's estate were leased at £16 and sold for £230 in 1912. For the relatively well-off a house in Sylvan Road could be leased at £25 and bought for £315 in 1914.[67]

Leisure was increasing under the stimulus of legislation. The council had first discussed the earlier closing of the markets in 1874 but it was not till 1910 that the decision was taken to close them at 10 o'clock on Saturday nights.[68] Action under the Shop Hours Acts provoked an unsuccessful petition from the small traders who suggested that their premises should be allowed to remain open till 8.0 p.m. on four days a week and till 10.0 p.m. on Saturdays with early closing at 2.0 p.m. on Wednesdays. Nevertheless, the assumption that the lot of most men was one of unrelieved labour was weakening. So too was the harsh attitude of the nineteenth century to the unfortunate and the unsuccessful. In 1908, after repeated rejections of the proposal in previous years, the corporation of the poor agreed that each adult in receipt of outdoor relief should receive an additional 1s. and each child 6d. for Christmas.[69] The matron at the workhouse was allowed a small sum for games. Girls in the workhouse were taught swimming. In 1910 the corporation of the poor supported the Charlton union in urging the deletion of the description 'pauper' from notices of death sent out from asylums on the grounds that such a description was not only unnecessary but was 'absolutely harmful to the feelings of the relatives at a time of deep distress and bereavement.'[70]

To occupy increased leisure the cinema was making its contribution by the eve of the first World War. It was suggesting not only adventure but luxurious living and standards of behaviour hitherto unimaginable. In so doing it provided a new solvent of the traditional society. By 1911 the Exeter Electric Cinematograph Company, proprietor of the new Exeter Electric Theatre, offered 'an entertainment to suit the most fastidious and combining pleasure and instruction.' The Empire was said to be 'luxurious, warm and comfortable.' Its clients could come and go as they pleased from 2.30 p.m. to 10.30 p.m. daily and the prices ranged from 3d. to 1s.[71]

Progress is an ambiguous term. But the vast improvement in the amenities of life for the great majority of Exeter's citizens in the period 1900 to 1914 is undeniable. The city's Victorian afternoon was its age of progress measured by economic growth, the humanity of its public attitudes, the higher standards of living, the increase of leisure and the more varied opportunities for amusement. It was not fortuitous that this period also saw the final dissolution of the old social order, for Exeter was at last involved, as a residuary legatee rather than as an active participant, in the progress of nineteenth-century England.

XIV

EXETER IN 1914

'The sunshine was truly golden, the convolvulus bell really white and miraculous sixty years ago.'[1]

THE conception of the year 1914 as a golden moment of a late summer afternoon is based on the assumption that the first World War and its aftermath marked the end of a humane and humanist culture. As a modern historian has demonstrated, antithetical pictures, each of equal validity, can be presented for most aspects of life during the Victorian period.[2] Matthew Arnold's 'jasmine – muffled lattices, And groups under the dreaming garden-trees' did not purport to portray the world of the slum-dweller, the workhouse inmate and the unemployed. In great measure nostalgia for the world as it was in 1914 is derived from loss of the unshaken sense of safety which was an ameliorating factor even at a time of severe economic and social stress.[3]

Some generalizations, however, are necessary. Exeter was a city of the middle classes, middle-class in income, function and standards, living within and under the influence of a rural environment. Its standards were not set by businessmen such as Mr Millbank in Disraeli's *Coningsby*. In literary terms, it was the world of Mr Podsnap and Mr Vholes, Mr Bold and Archdeacon Grantly, in a setting depicted in all its earthy humanity by Surtees. Dickens, Trollope and Surtees had written of an older England which still existed in and around the Exeter of 1914. In some eighty years of Victorian life the city had survived, and ultimately had prospered, by means of a slow adaptation to a changing environment, a belated response to external stimuli. If some looked back to the past with a vague feeling that history had passed them by, those communities and individuals who have no share in the making of history are nevertheless themselves a part of history: 'A fair field full of folk . . . Of all manner of men, the meaner and the richer, working and wandering, as the world asks of them.'[4] Their setting was the world of the bishop and the parson, the landowner and the farmer, merchant and shopkeeper. The glimpses of wooded hills and fields, the glint of water from so many streets, the elms and oaks and ilex for which Exeter had been for so long renowned, all these were reminders of the ancient life of rural England driven back to the perimeter of the nation by urbanization and industrialism. The people of Exeter could not be other than the creatures of their environment. Not for them were the shipyards of Tyneside and the Clyde, the pits and blast furnaces, the docks and mills, high finance and political power.

Exeter's Conservatism was the conservatism of a static society. The city's Liberalism was rarely Radical. True Radicalism, involving a demand for fundamental change in the economic and social structure of the city, required the millowners and steel masters, the industrialists, inventors and financiers, and the thousands who flocked to seek fortune in the conditions they created. For such as these Victorian Exeter offered little. In 1914, as in 1837, the dominant social pattern was still that of the banker, lawyer and clergyman, surgeon and merchant. The carriages of the county gentry were still observed by all in the streets. The great towers of the cathedral, the towers and spires of lesser parish churches, were still the dominating architectural features of the city. In church and chapel, Exeter adhered to that religious observance which is one of the characteristics of the Victorian era. Standards set by the clergyman, doctor and lawyer, by the Nonconformist businessman giving time and money in pursuit of 'fruit unto holiness,' however indequate for the radical reformer, represented moral values and a practical neighbourliness which had mitigated the harshness of life for many and which inspired the conscientious though unadventurous expansion of the social responsibilities of the council.

The overwhelming victory of the Liberals in the council elections of 1900 was a revolt against the authority of traditional society. When in 1913 the railwayman Councillor

Gayton tabled in the council a motion to the effect that all employees should receive a minimum wage of 21s. a week,[5] it was a sign that economic change and the expansion of the city had carried change a stage further, to the point of the admission to power of a class which stood outside middle-class Liberalism. Exeter, still a small city, was yet becoming too large for the old social influences to be effective.

The growth in the size of the city, which coincided with the change in the composition of the council was remarked on, and often lamented, by contemporaries. By 1908 there were wistful backward glances at the loss of natural beauty, regret for the lost peace, the bird song and autumn colours which, in their due season, had distinguished Hoopern Fields in the years before Diamond Jubilee. In 1914 there were laments for the loss of the noble elms of Cowick Fields, the disappearance of good meadow land and the spoiling of the best walks near Exeter.[6] The dreariness of the approach to Exeter along the Pinhoe Road gave rise to regrets in the press that the city council had then no power, in 1914, to control building development on the Polsloe Estate.

Slum clearance schemes and business development, necessary in themselves, involved both the disappearance of part of Exeter's former beauty and a breach of the continuity between past and present. They required the disappearance of Cornish's Court and Barbican Place in Paul Street; courts and alleys with ancient beams and casement windows, yet accessible to sunshine which emphasized the contrasting patterns of light and shade; the old houses in Bradninch Place which gave way to the University College extensions. When in 1908 the chief constable had explained to the watch committee that Exeter was on the main road to the west, he was not only summarizing the city's history but forecasting the problems of the twentieth century.[7] Reporting on his attendance at the Town Planning and Garden City Conference in London, Councillor Ross told the parliamentary committee 'It was admitted, and the remark was favourably received, that the future of Town Planning was to carry out the character of the past, not to destroy it.'[8] The principle required an imaginative approach on the part of councillors and ratepayers that was not easy to acquire.

The first meeting of the council's town planning committee was held in 1910. By 1914 Exeter was embroiled in the controversy, which still endures, over the development of the heart of the city in the angle between Queen Street and the Guildhall. The architect T. H. Mawson, called in by the council, drew up plans with the purpose of giving the buildings in the area 'the setting of greenery which is essential in every case if architectural erections are to receive the full aesthetic treatment.'[9]

There were inevitable complaints that so large a sum as £315 should have been paid to an outside adviser when, it was suggested, local architects could have told the council how to proceed; but the press informed the city that the clearances in Paul Street and the acceptance of a Carnegie grant for a public library had created a unique situation and 'one in which the experience of other cities was in the highest degree necessary.'[10]

The central area controversy was shelved on the outbreak of war in 1914 to be revived some fifty years later. Mawson's report, and the controversy which followed it, were signs of a growing awareness of the problems and ambiguity of progress which itself marked the city's emergence from Victorianism. It was in accordance with this trend that the council decided, not without opposition, to acquire and preserve historic buildings such as St Nicholas Priory off Fore Street, and Rougemont House, once the home of Somers Gard, on Northernhay.

For the housewife of St Thomas, enjoying a tram ride up Fore Street, and for thousands like her, life in Exeter before the first World War represented indubitable progress. The transformation of High Street in recent years had not only been a sign of business activity but of new standards for customers, such as Messrs Walton's innovation of a tea-room in 1913. Despite the building activity of the past twenty-five years Exeter still preserved the atmosphere and amenities of a small country town. The low roof levels were subservient to the hills. Pinhoe and Whipton were villages in rich farmland. From St Leonard's to Countess Wear was still a country walk. Lanes, which have since lost all but their names, then were lanes indeed, rambling under high banks and hedges where children could play and lovers wander between the wild roses and the honeysuckle; but on the main roads in that hot June of 1914 motor traffic was raising clouds of dust to an extent which induced the council to discuss tarring.

At the time of the census of 1911[11] the population of Exeter was only 48,000. It had grown by 3.1 per cent. in the previous decade, half the increase of contemporary Brighton. York had grown by 5.6 per cent., Leicester by 7.4 per cent. and Nottingham by 8.4 per cent. Out of seventy-five large towns only seven had had a lower rate of population growth than had Exeter. The largest single source of employment for males was building and works of construction employing 887 males per ten thousand, a larger proportion than the 715 per ten thousand of the urban districts and boroughs of England and Wales as a whole. Food, tobacco, drink and lodging followed with 845 males per ten thousand compared with 734 in the urban areas of England and Wales. Third place was taken by railway employment with 541 males per ten thousand. Only fifteen out of over 120 towns with a population exceeding fifty thousand had a larger proportion of males employed on the railways. In the census group described as retired or unoccupied the proportion of males in Exeter was 1,918 per ten thousand, a substantially higher figure than the 1,578 per ten thousand in the urban areas of England and Wales as a whole. Exeter remained, as in the 1830s, a centre of relatively cheap and quiet retirement.

For females the largest occupational group was still domestic service which, including ancillary occupations such as charring and laundry work, employed 2,253 women and girls or over one-quarter of those in occupations at the time of the census of 1911. Indoor domestic service employed 1,021 females per ten thousand. Out of over 120 boroughs and urban areas only twenty-eight showed a higher proportion of females employed in domestic service and these included thirteen in the special conditions of the London area. The highest proportion was in comfortable and expanding

v

residential towns such as Eastbourne, where the proportion was 1,658 per ten thousand, and Hastings where it was 1,402. In ancient county capitals such as York and Gloucester the proportion was 812 and 751 per ten thousand respectively. In industrial Leicester it was only 440. The proportion of females employed in domestic service and similar occupations had fallen significantly between 1901 and 1911; domestic indoor service from 1,287 to 1,021 per ten thousand, charwomen from 158 to 129, and laundry and washing services from 235 to 165. Dressmaking was the second largest occupational group for women and girls, employing in 1911 391 females per 10,000. Female employment was still traditional though alternative occupations in the modern fashion were increasing. Female employment in the civil service and in the telegraph and telephone services had increased from fifteen to twenty-seven per ten thousand; municipal, parish and hospital employment from forty-six to fifty-three; employment in commerce, banks and insurance from thirty-three to sixty. In this last category Exeter was lagging. The proportion was eighty-three per ten thousand in England and Wales as a whole and 1,000 per ten thousand in the boroughs and urban areas generally. Feminine leadership in the public life of Victorian Exeter had been confined to Miss Temple and Miss Jessie Montgomery, both with the assured social position and independence required for feminine activity in public affairs in the Victorian era. After 1900 there were women members of Exeter's board of guardians and the education committee but when the question of women's role in public affairs had been discussed in 1913 it was suggested, no doubt with truth at the time, that educated women did not seek election to the council.[12]

According to the mayor's statement to the twenty-eighth congress of the Royal Sanitary Institute, held in Exeter in 1913, the standards of the council had themselves declined. Exeter's local government, it was said, was ceasing to attract those who would be the most valuable members by reason of 'education, leisure, business training or strong personality.'[13] Three years previously a letter to the *Flying Post* had lamented the passing of the 'fine, typical Exonians and businessmen who formerly governed our city.'[14] This complaint was as old as the council itself. It had been heard repeatedly since 1837, usually in order to blame the opposite political party as when, in 1883, the *Flying Post* complained that 'the Radicals have made the duties of a Town Councillor so irksome and distasteful that it is difficult to find men to come forward.'[15] Somewhat similar comments were to be made well into the twentieth century. On the other hand it is not uncommon to hear those who today can still remember the city of the early decades of the century extol the vigorous personalities of a previous generation. In 1913 the *Flying Post* made its own analysis of occupations on the council.[16] The list included solicitors, builders, doctors and representatives of the licensed trade, bakers and grocers, all of them occupations consistently represented on the council since 1837. The most striking change, perhaps, was the reduction of wine and spirit merchants, brewers and innkeepers from nine on the smaller council of 1898 to three, the absence of bankers and newspaper proprietors in 1913 and, in contrast, the appearance of two railway employees.

If a detailed comparison were to be made between the circumstances of each member of the council in 1837 and on the eve of the first World War it would be found that the former did in fact represent a much higher proportion of the wealth and social status of the city, a change which can hardly be regarded as being for the worse, however much it might be deplored by the standards acceptable in the early years of the Victorian era. It was this change, however, which inspired the comments in the Conservative press at the time of the Liberal victory in 1900. By the twentieth century the growing complexity of local government and its increasing professionalism implied a reduction in the initiative of individual members. With the extended parliamentary franchise, and the change in the composition of parliament itself, there was no longer in 1914 that close link between the council and county society and politics which had been so marked in 1837 and which had been retained, though in gradually more attenuated form, for so long.

The *Flying Post* was to be sold by auction in 1917. The

Devon and Exeter Gazette was to be amalgamated with the
Western Morning News in 1932; the former's editor G. F.
Gratwicke, the last of the old-style editor politicians
appointed in 1885, died in 1912. More important figures in
the local political world had gone by 1914 and with them the
old traditional pattern of politics; for, in the small, conservative world of Exeter, tradition and personality had
perpetuated the habits and attitudes of the past.

W. J. Richards, the reorganizer of the Conservative
political machine, had died in 1903; his former partner
Joseph Harding, first elected for St Paul's ward in 1856 and
mayor in 1871, in 1908. Their political heirs were Robert
Pople, the former Bridgwater tile worker, whose New London
Inn was a Conservative stronghold, 'a great racegoer and a
strong churchman,' who died in 1909; Walter Pring the
brewer, member of the city council from 1875 to 1893,
president of the Exeter Conservative Working Men's Conservative Union, one of the founders of the Constitutional
Club, in 1910. Edward Sanders himself, upright and
honourable, never a target for political obloquy, died in
1905. His position as banker and his relationship with the
Courtenays of Powderham had linked the city with the
landed interest in its Victorian heyday. Sanders had seconded
the nomination of Sir William Follett in the days when
Peel was laying the foundations of the Conservative party.
He had appeared on the platform with the Edwardian figure
of Sir Edgar Vincent. He had seen the apotheosis of empire.
Men such as these left no successors.[18] They had flourished
in an environment which no longer existed. That environment was rural England which was followed, in the southwest,
by suburban England, 'land of the lobelias and tennis
flannels,' civilized, tolerant, less local in character.

If Edward Sanders had lived a few more years he would
have reached his hundredth birthday and could have looked
back on seventy years of Victorian Exeter. He would have
recalled the terrible cholera year of 1832, the year of the
Great Reform Bill, when Exeter was still a Tudor city within
a Georgian setting, a city of gables and lath and plaster
houses, of narrow passages and courts, of abandoned drying

racks, the relics of the old cloth industry; a compact city above an unpolluted river where salmon were plentiful, a city of trees, set in orchards and gardens, but still virtually unpaved, unlit and unpoliced.

In 1914 the cathedral remained the dominating feature of the city, as Mawson had explained to the council; silver-grey in sunshine, dark and lustreless under cloud, it stood as it stands today. In 1914 it was the supreme architectural achievement of a culture that was still Christian in practice as well as by descent and unchallenged by the architectural self-expression of the twentieth century. The bishop was still in his palace, though Victorian Exeter had so often been alarmed or invigorated by the spectacle of an endangered church. If bishops were no longer the giant figures of Phillpotts and Temple they were not liable to be burnt in effigy or rabbled at public meetings. The fifth of November had ceased to be celebrated in the smoke and flames of the great bonfire before the west door of the cathedral while police and yeomanry strove with the mob. The surplice appeared each Sunday in the pulpit and no man remarked it.

Hunger, like religious issues, no longer caused rioting. Soldiers had been called out for the last time in 1879 when the barricades had been erected for the defence of the City Bank and the Riot Act had been answered by cries of 'Cheap Bread.' Indeed, old Mr Sanders might have reflected, manners everywhere were milder. Gone were the riotous and drunken elections, the uproar over the mayor-choosing in the Guildhall, the stir over council elections as if the fate of England depended on the outcome. Drunkenness had declined. In 1913 the chief constable drew attention to what he described as the remarkable decrease in drunkenness as compared with the average for the eight years prior to 1912.[19] There was no serious crime.

Business had unquestionably turned the corner since the seventies and if the purchasing power of the county was no longer important, a wider effective demand especially for capital investment in houses, new tastes and higher standards had brought a more widely diffused prosperity than ever before. Wages had risen. Even the council's sweepers were paid 20s. a week and grave diggers and water department labourers 5½d. to 6d. an hour. Progress was demonstrated by cheap gas and electricity, by the trams which brought the people from Heavitree and St Thomas to work or shop in the city at a profit to the council itself, by the long lines of artisans' houses, the new shop fronts in High Street and Fore Street.

Visitors were bringing money into the city. To attract the new tourists the council in 1912 had ordered ten thousand posters for railway stations and views of the city for G.W.R. railway carriages.[20] Hotels, including temperance hotels, had increased to twenty-eight by 1914, as compared with fifteen in 1883 and twenty in 1901. Exeter traders were beginning to take up the new opportunities offered by the transformation of women's fashions into a large-scale industry. A hair-waving establishment first appeared in Exeter in 1914. The number of hairdressers in the directories rose from twenty-five in 1883 to forty-five in 1901 and to fifty-three by 1914. Travel was easier, faster, more comfortable and cheaper. In Sanders's youth a journey to London on the outside of the Telegraph coach had cost £2. By 1910 an excursion ticket to London cost only 6s. return. Already, by 1912, an alleged decline in church-going had been attributed to the new tendency 'to rush about the country in a motor car on Sundays.'[21] In 1914 a char-à-bancs with thirty or forty visitors was observed in the High Street. It was worth remark that the visitors would be back in north Devon by a reasonable hour that same evening.[22] New technical developments were bringing new business opportunities to the city. As a businessman Sanders would have been unlikely to see anything to deplore in Exeter's economic revival between the Boer War and 1914.

A man of Sanders's background and connections would also have been unlikely to have assessed changes in his lifetime purely in terms of material progress. He could have looked back to the days of his mayoralty, the year when the city was host to the landed interest and Exeter's bishop was convicting the primate of bad theology. He could have remembered the Exeter of his boyhood when the chamber was strictly Anglican and included members such as Edward Upham, the learned bookseller, mayors like Edward Woolmer, of the *Gazette*, and Philip de la Garde, surgeon and archaeologist. In those days Exeter had still been the city described by Defoe as 'full of gentry and good company.' Those days had been doomed by the Municipal Corporations Act and, more decisively, by the transfer of power from rural to urban England, though their influence had lingered long in Exeter. Exeter had retained its Conservatism, but the social composition and background of the council had changed. The Municipal Corporations Act had not noticeably improved the standards of the council as a whole. It had necessitated the rough methods of the forties to secure election in the place of the more decorous methods of the past. Influence in city affairs passed to new men, and as the smaller world of the provincial England of the west country lost its status and independence so the council became less congenial to members of the old governing class.

The typical representatives of Exeter in the years between 1900 and 1914 were not bankers but the professional men, shopkeepers, traders and artisans, some Liberal in their politics, others Conservative, but even these less influenced by the standards and traditions of clergy and county. These could congratulate themselves with some reason that their lot had fallen in a fair ground. The young middle-class housewife who had married in June 1880 would have found no significant change in prices if she had looked over her old accounts on her wedding anniversary in June 1914. Eggs would have cost her 1s. for twelve instead of for thirteen, butter 17d. to 18d. per lb. instead of 11d. She would have paid 5s. to 5s. 6d. for a couple of fowls in June 1880, and 6s. to 7s. 6d. in June 1914. The top price for beef had risen from 10d. to 11d. per lb. The price of potatoes had remained unaltered at 1d. per lb. In 1914 a leg of mutton could be bought for 9d. per lb., shoulder at 7d. to 8d., chops at 10d. to 1s., sirloin and topside at 9d. per lb.[23] Servants' wages had risen substantially. The housewife who began her married life in 1880 would have paid a cook about £14 a year and a housemaid rather less. In 1914 a good cook would have expected £30 to £45 a year. Rates and taxes were rising and insurance stamps were an unpopular innovation though in 1914 even the borough rate was reduced by 2*d*. in the £ and the poor rate by 1*d*. Gas was cheaper than ever before. Electricity was more widely used. The middle-class housewife did not represent all Exeter. But she did represent an important element of the city.

The artisans had more cause for concern over pennies and with the rise in prices which had brought food prices in England as a whole to some 14½ per cent. over the level of 1900.[24] But if the council is taken as a guide, wages in Exeter were being raised repeatedly, from an admittedly low level, between the Boer War and the first World War. There was a generally high level of economic activity in the city. Opportunities for more skilled work at higher pay were widening. In housing, sanitation and education the working classes as a whole were infinitely better off than ever before. On the basis of the 'hard facts of food, health and shelter'[25] there had been undoubted progress. Photographs of Messrs Colsons' staff picnics at this period record a new individual freedom: the men in the ubiquitous straw hat or even hatless, one smoking a cigarette, the women in the wide-brimmed hats and simple skirts and blouses of the period.[26] For such as these there was much to enjoy in that golden early summer of 1914, as yet unshadowed by war.

The material benefits of life were enjoyed in a city which was still remarkable for the rural setting once common to most urban communities. Exeter had survived and finally prospered not through its own exertions but as the beneficiary of economic change and social habits in the country as a whole. The great industrial areas of Victorian England had transformed the country at a cost both in human happiness and in the aesthetics of urban life. Exeter had waited, preserving much of its beauty as a city as well as the attitudes and traditions of preindustrial England, until the new waves of energy created elsewhere reached the southwest down the railways and roads which still converged at the river-crossing on the lower reaches of the Exe. The city had never lost its position as a centre of administration, business and amusement, of distribution and communications. In all these capacities the city was being revitalized and used by larger numbers than ever before, drawn from wider areas, with new tastes but not in the aggregate with less purchasing power. For the preservation of the rural background, the setting of woods and fields, its trees and water meadows, Exeter had also paid a price, as the food riots and unemployment problem of the nineteenth century testify. Relatively to the size of the city this price had not been much lower than the price paid elsewhere for industrial success; but the effect had been that the city's beauty had survived the heyday of economic *laissez faire* until the age of town planning began. This was an advantage which many larger cities did not share. Exeter had escaped, too, the economic tensions and class cleavages which were rending England in the years before the first World War. A small, relatively homogenous city, moderate alike in its wealth and social divisions, slow-moving, it had never on any significant scale seen the emergence of 'The Two Nations' of Disraeli's *Sybil*.

The old social order, in its essence the world of the county, by 1914 was dying of obsolescence not through direct assault, at least in Exeter itself. That social order had remained the power-house of leadership in the city. Its Conservative characteristics survived when the leadership perished. Thesis and antithesis had been followed by a new synthesis on another level, in the material sense on a higher level. It was no longer the world of Richard Ford, a world which had lingered longer in Exeter than in most cities; but 'social change, however profound, may be sign of renewal, not of collapse.'[27]

In the early summer of 1914 Exeter, sheltered from and untouched by the industrial unrest of early twentieth-century England, in spirit still remote from the more turbulent and creative aspects of national life, was reading of troop movements in Ulster and of a reduction in the rates. The problems of Anglo-German relations had not escaped notice. In 1912 they had been discussed at a peace meeting at the Guildhall. But Exeter as a whole was less alive to the significance of

international events than it had been in the eighteenth
century when it had carried on an extensive trade with
Europe from the Tagus to the Elbe. On 4 July a small
paragraph in the *Flying Post* reported the murder of the
Archduke Franz Ferdinand and his wife six days previously;
but at the end of the month the emphasis in the local press
was still on the threat of civil war in Ireland. On 1 August the
city was informed for the first time that a general European
conflagration was a 'hideous possibility.'[28] Three days later
special editions announced that Britain was at war. The
announcement was followed by rumours of attempts to
tamper with the city's water supply.[29] For the first time since
the Napoleonic wars, when Devon had prepared evacuation
schemes, war was more than an adventure in foreign parts.
It was the end of the Victorian era.

OCCUPATIONS OF MEMBERS OF THE CHAMBER AND COUNCIL OF EXETER
1835–1914

THE following lists show the occupations of members of the unreformed corporation in the last year of its existence and of the council in 1836–37, 1848–49, 1867–68, 18 70–71, 1881–82, 1898–99 and 1901–02. An analysis of occupations for the year 1913–14, originally published in the *Flying Post* of 20 December 1913, is also included. To provide a broader view of the composition of the council than can be obtained from any one year lists of councillors and their occupations have been compiled for the years 1837–46, 1868–77 and 1896–1905. Summaries of these lists have also been compiled. The years 1835/1836–37 and 1898–99/1901–02 have been chosen to show the effects of change in two critical periods at either end of the Victorian period. The year 1848–49 was selected as about the time when local power was devolving on new men and particularly on the city boss, the builder Henry Hooper. The year 1867–68 was selected to show the composition of the council at the time of the second Reform Bill; 1870–71 because it was the beginning of the rule of the licensed trade; 1881–82 because it was the time of the brief Liberal revival.

The sources are the directories, the local lists of voters and voting in the parliamentary elections of 1831, 1832, 1835, 1864 and 1868; council minutes; and the newspapers. None of these is self-sufficient. The term gentleman was often used, both in the directories and in the voting lists, in a manner which would not have satisfied a contemporary social purist. Wherever possible this description has been discarded in favour of the original or actual trade or profession of the individual concerned. This, of course, does not involve moral judgements. The newspapers are an invaluable source of information with their comments on local personalities which often include vivid thumb-nail sketches of the character and interests of individuals. These are useful when it is necessary to make a choice between two individuals with the same names and status. Unfortunately Victorian newspaper files are voluminous and it cannot be guaranteed that pertinent information has not been overlooked. From the 1870s the newspapers sometimes, but not always, published the nomination lists which often included the occupation of the candidates; but the occupation given was too often a vague term such as merchant or gentleman.

Contemporary opinion reiterated laments over the decline in the standards of the council. The Conservative *Gazette* at first was hopeful. 'The burgesses have made a most judicious choice' said an editorial on 2 January 1836, 'for we know of scarcely any individual, who may not be entitled to that distinction, as regards integrity, respectability and habits of business.' But on 11 November 1870 the Liberal *Western Times* complained that 'people of competent means and position care not to enter into the Town Council.' 'Years ago,' declared the Conservative *Flying Post* on 8 November 1882, 'men of position, wealth and leisure were proud to serve the public offices in the city, and the city was well served by men who gave dignity to the municipal life . . . But now the difficulty is to find men of position to have anything to do with public work.' The Liberal victory of 1900 gave control of the council, according to the *Flying Post* of 2 November 1900, to 'men to whom the majority of . . . citizens could scarcely give a moment's thought in ordinary times, faddists, extremists of all sorts, men of parochial minds.' And after the Conservatives were returned to power the mayor was reported by the *Flying Post* of 12 July 1912 as stating that 'from a variety of reasons those who, by virtue of their education, leisure, business training or strong personality would and should be the most valuable members in the public service, stood aside in greater numbers and declined to serve.'

The composition of the council to which these remarks referred is shown below. There were occasions when laments over declining standards were in part political propaganda; in part they were based on the undoubted fact that membership of the council spread to circles who had neither the social status, by local standards, nor the wealth, of their predecessors. This is difficult to demonstrate statistically. It involves appreciating the difference between, for instance, John Carew, mayor 1840–41 and A. E. Dunn, mayor 1900–1902. Both were lawyers, but the first was a member of a county family, a wealthier man and one who carried more weight in a society where status and wealth mattered.

Nor does an analysis of the council necessarily disclose the real seat of power, though it shows the over-representation, proportionately, of the lawyers throughout the period and the weight carried by the licensed trade at a time when the liquor question was a burning political issue. As the *Flying Post* pointed out on 20 October 1900 'Some innocents without political guile might imagine that all business of the city is, or ought to be, conducted within the walls of the council chamber; but every man and woman of the world is aware that there must be informal discussion and consideration of various matters.' It may be inferred, though it cannot be proved, that for the greater part of the period the most influential voice on important issues was that of Edward Sanders, a descendant of the Courtenays of Powderham, educated at Harrow and Oxford, banker, and for some sixty years chairman of Exeter's Conservative parliamentary candidates' committees. Yet Sanders only once took an active part in council affairs when a mayor of suitable social status and wealth was required for the year of the Royal Agricultural Show of 1850.

THE CHAMBER OF EXETER 1835

Accountant
Lee, W.
Attorney
Turner, C. H.
Banker
Sanders, R. R.
Doctor, surgeon
Besley, W. H.
de la Garde, P. C.
Gurney, B.
Harris, J.

James, J. H.
Johnson, B. W.
Norris, T.
Shapter, T.
Walkey, S. C.
Leather, glove mfr.
Tanner, J.
Newspaper proprietor
Woolmer, E. – *Exeter and Plymouth Gazette*

Postmaster
Measor, P.
Licensed trade etc.
Crockett, W.
Hirtzel, H. L.
Kennaway, W.
Smith, T.

Gentleman, retired
Blackhall, H.
Carter, Capt. J. S.
Hart, J.
Payne, Capt. W.
Were, J.

EXETER CITY COUNCIL 1836–37

Attorney
Drake, T. E.
Ford, H. M.
Furlong, W. E.
Kennaway, M.
Pitts, J.
Banker
Nation, W.
Sanders, J. B.
Snow, T.
Doctor, surgeon
Barnes, S.
Ham, J.
Harris, J.
Kingdon, W. B.
Tucker, J.
Druggist
Evans, R.
Hill, C.
Builder, surveyor
Clark, J.
Cornish, R.
Ironmonger
Beal, W.
Kingdon, S.
Kingdon, W.
Postmaster
Measor, P.
Newspaper proprietor
Trewman, R. J. – *Flying Post*
Woolmer, E. – *Exeter and Plymouth Gazette*

Licensed trade etc.
Bastard, R. – spirit and hop mercht.
Bastard, S. S. – hop mercht.
Bastard, W. S. – spirit and hop mercht.
Clench, J. – brewer
Drewe, W. – wine and spirit mercht.
Hill, W. B. – wine and spirit mercht.
Kennaway, W. – wine and spirit mercht.
Sayell, J. – maltster
Wilkinson, W. J. P. – wine and spirit mercht.
Others
Arden, C. – mercer
Burt, J. – picture dlr.
Davy, C. – currier
Davy, D. B. – candle and soap mercht.
Hayman, J. – coach mfr.
Sercombe, J. C. – grain mercht.
Skinner, J. – watchmaker
Snell, W. W. – grocer
Strong, J. – miller, timber mercht.
Tuckett, N. – candle and soap mercht.
Wilcocks, J. C. – draper
Upjohn, J. – watchmaker

Wilcocks, J. C. – draper
Gentleman, retired
Bond, Capt. F. G.

Golsworthy, J. – ex water-
works prop.
Langston, S.

EXETER CITY COUNCIL 1848–49

Attorney
Brutton, C.
Carew, J.
Drake, T. H.
Flood, T.
Force, E.
Furlong, W. H.
Hirtzel, H. E.
Hooper, H. W.
Moore, W. D.
Richards, C.
Toby, J.
Turner, C. H.
Doctor, surgeon
Harris, J.
Kingdon, W. P.
Land, W.
Shapter, T.
Builder, auctioneer
Force, C.
Hooper, H.
Hooper, W. W.
Taylor, R.
Newspaper prop., editor
Latimer, T. – *Western Times*
Trewman, R. J. – *Flying Post*
Woolmer, E. – Devon *Exeter and Plymouth Gazette*
Licensed Trade etc.
Bastard, R. – spirit and hop mercht.

Bastard, W. S. – spirit and hop mercht.
Cockram, J. – prop. New London Inn
Hirtzel, F. – wine mercht.
Lisson, P. – prop. Acland Arms
Norman, J. E. – wine mercht.
Richards, W. – prop. Turk's Head
Sayell, J. – maltster
Trehane, J. – wine and spirit mercht.
Others
Arden, C. – mercer
Burrington, J. – watchmaker
Brunskill, S. – tailor
Davies, S. – grocer
Duchemin, G. – paper mfr.
Ferris, G. – jeweller
Franklin, F. – coachbuilder
Kingdon, W. – ironmonger
Nicholls, J. – upholsterer
Nicholls, J. P. – furniture dlr.
Piper, W. – perfumer, hairdresser
Sercombe, G. – grain and seed mercht.
Wilcocks, J. C. – draper
Worthy, T. D. – woollen mfr.

EXETER CITY COUNCIL 1867–68

Attorney
Buckingham, W.
Burch, A.
Drake, T. E.

Force, E.
Ford, B. J.
Head, R. T.
Huggins, W.

Rogers, W. G.
Turner, C. H.
Banker
Snow, T.
Builder, surveyor, timber mercht.
Cornish, R. S.
Hooper, H.
Moass, J.
Ware, J.
Newspaper prop., editor
Bellerby, J. – *Flying Post*
Wescomb, C. – *Exeter and Plymouth Gazette*
Sharebroker
Down, G.
Dentist
King, N.
Toll contractor
Norris, T. G.
Licensed trade etc.
Bastard, S. – hop mercht.
Birkett, W. – prop. Royal Clarence
Harding, J. – brewer
Hadley, P. M. – wine and spirit mercht.
Richards, W. J. – brewer
Thomas, H. D. – brewer
Trehane, J. – wine and spirit mercht.

Others
Brooking, J. R. – silversmith, pawnbroker
Carter, W. – draper
Chalk, J. – sadler
Clifford, W. – bookseller
Cuthbertson, W. – confectioner
Damerel, J. – ironmonger
Dipstale, E. – decorator
Davy, W. – currier
Franklin, F. – coachbuilder
Hughes, H. – ironmonger
Kendall, W. – draper
Moore, W. – hatter
Nichols, J. P. – furniture dlr.
Norrington, H. – agric. implement dlr.
Norris, W. – woollen mercht.
Pearse, S. – ironmonger
Popham, A. T. – oil and colour mercht.
Sclater, C. – nurseryman
Trimble, J. T. – pawnbroker
Vickary, J. – iron and brass founder
Gentleman, retired
Whistler, T.

EXETER CITY COUNCIL 1870–71

Solicitor
Buckingham, W.
Burch, A.
Drake, T. E.
Gidley, B. C.
Head, R. T.
Huggins, W.
Rogers, W. G.

Builder, surveyor, timber mercht.
Abell, T.
Cornish, R. S.
Moass, J.
Ware, J.
Surgeon-dentist
King, N.

Toll contractor
Norris, T. G.
Licensed trade etc.
Birkett, W. – prop. Royal Clarence
Hadley, P. M. – wine and spirit mercht.
Harding, J. – brewer
Gardner, T. – prop. Half Moon Hotel
Lawless, H. – wine and spirit mercht.
Pople, R. – prop. New London Inn
Pridham, J. – prop. Bude Hotel
Richards, J. – brewer
Trehane, J. – wine and spirit mercht.
Salter, T. – wine and spirit mercht.
Thomas, H. D. – brewer
Others
Brooker, J. – watchmaker, pawnbroker
Carter, W. – grocer

Clifford, W. – bookseller
Cooper, G. – druggist
Davy, W. – currier
Dipstale, E. – decorator
Ellis, H. S. – jeweller
Franklin, F. – coachbuilder
Grant, F. – fancy warehouse
Hughes, H. – ironmonger
Kendall, W. – draper
Knapman, E. – draper
Lloyd, H. C. – tobacco mercht.
Norrington, H. – agric. implements, manure mercht.
Pearse, J. – draper
Pearse, S. – ironmonger
Popham, A. T. – oil and colour mercht.
Rookes, W. – horse dealer
Sclater, C. – nurseryman
Smith, W. – butcher
Trimble, J. T. – silversmith, pawnbroker
Wilcocks, H. – tea, coffee, spice dlr.
Wills, J. – tallow chandler

EXETER CITY COUNCIL 1881-82

Solicitor
Buckingham, W.
Burch, A.
Daw, R. R. M.
Friend, J. W.
Hirtzel, G.
Roberts, C. T. K.
Accountant
Andrew, T. – high bailiff
Southcott, R.
Bank manager
Cotton, W.

Builder, architect, auctioneer
Commings, W. J.
Force, S. R.
Fulford, E. B.
Huxtable, W.
Luscombe, F. L.
Packham, G.
Ware, C. E.
Draper, outfitter
Armstrong, R.
Brown, W.
Courtney, J.

w

Davy, S.
Knapman, E.
Pearce, T.
Samuel, H.
Tuckwell, H.
Tuckwell, J. C.
Doctor, surgeon
Domville, E.
Licensed trade
Finch, G. P. – wine and spirits
merch t.
Hexter, H. – prop. Queen's
Hotel
Jones, S. – wine and spirit
merch t.
Norman, J. J. – wine and
spirit merch t.
Pring, W. – brewer
Richards, W. J. – brewer
Wilkinson, R. C. – wine and
spirit merch t.
Williams, F. J. – wine and
spirit merch t.
Journalist, printer
Pollard, W.

Wreford, W.
Others
Badcock, J. – provision
merch t.
Dark, J. J. – grocer
Eland, H. S. – stationer
Ellis, W. H. – jeweller
Guest, J. C. – music seller
Hart, M. – furnisher
Hughes, H. – ironmonger
Norton, W. – confectioner
Pearse, S. – ironmonger
Peters, W. – grocer
Pidsley, W. – grocer
Rowe, T. – oil merch t.
Sclater, W. H. – nurseryman
Stockham, J. – cork merch t.
Turner, E. – cabinet maker
Wilcocks, H. – tea and spice
merch t.
Wippell, G. – ironmonger
Gentleman, retired
Martyn, A. – major
Owen, W. H.
Peters, E.

EXETER CITY COUNCIL 1898–99

Solicitor
Baker, C.
Campion, H.
Caunter, W. A.
Daw, J. E.
Daw, R. R. M.
Dunn, A. E.
Gidley, J.
Houlditch, G. H.
Luke, E. W.
Orchard, H. H.
Roberts, C. T. K.
Accountant
Andrew, T.
Fulford, E. T.

Artist
Widgery, F. W.
*Builder, architect, house-
agent etc.*
Cole, C.
Force, S. R.
Lucas, J. S.
Jerman, J.
Rippon, H. E.
Scadding, F. H.
Stile, G. L.
Thompson, A.
Ware, C. E.
Doctor, surgeon
Domville, E. J.

Steele Perkins, A. R.
Steele Perkins, E. B.
Insurance manager
Templeton, J.
Journalist
Wreford, W.
Liberal agent
Perry, E. C.
Sharebroker
Yeo, H.
Licensed trade etc.
Birkett, E. W. – brewer
Finch, C. T. W. – prop. Half Moon Hotel
Finch, G. P. – wine and spirit mercht.
Norman, J. J. – wine and spirit mercht.
Pople, R. – prop. New London Inn
Pring, T. C. – brewer
Pring, W. – brewer
Williams, J. W. – wine and spirit mercht.

Others
Edwards, W. H. – grocer
Gadd, H. – druggist
Ham, C. – aerated water mfr.
Hamlin, H. P. O. – provision mercht.
Herbert, S. T. – watchmaker
Hutchings, A. M. – butcher
Kelland, P. – baker
Linscott, T. – pawnbroker
Loram, J. A. – grocer
Munro, H. C. J. – dairyman
Oliver, A. T. – general mercht.
Pulsford, J. – draper
Peters, J. – mercht.
Rowe, T. B. – lead mercht.
Stokes, J. – fruit mercht.
Surridge, J. – miller
Turner, E. – cabinet maker
Varwell, H. B. – coal mercht.
Wards, S. – coal mercht.
Wilson, T. – decorator
Gentleman, retired
Dunn, W. H.
Jarman, W.

EXETER CITY COUNCIL 1901–02

Solicitor
Baker, C.
Brown, W. L.
Campion, H.
Daw, J. E.
Dunn, A. E.
Gidley, J.
Roberts, C. T. K.
Artist
Widgery, F. J.
Builder, architect, house-agent, surveyor
Challice, R. M.
Cole, C.
Courtney, J.

Jerman, J.
Lucas, J. A.
Stocker, J.
Draper, outfitter
McCrea, A.
Pulsford, J.
Wilson, J.
Journalist
Wreford, J.
Merchant, dealer
Knapman, E. T. – oil and colour
Oliver, A. T. – fruit
Oliver, W. H. – general
Rowe, C. E. – lead

Rowe, T. B. – lead
Stokes, J. E. – fruit
Tucker, J. – coal
Varwell, H. B. – coal
Paper manufacturer
Reed, W. H.
Professor of music
Noble, H.
Railway official
Campfield, J.
Secretary, Liberal Assoc.
Perry, E. C.
Sharebroker
Yeo, H.
Surgeon
Domville, E. J.
Licensed trade, etc.
Pring, T. C. – brewer
Pring, W. – brewer
Finch, C. T. W. – prop. Half Moon Hotel
Howard, T. – prop. Seven Stars Hotel

Pople, R. – prop. New London [Inn
Others
Bates, J. – brasscaster
Hawke, W. – smith
Herbert, S. T. – stationer
Hodson, F. G. – jeweller, silversmith
Kelland, P. – baker
Linscott, T. – pawnbroker
Loram, A. T. – dairyman
Loram, J. A. – grocer
Mallet, W. R. – miller
Munro, H. J. – dairyman
Mansfield, F. G. – cabinet maker
Peters, J. – furnisher
Rowe, B. – stationer
Turner, E. – cabinet maker
Taylor, C. M. – ironfounder
West, H. E. – butcher
Gentleman, retired
Dunn, W. H.
Jarman, W.

EXETER CITY COUNCIL 1913–14

Analysis of occupations published in the *Flying Post* on 20 December 1913.

Retired	6	Railway employees	2
Solicitors	5	Bank manager	1
Furniture trade	5	Artist	1
Jewellers	4	Brewer	1
Builders	4	Cloth merchant	1
Architects	3	Outfitter	1
Doctors	3	Coal merchant	1
Merchants	3	Motor dealer	1
Paper mfrs.	2	Hardware mercht.	1
Printers	2	Market gardener	1
Grocers	2	Marine store dlr.	1
Bakers	2	Fish dealer	1
Licensed trade	2	Secretary	1
Pawnbrokers	2	Timber trade	1

Dentist	I	Engineering	I
Butcher	I	Cycle dealer	I
Smith	I	Fruit mercht.	I
Game dealer	I	Forage dealer	I
Laundry prop.	I		

OCCUPATIONS OF MEMBERS OF THE EXETER CITY COUNCIL 1837-46

Arden, C. – mercer

Barnes, S. – surgeon

Bastard, R. – spirit and hop mercht.

Bastard, S. S. – hop mercht. and wholesale dlr.

Beal, W. – ironmonger

Bishop, D. B. – hemp and iron mercht.

Bond, F. G. – Capt. R.N. (Rtd.)

Browne, E. – butcher

Brunskill, S. – tailor

Brutton, C. – attorney

Burt, J. – picture dlr.

Carew, J. – attorney

Clark, J. – builder

Clench, J. – brewer, maltster

Commin, N. – maltster

Cornish, R. – timber mercht. builder

Cornish, R. S. – builder, surveyor

Davy, C. – currier

Davies, S. – grocer

Daw, J. – attorney

Dewdney, J. S. – printer, paper mfr.

Drake, T. E. – attorney

Drewe, W. – wine and spirit mercht.

Duchemin, G. – paper mfr.

Evans, R. – druggist

Ferris, G. – jeweller, silversmith

Floud, T. – attorney

Force, E. – attorney

Ford, H. M. – attorney

Froom, W. J. – druggist

Furlong, W. H. – attorney

Gill, J. – builder

Golsworthy, J. – water works prop.

Ham, J. – doctor

Harris, J. – surgeon

Hannaford, P. A. – bookseller

Harding, W. – maltster

Hayman, J. – coach mfr.

Helmore, N. – ironmonger

Hill, C. – druggist

Hill, W. M. – wine and spirit mercht.

Hirtzel, H. – attorney

Hooper, H. – builder

Hooper, H. W. – attorney

Hooper, W. – builder

Hubbard, C. – caterer

Kennaway, M. – attorney

Kennaway, W. – wine and spirit mercht.

Kingdon, S. – ironmonger

Kingdon, W. – ironmonger

Kingdon, W. P. – surgeon

Langston, S. – gentleman

Land, W. – surgeon

Latimer, T. – editor, *Western Times*

Lee, W. – accountant
Macgowan – doctor
Maunder, S. – boot and shoe maker
Measor, P. – postmaster
Moore, W. D. – attorney
Nation, W. – banker
Osborn, J. D. – glass and china merry.
Pain, R. – innkeeper
Piper, W. – perfumer
Pitts, J. – attorney
Richards, C. – attorney
Richards, W. – maltster, inn-keeper
Salter, B. – brewer
Sanders, J. B. – banker
Sayell, J. – maltster
Sercombe, J. C. – grain merry.
Shepherd, J. – wine merry.
Sheppard, J. – mercer, draper
Skinner, J. – watchmaker

Smith, T. – spirit dlr., hop merry.
Snell, W. W. – grocer
Snow, T. – banker
Strong, J. – miller, timber merry.
Strong, W. – attorney
Tanner, F. – tanner
Tanner, J. J. – glove merry.
Taylor, R. – auctioneer
Toombs, W. – banker
Trewman, R. J. – printer, newspaper prop.
Tucker, J. – surgeon [dlr.
Tuckett, N. – candle and soap
Turner, C. H. – attorney
Upjohn, J. – watchmaker
Woolmer, E. – newspaper prop. *Exeter and Plymouth Gazette*
Wilcocks, J. C. – draper
Wilkinson, W. J. P. – wine and spirit merry.

OCCUPATIONS OF MEMBERS OF THE EXETER CITY COUNCIL 1868–77

Abell, T. – timber merry.
Angel, O. – photographer
Barnes, S. – surgeon
Bastard, S. – hop merry.
Bellerby, J. – editor, *Flying Post*
Birkett, W. – prop. Royal Clarence Hotel
Bodley, O. A. – brassfounder
Brooking, J. R. – silversmith, pawnbroker
Brown, W. – draper
Buckingham, W. – attorney
Burch, A. – attorney
Carter, W. – grocer
Clifford, W. – bookseller

Chalk, J. – saddler
Cooper, G. – druggist
Cornish, R. S. – builder, surveyor
Courtney, J. – draper
Damerel, J. – ironmonger
Davey, W. – currier
Dey, T. – plumber
Dipstale, G. – painter, decorator
Down, G. – sharebroker
Drake, T. E. – attorney
East, S. – boot and shoe maker
Edwards, J. – hatter
Ellis, H. S. – jeweller, optician

Follett, C. J. – attorney
Force, E. – attorney
Force, S. R. – auctioneer, house agent
Ford, B. J. – attorney
Franklin, F. – coachbuilder
Friend, J. W. – attorney
Gardner, T. – prop. Half Moon Hotel
Gidley, J. – attorney
Grant, F. W. – boot, glass, china dlr.
Green, E. – mercer, draper
Hadley, P. M. – wine mercht.
Harding, J. – wine mercht., brewer
Harris, J. O. – builder
Head, R. T. – attorney
Hirtzel, G. – attorney
Hooper, H. – builder
Huggins, W. – attorney
Hughes, H. – ironmonger
Huxtable, W. – builder
Jeboult, H. R. – glass and china dlr.
Jones, S. – wine mercht.
Kendall, W. – draper
King, N. – surgeon dentist
Knapman, E. – draper
Lawless, H. – wine mercht.
Lloyd, H. C. – tobacco mfr.
Melhuish, J. W. – hosier
Moass, J. – builder
Moore, W. – builder
Nichols, J. P. – furniture dlr. cabinet mkr.
Norrington, H. – agricultural implement and manure mercht.
Norris, T. G. – toll contractor
Norris, W. – woollen mercht.
Pearse, S. – ironmonger

Pollard, W. – printer, stationer
Popham, A. T. – oil and colour mercht.
Pople, R. – prop. New London Inn
Pridham, J. – prop. Bude Hotel
Pring, W. – brewer
Richards, W. J. – wine and spirit mercht., brewer
Rogers, W. G. – attorney
Rookes, W. – horse dealer
Roper, C. H. – surgeon
Rouse, R. – plumber
Salter, T. – wine and spirit mercht.
Sclater, C. – nurseryman
Sclater, W. H. – nurseryman
Smith, W. – butcher
Snow, T. – banker
Stile, J. – builder
Thomas, F. – hatter
Thomas, H. D. – wine and spirit mercht., brewer
Trehane, J. – wine and spirit mercht.
Trimble, J. T. – silversmith, pawnbroker
Vickary, J. – ironfounder
Ware, J. – builder
Welsford, H. – auctioneer, house agent
Wescomb, C. – printer, financier
Whistler, T. – gentleman
Wilcocks, H. – tea, coffee and spice mercht.
Wilkinson, R. C. – wine and spirit mercht.
Wills, J. – tallow chandler
Wippell, G. – ironmonger

Occupations of Members of the Exeter City Council 1896–1905

Acott, R. P. – draper
Alford, A. M. – solicitor
Andrew, S. – solicitor
Andrew, T. – accountant, High
Baker, C. – solicitor   [Bailiff
Bates, J. – brasscaster
Birkett, E. W. – brewer
Bowden, A. – coal merchant
Brown, W. L. – solicitor
Burch, A. – solicitor
Campfield, J. – railway official
Campion, H. – solicitor
Casley, W. H. – grocer
Caunter, W. A. – solicitor
Challice, G. M. – sanitary
  engineer
Challice, R. M. – architect,
  surveyor
Clapp, C. R. W. – solicitor
Cole, C. – architect
Commin, J. G. – bookseller
Courtney, J. – surveyor,
  architect
Daw, J. E. – solicitor
Daw, R. R. M. – solicitor
Depree, F. T. – goldsmith
Domville, E. J. – surgeon
Dunn, A. E. – solicitor
Dunn, W. H. – gentleman
Edwards, W. H. – grocer
Ellis, H. – tailor, draper
Finch, C. P. – wine and spirit
  mercht.
Finch, C. T. W. – prop. Half
  Moon Hotel
Fulford, E. T. – accountant
Gadd, H. – druggist
Gidley, J. – Solicitor
Gratwicke, C. F. – editor,
  Devon and Exeter Gazette

Guest, J. C. – music seller
Ham, C. – aerated water mfr.
Hamlin, H. P. O. – grocer
Hawke, W. – smith
Herbert, S. T. – watchmaker
Hodson, F. G. – jeweller,
  silversmith
Houlditch, E. H. – solicitor
Howard, T. – prop. Seven
  Stars Hotel
Hutchings, A. M. – butcher
Jackson, W. J. – gentleman
Jarman, W. – gentleman
Jerman, J. – architect,
  surveyor
Jones, S. – wine and spirit
  mercht.
Kelland, P. – baker
Knapman, E. – oil and colour
  mercht.
Linscott, T. – pawnbroker
Lisle, W. R. – watchmaker
Loram, A. T. – dairyman
Loram, J. A. – grocer
Lucas, J. A. – auctioneer,
  house agent
Luke, E. W. – solicitor
Mallett, W. R. – miller
Mansfield, F. G. – cabinet
  maker
McCrea, A. – draper
Merrick, A. B. – oil and
  colour mercht.
Munro, H. J. – dairyman
Noble, H. – professor of
  music
Norman, J. J. – wine and
  spirit merchant, grocer
Oliver, A. T. – fruit mercht.
Oliver, W. H. – general mercht.

Perkins, A. R. Steele – surgeon

Perkins, E. B. Steele – doctor

Perry, E. C. – political agent

Peters, J. – house furnisher

Peters, R. – merchant

Pople, R. – prop. New London Inn

Pring, T. A. – brewer

Pring, W. – brewer

Pulsford, J. – draper

Reed, W. H. – paper mfr.

Rippon, H. E. – auctioneer, house agent

Roberts, C. T. K. – solicitor

Roper, A. H. – surgeon

Ross, C. J. – outfitter

Rowe, C. E. – lead mercht.

Rowe, B. – stationer

Rowe, C. E. – lead mercht

Rowe, T B. – lead mercht.

Scadding, F. H. – builder

Southwood, W. H. – printer

Stile, G. L. – builder

Stocker, J. – builder

Stokes, S. – fruit mercht.

Surridge, J. – corn mercht., miller

Tarbet, W. H. – solicitor

Taylor, C. M. – ironfounder

Templeton, J. – insurance manager

Tolson, H. – gentleman

Tucker, J. – coal mercht.

Turner, E. – furniture dlr., cabinet maker

Upright, R. C. – miller

Varwell, H. B. – coal mercht.

Ware, C. E. – civil engineer

West, H. E. – butcher

White, J. – poulterer

Widgery, F. J. – artist

Williams, F. J. – wine and spirit mercht.

Williams, J. W. – builder

Wilson, T. – decorator

Wreford, W. – journalist

Yeo, H. – sharebroker

SUMMARIES

1836–47

Wine and spirit mercht., brewer, hotel prop., innkeeper, maltster, hop merchant	16
Attorney	16
Builder, auctioneer, timber mercht., surveyor	8
Doctor, surgeon	7
Merchant, dealer	5
Editor, paper mfr., printer	5
Banker	4
Draper, mercer, tailor	4
Currier, leather mercht., boot and shoe mfr., tanner	4
Ironmonger	4
Druggist	3
Jeweller, silversmith, watchmaker	3
Gentleman, retired	3
Confectioner, baker, caterer	2
Grocer	2
Accountant, bookseller, coach mfr., perfumer, postmaster	5
	91

1868–77

Wine and spirit mercht., brewer, hotel prop., innkeeper, maltster, hop mercht.	15
Attorney	12
Builder, auctioneer, timber mercht., surveyor	11
Draper, hatter, hosier, tailor, woollen mercht.	9
Merchant, dealer	8
Ironmonger	4
Doctor, dentist, surgeon	3
Editor, printer	3
Jeweller, silversmith, pawnbroker	3
Brasscaster, ironfounder	2
Currier, boot and shoe mfr.	2
Nurseryman	2
Plumber	2
Banker, bookseller, butcher, coachbuilder, decorator, druggist, gentleman, grocer, photographer, saddler, sharebroker, tobacco mfr., toll contractor	13
	89

1896–1905

Solicitor	16
Merchant, dealer	13
Builder, auctioneer, house agent, civil engineer	12
Wine and spirit mercht., brewer, hotel proprietor, innkeeper	11
Draper, outfitter	7
Cabinet maker, furnisher, decorator	5
Goldsmith, jeweller, pawnbroker, watchmaker	5
Doctor, surgeon	4
Editor, printer, paper mfr., journalist	4
Grocer	4
Gentleman, retired	4
Butcher, poulterer	3
Miller, corn mercht.	3
Accountant	2
Dairyman	2
Aerated water mfr., artist, baker, bookseller, brasscaster, druggist, insurance manager, ironfounder, music seller, professor of music, political agent, sharebroker, smith	12

107

SOME WAGES IN EXETER 1834–1914

THE following figures are not intended to support any claim that all members of the various categories referred to necessarily earned the wages recorded. Some, of course, did. All police constables, for instance, were on the same basic rate of pay. The wages of artisans, domestic servants and labourers depended to a great extent on the individual circumstances of each case, even in 1914. Throughout most of the nineteenth century there was a great deal of variation, with the result that individual cases can be cited in apparent contradiction of general statements. In 1838, for example, the council paid a carpenter 3s. 6d. for a day's work; but the pay of the carpenters in the regular employment of the council at this period ranged from 2s. 4d. to 2s. 10d. a day. In 1860 Mark Kennaway paid a labourer 2s. 4d. for a day's work 'assisting painters with ladders' at Hoopern House. This was the same rate received by a labourer employed by the council on digging pits for horse posts at the Bonhay Fair in 1834. Even at the end of the period the statistics of the board of trade suggest a greater uniformity of wages than is safe to accept. Carpenters in Exeter earned 33s. 5¼d. a week at summer rates according to the report (Cd.5085) of 1910; but in 1898 a carpenter claiming under the Employers Liability Act was stated to have been earning 35s. a week. In 1914 the Exeter City Asylum paid artisans such as painters, masons and plumbers from 25s. to 29s. a week. The asylum's non-resident gardener was paid 20s. a week in 1914; but the gardener at Hoopern House received 25s. a week in 1874. Wages in domestic service were even more dependent on the age and experience of the employee and on the circumstances of the employer.

Wages have been given at weekly rates but these are often hypothetical. The mason paid 3s. 8d. for working on the wall of the piggery at Hoopern House in 1859 was not necessarily earning 22s. a week.

A. General

	1834–42	1865–70	1890–1900	1907	1914
Bricklayers	25s.	26s. 7½d.	31s. 9½d.	35s. 8d.	37s. 10d.
Bricklayers' labourers	—	—	—	22s. 3½d.	—
Carpenters	14s.–21s.	23s. 6½d.– 26s. 7d.	28s. 4½d.– 35s. 5½d.	33s. 5½d.	35s. 8d.
Carters	—	—	—	21s.	22s.
Carters with carts	6s. per day	—	—	22s.	23s.
Draymen	—	—	18s.	—	—
Foundry workers	—	12s.	—	—	—
Gardeners	—	—	17s.–24s.	—	—
Labourers (canal)	10s.–14s.	—	—	21s. 2d.	22s.
Labourers (skilled)	12s.–14s.	14s.–15s.	18s.–20s.	21s.	25s.–27s.
Labourers (unskilled)	8s.–10s.	—	18s.	—	19s.–20s.
Masons	21s.	27s.	28s.	35s. 8d.	38s. 3d.
Masons' labourers	—	18s.	22s. 3½d.	—	—
Painters	—	—	28s. 11¾d.	28s. 11¾d.	31s. 2½d.
P.O. sorting clerks (male)	—	20s.	—	15s.	—
P.O. sorting clerks (female)	—	—	—	12s.	—
Postmen	—	16s.	—	15s. and allowances	—
Telephonists	—	—	—	10s.	—
Police constables	16s.	17s.	21s. 6d.	22s. 6d.	24s. 6d.
Plumbers	18s.–21s.	—	35s.	35s.	36s.
Plasterers	20s.	—	28s. 4½d.– 35s. 5¼d.	33s. 5¾d.	—
Plasterers' labourers	—	—	22s. 3½d.	22s. 3½d.	—

	1834–42	1865–70	1890–1900	1907	1914
Rly. engine drivers	—	—	25s.–40s.	—	—
Rly. guards	—	—	25s.–30s.	—	—
Rly. porters	—	—	10s.–15s.	—	—
Scavengers	—	18s.	19s.	21s.	22s. 6d.
Sweepers	—	—	—	20s.	21s.
Tram motor men	—	—	—	22s.	22s.
Tram conductors	—	—	—	17s.	17s.
Tram ticket clerk	—	—	—	22s. 6d.	27s. 6d.
Van drivers	—	—	20s.	—	—
Slaters	—	—	—	33s. 5¼d.	—
Wheelwrights	—	—	23s. 6d.	27s.	—

B. DOMESTIC SERVICE

	1871	1888	1900	1913–14
Superior cooks	£20–£21	£35	£36–£50	£40–£45
Plain cooks	£12–£16	£14–£22	£18–£30	£20–£30
Cook generals	—	—	£18	£20–£25
Housemaids	£8–£14	£14–£16	£15–£28	£16–£28
Parlour maids	£8–£14	£16–£18	£18–£30	£22–£26
General servants	£7–£15	£16	£10–£18	£16–£24
Children's nurses	£10–£18	—	—	—
Hotel waitresses	—	£14	—	—
Hotel kitchenmaids	—	£20	—	—
Kitchenmaids	—	£12	£14–£18	£20

ABBREVIATIONS

A.R.	Annual Register
C.A.B.	Chapter Act Books
C.L.	Cathedral Library
C.M.	Council Minutes
Colson Papers	Miscellaneous papers lent by Messrs Colsons of Exeter
Constabulary Report	*First Report of the Commissioners appointed to inquire as to the best means of establishing an efficient Constabulary Force in England and Wales*, 1839 (169) xix
Corporations Commission Proceedings	Proceedings of the Municipal Corporations Commissioners at Exeter, 1 – 6 November 1833
C.P.	Corporation of the Poor, Minutes of the Court
C.T.V.	Exeter City Treasurer's Vouchers
D.A.	Transactions of the Devonshire Association
DEI	Devon and Exeter Institution
D.N.B.	Dictionary of National Biography
DRO	Devon County Record Office
ECA	Exeter City Archives
Ellis Memoirs	Memoirs of Henry Ellis, written by himself, 1799–1859
Exeter Election 1831	List of voters and record of votes, parliamentary election, 1831, in *Besley's Itinerary and General Directory*
Exeter Election 1832	List of voters at the parliamentary election of December 1832 in *Besley's Exeter Directory*, 1833
Exeter Election 1835	List of voters at the parliamentary election of January 1833 in *Besley's Exeter Directory*, 1835
Exeter Election 1864	*The List of Persons in the Borough of Exeter who voted or were entitled to vote at the election of a member to sit in Parliament to fill the vacancy caused by the death of Edward Divett Esq.*, 1864

Exeter Election 1868	*A complete list of persons in the borough of the city of Exeter who voted or were entitled to vote at the General Parliamentary Election*, 1868
E.S.B.	Exeter School Board, Minutes
Exeter Valuation 1838	*Valuation of the Houses and Lands in the City of Exeter made by Messrs Rowe, Cornish and Hooper . . . and completed 25 July*, 1838
F.P.	*Exeter Flying Post*
Force Papers	Volumes of notes of sales and advertisements lent by Messrs S. R. Force and Sons, of Exeter
Gazette	*Devon and Exeter Gazette*
I.C.	Improvement Commissioners, Minutes
Inquiry Transcript, 1867	Transcript of the proceedings of the Government Inquiry before Arnold Foster Esq., Inspector from the Home Office
M.O.H.	Reports of the Exeter Medical Officer of Health
Municipal Corporations, 1835	*Municipal Corporations (England and Wales) First Report of Commissioners* 1835 (116) xxiii
P.L.B.	Poor Law Board
P.L.C.	Poor Law Commissioners
Religious Worship, 1851	*Census*, 1851. *Religious Worship, England and Wales*, 1852–53 (1690) lxxxix
Shapter, Report on Exeter, 1845	'Report on the Sanitary Condition of Exeter' by Thomas Shapter, M.D., pp 350–380 Appendix, *Second Report of the Commissioners of Inquiry into the State of Large Towns and Populous Districts* 1845 (602) xviii
State of Towns, 1845	Report of Commissioners 1845, see above
Voters for Exeter	Register of Electors for Members of Parliament
W.C.	Exeter Watch Committee, Minutes
W.T.	*Western Times*

NOTES

Introduction

1 G. B. A. M. Finlayson, 'The Politics of Municipal Reform' *Eng. Hist. Review* lxxvi, No. 321, Oct. 1966, p. 687.
2 Quoted by W. G. Hoskins, *Two Thousand Years in Exeter*, (1960) p. 79.
3 T. Shapter, *Report on Exeter*, 1845, p. 357.
4 R. E. Prothero, *The Letters of Richard Ford 1797–1858*, (1905) p. 135.
5 ECA: Lady Paterson's Diary, 1831–35.
6 E. Howard, *An Essay read to the Members and Friends of the Exeter Society*, (1850) p. 41.
7 W.T. 24.2.1871.
8 PP: Royal Commission on Secondary Education, vi. *Reports of the Assistant Commissioners*, p. 88.
9 F.P. 27.4.1881.
10 W.T. 2.2.1900. The speaker was H. A. Willey.
11 M. E. Sadler, *Report on Secondary and Higher Education in Exeter*, (1905) pp. 63–64.
12 PP: *Select Committee on Scientific Instruction* 1868. Q. 8328–8329.
13 *Luminary* 13.11.1837; W.T. 26.10.1839; 3.1.1835.
14 W.T. 20.11.1868.
15 Mayor Andrew; F.P. 18.10.1882.
16 For these four quotations: W.T. 29.10.1875; F.P. 3.11.1886; 8.11.1882; 12.7.1931.
17 F.P. 28.4.1875.
18 W.T. 22.11.1889.
19 Langland in Nevill Coghill's translation.
20 Ellis Memoirs iii, f. 314.
21 G. M. Trevelyan, *Illustrated English Social History*, i (1949), p. xiii, quoted with approval by J. H. Plumb, *Men and Places*, (1963) p. 225.
22 W.T. 30.1.1863.
23 *Athenaeum* No. 2181 of 14.8.1869, p. 203.
24 G. M. Young, 'Portrait of an Age,' in *Early Victorian England* (1951), ii, p. 432.

Chapter I

1 There is ample evidence that the terms Conservative and

Liberal were widely used in Exeter at this time. Thus the reformist *Western Times* of 5.11.1837 described a meeting of 'Liberal councillors' to discuss the mayoralty. On 12.11.1837 the Conservative *Gazette* reported the views of 'the Conservatives' on the same issue.

2 W.T. 12.11.1836. The speaker was the Wesleyan grain merchant, J. C. Sercombe.

3 F.P. 14.6.1837.

4 W.T. 27.5.1837.

5 *Gazette* 30.6.1837.

6 Ellis Memoirs, v. 1835–40, f. 143.

7 W.T. 3.1.1835.

8 W.T. 24.6.1837.

9 *Ibid* 21.6.1837; 1.7.1837.

10 Ellis Memoirs, v. 1835–40, f. 143.

11 W.T. 1.7.1837.

12 *Ibid* 3.1.1833.

13 *Journal of Lady Charlotte Guest,* (1950) p. 66.

14 For Follett's career see D.N.B. xix and obit. in W.T. 5.7.1845.

15 *Gazette* 29.12.1832.

16 Ellis Memoirs, vii, f. 130.

17 This account is from the contemporary newspapers, particularly F.P. 27.7.1837.

18 G. M. Trevelyan on 'Natural Beauty,' *An Autobiography and other Essays,* p. 95.

19 Alexander Jenkins, *Civil and Ecclesiastical History of the City of Exeter,* (1806) pp. 212–213. 'The spirit of improvement began now to manifest itself in the city, and it may justly date its beginning from the public spirit of William Mackworth Praed Esq' who opened the Clarence Hotel in 1769.

20 T. Risdon, *Survey of the County of Devon,* (1811) p. 103.

21 G. Oliver, *The History of the City of Exeter,* (1861) pp. 174–175.

22 *Besley's Guide,* 1836, p. 38. The style of course was conventional. Catherine Morland would have made similar comments at Bath and Clifton some forty years previously.

23 *Gazette* 17.6.1868.

24 *Ibid* 22.7.1837.

25 T. Shapter, *The History of the Cholera in Exeter in 1832,* (1849). Shapter took an active part in combating the epidemic. He himself lived till 1902.

26 F.P. 28.9.1837.

27 G. Oliver, *op. cit.* p. 169. And despite the growing interest in Gothic – Salvin had made his reputation with Mamhead, near Exeter, in 1828.

28 *Sporting Magazine* 2nd ser., xiii No. lxxxv, p. 213.

29 *Gazette* 13.11.1837.

30 W.T. 8.7.1832.

31 Ellis Memoirs, v. f. 48.

32 W. G. Hoskins, *Industry, Trade and People in Exeter* 1688–1800, p. 39.

33 T. Shapter, PP: *Report on Exeter*, 1845, pp. 353, 357. Hoskins, *op. cit.* p. 148, points out that Shapter exaggerated the industrialization of the city in 1800.

34 PP. *Municipal Corporations*, 1835, Appendix p. 495.

35 E. A. Clarke, *The Ports of the Exe Estuary* 1660–1860, pp. 198, 199–200.

36 C.M. 6.12.1836.

37 F.P. 23.2.1837.

38 ECA: Lady Paterson's Diary 9.7.1831; 18.7.1831.

39 PP: *Report on the City and County of Exeter*, 1831–1832 (141) xxxvii, pp. 121–123.

40 H. E. Prothero, *The Letters of Richard Ford* 1797–1858, p. 135.

41 *Besley's Guide*, 1836, p. 22.

42 *Ibid* 1835, p. 22.

43 Ellis Memoirs, v, p. 15.

44 W.T. 8.2.1834. PP: *Municipal Corporations*, 1835. Appendix p. 488 gives his profession as 'of the record office.'

45 *Gazette* 31.10.1871.

46 ECA. Lady Paterson's Diary 8.3.35; 31.3.37.

47 *Ibid* 26.8.1831; 2.10.1834.

48 *Ibid* 22.12.1831.

49 He opened Sadler's Wells, Islington, and produced Shakespeare with success for twenty years.

50 W.T. 30.9.1837.

51 At the Bachelors' Ball of 1835; cf. ECA: Lithograph D 8692/009.1.

52 W.T. 9.7.1836.

53 *Ibid* 16.9.1837.

54 PP: *Poor Laws. Reports from Commissioners*, 1834. (44) xxviii. Appendix A, Assistant Commissioners Reports, Pt. I, pp. 519, 521.

55 ECA: CTV Box 1. Paysheets for 1836 show that two men

350 VICTORIAN EXETER 1837-1914

described as ships' carpenters were paid 3*s*. 6*d*. a day. Four men out of a gang of seven received 2*s*. 9*d*. but one received 1*s*. on another occasion.

56 C.M. 12.12.1838 which approved the reduction of wages of men provided with a house and garden from 14*s*. to 13*s*. a week. The wages of one employee were raised to 14*s*., 'he not having a house and garden.'

57 F.P. 5.1.1837.

58 *Gazette* 21.1.1837.

59 Ellis Memoirs, v, f. 58. She began 'as an assistant in the front shop' at 12 guineas in 1832.

60 P.L.C. 12*th Annual Report*, 1846, p. 131.

61 F.P. 5.1.1837.

62 There were forty-four charitable and benevolent organizations in 1837, eight of which were engaged in various forms of poor relief. The majority had religious and educational objects.

63 *Luminary* 15.1.1838.

64 PP: *Poor Laws, Reports from Commissioners*, 1834 (44) xxviii, Appendix A. i., p. 519.

65 PP: Shapter, *Report on Exeter* 1845, p. 357.

66 P.L.C. 9th An. Rept. 1843, report by E. C. Tuffnell on 'The Administration of the Poor Law in the City and County of Exeter.'

67 PP: *Select Committee on Education of the Poorer Classes* 1837–1838, (589) vii, pp. vii and viii; tables pp. vii and ix.

68 *Ibid.* Min. of ev. Q. 98.

69 The complex character of Henry Phillpotts is beyond the scope of this book. He is the subject of R. N. Shutte's unfinished biography, *The Life, Times and Writings of the Right Rev. Dr Henry Phillpotts*, (1863) and G. C. B. Davies's *Henry Phillpotts, Bishop of Exeter*, (1954). Phillpotts is also the villain of R. S. Lambert's vivid study of Thomas Latimer, *The Cobbett of the West*, (1939).

70 F.P. 26.2.1850.

71 W.T. 6.11.1847.

72 DRO: Phillpotts to Barnes, No. 31. of 14.12.1830.

73 CL: Correspondence of Bishop Phillpotts, letter dated 4.12.1830.

74 e.g. DRO: correspondence entitled 'Pluralists, 1831.'

75 *Gazette* 10.6.1837.

76 ECA: Lady Paterson's Diary 10.2.1833.

77 *Western Times* 7.6.1839.
78 CL: Chapter Act Books 30.12.1837; 3.2.1838.
79 B. Le Messurier, *A History of the Mint Methodist Church, Exeter*, pp. 16–18; A. A. Brockett, *Nonconformity in Exeter*, (1962) pp. 233–234.
80 J. D. Osborn, W. W. Snell, W. T. P. Wilkinson and J. C. Sercombe were all Nonconformist, the first two being Unitarian.
81 W.T. 25.4.1835.
82 *Ibid* 30.3.1837.
83 ECA: Corporations Commission Proceedings 5th day p. 66.
84 S. Kingdon (1836), Unitarian, ironmonger; W. J. P. Wilkinson (1837–38) Independent, wine and spirit merchant; W. Drewe (1839–40), Unitarian, wine and spirit merchant. Dr E. Macgowan (1838–39) was an Evangelical.
85 C.M. 12.5.1859.
86 W. T. MacCaffrey, *Exeter 1540–1640* (Harvard 1958) p. 1.
87 S. and B. Webb, *English Local Government*, 'The Borough,' ii (1963), p. 718.
88 PP: *Municipal Corporations in England and Wales*, R. Com. 1st Rept. 1835 (611) xxiii, appendix p. 498.
89 Ellis Memoirs, v. f. 15.
90 See ECA: *Proceedings of the Municipal Corporations Commission at Exeter taken by Thomas Latimer*, 1833.
91 ECA: Commission Proceedings, 5th day, p. 72.
92 ECA: Commission Proceedings, 5th day, p. 55.
93 *Ibid.*
94 *Ibid* 3rd day, p. 15.
95 *Ibid* pp. 20–21.
96 *Ibid* p. 37.
97 ECA: Commission Proceedings 3rd day, p. 37.
98 W.T. 15.6.1835.
99 PP: *Municipal Corporations*, 1835, para 72.
100 *Ibid* para 73.
101 ECA: Commission Proceedings 1st day pp. 27–28.
102 W.T. 15.9.1835.
103 *Ibid* 9.2.1833.
104 *Ibid* 15.9.1835.
105 S. E. Finer, *The Life and Times of Sir Edwin Chadwick*, (1952) pp. 12–13.
106 *Gazette* 19.12.1835.
107 The parliamentary commissioners reported that the Reform

Bill had increased the electorate to 2,952 including 586 freemen. The electorate at the time of the election of July 1831, was 1,125 – see PP: *Municipal Corporations*, appendix p. 498 and ECA. Exeter Election 1831. But parliamentary returns exaggerated the electorate by including all who were registered in respect of different properties and as both freemen and property owners. *White's Directory*, 1850 p. 68 suggests that about 2,800 was the true figure. This seems to be approximately correct. ECA: Ward Poll Books record 1,914 local electors in 1836 and 1920.

108 For the following statements see ECA. *Besley's Directory*, 1831 and 1833 which give the details of the voting in the elections of July 1831 and Dec. 1832.

109 He was reported as having left £250,000 when he died in 1857 – W.T. 19.11.1872.

110 W.T. 20.11.1868. The statement is supported by the published reports of five parliamentary elections in ECA.

111 See analysis of the occupations of the chamber and council in Appendix I.

112 *Athenaeum* No. 2181 of 14.8.1869, p. 203.

113 F.P. 6.11.1861.

114 Ellis Memoirs, v. f. 17.

115 The six wards were: St Paul's, including the old parishes of St Paul, St Lawrence, Allhallows, Goldsmith Street, St Pancras and St Kerrian, and part of St David; St Mary Major's, including the parishes of St Mary Major, St Stephen, St George, and the precincts of the Cathedral Close and Bedford; Trinity, including the parishes of Holy Trinity, St Edmund and St Mary Steps; St Petrock's, including the parishes of St John, Allhallows on the Walls, St Olave, St Mary Arches, St Martin and St Petrock; St Sidwell's, including the greater part of St Sidwell's parish southeast of the St Sidwell's – Black Boy road; and St David's which included part of St Sidwell's parish.

116 W.T. 3.1.1835.

117 W.T. 12.11.1836.

118 *Hansard* 3rd ser. ccxi/1323; 6.6.1878.

119 W.T. 12.11.1836.

120 *Ibid.*

121 Ellis Memoirs, v. ff. 17 and 20.

122 W.T. 3.6.1837.

Chapter II

1 According to S. Bastard – *Luminary* 13.11.1837 and W.T. 26.10.1839.
2 *Ibid* 12.9.1835.
3 *Ibid* 4.11.1840.
4 *Gazette* 12.12.1846; W.T. 13.4.1839.
5 W.T. 22.12.1838.
6 *Hansard* 3rd ser. xxviii/544; 5.6.1835.
7 *Gazette* 2.1.1836.
8 F.P. 8.11.1882.
9 W.T. 12.11.1836.
10 W.T. 5.11.1837.
11 *Ibid* 11.11.1837.
12 *Ibid*.
13 *Ibid*.
14 *Luminary* 13.11.1837; W.T. 18.11.1837.
15 W.T. 4.1.1840 in discussing the religious practices of the mayors.
16 *Luminary* 4.11.1839.
17 W.T. 31.8.1838.
18 *Luminary* 5.11.1838.
19 W.T. 31.8.1838.
20 W.T. 25.10.1838 and 3.11.1838.
21 *Ibid* 15.5.1840.
22 *Luminary* 12.11.1838.
23 W.T. 9.11.1839.
24 ECA: Papers relating to Regina v Macgowan, Box 55 City officials; C.M. 12.12.1838; 13.2.1839.
25 C.M. 6.7.1840; 10.8.1840. W.T. 15.5.1840 describes Kennaway's role. For the reversal of the previous decision see C.M. 12.12.1840.
26 Ellis Memoirs, v, f. 399.
27 *Luminary* 4.11.1845. In 1838 'The operative Conservative Association took the field . . . within two years we were able to congratulate ourselves on the election, once more, of a Conservative Mayor.'
28 W.T. 31.10.1840.
29 Ellis Memoirs, v, ff. 399–400.
30 C.M. 6.12.1836.
31 ECA: Borough Fund Accounts 1.9.1836–1.9.1837.
32 C.M. 7.1.1836.
33 ECA Committee on municipal officers 25.3.1836. An interesting report on council staff and their duties.

34 *Ibid.*
35 C.M. 26.8.1837.
36 ECA: Bill in Exeter Markets, Box 3. It was not till 1888 that the town clerk's office ceased to be the administrative office of the council.
37 C.M. 4.11.1837.
38 J. Cossins, *Reminiscences of the City of Exeter* (1877), p. 41.
39 W.T. 28.5.1837 and 7.5.1836. C.M. 9.11.1836.
40 ECA: *Exeter Borough Fund* 1837–38.
41 C.M. 21.1.1836.
42 *Ibid* 28.1.1836.
43 C.M. 24.5.1837.
44 Finance committee 21.8.1837.
45 C.M. 14.10.1840 incorporating a financial statement for the years 1836–1840.
46 ECA: Council Letters 1837–1841; Box 23.
47 C.M. 27.12.1837. The papers on the market controversies are voluminous. No more than a brief summary can be attempted.
48 Local Act. 4 Wm. IV. cap. 8.
49 Local Act. 3 and 4 Vict. cap. cxxii.
50 C.M. 14.5.1845.
51 *Gazette* 11.4.1846, which is also the authority for Salter's remarks.
52 C.M. 14.5.1845.
53 There is a useful summary of this affair dated 12.7.1880 by B. C. Gidley, Town Clerk; ECA: box entitled 'Documents relating to negotiations between the Mortgagees of the Exeter Canal and the Corporation.'
54 Finance committee 1.4.1846; special committee, C.M. 9.12.1846; F.P. 23.4.1846.
55 25 Geo. III cap. 21.
56 C.M. 8.3.1848. Report of finance committee.
57 W.T. 16.9.1848.
58 ECA: Ward poll books 1835–1847.
59 W.T. 6.11.1847.
60 *Ibid* 28.3.1857.
61 See Appendix I.
62 W.T. 6.11.1847.
63 W.T. 14.7.1868, *obit.*
64 *Ibid.*
65 *Gazette* 17.7.1868, *obit.*
66 W.T. 14.7.1868.

67 Ellis Memoirs, viii, f. 130.
68 W.T. 12.6.1841.
69 F.P. 12.6.1841.
70 Ellis Memoirs, vi, f. 18.
71 W.T. 12.6.1841.
72 *Ibid* 19.6.1841.
73 *Gazette* 12.6.1841.
74 Ellis Memoirs *op. cit*. f. 19. Ellis gives an entertaining account of the canvassing and describes the difficulties which a substantial tradesman could experience with good customers.
75 *Gazette* 12.6.1841.
76 F.P. 1.7.1841.
77 W.T. 3.7.1841.
78 He was the son of Admiral Sir John Duckworth and Susannah Catherine, daughter of Dr W. Buller, Bishop of Exeter.
79 F.P. 10.7.1845.
80 *Ibid.*
81 *e.g.* F.P. 3.6.1841 reporting meetings of the Devon Agricultural Society and the Barnstaple and North Devon Agricultural Society.
82 W.T. 8.5.1841 in an editorial on Russell's proposals for a fixed duty on imported corn.
83 F.P. 28.1.1846.
84 Vividly described in R. S. Lambert's *The Cobbett of the West*, (1939).
85 *e.g.* W.T. 7.12.1844.
86 The thirty-seventh.
87 CL: Correspondence ED 11/24 letter to Rev. T. Baker 10.1.1842. Yet J. H. R. Moorman, *A History of the Church of England*, (1954) p. 354, describes Phillpotts as a Tractarian.
88 Ordination Sermon, 1843.
89 CL: No. 7170/41, Letter to Barnes. The general chapter was the cathedral chapter with the addition of the archdeacons and prebendaries.
90 CL: T. Shapter. MS. account of the Surplice Riots, f. 4.
91 W.T. 7.12.1844.
92 CL: No. 7170/41 letter to Barnes p. 4.
93 CL: No. 7170/41 Surplice Questions. Notes in Barnes' handwriting. Barnes considered that the publication of the memorial was an attempt to lead the public to expect that the archbishop would support the chapter. He recorded that Canon Bull had indulged in 'unmeasured language in public.'

94 R. E. Prothero, *Letters of Richard Ford* 1797–1858, (1905), pp. 194–195.
95 Shapter *op. cit.* f. 17.
96 Ellis Memoirs, vii, f. 112.
97 W.T. 27.7.1832.
98 *Gazette* 13.8.1835.
99 *Ibid.*

Chapter III

1 E. Halevy, *England in* 1815 (1959), p. 44.
2 G. M. Young in *Early Victorian England*, (1951), ii p. 432.
3 PP: *Constabulary Report*, 1839, p. 107. See, too, Chapter 8 of Donald Read's *Peterloo*, (1958).
4 *Gazette* 8.5.1847.
5 W.T. 22.5.1847.
6 PP: *Municipal Corporations*, 1835, Appendix p. 439.
7 *Hansard* 3rd ser. xxviii/554; 5.6.1835.
8 *Gazette* 2.1.1836.
9 C.M. 16.8.1839.
10 C.M. 19.2.1856.
11 W.C. 7.5.1886.
12 *Ibid* 18.1.1836.
13 Improvement commissioners 8.5.1837.
14 C.M. 12.8.1847.
15 The minutes of the watch committee in the Exeter city archives contain a full record of the evolution of the police.
16 W.C. 6.1.1838; 15.9.1838. For John Coles, W.C. 4.12.1847; for John Ginham W.C. 6.1.1849.
17 W.C. 10.10.1836.
18 W.C. 1.11.1838.
19 *Ibid* 23.1.1836.
20 There were occasions when the mayor gave instructions without reference to the superintendent. One mayor supported a sergeant who complained that patrolling was inconsistent with his traditional duties. See W.C. 6.11.1847.
21 W.C. 10.6.1836.
22 *Ibid* 4.7.1836.
23 W.C. 23.9.1837.
24 *Ibid* 20.12.1841; 1.1.1842.
25 ECA: Council Letters 1837–1841.
26 W.C. 12.8.1837; *Gazette* 15.2.1847.
27 C.M. 14.4.1847; 12.5.1847; 16.6.1847.

28 *Gazette* 3.7.1847.
29 C.M. 14.7.1847.
30 *Gazette* 31.8.1847.
31 *Ibid.*
32 C.M. 13.5.1891.
33 W.T. 20.8.42.
34 W.T. 20.8.1842; 8.4.1843.
35 *Ibid* 19.2.1842; 26.3.1842.
36 W.T. 24.2.1844.
37 The full story is in W.T. 24.2.1844.
38 W.C. 3.8.1839.
39 W.T. 8.6.1844; 6.7.1844.
40 W.C. 11.11.1843.
41 W.T. 11.11.1848 describing the events of 1847 as well as of 1848.
42 In ECA. The following figures are compiled from this record.
43 ECA: Gaol Calendar Book 23.7.1840; 5.7.1840; 19.3.1840 and 18.10.1840; 14.3.1840; 19.7.1847.
44 W.C. 2.9.1848.
45 W.T. 15.4.1837.
46 *Ibid* 25.3.1845.
47 A.R. 1840, p. 5.
48 *Hansard*, 3rd ser. xcii/672–3, 11.5.1847.
49 ECA: Gaol Calendar Book, 20.3.1847.
50 W.T. 20.3.1847.
51 *Ibid* 15.5.1847. The following account is taken from W.T. of this date and 22.5.1847 and *Gazette* 22.5.1847.
52 W.T. and *Gazette* 22.5.1847; ECA: Gaol Calendar Book 22.6.1847.
53 *Hansard* 3rd ser. xcii/952, 17.5.1846.
54 W.T. 3.7.1847.
55 In June the grand jury reported 'the strong and unanimous expression of their opinion, that had the police been on their legitimate duty, and under a more efficient and vigilant superintendent, the late riot and tumult . . . might easily have been suppressed.' W.T. 3.7.1847.

Chapter IV

1 T. Shapter, *Report on Exeter*, 1845, pp. 333 and 357.
2 F.P. 27.4.1881.
3 W.T. 2.2.1900.
4 W. Hoskins, *Industry, Trade and People in Exeter* 1688–1800, (1935), p. 18.

5 W.T. 6.11.1847.
6 F.P. 14.1.1847; *Gazette* 9.2.1849.
7 W.T. 13.2.1847.
8 *Gazette* 4.1.1845; 10.10.1846.
9 ECA: Lady Paterson's Diary 1831–1835.
10 *Gazette* 15.7.1837.
11 *Census* 1821, 1831. The population of St Leonard's rose from 206 to 407 and then to 1,129; Heavitree from 1,253 to 1,932 and 2,812.
12 Mount Radford, *Gazette* 1.7.1837; Elm Field, W.T. 13.11.1841.
13 *Gazette* 27.1.1838.
14 *Census* 1831. Heavitree contained 393 families with 184 servants, Crediton 394 families with 94 servants.
15 For these and the following figures see *Census* 1841, Occupation Abstract I.
16 ECA: *Lady Paterson's Diary* 3.6.1834.
17 J. E. Daw, *John Daw* 1764–1849 (privately printed 1939).
18 *Gazette* 23.1.1836; W.T. 23.1.1850.
19 There is a useful note on the rise of Colsons by Mr William Hoyle, dated September, 1490, in the miscellaneous Colson Papers kindly made available by the managing director Mr G. Alderman. Colsons of Exeter, of course, is still prominent in the city.
20 *Ellis Memoirs*, iii, ff. 322–323.
21 *Ibid* f. 313.
22 *Ibid* viii, f. 24, letter dated 27.8.1850.
23 *Trewman's Exeter Journal* 1837.
24 *Gazette* 2.12.1837.
25 The figures in this paragraph are from the *Exeter Valuation*, 1838.
26 W.T. 29.12.1838.
27 *Ibid* 15.5.1847.
28 In *Ask Mamma*, (1858).
29 F.P. 14.11.1850.
30 *Exeter Valuation* 1838; *White's Directory* 1950.
31 *Exeter Valuation* 1838, pp. 46, 47, 49.
32 *Census* 1851, II, i, pp. 404–405.
33 Figures from the Exeter Probate Records. They refer to personal estate only and are an indication rather than an exact record of wealth.
34 Ellis Memoirs, i, f. 124.
35 A. Vincent, *Memoir of the Late John Dinham of Exeter*, (Exeter 1877), pp. 25, 52–53.

36 Ellis *Memoirs*, viii, f. 42.
37 *Census* 1851, St Edmund, 1,472; St Mary Major 3,691; St Mary Steps 1,362. Shapter, *Report on Exeter* 1845, p. 374.
38 *Ibid* pp. 373, 377.
39 *Ibid* Tables I, VI, XV, XXVI.
40 PP: *State of Large Towns* 1845, Appendix p. 240. The quotation is from G. M. Young, *Early Victorian England*, ii, p. 500.
41 Shapter *op. cit.* Table XXVI, p. 377; Table XIX, p. 370.
42 *Ibid* p. 366; PP. *State of Large Towns*, 1845, Report p. 49.
43 C.P. 1.9.1846.
44 *Hansard* 3rd ser. xcii/716, 18 June, 1846. Buck had been member for Exeter 1826–1832.
45 W.T. 18.3.1847.
46 *Royal Commission on the Housing of the Working Classes* (C – 4402 – 1), ii, p. 707.
47 F.P. 10.1.1850.
48 T. Shapter, *Report on Exeter* 1845, p. 374.
49 T. Shapter, *Report on Exeter* 1845, p. 375.
50 W.T. 21.10.1848.
51 *Royal Commission on Housing op. cit.* p. 707.
52 For these examples see C.T.V. Box 12, paysheets for 22.12.1841 and 11.5.1842; Box 19, paysheet for 18.6.1845; Box 34, paysheet for 8.6.1853.
53 C.T.V. Box 34, paysheet for Sept. 1852; Box 1, 19.5.1836.
54 For the carpenters C.T.V. Box 12, 22.12.1841; Box 29, 12.11.1850; other examples paysheets generally in Box 2; carpenters in 1850, Box 29, 12.11.1850; mason, Box 34, Sept. 1852; plumber, Box 23, 10.6.1846.
55 C.T.V. Box 23. Paysheet order 9.11.1847.
56 F.P. 3.3.1842 reporting proceedings at the bank's twenty-sixth annual general meeting.
57 Ellis *Memoirs*, v, p. 156.
58 P.L.C. 9th annual report, 1843, p. 127.
59 Prices are obtained from the market prices reported weekly in the local papers. The reports are as near as possible to the middle of January, June and November each year and were selected as an indication of prevailing prices.
60 P.L.C. *op. cit.* p. 131.
61 F.P. 12.11.1846.
62 *Gazette* 23.9.1837.
63 *Ibid* 4.1.1845.
64 *Ibid* 23.9.1837.

65 For the workhouse, see C.P. 30.4.1837.
66 *Gazette* 23.9.1837; 16.11.1850; for Mark Kennaway's purchases see ECA. Kennaway Papers, Box 3, Family vouchers.
67 Ellis Memoirs, iii, f. 210.
68 C.T.V. Box 14, paysheet 22.1.1843.
69 The newspapers from which these figures are taken reported the annual meeting of the Exeter relief society each January.
70 P.R.O: M.H. 12/2239 Exeter Correspondence 1846/1855. Return dated 23.3.1847.
71 W.T. 15.5.1847; 7.8.1847.
72 P.L.C. *9th An. Rept.* 1843, p. 125.
73 *Ibid* pp. 124–125.
74 P.L.C. *13th An. Rept.* 1847, p. 6.
75 W.T. 17.4.1848.
76 F.P. 11.1.1849.
77 W.T. 15.11.1845.
78 F.P. 29.1.1850.
79 This description of the amenities of Exeter at this period is largely derived from Cossins, *Reminiscences of Exeter Fifty years since*, (1877), as well as from the contemporary press.
80 ECA: Lady Paterson's Diary, 27.5.1835.
81 F.P. 28.1.1839.

Chapter V
1 W.T. 4.5.1844, the source of this quotation, and *Gazette* of the same date describe the arrival of the first train in detail.
2 Ellis Memoirs, vii, f. 20, v, f. 149.
3 W.T. 4.5.1850.
4 Ellis Memoirs, v, f. 1490.
5 W.T. 18.5.1850.
6 W.T. 10.11.1849.
7 The Supplement of the *Gazette* and W.T. of 20.7.1850 are the sources for this account.
8 Newspaper market reports.
9 *Gazette* 20.7.1850.
10 *White's Directory*, 1850, p. 63.
11 Ellis Memoirs, viii, f. 18.
12 F.P. 28.3.1850.
13 P.L.B. 4th *An. Rept.*, 1851, p. 2.
14 P.L.B. 1st *An. Rept.*, 1848, appendix 2, p. 60; 4th *report* 1851, p. 2.
15 F.P. 24.1.1850 reported that the society had assisted 887 families in 1849. The *Gazette* of 7.1.1854, reviewing the society's activi-

ties over four years, said that the society assisted 1,131 'cases' in 1850. The figure rose to 1,704 in the following year and to 3,660 by 1855. The records of the society no longer exist. From the newspaper reports it appears that 'cases' referred sometimes to families and sometimes to individuals.

16 F.P. 11.4.1850.
17 *White's Directory*, 1850, p. 50.
18 *Census* 1841 and 1851.
19 F.P. 17.1.1850.
20 PP: *Religious Worship, England and Wales;* 1852–1853, (1690) lxxxix, p. clviii.
21 PP: *Religious Worship, England and Wales:* 1852–1853, (1690) lxxxix, p. clxii.
22 K. S. Inglis, 'Patterns of Religious Worship in 1851,' *Journal of Ecclesiastical History*, ii, 1960, p. 80.
23 For all practical purposes these figures are the same as those arrived at by A. A. Brockett, *Nonconformity in Exeter 1650–1870* (1962) p. 233.
24 See Brockett *op. cit.* pp. 233–234.
25 *Ibid* p. 60.
26 *Ibid* p. 186 and Chapter XII generally on 'The Decline of George's Meeting.'
27 F.P. 20.9.1865.
28 PP: *Religious Worship* 1851, *op. cit.* p. viii.
29 W.T. 2.2.1850.
30 *Luminary* 14.6.1851.
31 CL: Letter to Barnes dated 28.11.1849. No. 42. 1849.
32 W.T. 7.6.1839.
33 F.P. 4.4.1850.
34 *Census* 1851, *Education, England and Wales;* PP. 1852–53 (30) xc, Summary tables, Proportion of scholars to population.
35 Quoted by W. G. Hoskins, *Industry, Trade and People in Exeter 1688–1800*, pp. 78–79.
36 W.T. 15.8.1835.
37 F.P. 5.11.1857.
38 ECA: Ward Poll Books.
39 W.T. 17.11.1849.
40 The Gorham Controversy forms part of the history of the Church of England. It is set out in detail in E. J. Moore, *The Case of the Rev. G. C. Gorham against the Bishop of Exeter*, (1852) and analysed in J. C. S. Nias, *Gorham and the Bishop of Exeter*, (1951).

41 *Luminary* 5.11.1850.
42 *Luminary* 24.12.1850.
43 F.P. 19.9.1850.
44 W.T. 24.4.1852.
45 W.T. 4.4.1857.
46 The manners and methods of Richard Brembridge emerge clearly from the inquiry into the Barnstaple election of 1852. There is much correspondence between the three firms of solicitors in the Iddesleigh Papers in the British Museum. Add. MSS. 50,035 ff. 107–128
47 Iddesleigh Papers, Add. MSS. 50,035 f. 123
48 *Ibid* 50,035 ff. 107–108, 128.
49 *Ibid* 50,035 f. 126.
50 W.T. 5.11.1853.
51 *Ibid* 16.11.1846; 11.11.1854.
52 In a letter from Gard's committee room 16.3.1857. ECA: Sheriff's Records, Box 2.
53 ECA: Sheriff's Records, Box 2.
54 W.T. 11.11.1843.
55 PP: *Return of Population etc.* 1852–53 (106), lxxxiii.
56 PP: *Reports from Commissioners; Boundary Commission* 1867–68 (3972), xx.
57 ECA: *Exeter Election* 1864 and 1868.
58 *Hansard* 3rd ser. clxxxii, 1821; 20.4.1866.
59 PP: *Electoral Returns* 1866 (3626) lvii. Return B.
60 The figures given above are taken from the local records of the elections for the years stated.
61 ECA: *Exeter Election* 1864.
62 *Gazette* 6.3.1852. On 17.7.1852 the *Gazette* published a list showing how the clergy voted.
63 *Exeter Valuation*, 1838.
64 Figures from *Exeter Election* 1864 in ECA.
65 W.T. 20.10.1857.
66 C.M. 21.1.1854.
67 C.M. 14.10.1857.
68 Iddesleigh Papers, Add. MSS. 50,034 f. 30. Draft in Northcote's handwriting headed 'Address to the electors of Exeter, 1852.'
69 W.T. 24.4.1852.
70 *Ibid* 17.5.1851; 21.4.1852.
71 *Gazette* 10.7.1852.
72 According to *Gazette* 17.7.1852.

73 Iddesleigh Papers, Add. MSS. 50,034, 78, letter dated Exeter 19.4.1853.
74 ECA: Poster in Sheriff's Records, Box 2.
75 *Gazette* 18.9.1868. *Obit.*
76 W.T. 28.3.1857.
77 *Ibid.*
78 W.T. 28.3.1857.
79 This affair, necessarily summarized, is given in detail in F.P. 27.5.1858; 10.6.1858; 24.6.1858; see also W.T. 30.6.1857 and 20.6.1858 and C.M. 14.7.1858 and 8.9.1858.
80 F.P. 11.11.1858.
81 *Gazette* 13.11.1858.
82 F.P. 11.11.1858.
83 W.T. 17.5.1867 and *obit* 25.6.1869.
84 W.T. 25.6.1869.
85 Iddesleigh Papers, Add. MSS. 50,036, f. 230, letter dated Exeter, 29.4.1866.
86 W.T. 25.6.1869.
87 *Gentleman's Magazine*, 1865, ii, p. 78.
88 C.M. 19.10.1865.
89 W.T. 2.11.1866.
90 *Ibid* 5.11.1867.
91 W.T. 5.11.1867; 10.11.1868.
92 W.C. 11.5.1851; 6.9.1851.
93 *Ibid* 4.1.1862.
94 W.C. 7.7.1866.
95 *Ibid* 4.1.1850.
96 *Ibid* 7.1.1854.
97 *Ibid* 13.8.1867.
98 W.C. 9.6.1851.
99 PRO: Home Office 45/7992. Letter from the mayor 15.11.1867.
100 PRO: Home Office 45/7992 *op. cit.*
101 19 and 20 Vic. cap. 69.
102 C.M. 12.5.1858.
103 *Ibid* 9.1.1861.
104 *Ibid* 11.2.1857; W.T. 14.2.1857; C.M. 11.2.1857.
105 Local Act 21 and 22 Vic. cap. 73.
106 ECA: *Exeter Borough Fund*, accounts for 1850–51 and 1870–71.
107 I.C. 12.8.1839.
108 C.M. 12.9.1865.

109 *Annual Register* 1866, pp. 182–183.
110 C.P. 11.8.1866.
111 *Ibid* 11.8.1866; 21.8.1866; 16.10.1866.
112 C.M. 23.1.1867; 20.3.1867. Special committee 1.4.1867. ECA: Reports of special committees 1866.
113 *Gazette* 26.2.1867.
114 ECA: Inquiry Transcript, 1867. The manuscript record is in two parts divided by blank pages.
115 ECA: Inquiry Transcript 1867, ii, p. 7.
116 *Ibid*, p. 27.
117 *Ibid*, p. 32.
118 ECA: Inquiry Transcript 1867, ii, p. 26.
119 30 and 31 Vic. cap. 123.
120 ECA: Special committees *op. cit.* 1.4.1867.
121 ECA: Special committees *op. cit.* 10.6.1887.
122 W.T. 11.11.1870.
123 *Gazette* 25.3.1857.
124 *Ibid* 14.3.1857; *Luminary* 30.8.1849.
125 E. H. Coleridge, *Life of Lord Coleridge*, (1904) ii, p. 32.
126 W.T. 29.1.1864.
127 *Complete Peerage*, iv, p. 338.
128 W.T. 2.8.1864.
129 *Ibid* 9.8.1864.
130 *Gazette* 6.7.1867.
131 *Ibid* 17.11.1867.
132 Iddesleigh Papers. Add. MSS. 50,015, f. 160. Letter to Disraeli 12.11.1866.
133 And was also said to be the translator of German hymns specially selected by the queen, see *Men of the Time* ed. Thomas Cooper, 10th ed. (London 1879), pp. 136–137.
134 W.T. 7.8.1868.
135 Electoral address in W.T. 8.9.1868.
136 H. J. Hanham, *Elections and Party Management*, (1959) p. 68 and p. 92 footnote 2 for analysis of electoral results in the large towns.
137 W.T. 20.11.1868.
138 Ellis Memoirs, vi, ff. 20–25.
139 For the 1868 voting figures see ECA: *Exeter Election*, 1868.
140 ECA: *Exeter Election*, 1864.
141 W.T. 17.11.1868.
142 *Gazette* 20.11.1868.
143 *Ibid* 14.11.1868.

144 *Ibid* 20.11.1868.
145 N. Gash, *Politics in the Age of Peel*, (1965), p. 96.
146 F.P. 12.11.1835.
147 *Ibid*.

Chapter VI

1 A. Jenkins, *History of the City of Exeter*, (1806), p. 212.
2 Cf. Asa Briggs *Victorian Cities*, (1963) p. 372 quoting the *Athenaeum* no. 2237 of 10.9.1870, p. 327.
3 *Athenaeum* no. 2182 of 21.8.1869, p. 243.
4 *Gazette* 21.7.1860.
5 Shapter, *PP: Report on Exeter* 1845, p. 353.
6 *Ibid* pp. 356–357.
7 G. M. Young in *Early Victorian England*, (1951) ii, p. 432.
8 For the following figures of population and houses see the Census Reports. A useful summary of the rate of urban growth from 1861 is in 1911 *Census Summary Tables* (cd. 7929) 1915, Table 15.
9 C.M. 9.1.1839; 14.1.1839.
10 I.C. 24.1.1838.
11 Shapter, *op. cit.* pp. 378–386.
12 W.T. 4.3.1848.
13 *Ibid* 26.2.1848.
14 ECA: Inquiry Transcript, 1867, ii, p. 11.
15 F. W. Dendy, *Three Lectures delivered to the Literary and Philosophical Society, Newcastle upon Tyne* (Newcastle, 1921), p. 15.
16 *Exeter Valuation*, 1838.
17 W.T. 8.10.1836; F.P. 5.1.1837.
18 *Besley's Guide* 1836, p. 63.
19 *Ibid* p. 69.
20 *Besley's Guide* 1836, p. 63.
21 *Billing's Directory*, 1857, p. 90.
22 ECA: Lady Paterson's Diary 12.1.1834; 14.1.1834; 16.1.1834.
23 W.T. 25.9.1847.
24 These buildings can be dated approximately by the improvement commissioners' map of Exeter, 1840, and by the water company's rent books, both in the Exeter City Archives. There is a gap in the rent books from 1843–1847. Houses in Bystock Terrace were offered for sale in W.T. 25.9.1847.
25 John Claudius Loudon 1783–1843. For a discussion of his architecture and its influence cf. J. Gloag, *Victorian Taste*, (1962), Chapter IV.

26 I.C. 14.3.1863.
27 W.T. 10.2.1864; I.C. 14.3.1864.
28 Richardson and Gill, *Regional Architecture in the West of England*, (1924), p. 19.
29 W.T. 29.1.1869.
30 *Exeter Valuation*, 1838.
31 PP: *Parl. Representation. Electoral Returns* (Boroughs and Counties) 1865–1866 (3626) lvii. Return E. *Exeter Valuation*, 1838.
32 Streets committee 3.7.1869; 28.8.1869; for Newtown 14.8.1869.
33 W.T. 13.12.1848.
34 ECA: Water company's rent books 1867 and 1870.
35 *Ibid* 1851 and 1871.
36 *Gazette* 18.5.1888.
37 Streets committee 1.2.1868.
38 *Ibid* 7.12.1867; 28.12.1867.
39 *Ibid* 3.7.1869.
40 W.T. 14.3.1857; 4.4.1857.
41 W.T. 29.9.1869.
42 *Ibid* 10.7.1847.
43 *Ibid* 6.10.1865.
44 *Ibid* 25.6.1869.
45 W.T. 15.10.1869.
46 *Ibid* 16.6.1863; 13.1.1865.
47 Richardson and Gill *op. cit.* p. 176 and p. 21 for the quotation below.
48 W.T. 29.6.1869; 20.10.1869.
49 William Gibbs, of Tyntesfield, near Bristol, gave £20,000 for the completion of the church.
50 There is an interesting account of George Oliver's life and times by W. G. Hoskins, 'George Oliver, D.D. 1781–1861' in the *Downside Review*, autumn, 1961.
51 ECA: Inquiry Transcript, 1867, ii, p. 13.
52 James Cossins, *Reminiscences of Exeter*, (1877), preface.
53 Thomas Sharp, *Exeter Phoenix*, (1946), p. 36.
54 *White's Directory*, 1878, p. 327.
55 I.C. 14.9.1863.
56 Streets committee 5.7.1870.
57 R. S. Surtees, *Mr Facey Romford's Hounds*, (1950 ed.), p. 60.

Chapter VII

1 *e.g.* G. D. H. Cole and R. Postgate, *The Common People, 1746–1946*, (1962), p. 351.

2 *Gazette* 14.1.1870; W.T. 21.8.1858; 19.7.1870.

3 ECA: Kennaway Papers 58/59 Box 9.

4 *Ibid* Box 3, accounts and receipts 1819–1839, 'easing doors, fixing beaded listing, repairing locks, etc.' 3 days, 11*s*. 6*d*.

5 W.T. 7.1.1854.

6 W.T. 7.1.1854. The following account is taken primarily from *Gazette* and *W.T.* of this date.

7 *Gazette* 7.1.1854.

8 C.P. 3.1.1854. For the scale of relief below C.P. 3.10.1848.

9 *Gazette* 7.1.1854, which is the authority for the following details.

10 W.T. 14.1.1854.

11 *Gazette* 14.1.1854. Following account taken from *Gazette* and *W.T.* of this date.

12 W.T. 14.1.1854. Edward Trood's evidence in *Reports of the Special Assistant Poor Law Commissioners* (H.M.S.O. 1843), p. 95.

13 A.R. 1854, Chronicle, p. 9.

14 Editorial in W.T. 14.1.1854; *Gazette* 14.1.1854.

15 W.T. 5.11.1867. The following account is taken from the issues of this paper of 5.11.1867 and 8.11.1867.

16 *Gazette* 5.11.1867.

17 For a summary of incidents in Devon see W.T. 8.11.1867.

18 *Times* 7.11.1867.

19 *Gazette* 8.11.1867.

20 PRO: Home Office 45/7992. Letter from the mayor of Exeter 15.11.1867.

21 C.P. 28.9.1867; 21.3.1867; 21.3.1868.

22 P.L.B. *21st An. Rept.* 1868–69 (1869) p. 232. For the Exeter prices C.P. 28.9.1867.

23 C.P. 7.12.1867; 8.12.1866.

24 W. G. Hoskins, *Devon*, (1959), p. 139.

25 *Cf.* J. Simmons, 'South Western v. Great Western: Railway Competition in Devon and Cornwall,' *The Journal of Transport History*, iv. No. 1, May, 1959.

26 W.T. 10.2.1867.

27 *Gazette* 1.1.1869.

28 ECA: Kennaway Papers, Box 10, Estate of Mark Kennaway Esq. These papers form an interesting record of the investments of a prosperous Exeter lawyer.

29 The following statements are based on *Census* 1861 and 1871 occupational tables.

30 See R. S. Surtees, *Mr Sponge's Sporting Tour*, (1853).
31 ECA: Kennaway Papers, Box 14, 'Hoopern House Estate, Accounts and Receipts 1855–73.'
32 W.T. 12.6.1858.
33 *Ibid* 18.6.1869; 22.6.1869.
34 *Ibid* 11.6.1872; Cole and Postgate, *The Common People*, p. 302.
35 W.C. 1.6.1872.
36 ECA: Kennaway Papers *op. cit.*
37 W.T. 10.6.1873.
38 *Ibid* 5.5.1863.
39 *Ibid* 24.12.1854; 10.3.1871; 17.3.1871.
40 ECA: Kennaway Papers, Box 9, Butler's Diary.
41 W.T. 29.1.1869; 14.8.1858.
42 For Strong's Cottages W.T. 5.9.1857; William Clement ECA: Kennaway Papers, Box 27, Lease.
43 *Gazette* 14.6.1851.
44 *Ibid* 15.2.1852; W.T. 17.3.1865.
45 W.T. 30.1.1862; 13.3.1863.
46 *Ibid* 24.4.1873.
47 Sanitary committee 21.3.1870; W.T. 19.10.1869.
48 Market reports; C.P. 27.4.1850 and 24.9.1870.
49 C.P. 28.10.1850; 24.9.1870.
50 W.C. 13.10.1849; 16.2.1852; 4.2.1871.
51 W.C. 27.4.1850; 24.9.1870.
52 Moleskins, W.T. 1.11.1870; *Gazette* 14.1.1845.
Trousers W.T. 1.11.1870; *Gazette* 5.1.1850.
Suits W.T. 5.1.1850; 1.11.1870.
Hats W.T. 1.11.1850; 20.5.1870.
53 W.T. 20.5.1870; *Gazette* 23.1.1836.
54 *Gazette* 8.1.1869.
55 *Ibid.*
56 C.P. 4.9.1855.
57 *Gazette* 19.2.1869 giving a 'write-up' of the post office.
58 W.T. 15.5.1860.
59 *Ibid* 30.5.1857.
60 *Ibid* 3.2.1863.
61 *Gazette* 21.2.1870.
62 W.T. 19.3.1869.
63 C.P. 23.2.1856; 21.4.1856.
64 C.P. 10.3.1860.
65 *Ibid* 22.6.1856; 9.3.1858.
66 *Ibid* 7.8.1860.

67 *Ibid* 26.4.1856.
68 C.P. 22.3.1857.
69 *Ibid* 7.6.1858.
70 *Ibid* 30.11.1858.
71 *Ibid* 4.2.1862.
72 C.P. 17.6.1862.
73 *Ibid* 5.10.1869.
74 W.T. 28.8.1858.
75 *Ibid* 23.1.1858.
76 C.P. 19.6.1860.
77 Sanitary committee 22.7.1867.
78 *Ibid* 25.4.1870.
79 *Royal Commission on the Housing of the Working Classes* 1885 (c. 4402.1) ii, p. 707.
80 *Gazette* 15.3.1869.
81 Sanitary committee 21.3.1870.
82 George Oliver, *History of Exeter*, (1861), p. 175.

Chapter VIII

1 *Gazette* 12.11.1869.
2 L. C. Sanders (ed.) *Lord Melbourne's Papers* (London, 1889, p. 496, quoting a letter from Melbourne to Lord John Russell of 9.1.1839.
3 For these views of Phillpotts the authorities are F.P. 22.9.1869; W.T. 24.9.1869; CL: Correspondence ED 11/26, letter from Gladstone of 4.10.1851; CL: T. Shapter, Surplice Riots, f. 18; F.P. 29.9.1869.
4 Obituaries *Gazette* 22.2.1869; F.P. 24.2.1869. W.T. 22.2.1869.
5 For this incident see W.T. 13.8.1859; 20.8.1859; 27.7.1859.
6 F.P. 5.12.1850.
7 W.T. 12.11.1838.
8 Sayell: W.T. 27.10.1865; Bastard: W.T. 31.10.1871.
9 W.T. 1.11.1870.
10 *Gazette* 22.9.1869.
11 Davidson and Benham, *Life of Archibald Campbell Tait*, (1891), 2 vols. ii, p. 59.
12 *Gazette* 3.12.1869.
13 F.P. 12.1.1870.
14 W.T. 19.7.1870.
15 W.T. 3.1.1871.
16 F.P. 15.1.1873.
17 *Census* 1831, 1871.

18 J. G. Harrod & Co., *Royal County Directory of Devonshire*, (1878), p. 197.
19 Sir John Daw, *Reminiscences* 1866–1957, p. 10.
20 See Appendix I.
21 C.M. 10.10.1867 and 10.4.1867; 9.10.1873 and 9.4.1873. The rate was levied in two instalments.
22 According to the reports of the annual meetings of the society. For the regular relief PP: *Sessional Papers, Poor Rates and Pauperism*, returns 1870 and 1871.
23 *Gazette* 3.2.1871.
24 DEI: *Report of the Administrative Committee . . . for the relief of the unemployed labourers at Exeter*. Tracts. vol. 129.
25 *Ibid*.
26 W.T. 18.1.1870.
27 F.P. 26.1.1870.
28 *Ibid*.
29 DEI: *Neglected and Destitute Children;* report of Guildhall meeting on 5.1.1869, Tracts vol. 129.
30 W.T. 7.6.1851.
31 DEI: *Neglected and Destitute Children op. cit.*
32 W.T. 20.6.1871 reporting the results of the investigations of the Exeter school board.
33 *Ibid* 23.11.1870.
34 *Minutes of Committee of Council on Education* 1869–1870 p. 44.
35 PP: 1886 (191) ix Endowed Schools Acts. *Sel. Cttee. Rep.*, Mins. of ev. Questions 1077–1078. Evidence of J. G. Fitch.
36 PP: *School Inquiry Commission*, 1868, xiv, Southwestern Division, Reports by Special Commissioners pp. 300–301.
37 *Ibid* xiv. Mins. of ev. Pt. I, pp. 734–738.
38 *Ibid* i. Rept. Appendix VII. Tables X-XV.
39 DEI: *Report of the Diocesan Board of Education* with report of the Rev. G. Martin and the Rev. O. Headley in accordance with the decision of the diocesan board of March, 1840.
40 *Report of the Committee of Council on Education* 1870–1871, p. 368.
41 *Gazette* 27.11.1872.
42 G. Donisthorpe, *An Account of the Origin and Purpose of the Devon and Exeter Albert Memorial Museum*, p. 1. DEI: Tracts vol. 129.
43 *Ibid* pp. 18–19.
44 F.P. 2.2.1870.

45 1831–1900. Son of mine-owner. M.P. 1874–1886. Owner of the *Newcastle Chronicle*. Admirer of Kossuth, Mazzini and Garibaldi.
46 W.T. 30.12.1870.

Chapter IX

1 F.P. 6.2.1909.
2 *Ibid* 20.10.1906.
3 W.T. 10.11.1882.
4 Sung at Conservative meetings in 1872, cf. F.P. 31.1.1872.
5 Letter to Thomas Andrew dated 7.6.1868 and bound in what is evidently Andrew's canvassing book for the election of that year. Exeter Reference Library.
6 By Ralph Sanders, the banker, F.P. 17.12.1873.
7 F.P. 4.7.1903.
8 Bishop of Peterborough 1868–1891. Archbishop of York 1891.
9 W.T. 15.12.1871.
10 *Ibid* 26.1.1872.
11 *Ibid* 9.4.1872; 23.9.1872. *The Times* 1.2.1872; 3.2.1872; 8.4.1872.
12 W.T. 23.9.1872.
13 W.T. 10.12.1875; F.P. 26.2.1873.
14 F.P. 22.10.1875.
15 W.T. 29.11.1872.
16 J. H. Clapham, *Economic History of Great Britain*, ii (1932), p. 186.
17 J. L. Garvin, *Life of Joseph Chamberlain*, i (1932), p. 432.
18 F.P. 19.11.1873 which is also the authority for the following statements.
19 F.P. 19.11.1873; and for the meetings at Heavitree and in the Temperance Hall in the following para.
20 F.P. 19.11.1873.
21 F.P. 26.11.1873.
22 *Ibid* 3.12.1873.
23 *Ibid* 10.12.1873.
24 Iddesleigh Papers. Add. MSS. 50,037, f. 172, letter from Mr Pye of 12.9.1868.
25 Iddesleigh Papers. Add. MSS. 50,016, f. 152, letter to Disraeli dated 10.9.1873.
26 As published in W.T. 21.11.1873.
27 W.T. 19.2.1873.
28 F.P. 10.12.1873.

29 W.T. 6.2.1874.
30 F.P. 17.12.1873.
31 W.T. 18.11.1873.
32 Iddesleigh Papers. Add. MSS. 50,016, letter dated 15.6.1874 and Northcote to Disraeli 16.6.1874.
33 W.T. 9.2.1875 quoting the parliamentary returns.
34 F.P. 5.1.1881.
35 W.T. 9.4.1880.
36 F.P. 31.3.1880.
37 W.T. 27.11.1885.
38 W.T. 5.2.1892.
39 City of Exeter Extension Act, 1877, 40 and 41 Vict. cap, cxii.
40 W.T. 3.10.1876.
41 *Ibid* 13.11.1876.
42 W.T. 21.2.1873; F.P. 2.8.1873.
43 W.C. 8.3.1873.
44 W T 1.4.1873.
45 *Ibid* 25.2.1873.
46 F.P. 23.4.1873.
47 The title of the post was changed to chief constable, W.C. 8.3.1873.
48 W.C. 4.12.1875; 6.12.1875; 1.1.1876.
49 W.C. 20.1.1886.
50 C.M. 22.4.1874.
51 C.M. 20.7.1879.
52 C.M. 10.6.1879.
53 C.M. 13.8.1879.
54 L.G.B. 11*th Annual Report* (C. 3337) 1882, p. 412.
55 F.P. 22.10.1879.
56 W.T. 3.11.1882.
57 F.P. 21.11.1883.
58 F.P. 3.11.1886.
59 C.M. 24.5.1882.
60 *Ibid* 10.10.1888; 15.10.1888.
61 Special committee 20.8.1905.
62 C.M. 20.6.1880; 12.7.1880.
63 W.C. 2.5.1891; C.M. 15.3.1891.
64 F.P. 12.11.1879, gives an account of this riot.
65 Market committee 9.3.1882; C.M. 14.3.1883 and 25.4.1883.
66 C.M. 4.4.1880; 24.11.1880.
67 C.M. 28.7.1880; 27.1.1883.

68 *Ibid* 24.11.1883. The following quotation is from the souvenir programme for the opening of the new Exe Bridge and the Electric Tramways, p. 10. ECA: Exeter Electric Tramways, Box 1.
69 Streets committee 25.10.1894.
70 A.R. 'Chronicle' p. 42. W.T. 6.9.1887; 9.9.1887; 16.9.1887; 23.9.1887.
71 F.P. 2.3.1887.
72 C.M. 11.4.1888.
73 *Ibid* 13.6.1888.
74 WT. 5.2.1892.

Chapter X
1 Von Raumer, *England in 1835*, (1836), iii, p. 36.
2 W.T. 7.11.1871.
3 T.D.A. v, 1872, p. 26.
4 F.P. 17.1.1883.
5 W.T. 15.12.1871.
6 *Ibid* 20.1.1871.
7 W.T. 22.3.1870.
8 W.T. 25.8.1874; 8.9.1874; 6.10.1874 and F.P. 21.10.1874; 4.11.1874.
9 F.P. 4.11.1874.
10 *Ibid* 2.2.1876.
11 W.T. 15.6.1875; F.P. 27.9.1882.
12 F.P. 27.5.1874.
13 *Gazette* 17.4.1874.
14 F.P. 23.1.1904.
15 W.T. 3.7.1883.
16 W.T. 29.11.1872; F.P. 1.1.1879.
17 W.T. 26.3.1871.
18 *Ibid* 15.4.1890.
19 F.P. 30.6.1880; PP: *Select Committee on the Education of the Poorer Classes in England and Wales*, 1838.
20 F.P. 4.10.1902.
21 Forster's speech on the introduction of the Bill. Hansard 3rd ser. cxcix/440–466, 17.1.1870.
22 For this summary see *Report of the Endowed School Commissioners* (Cd. 524) 1874. Appendix 2.
23 PP: *Evidence given before the Select Committee on the Endowed Schools Act 1873* (253) viii. Sel. Cttee. Rep. Mins. of ev. Q. 2468.
24 *Endowed Schools, Commissioners Report* 1872, para. LI.

25 The history of Exeter's charitable endowments is summarized in PP: *Endowed Charities (County Borough of Exeter)* 1909 (37). This reprints the report of 30.6.1821.

26 PP: *Public Charities (Schools)* 1843, xviii (435) p. 23.

27 Sanders, *Observations on the Memorandum in Reference to the Reorganisation of the Exeter Education Endowments,* (Exeter 1872) p. 5. DEI. Tracts vol. 129.

28 Prospectus, 1853, p. 4. bound in DEI: Tracts vol. 129.

29 For this summary of Hele's see PP: *Education Commission* 1861, iv. Reports of assistant commissioner p. 288.

30 *Gazette* 1.3.1872.

31 M. Sadler, *Report on Secondary and Higher Education in Exeter* (1905) p. 3.

32 F. K. Aglionby, *Life of Edward Henry Bickersteth,* (1907), p. 117.

33 W.T. 17.1.1871.

34 *Ibid* 20.1.1871.

35 W.T. 20.1.1871.

36 *Gazette* 13.11.1871.

37 W.T. 10.1.1871.

38 *Ibid* 24.1.1871.

39 W.T. 26.1.1871.

40 *Ibid* 3.2.1871.

41 A. A. Brockett, personal communication.

42 *Gazette* 27.1.1871; W.T. 31.1.1871.

43 W.T. 24.1.1871.

44 *Gazette* 20.1.1871.

45 The results are analysed by F.P. 25.1.1871 and 1.2.1871.

46 E.S.B. 3.2.1871; W.T. 17.2.1871.

47 E.S.B. 9.3.1871; 16.3.1871.

48 The report of the committee was published in detail. The original does not appear to have survived. The figures quoted are from W.T. 20.6.1871.

49 W.T. 23.6.1871.

50 E.S.B. 29.6.1871; W.T. 4.7.1871.

51 W.T. 4.7.1871 fills in the details of E.S.B. 29.6.1871.

52 Regulations E.S.B. 12.10.1871; fees 14.12.1871; prayers *et al.* 14.12.1871.

53 E.S.B. 8.8.1872. Comparative Returns.

54 *Ibid.* 15.1.1874. F.P. 13.10.1875.

55 F.P. 3.3.1880.

56 W.T. 19.12.1871.

57 E.S.B. 11.11.1875. F.P. 17.11.1875.
58 F.P. 9.12.1875.
59 PP: *Statistical Report of Commissioners appointed to inquire into the Elementary Education Act* (C-4385-II) 1888 Table B. Average attendance 2,552 in voluntary schools, 1,440 in board schools.
60 *Report of the Committee of Council on Education* 1884–1885, p. 24.
61 *Ibid* p. 248.
62 *Report of the Committee of Council on Education* 1897–1898, Appendix Pt. I. Table 9, p. 24.
63 *Report of the Board of Education* 1899–1900, iii Appendix (Elementary Education) Table 6, p. 13.
64 *Report of the Board of Education* 1899–1900, iii Appendix (Elementary Education) Table 13, p. 52.
65 *Ibid.*
66 F.P. 3.2.1900.
67 Letter to the mayor 5.2.1872. Printed in *Report of the Endowed Schools Commissioners* 1872, Appendix 6, p. 68.
68 *Ibid* p. 69.
69 W.T. 20.2.1872. *Gazette* 2.2.1872.
70 Letter to the mayor *op. cit.* p. 69.
71 Following account from *Gazette* 1.3.1872.
72 Observations on the Reorganization of the Exeter Educational Endowments (1872) p. 13. DEI: Tracts vol. 129.
73 C.M. 26.4.1871.
74 *Hansard* 3rd ser. ccxxv/788 and 950, 5.7.1875; ccxvii/134, 10.2.1876.
75 Summary in this paragraph from *Scheme Submitted to the Committee of Council on Education* (1874), No. 378.
76 PP: *Select Committee on Endowed Schools Act*, 1886. Q. 1077.
77 *Ibid.* Letter read by J. G. Fitch in giving evidence. Q. 1078.
78 PP: *Royal Commission on Secondary Education* 1895, vi. *Reports from Assistant Commissioners*, p. 88.
79 Letter in F.P. 3.1.1883.
80 M. E. Sadler, *Report on Secondary and Higher Education in Exeter* (1905), p. 3.
81 *Ibid* p. 9.
82 *Ibid* p. 18.
83 *University Extension Bulletin.* Jan. 1919, 'Memoir of Miss Montgomery.'

84 Sadler *op. cit.* p. 29; R. D. Roberts, address on 'University Extension' delivered at the Cambridge Summer Meeting on 29.7.1908; PP: *Royal Commission on Secondary Education* 1895, i, Reports from commissioners p. 56 and Miss Montgomery's letter p. 52.

85 W.T. 23.7.1895.

86 *Ibid* 7.7.1899.

87 Royal Albert Memorial, Minutes 12.6.1901.

88 C.M. 24.2.1901.

89 Sadlers, *op. cit.* p. 2.

90 *Exeter Evening Post* 25.10.1902.

91 *Ibid* 13.10.1902.

92 F.P. 1.11.1902.

93 Special committee on education 5.9.1903; C.M. 8.9.1903.

94 C.M. 8.9.1903.

95 Education committee 16.9.1903.

96 *Ibid.*

97 Education committee 16.9.1903.

98 *Education in Exeter in* 1908 published by the Exeter education committee.

99 C.M. 27.1.1909.

100 F.P. 6.1.1906 reporting his speech to the Devon Liberal Association.

101 F.P. 17.1.1883.

102 *Ibid* 7.2.1903.

103 *Ibid* 29.1.1890.

104 *Proceedings of the Thirty-fourth Church Conference* p. 1.

105 W.T. 23.4.1889; E.P. 15.4.1902.

106 F.P. 9.3.1887.

107 A. A. Brockett, *Nonconformity in Exeter* 1650–1875, p. 233, expresses the view that the percentage of churchgoers in Exeter probably increased towards the end of Queen Victoria's reign. The evidence supports this view.

108 N. Pevsner, *The Buildings of England; South Devon*, (1952), p. 148.

109 F.P. 11.4.1914.

Chapter XI

1 F.P. 27.4.1881.

2 W.T. 28.4.1899.

3 W.T. 2.2.1900.

4 *Gazette* 14.2.1879.

5 F.P. 1.1.1894.

6 *Devon Evening Express* 27.2.1903.
7 *Complete Peerage*, xi, (1949) p. 76.
8 F.P. 31.12.1879.
9 A.R. 1879, p. 1.
10 F.P. 11.12.1878.
11 F.P. 20.10.1880 describes the extent of Thomas's business ventures.
12 F.P. 15.1.1879.
13 *Ibid* 4.2.1880.
14 F.P. 28.4.1875.
15 W.T. 22.11.1889.
16 *Royal Commission on the Housing of the Working Classes* (Cd. – 4402 – 1) 1885, ii, p. 707.
17 W. G. Hoskins, *Two Thousand Years in Exeter*, (1960), p. 117.
18 T. Shapter. PP: *Report on Exeter* 1845, p. 357.
19 The following figures are derived from *Census* 1871 Population Abstracts (Cd. 872) 1873. (The reference is not repeated unless required by the context).
20 These, and the following figures, are from *Census, England and Wales* 1901. General Report (Cd. 2174) 1904, Appendix A. Table 39. For details see *County of Devon* (Cd. 1,271) 1902.
21 E. T. MacDermot, *History of the Great Western Railway*, i, pp. 190, 642–5.
22 J. Simmons, 'South Western v. Great Western: Railway Competition in Devon and Cornwall,' *The Journal of Transport History*, iv, May 1959, p. 29.
23 W.T. 21.6.1898.
24 *Census* 1911. *Summary Tables*. (Cd. 7929) 1915.
25 Figures from streets committee minutes.
26 Streets committee 8.4.1876.
27 Sandford Street, etc. Streets committee 15.1.1877; Portland Street 4.3.1878.
28 Streets committee 4.3.1878; 3.6.1878; 5.7.1878. For the, railwaymen see *Besley's Directory*, 1901.
29 Streets committee 23.1.1896.
30 *Ibid* 19.1.1888.
31 *Besley's Directory*, 1901.
32 F.P. 2.1.1897.
33 J. Gloag, *Victorian Taste* (1962) p. 78.
34 F.P. 27.2.1884.
35 W.T. 27.6.1899.

36 W.T. 4.7.1899.
37 *Ibid* 7.11.1896.
38 F.P. 27.2.1903.
39 Newtown, F.P. 27.7.1881; Jubilee Road, W.T. 6.4.1900; Toronto Road, Force Papers, adverts. 1904.
40 Mansfield Road, F.P. 21.9.1895; Force Papers, advert. 1898; *Besley's Directory*, 1901.
41 Force Papers, adverts. 1899.
42 F.P. 7.5.1887; Force Papers, adverts. 4.2.1904; 19.7.1904.
43 Force Papers, adverts. 1899.
44 W.T. 1.3.1898.
45 F.P. 27.10.1880.
46 W.T. 2.3.1879.
47 *Ibid* 16.3.1839.
48 F.P. 21.2.1872.
49 Exeter local board, 21.3.1870.
50 *Gazette* 15.3.1869.
51 W.T. 9.5.1873; F.P. 21.5.1873 for details of rents etc.
52 F.P. 7.7.1875.
53 *Ibid* 26.6.1872.
54 Sanitary committee 11.5.1868; 9.
55 *Ibid.*
56 *Ibid* 22.7.1867.
57 Exeter local board 27.8.1877.
58 M.O.H. 1901 p. 34.
59 F.P. 1.5.1872.
60 Exeter local board, 1878.
61 Sanitary committee 20.7.1876.
62 *Ibid* 24.9.1877; and for the following details 26.11.1877; 21.1.1878.
63 Sanitary committee 3.12.1873.
64 Exeter local board 16.6.1870.
65 Exeter local board 4.4.1871; W.T. 6.4.1871.
66 *Gazette* 14.4.1871.
67 Exeter local board 13.11.1871.
68 Sanitary committee 18.3.1880.
69 *Royal Commission on Housing* (Cd. – 4402 – 1) 1885, p. 707 .
70 Sanitary committee 13.9.1899.
71 F.P. 17.10.1896; 21.8.1897.
72 W.T. 14.6.1898.
73 F.P. 19.8.1874.
74 Sanitary committee 20.9.1875.

75 *Ibid* 24.4.1876.
76 *Ibid* 19.2.1877. Report of Mr C. W. Stevenson 15.2.1877.
77 C.M. 21.3.1878.
78 C.M. 24.7.1879.
79 Sanitary committee 19.7.1880.
80 Sanitary committee 16.1.1882.
81 C.P. 7.1.1879.
82 W.T. 12.1.1875.
83 Sanitary committee 21.11.1885.
84 *Ibid* 20.4.1889.
85 Sanitary committee 25.11.1885.
86 M.O.H. *Annual Report*, 1902, p. 10.
87 PP: Shapter, *Report on Exeter*, 1845, p. 377.
88 The strike was reported in W.T. 2.5.1873; 9.5.1873; 3.6.1873.
89 *Statistical Tables and Report on Trade Unions.* Second Report (Cd. – 5505) 1888.
90 C.T.V. Box 40.
91 W.T. 27.5.1890.
92 E.P. 18.8.1890.
93 W.T. 8.7.1890.
94 F.P. 17.1.1890 which published the balance sheet.
95 *Building and Woodworking Trades in* 1906 (Cd. 5086) 1910.
96 W.T. 23.5.1890; 3.6.1890.
97 Board of trade, *Statistical Tables and Report on Trade Unions* (Cd. – 5505) 1888.
98 W.T. 10.5.1898.
99 Board of trade, *Eighth Annual Report of Labour Statistics* 1900–01 (Cd. 1124) 1902.
100 Analysis of deposits in *Gazette* 12.2.1857; *Annual Statement* 1891.
101 Figures from adverts. in W.T. of 1871 and 1900. See also Appendix II.
102 F.P. 11.1.1896.
103 Survey by watch committee, 7.3.1900.
104 W.T. 8.7.1890.
105 B. S. Rowntree, *Poverty, a study in Town Life*, p. 54, pp. 60–65.
106 W.C. 7.11.1874; 9.2.1901.
107 C.P. 3.3.1891.
108 F.P. 18.2.1901.
109 Gatty's Court: F.P. 3.1.1891; Smythen Street 26.12.1891; Preston Street 15.11.1893.

z

110 L.G.B. 27th An. Rpt. 1898–1899 (C. 9444) 1899 p. 128.
111 C.P. 24.9.1870; 22.9.1900.
112 W.T. 27.5.1890.
113 F.P. 27.9.1894.
114 *Ibid* 12.6.1872.
115 *Ibid* 18.8.1875.
116 *Ibid* 25.10.1894.
117 F.P. 12.9.1896.
118 *Ibid* 3.8.1895.
119 W.T. 22.2.1898.
120 *Gazette* 23.11.1900; 14.1.1900.
121 W.T. 14.4.1899.

Chapter XII

1 E. A. Freeman, *Exeter*, p. 239.
2 W.T. 2.2.1900.
3 H. Rider Haggard, *Rural England*, (1902) i, p. 216.
4 *Census* 1901. *County of Devon*. (Cd. 1,271) 1902, Table 36.
5 Exeter Probate Records from which the following statements are also taken.
6 W.T. 28.12.1900.
7 W.T. 16.2.1900.
8 L.G.B. *29th An. Rpt.* 1899–1900 (Cd. 292) p. 102.
9 W.T. 23.2.1900.
10 Royal Commission on Local Taxation, *Appendix to Final Rept.* (Cd. – 1221) 1902, p. 118. Bath £5.13.0, Brighton £6.14.0, Cheltenham £5.14.0, York £5.3.0, Leicester £3.17.0, Norwich £3.5.0.
11 *Census* 1901. *County of Devon*.
12 St Leonard's and Pennsylvania, W.T. 2.1.1900; Polsloe Road W.T. 5.1.1900.
13 According to W.T. 14.1.1870 and 16.1.1900.
14 W.T. 4.5.1900.
15 ECA: Report to the education committee 1908.
16 Southwood & Co., D.W.T. 27.7.1900; Townsend & Sons, W.T. 26.6.1900.
17 Exeter Corporation Act, 63 & 64 Vict. cap. cxxxi.
18 F.P. 2.11.1900.
19 W.T. 24.10.1893.
20 *Gazette* 2.11.1900.
21 F.P. 2.11.1900.

22 ECA: *Borough Fund* and *Urban Sanitary Authority Accounts* for the years mentioned. For loan expenditure L.G.B. 28th Annual Rept. 1898–1899 (C. – 9444) 1899; 29th Annual Rept. 1899–1900 (C. – 292) 1900.
23 See Appendix.
24 W.T. 30.1.1848.
25 F.P. 23.1.1884.

Chapter XIII

1 F.P. 23.10.1899.
2 D.N.B. 1941–1950; *The Times* 3.11.1941.
3 F.P. 30.5.1903; 18.4.1903.
4 F.P. 7.2.1903; 11.4.1903.
5 F.P. 13.4.1911.
6 G. W. Kekewich, *The Education Department and After*, p. 240.
7 *Ibid.*
8 The streets selected as a sample are Buller Road, Dean Street, Hoopern Street, Rosebery Road, Toronto Road, Victoria Road. *Besley's Directory* for 1905 was compared with the electoral roll 1906.
9 Kekewich op. cit. p. 252.
10 W.T. 8.10.1909; F.P. 9.10.1909.
11 For St Maur's career see *The Times* 5.2.1910; for Duke, later Lord Merrivale, *The Times* 22.5.1929; D.N.B. 1931–1940; *Who was Who* 1929–1940.
12 F.P. 5.2.1910.
13 *Ibid* 16.10.1909.
14 *Ibid* 29.1.1910.
15 F.P. 11.12.1909.
16 W. G. Hoskins, *Devon*, (1959), p. 190.
17 *The Times* 12.11.1910.
18 F.P. 10.12.1910.
19 *Ibid.*
20 The following account is based on the full reports in F.P. 8.4.1911 and 15.4.1911; and on *The Times* 12.4.1911. For Sir Edward Ridley's career and character below see *Who was Who* 1916–1923 and *The Times* 15.10.1928.
21 F.P. 15.4.1911.
22 The details of personal emoluments are from *Exeter Borough Fund Accounts* for the appropriate years.
23 Sanitary committee 14.1.1907.
24 ECA: Abstracts of Accounts 1901–1902, p. 289 and 1913–1914, p. 406, which include summaries of the rates 1896–1914.

25 F.P. 19.10.1904.
26 *Ibid* 4.11.1904.
27 F.P. 2.11.1912.
28 E.P. 9.3.1901.
29 Housing figures from streets committee minutes. M.O.H. Annual Reports 1903–1911 include figures for buildings completed and under construction. See M.O.H. 1908 p. 99 and 1914 p. 256. For monthly av. 1906–1908 see statement in Unemployed Workmen Act (Special committee) Min. 10.12.1908.
30 F.P. 25.10.1902.
31 Streets committee minutes 1905–1908 are the authority for the statements above.
32 Electric traction committee 23.11.1901.
33 C.M. 10.7.1902.
34 Electric traction committee 10.7.1902.
35 For this project see E.P. 15.1.1902; F.P. 1.3.1902 and E.P. 10.3.1902.
36 Electric traction committee. Report of 21.6.1902.
37 F.P. 20.5.1905.
38 For a summary of H. A. Willey's career see Hoskins, *Two Thousand Years in Exeter*, pp. 116–117; also obit. in F.P. 24.9.1904.
39 *Ibid* 7.11.1903.
40 Streets committee 17.3.1904.
41 F.P. 21.3.1908.
42 F.P. 31.10.1908.
43 L.G.B. 37th An. Rept. 1907–1908 (Cd. 4347, 1908 p. 317; 38th An. Rept. 1908–1909 (Cd. 4780) 1909 I p. 61. 39th An. Rept. 1909–1910 (Cd. 5260) 1910. p. 50.
44 F.P. 5.3.1910.
45 *Ibid* 25.2.1911.
46 According to summaries of trading accounts in possession of Colsons of Exeter Ltd.
47 F.P. 8.11.1913.
48 G. D. H. Cole and R. Postgate, *The Common People*, pp. 441–442, 497.
49 See Appendix II.
50 C.P. 16.3.1901; 21.3.1914.
51 W.C. 30.11.1911.
52 *Ibid* 14.1.1913.
53 Finance committee 19.2.1913. See Appendix II.

54 Board of trade, *Building and Woodworking Trades in* 1906, (Cd. 5085) 1910.
55 F.P. 3.4.1909 quoting civil service estimates.
56 Exeter *Borough Fund Accounts*.
57 Workmen's wages committee 10.2.1914.
58 C.T.V. Box 2.
59 City asylum committee 24.10.1901; 31.3.1914.
60 M.O.H. 1914, p. 13.
61 Infantile death-rate M.O.H. 1896, p. 6; 1902, p. 10; 1914, p. 16.
62 Death-rate: M.O.H. 1914, p. 13. Infantile death-rate M.O.H. 1896, p. 6; 1902, p. 10; 1914, p. 16. Scarlet fever: M.O.H. 1901, p. 34. Measles: M.O.H. 1907, p. 36, p. 39.
63 City extension committee 18.12.1912.
64 M.O.H. 1911, p. 77. Streets and sanitary committee, joint meeting 11.5.1910.
65 C.M. 20.7.1904; special committee 19.3.1906; 27.2.1907.
66 Streets and sanitary committee 13.7.1911.
67 Mansfield Road F.P. 31.3.1895; Force Papers, 'Newspaper Cuttings.' Portland Street F.P. 22.8.1908; Force Papers, 'Notes of Sales.' Sandford Street, Force Papers, 'Notes of Sales.' Lyndhurst Road, *ibid.* Hoopern Street, F.P. 7.3.1914. Knightly's, Force Papers, 'Newspaper Cuttings.' Sylvan Road, *ibid.*
68 Market and general purposes committee 25.6.1910.
69 C.P. 1.12.1908.
70 *Ibid* 28.6.1910.
71 F.P. 23.12.1911.

Chapter XIV

1 Edmund Blunden, in *Edwardian England* 1900–1914, (1964), p. 547.
2 W. L. Burn, *The Age of Equipoise*, (1964), especially Chapter 1
3 G. D. H. Cole and R. Postgate, *The Common People* 1746–1946, p. 454 and Chapter XXXVI generally.
4 *Piers Plowman*, ed. Nevill Coghill (1949).
5 C.M. 11.3.1913.
6 For Hoopern Fields F.P. 3.10.1908; Cowick Fields, F.P. 21.3.1914.
7 W.C. 9.7.1908.
8 Parliamentary committee 31.10.1910.
9 F.P. 21.3.1914.
10 F.P. 21.3.1914.

11 *Census* 1911, Summary Tables (Cd. 7929) 1915 is the authority for the following figures for males and female employment.
12 At a meeting organized by the National Union of Women Workers. F.P. 15.2.1913.
13 F.P. 12.7.1913. For the following quotations, F.P. 1.1.1910; 7.11.1883.
14 *Ibid* 1.1.1910.
15 F.P. 7.11.1883.
16 *Ibid* 20.12.1913. See also Appendix I.
17 F.P. 17.8.1912, obit.
18 For persons mentioned above see the following obituaries: Richards, F.P. 4.7.1903; Harding, F.P. 29.2.1908; Pople, F.P. 6.2.1909; Pring, F.P. 24.12.1910; E. A. Sanders, F.P. 25.3.1905.
19 W.C. 23.1.1914.
20 Finance committee 7.2.1912.
21 F.P. 22.7.1912.
22 *Ibid* 25.7.1913.
23 Prices on the authority of market reports in the newspapers for June 1880 and June 1914. For meat prices in 1914 personal communication from Mr. L. J. Seward, O.B.E. For servants' wages below, advertisements in 1880 and 1914.
24 J. H. Clapham, *Machines and National Rivalries*, (1938), p. 475.
25 J. H. Plumb on 'The Historian's Dilemma,' *Crisis in the Humanities* (1964), p. 39.
26 Colson Papers, in the possession of Colsons of Exeter (Ltd.)
27 G. Barraclough, *History in a Changing World*, (1955), p. 205.
28 F.P. 1.8.1914.
29 *Ibid* 14.8.1914.

BIBLIOGRAPHY

PRIMARY AUTHORITIES: MANUSCRIPT

A. Public Record Office
Bread Riots of 1867, H.O. 445/7992
Correspondence of the Exeter Guardians, 1843–1900

B. British Museum
Iddesleigh Papers, Additional Manuscripts 50,013–50,064

C. Devon County Archives
Visitation Reports
Bishop Phillpotts' Letters
Pluralists 1831, correspondence between Bishop Phillpotts and Ralph Barnes

D. Exeter Cathedral Library
Chapter Act Books
Correspondence concerning the Surplice Question, Chapter Papers 40.1844
Correspondence of Henry Phillpotts, Bishop of Exeter
Offices in the patronage of the Dean and Chapter, Chapter Papers 7076/91
Return to Church Revenue Commissioners, Chapter Papers 7076/91
Letter from Sydney Herbert to Dean Lowe, Chapter Papers 7170/41
Shapter, Thomas; Manuscript account of the Surplice Riots, ED/22

E. Exeter City Archives
No attempt has been made to record the full list of the various committees of the council which were consulted. These have been given in the footnotes together with the date of the relevant minute cited in the text. The minute book of the sanitary committee of the council is entitled Exeter local board for the period 1867–1875 after the adoption of the Local Government Act of 1875. From 1867–1876 the minutes of the streets committee were entitled Exeter local board, streets committee. From 1876 to 1878 they appear as Exeter urban authority, streets committee. The finance committee of the council acted as local board of Health and subsequently as urban sanitary authority. Separate minute books were kept but these became merged with the council minutes.

Canal; Papers relating to the Canal Mortgage 1846–54:
Trevillian *v* Mayor of Exeter

City Treasurer's Vouchers

City Council Minutes 1836–1914. These minutes were
printed in 1881 and from that date include the minutes of
committees bound in the same volume

City Council; Special Committees

Committee on Municipal Officers, 1836

Conference Point Book and Nominal Roll

Corporate Officers, Rates of Pay and Duties

Council Letters, 1836–41

Declaration Books of Aldermen, Councillors, Auditors and
Assessors, from 1835

Diary of Margaret, Lady Paterson, 1831–35

Exeter Local Board: Minutes of the Council acting as Local
Board of Health and Urban Sanitary Authority, 1867–68

Exeter Markets, 1836–96

Exeter School Board, Minutes 1871–1903

Exeter Shrievalty Records

Exeter Water Company, Rent Books

Gaol Calendar Book

Guardians of the Poor, Minutes of the Monthly Court

Improvement Commissioners, Proceedings of General Meetings to 1867

do.   Names and Declarations

do.   Transcript of Proceedings of
Government

Inquiry at the Guildhall before Arnold Taylor Esq., Inspector
from the Home Office, 1867

Kennaway Papers

Municipal Corporations' Commissioners; Proceedings at
Exeter 1–6 November 1833, taken by Thomas Latimer

Regina *v* Macgowan, papers relating thereto

Sanitary Condition of Houses, Extracts from Inspectors'
Reports, 1871

Special Constables, Lists

Ward List of Voters 1835–1914. Printed from 1872

Ward Poll Books; Election of Town Councillors 1835–71

F. George's Meeting, South Street, Exeter

Unitarian Minutes and Accounts 1818–80

G. Other Manuscript Authorities

Colson Papers; three boxes of miscellaneous material in the
possession of Messrs Colsons of Exeter

Force Papers; four volumes of notes of sales and advertisements for the period 1883–1938 in the possession of Messrs S. R. Force and Sons, Exeter

Memoirs of Henry Ellis 1790–1859; eight volumes lent by Mr Roger Ellis of 3, High Street, Harrow on the Hill

PRIMARY AUTHORITIES: PRINTED

A. **Parliamentary Papers**

Accounts and Papers relating to Parliamentary Representation. *Proposed Division of Counties and Boundaries of Boroughs. Reports from Commissioners.* Pts I, II, 1831–32 (141) xxxviii

Return of Freemen and Voters. Votes polled at the last contested election. 1831–32 (112) xxxvi

Poor Laws. Reports from Commissioners 1834 (44) xxviii

Expenses charged by Retiring Officers. Sel. Com. 1834 (591) ix

Municipal Corporations (England and Wales) First Report of Commissioners, 1835 (116) xxiii

Municipal Corporations Boundaries. Reports of Commissioners upon the Boundaries and Wards of Certain Boroughs, 1837 (238) xxvi

Education of the Poorer Classes in England and Wales Sel. Com. 1837–38 (589) vii

Public Charities (Schools). Reports from Commissioners 1834 (435) xviii

First Report of the Commissioners appointed to inquire as to the best means of establishing an efficient Constabulary Force in England and Wales, 1839 (169) xix

State of Large Towns and Populous Districts. Second Report of the Commissioners, 1845 (602) xviii

Return of Population etc., 1852–53 (106) lxxxiii

Return of Electors 1852–53 (863) lxxxiii

Constituencies, 1859 (141) xxiii

Return relative to the Poor Rates, 1859 (171) xxiii

State of Popular Education in England 1861 (2794 – IV)

Parliamentary Representation Returns, 1866 (3626) lvii

Reports from Commissioners, Boundary Commission 1867–68 (3972) xx

Education. Schools not comprised within the two recent Commissions on Secondary Education, I Report, 1867–68 (3966) xxviii; IV Pt. II, Minutes of Evidence 1867–68

(3966 – III); South-Western Division, *Special Reports of Assistant Commissioners*, XI, vol. XIV, 1867–68 (3966 – XIII) xxviii

Select Committee on Scientific Instruction. Provisions for giving instruction in Theoretical and Applied Science to the Industrial Classes, Sel. Com. Mins. of ev. 1867–68 (432) xv

Electors (Cities and Boroughs) 1868–69 (419) i

Parliamentary Boroughs (Poor Rates) 1868–69 (II) i

Endowed Schools Act. Sel. Com. Mins. of ev. 1873 (254) viii

Report of the Royal Commission on the Housing of the Working Classes, II, 1884–85 (C. 4402 – I) xxx

Secondary Education. Royal Commission. I General Report, 1895 (C. 7862) *VI Reports of the Assistant Commissioners*, 1895 (C. 7862 – v) xiviii

Endowed Charities (County Borough of Exeter) (Cd. 37) 1909

Census Reports 1821–1911

B. Other official reports and publications

Reports of the Special Assistant Poor Law Commissioners on the Employment of Women and Children in Agriculture, London, 1843

Hansard's Parliamentary Debates

Board of Education, *Reports*

Report of the Consultative Committee on Secondary Education, H.M.S.O. 1959

Committee of Council on Education, *Reports*

Dept. of Science and Art, *Reports* 1854–93

Earnings and Hours Inquiry; *Report of an Inquiry by the Board of Trade into the Earnings and Hours of Labour of Workpeople in the United Kingdom; III, Building and Woodworking Trades in* 1906. (Cd. 5086) 1910

Endowed School Commissioners. *Report to the Lords of the Committee of Her Majesty's Privy Council on Education.* (Cd. 524) 1872

Labour Statistics; *Eighth Annual Abstract for the United Kingdom*, 1900–01 (Cd. 1124) 1902

Local Government Board, *Annual Reports*

National Association for the Promotion of Technical Education; *Annual Reports*

Poor Law Board, *Annual Reports*

Poor Law Commissioners, *Annual Reports*

C. Printed reports and publications, Exeter City Archives

Annual Income and Expenditure of the City of Exeter; Estimate

laid before the Council, 8.3.1843
City Council Minutes, 1881–1914
City Council Committees, 1881–1914
Corporation of Exeter and the Exeter Gas Company; Report
of the Parliamentary Committee, 18.12.1878
Exeter Borough Fund Accounts and Market Accounts, 1836–1914
Exeter Canal; Report by the Special Finance Committee
Exeter Canal; Report by B. C. Gidley, 1880
Gidley, J. *An argument to show that, according to the Provisions
of the Acts for the Regulation of Municipal Corporations in
England and Wales, the Triennial Election of Aldermen
ought to take place before the Election of the Mayor and
before the Quarterly Meeting,* London, 1844
Reply to the Argument (Anon.), Exeter, 1844
Roll of Citizens, 1876–1914
Sadler, M. E., *Report on Secondary and Higher Education in
Exeter,* 1905
*Valuation of the Houses and Lands in the City of Exeter made
by Messrs Rowe, Cornish, and Hooper by order of the
Guardians of the Poor and the Improvement Commissioners
and completed the 28th of July,* 1838

D. Maps in Exeter City Archives
Boundaries of Exeter. Maps from the reports of the Boundary
Commissioners of 1831, 1837, 1868
1840. *Plan of the City of Exeter from Actual Survey;* Exeter
Improvement Commissioners
1851. *Map of the City of Exeter embracing all the Alterations
and Improvements to the present period.* Drawn, printed and
published by Featherstone & Co. Exeter
1877. *Plan showing City of Exeter and Parish of St. Leonard's,
Exeter Extension Act,* 1877
1900. *Exeter Corporation Act, 1900. Distribution of Wards*
1913. *Map showing the area included in the City and County of
the City of Exeter by the Exeter Extension Order,* 1913

E. Other printed sources in Exeter
(i) Devon and Exeter Institution
Acts of the Synod of Exeter, London, 1851
Albert Memorial Museum, Treasurer's Report, 1865; bound
in Tracts, vol. 129
Barnes, Ralph. *Report of the case of the Queen v. The President
and Chapter of the Cathedral Church of St. Peter in Exeter
regarding the Deanery of Exeter,* London, 1841

Birkmeyer, J. B. *Exeter School of Art*, Exeter, 1868, Tracts vol. 129

Charities; *The Report of the Commissioners concerning Charities containing that Part which relates to the City of Exeter*, Exeter, 1825

Donisthorpe, G., *An Account of the Origins and Progress of the Devon and Exeter Albert Memorial Museum*, Exeter, 1868; Tracts vol. 129

Devon and Exeter Central Schools, 24*th Annual Report*, 1905–06

Education in Exeter; Guide for visiting Canadian and American Teachers, Exeter, 1908

Exeter Diocesan Board of Education, *Reports and Proceedings*

Exeter Science Classes, 1*st Annual Report*, 1866, Tracts vol. 129

Howard, E. *An Essay read to the Members and Friends of the Exeter Literary Society at the Royal Subscription Rooms. Exeter*, 17*th May* 1850

Sanders, R. *Observations on the Memorandum in reference to the Reorganization of the Exeter Educational Endowments*, Exeter, 1872

Transactions of the Devonshire Association, from 1862

(ii) Cathedral Library

Bull, Rev. J. *A Letter addressed to Henry, Lord Bishop of Exeter*, Exeter, 1844

Phillpotts, H., Bishop of Exeter, *Collected Works* 1819–1852, 4 vols.

(iii) City Health Office

Annual Reports of the Medical Officer of Health, from 1896

F. Guides and Directories

1797–1877	*Exeter Pocket Journal*
1821	Woolmer, S. *Exeter and its Neighbourhood and adjacent Watering Places*, Exeter, 1821
1831	Besley, T. & H., *Exeter Itinerary and General Directory*, Exeter, 1831
1833	Besley, H., *Exeter Directory*, Exeter, 1833
1835	*Exeter Directory*, Exeter, 1835
1836	*Exeter Guide and Itinerary*, Exeter, 1836
1844	Pigot & Co. *Royal National and Commercial Directory and Topography*, London, 1844
1850	White, W. *History, Gazetteer and Directory of Devonshire*, Sheffield, 1850

1857	Billings, M. *Directory and Gazetteer of the County of Devon*, Birmingham, 1857

1857   Billings, M. *Directory and Gazetteer of the County of Devon*, Birmingham, 1857

1863   Palmer, G. *Handbook to Exeter*, Exeter, 1863

1866   Smith & Co., *Devonshire Directory*, London, 1866

1875   Mortimer, H. *A.B.C. Directory and Handbook for Exeter and its Neighbourhood*, Exeter, 1875

1877–1914 *Besley's Exeter Directory*

1878   White, W., *History, Gazetteer and Directory of Devonshire*, Sheffield, 1879

1884   Vincent, A. *Guide to Exeter*, Exeter, 1884

1907   Soper, H. T. *Exeter Illustrated*, Exeter, 1907

1913   Exeter City Council, *Exeter in 1913; Souvenir of the Royal Sanitary Institute*, Exeter, 1913

G. Parliamentary Elections

Details of the electorate and of the voting are provided by the following local reports of elections:

July 1831   'List of voters and record of votes,' T. & H. Besley, *Exeter Itinerary and General Directory*, Exeter, 1831

December 1832 'List of voters at the Exeter Elections (the first under the Reform Bill), which took place on December 10th and 11th 1832,' H. Besley, *Exeter Directory*, 1833

January 1835 'List of voters polled at the contest for the City in January, 1835,' Henry Besley, *Exeter Directory*, 1835

1864   *The List of Persons in the Borough of the City of Exeter who voted or were entitled to vote at the Election of a Member to serve in Parliament to fill the vacancy caused by the death of Edward Divett, Esq.*, Exeter, 1864

1868   *A complete list of Persons in the Borough of the City of Exeter who voted or were entitled to vote at the General Parliamentary Election*, Exeter, 1868

H. Newspapers

(i) Devon and Exeter Institution

Devon Weekly Times 1863–1899

Exeter Flying Post 1813–1867

Exeter and Plymouth Gazette 1819–1901; appears as the *Devon and Exeter Gazette* from 1887

Western Luminary 1823–1850
Western Times 1831–1901
(ii) Exeter City Archives
Evening Post 1884–1902
Flying Post 1903–1917

I.　**Periodicals**
Annual Register
Gentleman's Magazine

SECONDARY AUTHORITIES

To avoid inflating the bibliography unreasonably only secondary authorities of special local significance have been listed. The history of Victorian Exeter is, after all, part of the history of Victorian England and cannot be properly understood without some knowledge of the latter. Memoirs, biographies, general histories and special studies of Victorian England are legion and some of these are cited as required in the footnotes.

Andrews, J. H. B.　　*The Rise of the Bible Christians with reference to the state of the Church in North Devon in the early 19th century,* D.A. xcvi, 1964, pp 147–184

Acland, A. H. D.　　*Memoirs and Letters of the Right Honourable Sir Thomas Dyke Acland,* 1902

Aglionby, P. K.　　*Life of Edward Henry Bickersteth,* 1907

Baring-Gould, S.　　*Early Reminiscences 1834–1864,* 1923

Boggis, J. E.　　*A History of the Diocese of Exeter,* Exeter, 1922

Brockett, A. A.　　*Nonconformity in Exeter, 1650–1875,* Manchester, 1962

Briggs, A.　　*Victorian Cities,* 1963

Chick, E.　　*A History of Methodism in Exeter,* Exeter, 1907

Coleridge, E. H.　　*The Life and Correspondence of John Duke, Lord Coleridge, Lord Chief Justice of England,* 2 vols. 1904

Clark, E. A. G.　　*The Ports of the Exe Estuary, 1660–1860,* Exeter, 1960

Cossins, J.　　*Reminiscences of the City of Exeter Fifty Years Since,* Exeter, 1877

Davies, G. C. B.　　*Henry Phillpotts, Bishop of Exeter,* 1954

Daw, J.　　*John Daw, 1760–1849,* privately printed, 1939

John Daw 1803–1884, privately printed, 1951

Reminiscences 1886–1957, privately printed, 1957

Exeter City Library   *Mayors of Exeter from the 13th Century to the Present Day*, Exeter, 1964

Freeman, E. A.   *Exeter*, 1887

Harper, C.   *The Exeter Road*, 1899

Hele's School   *Born in Exeter: A Historical Survey*, Exeter, 1950

Hoskins, W. G.   *Industry, Trade and People in Exeter* 1688–1800, Manchester, 1935

Devon, 1959

Two Thousand Years in Exeter, Exeter 1960

'George Oliver, D.D. 1781–1861,' *Downside Review*, 1961

Hutchings, W. J.   *Out of the Blue: History of the Devon Constabulary*, Torquay, 1956

Jenkins, A.   *Civil and Ecclesiastical History of the City of Exeter*, Exeter, 1806

Kekewich, G. W.   *The Education Department and After*, 1920

Lambert, H. S.   *The Cobbett of the West*, 1939

Le Messurier, B. A.   *History of the Mint Methodist Church, Exeter*, Exeter, 1962

Little, B.   *Exeter and its Surroundings*, 1953

MacCaffrey, W. T.   *Exeter* 1540–1640, Harvard, 1958

Melville, C. H.   *Life of the Right Hon. Sir Redvers Buller V.C.*, 2 vols., 1925

Moore, E. J.   *The Case of the Rev. G. C. Gorham against the Bishop of Exeter*, 1852

Mortimer, The Right Rev., R. C.   *The Exeter Case*, D.A. xciv, 1962

Northey, T. J.   *Popular History of Exeter*, Exeter, 1885

Nias, J. C. S.   *Gorham and the Bishop of Exeter*, 1951

Oliver, G.   *History of the City of Exeter*, Exeter, 1861

Parry, H. L.   *The Founding of Exeter School*, Exeter, 1913

Exeter Guildhall; Exeter, 1936

Pevsner, N.   *The Buildings of England, South Devon*, 1952

Phelps, W. H. and Forbes-Roberston, J.   *The Life and Times of Samuel Phelps*, 1886

Prothero, R. E.   *The Letters of Richard Ford* 1797–1858, 1905

Richardson, A. E. and   *Regional Architecture in the West of*
Gill, C. L.   *England*, 1924

Sandford, E. C.   *Memoirs of Archbishop Temple*, 2 vols., 1906
                           The Exeter Episcopate of Archbishop Temple, 1869–1885, 1907

Sharp, T.   *Exeter Phoenix*, 1946

Shapter, T.   *The History of the Cholera in Exeter in* 1832, 1849

Shutte, R. N.   *The Life, Times and Writing of the Right Rev. Dr Henry Phillpotts, Lord Bishop of Exeter*, 1863

Stephens, W. B.   *Seventeenth Century Exeter*, Exeter, 1958

Vincent, A.   *Memoir of the late John Dinham of Exeter*, Exeter, 1877

Worthy, C.   *The History of the Suburbs of Exeter*, 1892

INDEX